Mastering Human Relations

2ND EDITION

Anthony Falikowski

Sheridan College

Prentice Hall Allyn and Bacon Canada
Scarborough, Ontario

Dedicated with love to the walking,
talking miracles of my life.

To Heather,
a strong-willed girl with great ideas,

to Michelle,
a creative and sensitive delight,

to Michael,
my son, a father's dream come true and

to my dear wife Pamela,
a friend and loving companion
to share with along the way.

You make it all worthwhile.

Canadian Cataloguing in Publication Data

Falikowski, Anthony, 1953-
    Mastering human relations

2nd ed.
Includes index.
ISBN 0-13-906173-8

1. Interpersonal relations. I. Title.

HM132.F34 1999   158.2   C98-931086-8

Prentice-Hall, Inc., Upper Saddle River, New Jersey
Prentice-Hall International (UK) Limited, London
Prentice-Hall of Australia, Pty. Limited, Sydney
Prentice-Hall Hispanoamericana, S.A., Mexico City
Prentice-Hall of India Private Limited, New Delhi
Prentice-Hall of Japan, Inc., Tokyo
Simon & Schuster Southeast Asia Private Limited, Singapore
Editora Prentice-Hall do Brasil, Ltda., Rio de Janeiro

ISBN 0-13-906173-8

Vice President, Editorial Director: Laura Pearson
Acquisitions Editor: David Stover
Marketing Manager: Kathleen McGill
Developmental Editor: Jean Ferrier
Production Editor: Andrew Winton
Copy Editor: Allyson Latta
Production Coordinator: Sharon Houston
Permissions/Photo Research: Susan Wallace-Cox
Cover Design: Sarah Battersby
Cover Image: Stephanie Power
Page Layout: Gail Ferreira Ng-A-Kien

2 3 4 5   03 02 01 00 99

Printed and bound in the United States of America.

Visit the Prentice Hall Canada web site! Send us your comments, browse our catalogues, and more at www.phcanada.com. Or reach us through e-mail at **phabinfo_pubcanada@prenhall.com**.

CONTENTS

PART THREE *Personal Growth and Development*   317

PREFACE TO THE SECOND EDITION

Good, better, best,
Never let it rest.
'Till your good is better
And your better is best!
                                        Anonymous

I begin the Preface to the second edition of *Mastering Human Relations* with a children's nursery rhyme. In its simple way, it captures the motivation and rationale behind this revision. Although it has been quite gratifying for me as the author to witness the success of this book in its first few years of publication, I'm not prepared to accept the notion that a good book can't be made better. In fact, it's my sincere hope that this "better" revised edition of *Mastering Human Relations* will turn out to be the "best" one to meet your needs as an instructor. For classroom teachers who have used the first edition and are troubled about having to do new course preparations, not to worry. I've left much as before in response to the positive feedback I've received. However, I have made significant changes to some things that were recommended by previous users of the book. These changes sometimes simplify matters, while at other times, substantially beef them up.

New Introduction: My new introduction provides a broad overview of the book and places its content into an understandable context for students. The introduction also establishes the importance to personal and professional success of mastering good human relations and interpersonal communication skills. Furthermore, the new introduction outlines the structure and organization of the text, previewing what is to be covered in each of the major parts and constituent chapters. By reading the introduction, you will see how each chapter applies to interpersonal communications and personal growth.

Simplified Learning Outcomes: Learning outcomes have been simplified in format to include both knowledge and skills objectives. Essentially the same goals will be achieved as before, but in a pedagogically more manageable and efficient manner. Learning outcomes are presented here in a cleaner, simpler fashion. This simplification should facilitate the achievement of desired exit competencies, and hence, the quality of your instruction.

Chapter Reorganization: Chapters 3 and 4 have been amalgamated into one chapter entitled "Psycho-Logical Defensiveness." Theoretical discussions in both previous chapters have been shortened, while other parts have been highlighted to emphasize how psychological defensiveness and irrationality constitute noise factors in the process of interpersonal communication.

Chapter 6 from the first edition has now been split into two separate ones — one entitled "Leadership Perspectives" and the other, simply

"Conflict." Fuller treatments of both these subjects should enhance generic skills development when it comes to resolving interpersonal differences and working with people in social and organizational settings.

Terminological Updates: In view of recent theoretical developments in the human relations field, a number of terminological changes have been made. For instance, in Chapter 9, where William Glasser's work is discussed, control theory psychology has been relabelled "choice theory" according to Glasser's wishes. Similarly, changes in enneagram terminology (Chapter 11) have also been made to reflect recent theoretical developments. On the subject of the enneagram, you will also notice that I've produced a better self-diagnostic in Chapter 11 to help students identify their enneagram character types with greater accuracy.

Weblinks: Another significant addition to this text is the Weblinks feature. In each chapter, you can now find web sites and online resources to help students in their research and personal growth, as well as in their journey toward human relations mastery. The human relations journey in the next millennium will take place, in part at least, in cyberspace.

In closing, let me underscore the fact that *Mastering Human Relations* still aims to integrate personal growth and interpersonal communications. It continues to offer interesting and useful content coverage. You will also still find the Built-In Student Study Guide and many creative enhancements to facilitate learning. I have made every effort to preserve the user-friendly, readable style of the text. I truly hope that you and your students achieve success in your quest for human relations mastery. Through use of this book, I will be supporting you all the way!

NOTE TO THE INSTRUCTOR

Mastering Human Relations, Canadian Second Edition, is an introductory-level textbook written specifically for Canadian post-secondary institutions. It has two basic objectives: it offers a program of general education that promotes the personal growth of students and develops a number of generic "people skills" that can be used in both private and professional life. Instructors using this text will help students establish a solid foundation for individual adjustment and for effective social functioning. Content coverage and skills development will also prepare students for lifelong learning and vocational success.

This book assumes that personal growth cannot occur in a social vacuum, while interpersonal communication skills cannot properly develop without self-awareness and self-understanding on the part of the communicator. Psychological insight improves interpersonal effectiveness; social interaction facilitates personal growth. To quote my daughter Heather on this point, "That's the way the world works!"

Mastering Human Relations adopts an outcomes-based approach to the teaching-learning process. Instead of emphasizing what the instructor will teach, it stresses the acquisition of knowledge and skills, shifting attention toward what the students will know and be able to do after studying each chapter. As an instructor using this book with its outcomes-based pedagogy, you will feel confident about your students achieving desired exit competencies specified at the beginning of each chapter. Students, as well, will be able to monitor their own progress through the use of learning aids included in the book. During difficult economic times, when classroom numbers are growing, when student-teacher contact is dwindling and when evaluation is becoming more sporadic, giving students a way to monitor their own individual progress is extremely valuable. *Mastering Human Relations* gives them a way with a built-in student Study Guide, described under *Special Features* and in the *Message to Students*. I invite you now to work with me as we travel together with our students down the difficult but exciting road to human relations mastery.

Special Features of Mastering Human Relations

Built-In Study Guide

As mentioned above, this text provides students with a built-in study guide to enhance academic performance. No additional workbook needs to be purchased. This guide is intended as an optional aid, not as a required tool. Certain instructors may wish to integrate some or all of the elements of the guide into their lesson plans as a way of complementing their teaching. Others may wish to have students use the guide primarily for independent study outside the classroom. Many aspects of the guide are suitable for workshops and tutorials. Regardless of how it's used, the guide offers many individual and group learning opportunities.

SQ3R Method of Learning: First of all, it should be noted that the built-in student study guide is based on the SQ3R method of learning. SQ3R stands for Survey, Question, Read, Recite and Review. Chapters are organized so that students can

- *Survey* the content to be covered
- Use focus *Questions* to direct their attention
- *Read* the material presented
- *Recite* and *Review* what was covered for self-testing.

In times of shrinking resources when teachers are forced to reduce instructional hours in the classroom and limit the frequency of evaluation, the SQ3R method is invaluable as a tool to promote academic success for students through guided self-study. Let's now look a little more closely at the elements comprising the SQ3R methodology, as well as at the creative enhancements which complement it.

Chapter Overviews: Each chapter begins with an Overview, providing students with an outline of what is to be covered. By simply glancing at the headings, students can survey the material they are expected to master.

Numbered Learning Outcomes: To facilitate the overview process, specific Learning Outcomes have been explicitly stated. By looking them over, students get an idea of what they will be expected to know and what they will be able to do upon successful completion of the chapter. To promote mastery of knowledge and skills, outcomes are numbered. These same numbers are placed alongside the text in which the corresponding outcomes are addressed. They are also found beside *Application Exercises* designed to help students achieve knowledge and skills mastery. After reading any particular chapter, students should review the listed outcomes to see if they have assimilated the information and developed the skills indicated. If not, they can go back to appropriate sections of the chapter for more study and practice.

Focus Questions: These questions, located just before the chapter Summaries, should be considered prior to reading the main text. The Focus Questions serve a dual purpose. First, they help students concentrate and reflect on important chapter information. Knowing in advance what questions to ask and what to look for helps learners to extract the most significant material for study purposes. *Focus Questions* offer direction when it comes to selecting what is essential from the reading. They also can be used by instructors for classroom purposes. For example, they can be given as written homework assignments for grading, or they can be adopted as a basis for classroom discussion. Student responses to these questions could also be used to partially determine classroom participation grades.

Highlighted Key Terms: Students should not have to guess what's important to note in any given part of the text. Thus, important concepts and key terms are boldfaced and a list of the *Key Terms* is found just before the *Progress Check* of each chapter.

Progress Checks: After reading each chapter, students can do the *Progress Checks* as part of the recitation and review process of the SQ3R methodology. Mastery of concepts should be reflected in the ability to answer questions contained in the Progress Checks. Answers are found in the *Appendix* located at the end of the book.

Summaries: Students are encouraged to study the chapter Summaries carefully before and after doing Progress Checks. Vital information is clearly and concisely presented to facilitate knowledge acquisition. The *Summaries,* like the *Progress Checks,* help to enhance the recitation and review process of the SQ3R methodology. They are also helpful aids for exam preparation.

Canadian Content

As the Canadian author of *Mastering Human Relations,* let me say that it is a textbook especially designed and developed to meet the needs of Canadian post-secondary students. Not surprisingly, then, it contains many examples and illustrations that are Canadian in context. It also contains numerous showcase profiles of prominent Canadian researchers whose work has had a significant impact on the field of human relations. The inclusion of Canadian content represents a refreshing change. The great majority of human relations textbooks used in the nation's schools are written and produced outside this country, or else they are merely Canadianized adaptations of American texts. While it is true that theories and skills don't have "nationalities" per se, the contexts in which they're presented do in fact reflect them. After waiting for years for someone to produce a truly Canadian text for my Human Relations course, I finally gave up and decided to write my own. I hope you like it, eh!

Creative Enhancements

Poems, comics, quotations, figures, tables, showcase profiles, photos and song lyrics are scattered throughout the text to make it more interesting and visually appealing for students. Sometimes simple quotations or comics can capture the essence of points made. At other times, they accent in an indirect and creative way what may otherwise be plainly expressed in theoretical, academic terminology.

Self-Diagnostics

Along with interpersonal effectiveness, this book stresses personal growth. To this end, opportunities are provided throughout the text for students to do self-assessments on such topics as personality type and communication style. Interestingly enough, self-assessments can facilitate understanding and appreciation of others. For example, by appreciating our own uniqueness, we can learn to understand and appreciate the uniqueness of others. Note that self-diagnostics are used in this book as thought-provokers, ones that encourage positive self-consciousness on the part of students. Don't see them as providing anything final or conclusive. Self-diagnostics simply provide opportunities for initial self-reflection.

Application Exercises

I've included *Application Exercises* to emphasize the benefits of mastering chapter material, as well as to consolidate learning. Some of these can be done individually, while others are designed to be done in groups. The *Application Exercises* of each chapter facilitate active learning and participation. Since it is possible to know a lot about human relations and still be terrible with people, it is important that students practise social interactions using the concepts covered. There's nothing as practical as a good theory as long as the theory gets applied, and that's what happens here!

Related Readings

For students and faculty wishing to do further research on topics covered in any one chapter, related readings are listed.

Weblinks

To further help students with their research and personal growth, Weblinks are now included in each chapter. These Web sites direct students to online resources that can facilitate more effective interpersonal communications and the mastery of human relations. This new special feature takes student learning beyond the textbook and the confines of the classroom and into the realm of cyberspace where personal discovery possibilities are virtually infinite.

Supplements

Instructor's Manual with Test Item File and Transparency Masters: Accompanying this text is an Instructor's Manual. It includes a sample course outline, overhead masters, lecture and discussion suggestions, key motivators for students and additional Application Exercises. The Instructor's Manual helps take much of the sting out of adopting a new textbook by having as much prepared for you as possible. The objective is to make *Mastering Human Relations* user-friendly for teachers, while at the same time interesting and useful for students. The Test Item File is also part of this package. It includes questions graded at three levels of difficulty; relevant chapter and textbook pages are cited along with the correct answer for each question. Questions formats include multiple choice, fill-in-the-blank, short answer and true/false.

    Computerized Test Item File: A computerized version of the Test Item File is also available for instructors. Questions can easily be selected and/or composed. Multiple versions of the same test can also be produced for instructors who teach different sections of the same course.

    Interactive Study Guide: Visit Prentice Hall Allyn and Bacon Canada's Web site and download the exciting new interactive electronic study guide that accompanies the second edition of *Mastering Human Relations*!

Based on the text's *Progress Checks*, the electronic study guide provides 400 questions designed to test and enhance understanding of core concepts in the text. Immediate feedback is provided, and the study guide also ties test questions to learning objectives in the printed text. In addition, a convenient online glossary of important terms is provided.

Users of *Mastering Human Relations*, Second Edition, can conveniently download the electronic study guide from Prentice Hall Allyn and Bacon Canada's Web site. Go to http://www.prenticehall.ca/falikowskimhr and follow the instructions.

MESSAGE TO STUDENTS

Mastering Human Relations Canadian Second Edition, is a textbook written with you, the student, in mind. It aims to promote personal growth and social skills development. I think you will find much in this book that is interesting, practical and fun. I hope you enjoy all of the comics, poems, song lyrics, visuals and other creative enhancements that are included to make the book not only relevant and insightful, but stimulating as well. On a personal note, I especially enjoyed including the quotations that are sprinkled throughout. I like to think of them as "Tonee Balonee's favourite zingers." For me, they are inspirational and thought provoking. I hope they are for you too!

Designed for your personal use, *Mastering Human Relations* includes a built-in student Study Guide. This guide is based on the SQ3R system of learning. SQ3R is an acronym that stands for *survey, question, read, recite* and *review*. If you follow this system, you're more likely to successfully complete your course and master human relations in the process.

Step One: Survey the Content to be Covered

Each of the chapters in *Mastering Human Relations* begins with an *Overview*. By simply glancing at the headings, you can *survey* ("S") the material you will be expected to master. Make sure, as well, to look over the *Learning Outcomes*. They have been explicitly stated here to make the overview and survey process easier. By perusing the outcomes at the outset, you can discover what you will be expected to know or to do by unit end. To promote mastery of content and skills, outcomes are numbered and placed where they are addressed. After completing a chapter, you should review the list of Learning Outcomes to ensure that you have assimilated the important information and have developed the skills marked for mastery. If not, you can go back and re-address the appropriate sections of the chapter.

Step Two: Direct your Reading Attention by Referring to the Focus Questions that can be Found after the Progress Checks.

Each chapter of this book contains *Focus Questions*, which make up the "Q" portion of the SQ3R methodology. You should examine the questions before actually reading the material contained in the chapter. The questions enable you to focus your attention while reading so that you know what is important. Your instructor may wish to use these questions for classroom discussion purposes. They can be helpful for your own personal reflections as well, as you get to know yourself better through the use of this text. By concentrating on the answers to the Focus Questions while you read, you will be better prepared for discussions, whether they take place in regular classes or in tutorials.

Step Three: Read the Chapter

Once you have an idea of what is in the chapter and what to look for, go ahead and read. I caution you to be patient. Reading theory is not like reading the newspaper or the comic strips. Don't be surprised if you find yourself going over the same paragraph more than once in order to understand what was stated. You are being introduced to a new subject of study with its own jargon and specialized vocabulary. What I would suggest you do while completing the first reading is highlight the important points. During your second reading, paraphrase the material you've highlighted, making sure you understand the notes you're taking. Just before writing your test on each unit, read the chapter a third time and memorize your notes on the information you now understand. Simply reading the text once or twice, the night before a test, and without notes and understanding, is not likely to result in success.

To assist you in your readings, I've boldfaced key terms. I don't wish to leave you guessing what's important. A list of *Key Terms* is also found just before the *Progress Check* of each chapter. Make sure you are familiar with each term in the list; also make sure you understand each term and, where appropriate, are able to define it.

Step Four: Recite and Review

After reading the chapter, you should start the recitation and review process by doing the *Progress Check*. Your mastery of the content is reflected in your ability to correctly answer questions contained in the check. Your responses to each of the Progress Checks can be verified for correctness by referring to the *Appendix* at the end of the book. (No cheating, remember!)

Step Five: Review the Summaries

Chapter end summaries also serve to comprise the recitation and review component of the SQ3R methodology. You may examine them before and/or after doing the *Progress Checks* to consolidate learning and to make sure that outcomes have been achieved. Reviewing the summaries is definitely something you should do at test time to maximize your chances for success.

As you now get started on the road to human relations mastery, I wish you well. Some self-discipline and hard work may be required, but the rewards in the end will make it all worthwhile. Good Luck!

Tonee Balonee
(Also known as the author)

ACKNOWLEDGMENTS

Mastering Human Relations, Second Edition, is a book that has been made possible through the coordinated efforts of many people. With this in mind, I would first like to say thank you to David Stover, acquisitions editor, for signing me to this project and looking after contractual matters. Other members of the editorial staff were also very instrumental to the realization of this book. Lisa Berland and Jean Ferrier, both developmental editors (I guess it takes two to develop my work!), helped to keep me on track and dealt with the many details associated with the publication of this book. Allyson Latta served as the copy editor and, without knowing it perhaps, provided me with a number of grammar and spelling lessons I should have learned many years ago. Thanks also to Andrew Winton, the production editor, for making sure that everybody was working together as smoothly as a symphony.

I would also like to thank William Glasser, president of the William Glasser Institute in California, for reviewing the section on Reality Therapy/Choice Therapy Psychology. I also wish to acknowledge the reviews done by Don Riso, president of the Enneagram Institute in New York City, and Carol Pearon, author of *Awakening the Heroes Within: Twelve Archetypes to Help Us Find Ourselves and Transform the World*. The fact that I studied and trained with all three of these individuals in the past made writing about their theories much easier. Thanks, everyone, for reading the manuscript and making sure I got descriptions of your work right!

Many other reviewers also helped to contribute to the substance and quality of this text. Of course, they are not to be held responsible for any deficiencies that may remain. But they do deserve a lot of credit for helping to make the final manuscript useful for instructors. In particular, I would like to thank the following individuals: Sue Bell, Georgian College; Paul Koziey, University of Alberta; R. Douglas Markle, Fanshawe College; Harry Havey, Red River Community College; Sara Pawson, Kwantlen College; Gary Anderson, Camosun College; Bev Brown, Niagara College; Jeffrey Arbus, Sault College; and Bill Gapen, George Brown College.

Finally, I wish to thank my family for their support and encouragement. "The Book" has become a source of humour around the house, as well as a cause for continuing celebration. Thank you, Pamela, Michelle, Heather, and Michael for just being you and giving me so much joy in my life. You have taught me more lessons than you could ever imagine. Always know that there's a special place for each and every one of you in my heart! I love you all!

ABOUT THE AUTHOR

Dr. Anthony Falikowski, better known to his students as Tony, is an internationally published author and full-time professor at Sheridan College. A graduate of the University of Toronto, he has spent the past 18 years teaching courses in psychology, philosophy and human relations. A certified Reality Therapist, enneagram teacher and personality type analyst, Tony conducts behavioural training and development workshops as a part-time consultant. He has been nominated for the President's Award of Teaching Excellence at Sheridan College, listed in *Who's Who in the Humanities*, and has also been included in *Profiles in Business and Management: An International Directory of Scholars and Their Research*, published by the Harvard Business School in Boston, Massachusetts.

Tony is happily married and lives with his wife, three children and pet cat Carl (Jung) in Oakville, Ontario. For fun, he likes to play hockey, spend time with his family, jog, camp, travel and watch mindless television, especially the Comedy Channel.

INTRODUCTION

As we get started, please allow me to say a heartfelt "Hello!" to you, to your classmates, and to your course instructor. Together, we are about to embark on a most important program of study. *Mastering Human Relations* is a book which I hope you'll find interesting, useful and fun. It is designed to facilitate your psychological adjustment and growth, while at the same time helping you to develop many of the "people skills" that will be essential to your future personal and professional success. Although technical or specialized knowledge and practical skills training are surely important for career advancement, they alone will not necessarily enable you to maximize your potential or to realize your vocational dreams. As a professor, I know from letters and personal contacts that employers demand more and more that colleges and universities produce graduates with good oral and interpersonal communication skills. They seek out and recruit mature, responsible and well-adjusted individuals who are confident, enthusiastic, friendly, articulate, motivated and "socially polished." Much to the chagrin of some highly intelligent and skilled people, landing a job is sometimes more about self-presentation and the ability to communicate well and get along with others in teams than it is about qualifications and expert knowledge. Many times I've witnessed candidates with fewer credentials get chosen for jobs over more highly qualified individuals primarily because the former were better able to work with people and because, therefore, they displayed greater leadership potential.

To help develop the "people skills" so important to your future, we will be examining in this text a number of psycho-social variables that influence the process of interpersonal communication. If you look at the figure paving the way for this Introduction, entitled Communication Dynamics, you will see a number of significant factors labelled within what has by now become a familiar model of communication. The standard model comprises sender, receiver, message, channel, noise, encoding and decoding (see Chapter 2, p.33). In this book, we will flesh out each one of these basic factors in some detail. For example, rather than discuss sender-receiver transactions in a purely abstract fashion, we will explore how personality type, individual motivation, temperament, ego states, gender and self-concept all influence the functions of message encoding and decoding. Senders and receivers are not

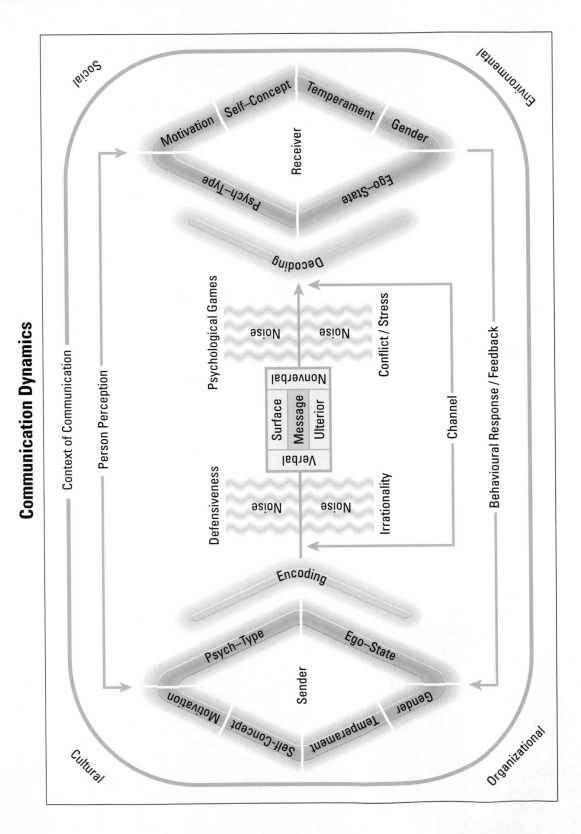

Communication Dynamics

abstract entities, but real live psychological beings displaying psychodynamic processes that must be understood if the process of communication is to be properly understood. In fleshing out the communication model, we will also see how messages can be sent by different channels and how they can be expressed in a variety of modes — verbal, nonverbal, surface and ulterior — depending on the intentions and behavioural cues exhibited by the communicator. Noise, too, will be one of our concerns. Interpersonal communication often gets bogged down, not only by environmental factors (e.g., loud construction work), but also by psychological interference. In this text, we will see how things such as conflict, stress, irrationality, defensiveness and psychological game playing all get in the way of productive dialogue. Though this text tends to focus more on the psychology of interpersonal relations, we will not forget how cultural and organizational factors impact on communication dynamics. For instance, you will learn how ethnic, linguistic and organizational variables such as leadership influence the nature and purpose of communication, and how human relations are affected by them.

This book contains three parts divided into 11 chapters. In the first chapter of Part I, you will be introduced to the notion of personality. You will learn about the work of Carl Jung and two important developers of his theory who have put forward a very insightful and informative concept of personality functioning. Knowledge gleaned from Chapter 1 will enable you to understand yourself and others better in terms of differing personality preferences. In Chapter 2, we will move on to a consideration of how these personality preferences influence the way messages are encoded and how, as a function of personality type, we all psychologically filter or decode messages that are received from external sources. In this chapter, you will also acquire information on how to make your communications with others "psych-smart." You will be cautioned against falling in love with your own personality-driven communication style, and encouraged to become more sensitive and accommodating to the preferences of others; that is, if you wish to communicate with them in more effective ways.

In Chapter 3, we will explore the nature of defensiveness and how it becomes a "noise" factor causing difficulties in interpersonal relations. By exposing some common defensive and irrational tendencies that many people display, we can become more understanding and forgiving of others and more aware of ourselves.

In Part II of *Mastering Human Relations*, we will look at interpersonal communications in more of a social context. Chapter 4 concentrates on interpersonal dynamics in terms of ego-state transactions. Using Eric Berne's theory of transactional analysis, we will come to appreciate how messages formulated by senders often have surface content that is different from their ulterior purpose. People don't always say what they mean or mean what they say. This kind of "game playing" adds again to the noise factor in interpersonal communication.

In Chapter 5, you will learn how to develop generic leadership skills useful when communicating with others in organizational settings or in social environments requiring someone to "take charge." Different leadership models are presented and you are invited to complete a self-diagnostic designed to help you identify your leadership temperament. Leaders and followers are not always the same in terms of their temperamental dispositions. Knowing, as a leader, how to appreciate and reward subordinates in light of temperamental differences, constitutes one big step forward in the direction of vocational success.

In Chapter 6, your human relations development is further facilitated by a treatment of conflict, another potential barrier or noise factor interfering with effective interpersonal communications. You discover in this segment how conflict can actually be used productively and how by employing appropriate conflict resolution strategies, damage and discontent can be minimized to the advantage of all.

Chapter 7 is about the self and person perception. Poor self-concepts and low self-esteem can, in some intuitively obvious ways, negatively influence how well we get along with others. Such things can also affect how others see and react to us. By facilitating greater self-awareness and appropriate self-disclosure, confidence and self-esteem can be built up. Furthermore, by building up self-esteem, we also hope in this section of the book to reduce errors when it comes to person perception. People who are unaware of themselves and how their own fears and insecurities influence social perception are more likely to fall prey to stereotyping and erroneous attributions of behaviour.

In Chapter 8, we examine gender, culture and nonverbal cues in the communication process. If "women are from Venus" and "men are from Mars," as one popular writer suggests, then perhaps it's not surprising that some research points to the fact that men and women display different communication patterns. We'll see if and how they do. In this chapter, we'll also see how both genders appear to display different moral orientations and ways of dealing with ethical dilemmas. No doubt, these kinds of differences can cause confusion and miscommunication in everyday human interactions.

Since interpersonal communication must take place in some kind of social and environmental context, we will examine the role of culture and location in Chapter 8. Linguistic, national and geographic factors can often impact on our communication transactions. In addition, nonverbal cues, also related to cultural and linguistic considerations, can set the tone for verbal communications or serve to emphasize or contradict what was said. In this section, it will be interesting and fun to explore the subtleties of body language and its role in the communication process. Finally, in this section, we will explore artifactual communication and how physical environments such as office space can send widely varying messages, intended or not.

In Part III of the text, efforts will be made to help you adjust and develop as an individual. In Chapter 9, which deals with human motivation, you will learn how to take better control of your life. By knowing what makes you and others "tick," you will be able to achieve greater stability and security in your everyday dealings with people. Chapter 10 will work toward this end as well, looking at the nature of stress and effective ways of coping with it. We also examine ineffective coping strategies and learn why they are best avoided. By reducing stress, we can begin to live more enjoyable and satisfying lives. We can also reduce a certain amount of psychological interference or noise in interpersonal communications. When stressed, people are often pre-occupied and inattentive to the messages sent by others. Effective and em-pathetic listening requires that we maintain a certain level of calm and attention.

In Chapter 11, we bring closure to our journey in *Mastering Human Relations*, only to pave a new road toward future self-transcendence. Understanding personality and using it for effective interpersonal commu-nications and vocational success is only a starting point. Our personality strengths and preferences, if idolized or taken to extremes, can become lia-bilities and obstacles to our fuller development as spiritual beings. Workshop leaders and professional development experts in the fields of business, edu-cation, medicine and social work, for example, have increasingly come to recognize that people comprise more than just mind and body; that they are made up of mind, body and *spirit*. We neglect the spiritual dimensions of life at our own peril. If we do so, we fail to find wholeness, meaning and a feel-ing of harmony with others in the world. I hope that my treatments of ar-chetypal psychology, Viktor Frankl's logotherapy and the ancient character typology of the enneagram, covered in Chapter 11, will help you to find di-rection and purpose for the next step of the glorious journey that is your life. On that note, let me wish you all a *Bon voyage*!

CHAPTER 1

There's only one corner of the universe you can be certain of improving, and that's your own self.

–Aldous Huxley

UNDERSTANDING PERSONALITY TYPES: A FIRST STEP TO HUMAN RELATIONS MASTERY

CHAPTER OVERVIEW

LEARNING OUTCOMES

After successfully completing this chapter, you will be able to

1.1   List the benefits of self-understanding

1.2   Form an hypothesis about your personality type

1.3   Understand psychological diversity in terms of four bipolar scales

1.4   Explain the differences between extraversion and introversion

1.5   Appreciate how sensors and intuitives gather information differently

1.6   Elaborate on how thinkers and feelers differ in their preferred ways of making decisions

1.7   Explain how judging and perceiving types orient to the external world.

1.1 ►

WHO AM I?

In today's highly competitive and fast-moving world there is often little time or inclination to reflect and ask the question "Who am I?" For many people, this question is simply too abstract or impractical to be taken seriously. Some may regard it as an exercise in navel-gazing; others may see the question as something more appropriately asked by philosophers, poets and dreamers. Most people are simply too busy trying to survive and earn a living to be concerned about matters of personal identity.

Benefits of Self-Knowledge

As a challenge to practical-minded "survivalists," let me suggest that the road to personal growth and interpersonal effectiveness begins with **self-knowledge**, an understanding of who you are and how your personality works for you. After all, if you wish to maximize your potential, you must know what that potential is. If you want to work on problems or limitations imposed by your **personality**, a combination of your unique behaviours, thoughts and feelings, you must recognize them in yourself. Furthermore, if you want to get along better with other people, you must understand how personalities differ and how each is perceived by the other. Without self-knowledge, your journey to human relations mastery will begin in darkness. Your direction will be uncertain and your destination unclear.

Self-knowledge has another practical importance. The German poet Goethe once said that if you wish to understand others, first examine yourself. Once you begin to appreciate the mechanisms of personality and how they operate in your own life, you will start to observe some of the universals of human behaviour. You will come to see how others are much like yourself. You may discover, for example, that your fears and insecurities are shared by other people. You may learn that the irritations and emotional conflicts you experience are quite similar to those experienced by people with whom you interact on a daily basis. On the other hand, as you discover some of the differences and unique qualities that set you apart from everyone else, you may then begin to appreciate the uniqueness of others. As you develop self-confidence and respect for yourself, trust and respect for others will naturally grow. This point underscores the spiritual insight that you can't love others until you love yourself. Once you begin reducing fear and insecurity and increasing respect and trust, your need to withdraw from others or to behave aggressively toward them will be reduced. Your interpersonal relationships will surely improve. In short, self-knowledge has a social payoff.

Studying how your personality functions can also present a range of possibilities that you may never have considered. Maybe you've always wanted to better yourself, but have never known how to do it. Consider a study of your personality, which can provide alternative behavioural paths toward per-

Socrates understood the importance of self-knowledge to personal growth and social functioning.

Know thyself.

Socrates

I am what I am and that's all what I am.

Popeye the Sailor

sonal growth and development. Perhaps you're at your wits' end when it comes to coping and getting along with "difficult" people in your life. A study of personality can sometimes help you to understand why such people present challenges for you, and you can begin to see these individuals from a different perspective. You can start to explore alternative and useful ways of handling those people you may have given up on.

> No man should part with his own individuality and become that of another.
>
> Channing

Understanding your personality can also help you to feel better about yourself. There is little worse than being down emotionally, but not knowing why. Maybe you're unaware of the things going on in your mind that are contributing to your bad feelings. A better understanding of personality can uncover things about yourself that you have never consciously realized, and it can help you to take more effective control of your life. It can free you from debilitating negative emotions, and it can open the door to new and positive experiences. Self-knowledge can help you to establish organized plans for your career and life in general. It can give you a framework for decision making and action by helping you to live and work more productively.

Since the turn of the 20th century, many different theories of personality have emerged. There have been psychoanalytic, humanistic and behavioural explanations. People such as Sigmund Freud, Abraham Maslow and B.F. Skinner have all offered their own accounts of human personality functioning. One account that has received widespread attention is an offshoot of Carl Jung's analytical theory of personality types. A mother-daughter team of Katharine Briggs and Isabel Briggs Myers has taken the original insights of Jung, added to them, and developed for practical use the **Myers-Briggs Type Indicator (MBTI®)**, an instrument used to help people identify their personality preferences. This instrument has been used by millions of people throughout the world for human resource development, team building and problem solving, as well as for personal counselling, therapy and education. The MBTI is a restricted psychological assessment tool that can only be used by trained and qualified personnel. (The MBTI is available from Consulting Psychologists Press in Palo Alto, California.)

For our purposes here, I have created my own personality self-diagnostic that is different from the MBTI in terms of wording and format, but is theoretically consistent with its ideas and assumptions. It can help you to start thinking about your personality preferences using concepts and insights discussed by Jung, Myers and Briggs. While my informal self-diagnostic obviously will not be as reliable and valid as the highly researched MBTI, it can nonetheless help you form an initial hypothesis about your **psychological type**, the way you perceive, make decisions and orient toward the world. Most people who have completed both the MBTI and my self-diagnostic have tended to arrive at similar results. My self-diagnostic can therefore serve as a valuable tool for preliminary self-reflection. For those who are seriously interested in verifying their personality type, I would strongly suggest taking the MBTI with a qualified counsellor at your college or university. Ideally, your instructor would be in a position to have it administered to you in class. If that's not possible, you may wish to complete Gordon Lawrence's (1983)

"Exercise: Thinking about Mental Habits" in *People Types and Tiger Stripes*, a source reference for my own work here. In any event, let us now establish our initial working hypothesis by completing Self-Diagnostic 1.1, Pinpointing My Personality Preferences.

Pinpointing My Personality Preferences

You can use this self-diagnostic tool to begin to understand yourself better. You're actually far too complex to "figure out" in one paper-and-pencil measure. Nonetheless, your results on this self-diagnostic can serve as a departure point for further self-exploration. See your results as a working hypothesis of who you are.

Instructions: Below are pairs of statements listed under lettered columns. Compare the statements in each pair and circle the letter beside the one that most accurately describes your preferences, behaviours or mental habits. Be sure to circle one—and ONLY one—letter in each pair. Some decisions may be difficult, especially when you like both statements. Simply pick the one for which you have the slightest preference. As well, choose the answer that feels right for you. Don't answer as you or others think you "should." Simply imagine yourself to be in a comfortable spot and answer the questions in a relaxed frame of mind. It's important to be accurate and honest. This is not your work self or student self answering; it is your "real" self.

Circle the statement of each pair below that describes you most accurately, E or I.

E	I
E I like fast living.	(I) I like quiet time and space to contemplate my affairs.
E I like the world outside.	(I) I like the inner world.
E I like people and things.	(I) I like ideas, thoughts and meanings.
(E) I like to be talkative and outgoing.	I I like to be quiet and reserved.
E I like to be sociable with many.	(I) I like to be introspective with few.
E I like to be energized by activity.	(I) I like to be energized by depth and intimacy.
(E) I like to seek out new experiences.	I I tend to avoid new experiences.
2 ⁱⁱ	TOTALS 5 ³

Add the number of both E and I statements circled. Place the letter with the highest total in the appropriate space below.

When it comes to E or I preferences, I tend to select __I__ more.

Circle the statement of each pair below that describes you most accurately, S or N.

S	N
S I tend to be practical.	(N) I tend to be idealistic.

(S) I like the concrete.

(S) I choose to use my eyes and ears and other senses to find out what's happening.

(S) I tend to be physically competitive.

(S) I prefer to be results oriented.

(S) I like to look at the facts.

(S) I enjoy using skills I've already learned.

N I like the abstract.

N I choose to use my imagination to come up with new possibilities and novel ways of doing things.

N I tend to be intellectually competitive.

N I prefer to be idea oriented.

N I like symbols, concepts and meanings.

N I enjoy using new skills more than practising old ones.

6 _____ TOTALS _____ 1

Add the number of both S and N statements circled. Place the letter with the highest total in the appropriate space below.

When it comes to S or N preferences, I tend to select **S** more.

Circle the statement of each pair below that describes you most accurately, T or F.

T

(T) I like to make decisions based on logic.

(T) I tend to notice ineffective reasoning.

(T) I prefer truthfulness over tact.

(T) I decide more with my head.

T I tend to focus on objective and universal principles.

(T) I like to deal with people firmly, when required.

(T) I give more attention to ideas or things.

F

F I like to make decisions based on feelings and values even if illogical.

F I tend to notice when people need support.

F I prefer tactfulness over truth.

F I decide more with my heart.

(F) I tend to focus on subjective and personal motives.

F I like to deal with people compassionately, when required.

F I give more attention to human relationships.

6 _____ TOTALS _____ 1

Add the number of both T and F statements circled. Place the letter with the highest total in the appropriate space below.

When it comes to T or F preferences, I tend to select **T** more.

Circle the statement of each pair below that describes you most accurately, J or P.

J

(J) I like closure, a sense of being finished.

(J) I prefer advance notice.

(J) I am task oriented.

(J) I like to plan and decide.

(J) I sometimes jump to conclusions prematurely.

P

P I like to hang loose and stay open to new things.

P I prefer spontaneous challenges.

P I am process oriented.

P I like to adapt and change.

P I tend to postpone decisions and procrastinate.

(J) I like to make things come out as they should.

(J) I like to finish one thing before starting another.

P I like to deal with unexpected and unplanned happenings.

P I like to do several things at the same time, though I have trouble finishing them.

___7___   TOTALS   ___0___

Add the number of both J and P statements circled. Place the letter with the highest total in the appropriate space below.

When it comes to J or P preferences, I tend to select __J__ more.

Summary of Results

Under each set of paired statements you indicated your preference. Now place the letters of your four preferences below. The four letters taken together represent your personality type according to this self-diagnostic (e.g., ENTJ or ISFP).

__I__   __S__   __T__   __J__   (My personality type preferences)

E or I   S or N   T or F   J or P

Explanation of Results

The self-diagnostic you just completed is an informal assessment tool based on the personality theory initially put forward by Carl Gustav Jung, later refined and developed by Katharine Briggs and Isabel Briggs Myers. According to Jung, Myers and Briggs, people's behaviour is not completely random. Personality types reflect patterns in the ways people perceive and make judgments about the world. You may be extraverted or introverted (E or I), sensing or iNtuiting (S or N), thinking or feeling (T or F), and judging or perceiving (J or P). Your results, then, serve as a summary statement about your perceptual and decision-making mental processes. The rest of this chapter explains these preferences, thereby debriefing your results. For now, you may wish to glance below at the summary description of your own type as well as the other possibilities. Each type has its preferred energy source, its preferred way of gathering information and making judgments about it, as well as its particular orientation to the external world.

Summary Chart of Your Personality Preferences

Personality Type	Energy Source	Information Gathered	Decides With	Orientation to Outer World
ENTJ	External	Intuitively	Head	Judging
ENTP	External	Intuitively	Head	Perceiving
ENFJ	External	Intuitively	Heart	Judging
ENFP	External	Intuitively	Heart	Perceiving
ESFJ	External	Sensorily	Heart	Judging
ESFP	External	Sensorily	Heart	Perceiving
ESTJ	External	Sensorily	Head	Judging
ESTP	External	Sensorily	Head	Perceiving
INTP	Internal	Intuitively	Head	Perceiving

INTJ	Internal	Intuitively	Head	Judging
INFP	Internal	Intuitively	Heart	Perceiving
INFJ	Internal	Intuitively	Heart	Judging
ISFP	Internal	Sensorily	Heart	Perceiving
ISFJ	Internal	Sensorily	Heart	Judging
ISTP	Internal	Sensorily	Head	Perceiving
ISTJ	Internal	Sensorily	Head	Judging

To learn all kinds of things, one must relate to all types of people.

Anonymous

You're only Jung once, but that's nothing to be a Freud about.

Anonymous

Carl Gustav Jung was the founder of analytical psychology.

PERSONALITY TYPES: RECOGNIZABLE PATTERNS OF DIVERSITY

According to Carl Jung, **human diversity** is not a completely random matter. At a psychological level, differences we see in people can be understood in terms of recognizable patterns. These patterns can be observed in the way people use their minds, particularly in the way they perceive the world and make judgments about it. **Perceptual mental processes** determine what we see or attend to in a situation. The **judgment function** influences how we make decisions about what we perceive. Jung also believed that differences in people can be understood in terms of **psychological attitude**. Attitude, in this context, refers to the energizing sources in life. Some individuals tend to focus their lives externally, while others tend to be more focused on the inner world of ideas.

> Having gifts that differ according to the grace given us, let us use them....
>
> Romans 12:6

As I mentioned earlier, Katharine Briggs and Isabel Briggs Myers made some minor modifications to Jung's work and elaborated upon it. They added to Jung's conception of type the idea of **external orientation**, the psychological stance adopted toward people, situations and events in the outer world. In what follows, you will find more detailed explanations of the orientations, attitudes, functions and mental processes that combine to establish type and type differences. The explanations will help you to understand better the results of Self-Diagnostic 1.1. They will also help you to appreciate for later purposes the usefulness and

Please Understand Me

If I do not want what you want, please try not to tell me that my want is wrong.

Or if I believe other than you, at least pause before you correct my view.

Or if my emotion is less than yours, or more, given the same circumstances, try not to ask me to feel more strongly or weakly.

Or yet if I act, or fail to act, in the manner of your design for action, let me be.

I do not, for the moment at least, ask you to understand me. That will come only when you are willing to give up changing me into a copy of you.

David Keirsey and Marilyn Bates

Source: Reprinted by permission of the Board of Prometheus-Nemesis Book Co.

practical applications of psychological type for personal growth and inter-personal communication. See the four psychological preference scales that follow, which depict how the 16 personality types can be formed.

The Four Psychological Preference Scales

Extraversion	or	Introversion
Sensing	or	iNtuition
Thinking	or	Feeling
Judging	or	Perceiving

Combining Preferences Leads to 16 Possible Personality Types

ISTJ	ISTP	ESTP	ESTJ
ISFJ	ISFP	ESFP	ESFJ
INFJ	INFP	ENFP	ENFJ
INTJ	INTP	ENTP	ENTJ

> Nothing is more wondrous than human beings when they begin to discover themselves.
>
> Chinese Proverb

Energy Source: Extraversion versus Introversion

Do You Have an Introverted or Extraverted Attitude?

Introvert to extravert: "Pardon me for speaking while you were interrupting."

Extravert to introvert: "Do you have any other speeds besides slow and stop?"

Probably by this time in your life you've referred to someone you know as being either introverted or extraverted. You likely have some common-sense notion of what these terms mean; however, you may not know that their technical psychological definition originates with the work of Carl Jung. According to Jung's analytical psychology, people differ with respect to the attitudes they adopt toward life. These attitudes are not something good or bad. Rather, think of them as approaches to life or psychological postures. Attitudes are characterized by what people find energizing. For instance, when you walk into a room full of people, do you feel excited? Or, is it more likely you feel drained? Your response here reveals much about your attitude. Some people like to mingle and interact with many (**extraverts**), while others prefer to speak with one or two people at a time (**introverts**). (By the way, the correct spelling of extravert is "extrovert." However, Carl Jung's misspelling of the term has now become the convention for type theorists. It continues to be a source of irritation for spelling-bee champions!)

Introverts — Life's Private "I"s

Attitudinal differences between introverts and extraverts are apparent when you look at the focus of their attention. Extraverts are more likely to focus their perceptions and judgments outwardly. The external world is their preoccupation. Introverts, by contrast, prefer to deal with the inner world of ideas; they are energized by concepts and inner reflections. This kind of individual (maybe you) would rather listen than talk. Intense and loud discussions are likely to be draining experiences. In order to "recharge," the introvert needs to be alone. Private time is important. "Alone, but not lonely" is a phrase that the introvert understands well.

If you are an introvert, chances are pretty good that sometime in your life you've felt underestimated. While I'm sure this happens to virtually everybody, this experience is more likely with introverts. The reason is that extraverts outnumber introverts by about three to one. Given the private nature of introverts, along with their smaller number, it's not surprising that many of the values and preferences of the extravert tend to dominate North American culture. Of course, many introverts learn to play the extraverted game of life very well. They become excellent at public relations and quite efficient in dealing with external matters. The problem is that they often feel drained, not energized, by becoming good at what they least prefer. (To appreciate why, do Application Exercise 1.1, Working in Your Wrong Hand.)

APPLICATION
EXERCISE
1.1

Working in Your Wrong Hand

This exercise, or some variation of it, is often used in workshops designed to help people appreciate the difficulties that arise when trying to operate with opposite or lesser preferred psychological functions.

Instructions: Write your name, address and telephone number on a piece of paper with your "wrong" hand. If you're right-handed, use your left hand. If you're left-handed, use your right hand.

For discussion: After finishing this task, evaluate your work. Is it better or worse than what you could have done with your preferred hand? How did you feel working with your "wrong" hand? What would be the effect on you if you were forced to operate all day long using your lesser preferred hand? What generalizations could you possibly make about people's behaviour using this experiential exercise?

Introverts: Recall a time when you were required to function as an extravert. Where were you? What did you have to do? How did you feel? What did you think? How did you experience this situation?

Extraverts: Recall a time when you were required to function as an introvert. Where were you? What did you have to do? How did you feel? What did you think? How did you experience this situation?

Extraverts — Life's Party Types

As you might guess, the extravert loves what the introvert least prefers. Extraverted types tend to be energized by people and action, and their orientation is outward. They generally enjoy being sociable, expressive and involved in external matters. Extraverts get their essential stimulation from the environment. As strong as the introvert's needs may be for privacy, so strong may be the extravert's need for social relationships. In contrast to the introvert, whose thoughts and reflections give depth to life, the extravert prefers breadth. (Do you complain about courses that are too superficial— an introvert's comment—or ones that are too narrowly focused and hence boring—an extravert's comment?)

By natural inclination, extraverts tend to act before thinking, whereas introverts reflect and then (maybe) act. Extraverts tend to think out loud. Introverts think to themselves. I suppose Alice in Wonderland exposed her extraverted preferences when she said at one point that she couldn't tell what she was thinking until she heard what she said. Like the proverbial extravert, she was "thinking out loud."

At this point, it is very important for you to note that we all display introverted and extraverted tendencies at different times; it's just that one is usually preferred and better developed. Nobody is entirely introverted or extraverted. We all show signs of both, but are energized as one.

Key Descriptors — Sources of Energy

Introverts (I)	Extraverts (E)
Focus on inner world	Focus on outer world
Depth	Breadth
Private	Social
Reserved	Outgoing
Think before acting	Act before thinking
Reflective	Active

Where does your preference fall?

Introversion   **Extraversion**

High   Moderate   Low   Low   Moderate   High

Take note: We all display introverted and extraverted tendencies, but usually prefer one over the other.

Information Gathering: Sensing versus Intuition

What Do You Pay Attention to When You Gather Information?

Not all people experience and gather information about the world in the same way. How we take in information is determined by the psychological functions of sensing and intuition. We all use both functions in our lives, but again, we typically display a preference for one, and feel more confident about it.

Sensors — The Realists

Sensors, or sensing type individuals, can be fairly described as realists. I like to think of them as no-nonsense, "meat and potatoes" people. Sensing types pay a great deal of attention to information that is received through sensory channels. For them, seeing is believing.

> We see things not as they are—but as we are.
>
> Ken Keyes, Jr.

Sensing types tend to focus on the here and now. They enjoy and experience what is currently happening, and focus less on what might or could be. Their present orientation causes them to concentrate on the facts and details of situations, people and events. Their greatest trust is placed in firsthand experience.

Scientists often use their sensing functions to formulate conclusions about minute and intricate processes.

A noticeable characteristic of sensing types is their preference for set procedures and established routines. Deviations and unexpected changes to usual ways of doing things may not be welcomed. Sensing types also enjoy looking at things in terms of their specific parts and pieces. They like things to be definite and measurable. Anything fuzzy and open-ended is not terribly appreciated. You can also notice that sensors have a sequential approach to life. They prefer to start at the beginning of things and methodically complete them, one step at a time. Sensors are at their best when allowed to work at things "hands on." The next time you meet a no-nonsense, concrete realist who's particularly interested in the facts and practical details, you're probably facing a sensor.

iNtuitives — The Innovators

Intuitives are unlike sensors insofar as they prefer to process information by way of a "sixth sense." They may downplay sensory-based information and opt for intuitive hunches. In contrast to the sensing types who prefer a routine, intuitives like exploring alternatives and change. Variety is the spice of life. This need for variety and change may make intuitives appear fickle or impractical, but this need is probably more reflective of their future orientation. Intuitives are possibility thinkers and always anticipate what might be or what could be. Intuitives therefore crave opportunities to be inventive because doing things in accepted routine ways is boring or limiting. Intuitives also don't seem to mind jumping in anywhere when tasks must be done. For them, "intuitive leaps" are commonly made of "sequential steps." In this vein, intuitives like to look for patterns, relationships and overall designs rather than concentrate on pieces and parts to make up the whole. The whole is the first object of attention.

Albert Einstein's intuitive ideas have helped to change our understanding of the physical world.

> Your imagination is your preview of life's coming attractions.
>
> Albert Einstein

Key Descriptors — Information Gathering

Sensors (S)	Intuitives (N)
Perspire	Inspire
Focus on present	Focus on future
Like routine	Choose variety
Enjoy	Anticipate
Conserve	Change
Stress facts	Stress innovations
Take sequential approach	Take random approach
Look for details	Look for patterns
Are practical	Are imaginative
Follow directions	Pursue hunches

Where does your preference fall?

Sensing   **Intuitive**

High	Moderate	Low	Low	Moderate	High

Take note: We all use sensing and intuitive processes, but usually prefer one over the other.

Decision Making: Thinking versus Feeling

Do You Prefer to Decide with Your Head or Your Heart?

The thinking-feeling dimension of personality explains how we make decisions about what we see. Remember that our perceptions are obtained through sensing-intuiting channels. Thinking-feeling processes establish our personal style of making judgments on what is seen or perceived. As with attitudes and perceptual functions, people differ in ways explainable by a bipolar scale. Though we all use both thinking and feeling as a basis of decision making at different times in our lives, we generally prefer one over the other. The results of your self-diagnostic should begin to give you insights as to whether you're a thinking type or feeling type.

Quotations that might appeal to the

Thinker: We are what we think; all that we are arises from our thoughts. With our thoughts we make the world.

Buddha

Feeler: The young man who has not wept is a savage, and the old man who will not laugh is a fool.

Confucius

Rodin's "The Thinker" captures the thoughtfulness of the T-type individual.

Thinkers — Life's Logicians

People with thinking preferences take a logical approach to life. Careful consideration is usually given to reasons justifying actions. **Thinkers** tend to consider carefully the consequences of actions in an unbiased, impersonal way. Decisions are taken objectively and based on truth or likelihood of truth. Thinking types desire to make firm decisions based on detached and impartial judgments. Thinkers thus tend to have an intellectual orientation to life. They can appear at times to be very "cerebral." They place great confidence in their mental and cognitive processes. When values or emotions play a part in their decision making, they are usually used to support logical conclusions. Given this, thinkers frequently choose to be truthful rather than tactful. They are sometimes less sensitive to people and more likely to be aware of rational considerations. They choose their heads over their hearts in most instances. Thinkers often consider it a greater compliment to be regarded as fair than as likeable or compassionate.

> The way to a thinker's heart is through his mind.
>
> Tonee Balonee

Feelers — Life's Lovers

People with feeling preferences, or "life's lovers," make decisions based on their emotions and personal values. When logic and reason are used to make decisions, they are typically employed to support values-oriented conclusions. We find, then, that **feelers** are more "people people," and that they're less likely to be regarded as detached and aloof, which is sometimes the case with objective-minded thinkers. Feeling types pick the heart over the head, preferring tact over truth. When hard decisions must be

Feeling types often base their decisions on emotion, which overrides what logic and reason dictate.

made, they are more likely to be compassionate than firm. They are not likely to stick to impersonal principles and rules at any cost. On this score, feeling types can be described as humane and personally involved. It's not that there's something wrong with the desire to be just and objectively fair, but for the feeler, subjective considerations and personal values take on a greater importance.

Key Descriptors — Ways of Making Decisions

Thinkers (T)	Feelers (F)
Objective	Subjective
Impersonal	Personal
Rational	Emotional
Head	Heart
Truthful	Tactful
Logic	Values
Firm	Compassionate
Just	Humane
Critical	Appreciative

Where does your preference fall?

Thinking   **Feeling**

High	Moderate	Low	Low	Moderate	High

Take note: We all display thinking and feeling processes, but prefer one over the other.

Orientation to the Outer World: Judging versus Perceiving

What's Your Preferred Way of Approaching External Reality?

By now you have learned something about what energizes you, what you pay attention to when gathering information, and how you go about making decisions. However, it is also insightful for you to consider your psychological orientation to people, places and events in the external world. What is your preferred **lifestyle orientation**?

By the use of this term, I'm not referring to your tastes in fashion or to your material possessions. Rather, the phrase refers to the psychological stance you assume vis-à-vis the world. Some of us tend to be judging types, while others are perceiving types. Be careful not to confuse judging with judgmental or perceiving with perceptive. No character evaluations are intended. It's just that people differ in their approaches to life. Neither approach is better or worse than the other. The judging-perceiving distinction points to how we relate to external reality. Some of us are decision makers; others are more comfortable as information gatherers.

Judgers — Life's Organizers

If you love making lists of things to do or if you like to use the expression "A place for everything and everything in its place," I would venture to guess that you are a judging type of person. **Judgers** create for themselves highly structured environments. Most activities are planned. For them, there may be a time and place for fun as well as an appropriate way to have it. For example, have you ever been to a party where there wasn't a moment of free time and where everything was organized and planned? If so, you simply couldn't do what *you* wanted since the party organizer had decided in advance what should be done and when.

Not only are judging types well-organized and highly structured in their approach to life, they are also decisive. Judgers need closure on matters and enjoy making decisions about what ought or ought not to be done in a given situation. They like to be definite and deliberate. Once plans or schedules are established, strong judgers like to follow them closely. This decisiveness gives judgers a sense of control and order. Once the target is fixed and the course is set, judgers enjoy taking action to achieve their goal.

If you are a judging type, you use either thinking (T) or feeling (F) as a preferred way of dealing with the external world. Your life may be organized in terms of impersonal considerations (e.g., time schedules and budgets) or in terms of interpersonal dealings (e.g., values and feelings). You can be decisive either with your head or your heart. Both are rational ways of making decisions. The judging type prefers one over the other.

Perceivers — Mellow Fellows and Females

People who display a strong preference for perceiving live noticeably different lifestyles compared to their judging cousins. In contrast to judgers who love to plan, schedule, organize and list, **perceivers** prefer to live spontaneously. Last minute changes to schedules, for example, may not be seen as problems, but rather as opportunities for new possibilities. Change is less of an enemy and more of a friend, because the perceiving person possesses the natural inclination to remain open to the unforeseen.

If you're a strong perceptive type, chances are pretty good that you feel uncomfortable when forced to come to quick conclusions. If you're typical of this type, then you prefer to adopt a tentative approach to life. Your conclusions will sound less like categorical judgments and more like testable hypotheses. You may feel a constant urge to learn more or gather additional information before making any final conclusions. In fact, the act of gathering information is probably a great source of pleasure for you. (Do you find researching a paper is more fun than writing it?)

Perceivers are distinguished by the tolerance and adaptability that they display. They are less likely to use words like "should" and "ought" when it comes to other people's lives. "Live and let live" is a saying that the perceiving person might use as a personal guideline. In short, perceptives tend to go with the flow of life and just let things happen.

If you are a perceiver, either sensing or intuition is your preferred way of dealing with the external world. An ESFP, for instance, relies most heavily on sensing, while, by contrast, an ESFJ is most reliant on feeling. Remember, sensing and intuition are perceiving functions, whereas thinking and feeling are decision-making processes. The last letter of your type (i.e., J or P) indicates whether you prefer perceptual processes (S or N) or decision-making processes (T or F) in your dealings with the external world. "J" points to T or F preferences. "P" points to S or N preferences.

Key Descriptors — Orientation to the Outer World

Judging (J)	Perceiving (P)
Structured	Flexible
Scheduled	Spontaneous
Ordered	Adaptive
Planned	Responsive to a variety of situations
Decisive	Wait and see attitude
Deliberate	Tendency to keep collecting new information
Definite	Tentative
Fixed	Flexible
Enjoy finishing	Enjoy starting

Where does your preference fall?

Judging   **Perceiving**

| High | Moderate | Low | Low | Moderate | High |

Take note: We all display judging and perceiving processes, but prefer one over the other.

TYPE CLASSIFICATIONS

In total there are 16 personality types, which are grouped into four categories. Find the four-letter combination that summarizes your personality preferences. What type are you?

Sensing-Thinking Types	Sensing-Feeling Types
ISTJ	ISFJ
ISTP	ISFP
ESTP	ESFP
ESTJ	ESFJ

Intuitive-Feeling Types	Intuitive-Thinking Types
INFJ	INTJ
INFP	INTP
ENFP	ENTP
ENFJ	ENTJ

My preferences indicate that I am probably a(n) _____ type.

ST	SF	NF	NT
S E N S I	S E N S I	I N T U I	I N T U I
N G & T	N G & F	T I V E	T I V E
H I N K	E E L I	& F E E	& T H I
I N G	N G	L I N G	N K I N G

SUMMARY OF TYPE CHARACTERISTICS

Sensing-Thinking People	**Sensing-Feeling People**
Focus on facts and details	Open to impulse and spontaneous acts
Speak and write directly to the point	Do what feels good
Adapt easily to established procedures and guidelines	Sensitive to others' feelings
Concerned with efficiency and utility	Decisions made according to personal likes and dislikes
Goal or task oriented	Prefer to learn through human interaction and personal experience
Emphasize accuracy	Enjoy activities involving emotional expression
Approach tasks sequentially	Persuasive through personal interaction
Focus on the present	Keen observers of human nature
	Interested in people

Intuitive-Feeling People	**Intuitive-Thinking People**
Open to the nonconventional	Need time to plan and consider consequences of an action
See facts and details as part of the larger picture	Like to organize and synthesize information
Express themselves in new and unusual ways	Focus on impersonal considerations
Adapt to new circumstances	Decisions based on evidence and logical thinking
Process oriented	Prefer to learn vicariously through books and symbolic forms
Highly interested in beauty, symmetry and form	Enjoy logical thinking activities
Enjoy exploratory activities	Persuasive intellectually
Focus on the future	Store huge amounts of knowledge and information
	Interested in ideas, theories and concepts

Classroom Chemistry

It's almost a cliché for educators to say that no two college or university classes are alike. However, to explain why this is the case is the challenge. Instructors are sometimes amazed how a single lesson plan and delivery method can work wonderfully well in one section of a course and bomb in another. As a student, you may also wonder about the quiet and impersonal nature of your introductory psychology class, especially when you compare it to the noisy and emotionally charged nature of the psychological counselling class taught by the same instructor. Course content and class size might have some influence on atmos-

phere, but then again, the differences may have something to do with the psychological makeup of the students. The different makeup of each course section could affect the "chemistry of the classroom."

Instructions: On the blackboard or flip chart, draw a type table similar to the one illustrated below. You could also draw the table on a transparency sheet for overhead projection. Decide whether you wish to keep a permanent record for yourself.

ISTJ	ISFJ	INFJ	INTJ
ISTP	ISFP	INFP	INTP
ESTP	ESFP	ENFP	ENTP
ESTJ	ESFJ	ENFJ	ENTJ

Invite students to put their names (or check marks) in the appropriate boxes as indicated by their psychological type. No student should be forced to do this. No reasons for refusal need be given. Respect everyone's privacy. Remember, no type is any better or worse than any other. After completing the type table, answer the following questions. (This may be done in small groups or all together as a class.)

Introversion versus Extraversion

1. How many introverts are in the class?
2. How many extraverts are in the class?

Letter of higher frequency _____ (I or E)

Discussion: Given what you know about introverted and extraverted preferences, what predictions about the class would seem reasonable? For example, will large or small group discussions flow more easily? Will class participation come readily? How could the introverted-extraverted chemistry of the classroom contribute to everyone's benefit? How could it pose challenges?

Sensing versus Intuition

1. How many sensing types are in the class?
2. How many intuitive types are in the class?

Letter of higher frequency _____ (S or N)

Discussion: Given what you know about sensing and intuiting preferences, what predictions about the class would be reasonable? Will the class be conducted in a routine way or will members opt for variety? Will people be more likely to perform in a step-by-step fashion or will they be more likely to jump in wherever they feel comfortable?

Thinking versus Feeling

1. How many thinking types are in the class?
2. How many feeling types are in the class?

Letter of higher frequency _____ (T or F)

Discussion: Given what you know about thinking and feeling preferences, what predictions about the class would seem reasonable? For example, will the group tend to be concerned with personal values or objective and emotionally detached considerations?

Judging versus Perceiving

1. How many judging types are in the class?
2. How many perceiving types are in the class?

Letter of higher frequency _____ (J or P)

Discussion: Given what you know about judging and perceiving preferences, what predictions about the class would seem reasonable? For example, will it be necessary for most students to function according to a strict timetable or will it be relatively easy to deviate from the lesson plans?

What are the four dominant preferences of your class? Is there anyone who is the "pure" classroom type—the one whose personality captures all the dominant preferences of the class?

_____ _____ _____ _____

    I or E   S or N   T or F   J or P

What are the class frequencies of

STs	Sensing-Thinking Types	_____?
SFs	Sensing-Feeling Types	_____?
NFs	Intuitive-Feeling Types	_____?
NTs	Intuitive-Thinking Types	_____?

Discussion: Given the chemistry of your class, what might be its strengths? What challenges might you anticipate? Who is likely to fit in most easily? What can be done to make others feel comfortable?

APPLICATION EXERCISE 1.3

TV Types Have Different Stripes

Now that you understand the basics of psychological type, it's time to apply your knowledge. Of course, there's nothing wrong in having a little bit of fun at the same time!

Instructions: Form small groups. Select a secretary and spokesperson for your group. Discuss the psychological profiles of the TV personalities and characters listed below. Place each name in the appropriate box labelled according to psychological preferences. If you need help, refer to the Summary of Type Characteristics (p. 21). For a variation of this activity, change any of the TV characters or personalities to suit the viewing tastes of the class.

Caution: Your group may choose to focus on particular features of the TV character or personality not emphasized by other groups. If your group's placements are different from those of other groups, use these differences as a basis for class discussion. In the end, the placement is less important than the rationale behind it.

TV Personalities/Characters

Frasier Crane	Deanna Troi	Dharma
Fox Mulder	Ren and Stimpy	Ellen Degeneris
Murphy Brown	Jessica Fletcher	Ally McBeal
Jerry Seinfeld	Homer Simpson	Brandon Walsh

ST	SF
NF	**NT**

STUDY GUIDE

Key Terms

self-knowledge (4)	processes (9)	sensors (14)
personality (4)	judgment function (9)	intuitives (15)
Myers-Briggs Type	psychological attitude	thinkers (16)
Indicator (MBTI)	(9)	feelers (17)
(5)	external orientation	lifestyle orientation
psychological type (5)	(9)	(18)
human diversity (9)	extraverts (11)	judgers (18)
perceptual mental	introverts (11)	perceivers (19)

Fill-in-the-Blank Questions

PROGRESS CHECK 1.1 ✔

Instructions: Fill in each blank with the appropriate answer from the list below.

intuitive-feeling	patterns
thinking	now
processes	innovators
bipolar	others
feeling	_____ (your type)
realists	inner
outer	analytical
decision making	future
life orientation	judging
perceptive	Jung

1. Self-understanding can help you to understand _____.

2. According to Self-Diagnostic 1.1, my personality type is _____.

3. Extraverts get their energy from the _____ world.

4. Introverts get their energy from the _____ world.

5. According to Myers and Briggs, there are four _____ scales that can be used to understand psychological type.

6. The Myers Briggs Type Indicator is based on Carl Jung's _____ psychology.

7. Sensing and intuition are perceptual _____.

8. Sensing types tend to be _____.

9. Intuitive types tend to be _____.

10. Sensing types focus on the _____.

11. Intuitive types focus on the _____.

12. People who adopt a highly rational or logical approach to life are probably _____ types.

13. People who prefer to make decisions in personal and value-oriented ways are _____ types.

14. Thinking and feeling are both _____ functions.

15. Judging and perceiving reflect our _____.

16. If you love to plan, organize, make lists and get things finished, then you're probably a _____ type.

17. If you prefer a tentative approach to life and often feel a need to gather more information, then you're probably a _____ type.

18. The mirror opposite of the sensing-thinking type is the _____ type.

19. While individuals are unique, there still are recognizable _____ of perception and decision making that we share with others.

20. If you're worried about being too _____, that's nothing to be a Freud about.

True/False Questions

Instructions: Circle the appropriate letter next to each statement.

T F   1. Learning about your own personality can help you to understand others.

T F   2. There are no patterns or recognizable mental habits in people's perceptual and decision-making functions.

T F   3. According to type theory, having an attitude refers to a character flaw.

T F   4. An ENFP is someone displaying extraverted, intuitive, thinking and perceiving preferences.

T F   5. An ST prefers sensing-thinking functions.

T F   6. Psychological type is made up of four bipolar scales.

T F   7. Introverts are necessarily lonely people.

T F   8. Extraverts are always good with people.

T F   9. Sensing types have an innate sense of innovation and future possibilities.

T F 10. Intuitive types like to look for meanings and relationships.

T F 11. Thinking types don't have feelings.

T F 12. Feeling types can't think logically.

T F 13. Judging types are necessarily judgmental toward others.

T F 14. Perceptive types can never make decisions on time.

T F 15. Type talk is terrific.

Focus Questions

1. Isn't it silly to ask, "Who am I?" What practical purpose could be served by finding an answer to this vague, disturbing question?

2. What makes me unique? What commonalities do I share with others?

3. What are the four scales explaining personality functioning according to Jungian psychology, as developed by Katharine Briggs and Isabel Briggs Myers?

4. What energizes people?

5. To what do people pay attention? How do some people perceive the world differently from others?

6. What are the two decision-making processes people use? How is one different from the other?

7. What are the two basic orientations to life people can adopt?

8. What four general categories can be used to summarize all 16 personality types?

Summary

1. Why is self-knowledge important?
   - it maximizes your potential
   - it develops your strengths
   - it works on your weaknesses
   - it increases self-awareness
   - it builds self-confidence
   - it helps you live more productively

2. How can self-knowledge help you socially?
   - discovering your personal uniqueness can help you to appreciate the uniqueness of others
   - your respect for others can increase
   - your defensiveness can be reduced by honouring yourself, thereby improving communications with others

3. What are the basic components of personality functioning according to Jung, Myers and Briggs
   - attitudes: how you're energized
   - perceptual processes: how you take in information
   - decision-making functions: how you make judgments on what you perceive
   - life orientations: how you deal with the external world

4. What are the two basic attitudes?
   - extraversion: outer world, breadth, active, sociable
   - introversion: inner world, depth, reflective, private

5. What are the two basic perceptual processes?
   - sensing: present, routine, factual, details, practical
   - intuiting: future, variety, innovative, larger picture, imaginative

6. What are the two basic decision-making functions?
- thinking: objective, rational, impersonal, head, firm, just
- feeling: subjective, emotive, personal, heart, compassionate, humane

7. What are the two basic life orientations?
- judging: structured, planned, decisive, ordered, scheduled
- perceiving: flexible, responsive, tentative, adaptive, spontaneous

8. What four categories can be used to capture all 16 types?
- sensing-thinking types
- intuitive-feeling types
- sensing-feeling types
- intuitive-thinking types

Related Readings

Barr, Lee and Norma Barr (1989). *The Leadership Equation: Leadership Management and the Myers-Briggs*. Austin, TX: Eakin Press.

Briggs Myers, Isabel (1995 10th Anniversary Edition). *Gifts Differing*. Palo Alto, CA: Consulting Psychologists Press, Inc.

Hirsh, Sandra and Jean Kummerow (1989). *Lifetypes*. New York: Warner Books.

Kroeger, Otto and Janet Thuesen (1992). *Type Talk at Work*. New York: Delacorte Press.

Weblinks

1. Resource materials on personality typing
   www.sunsite.unc.edu/personality/faq-mbti.html

   Visit this site for an extensive list of books and resource materials on the MBTI and psychological type.

2. DeVere Winter Associates
   www.deverewinter.mb.ca/products.htm

   Check out deVere Winter Associates for available services relating to the application of psychological type to individual and group consulting, negotiating, serving clients and productive group work.

3. Isabel Briggs Myers Memorial Library
   www.capt.org/library.html

   The Center for the Applications of Psychological Type houses the Isabel Briggs Myers Memorial Library, which is open to visitors during the CAPT's normal business hours.

4. Association for Psychological Type (APT)
   www.aptcentral.org/

   APT has outstanding training services, including its MBTI qualifying training program.

CHAPTER 2

Mend your speech a little, lest it may mar your fortunes.

—William Shakespeare

PSYCH-SMART COMMUNICATIONS: HOW TO COMMUNICATE EFFECTIVELY WITH DIFFERENT PERSONALITY TYPES

CHAPTER OVERVIEW

LEARNING OUTCOMES

After successfully completing this chapter, you will be able to

2.1   Spell out the importance of communication to effective interpersonal relations

2.2   Outline the process of communication

2.3   Explain how psychological type influences the communication process

2.4   Communicate more effectively with people displaying opposite type preferences

2.5   Appreciate the sunny and shadow sides of each communication style

2.6   Modify communication strategies to accommodate psychological diversity

2.7   Identify the features of your preferred communication style and explore possibilities for self-improvement in this area

2.8   Better prepare for job interviews by accommodating psychological type preferences of prospective employers

2.9   Structure and organize "psych-smart" presentations

THE IMPORTANCE OF COMMUNICATION

In the preceding chapter, you had an opportunity to explore your psychological preferences and habits of thought. I hope that you have been able to develop at least a working hypothesis of your personality type for future consideration and verification. I also hope that you have come to appreciate human diversity in a way that honours your uniqueness as an individual and respects differences in others. As you will see shortly, recognizing and accommodating psychological diversity is instrumental to more effective communication.

> I know you heard what I said, but I'm not sure you understand what I meant.
>
> Anonymous

It's difficult to overstate the importance of **communication**. By means of communication, we relate to others and express ourselves. If we couldn't somehow convey our feelings and thoughts, it would be very hard to meet our basic needs. If we couldn't communicate, nobody would ever know what we wanted. This problem would seriously undermine our ability to achieve our goals in life.

Communication helps us to relate and build relationships with others. Through communication we share, empathize and learn about one another. We form friendships and develop intimacy. By talking and interacting, we share our thoughts and discover what others want.

Effective communication has a professional payoff. Observations in the fields of entertainment, business, politics and education clearly indicate the advantages of being a good communicator. For example, motivational speakers such as Norman Vincent Peale (author of *The Art of Positive Thinking*) and Anthony Robbins (author of *Unlimited Power*) didn't become rich and famous because of poor communication skills. As you consider this point, think about any long-lasting relationship, corporate success story or accomplished person you know. Has the success been based on poor or excellent communication skills? Are good and long-lasting marriages based on faulty communication between partners? In truly successful companies and organizations, do managers and employees fail to communicate? Are people who get what they want from life generally unable to express their desires? I think the answers to these rhetorical questions are all fairly obvious. In short, developing good communication skills is very much in your interest if you wish to be successful in your personal and professional dealings with people.

> People understand me so little that they do not even understand when I complain of being misunderstood.
>
> Soren Kierkegaard, misunderstood philosopher

THE PROCESS OF COMMUNICATION

As you learned in the introduction to this book, the process of communication is multifaceted and can be explained from a number of different perspectives (e.g., cultural or nonverbal). For our practical purposes here, I've provided a very simple model for analysis. See Figure 2.1 below.

Sender

The communication process begins with a **sender**, someone who acts as the source of communication. The sender about to communicate may wish to convey to another person some thought, feeling or idea; in other words, a **message**. Prior to communication, the sender may have had experiences and mental images that were not verbalized, but are now ready to be translated into words and symbols. This step takes us to encoding.

Message Encoding

Once the sender identifies the thought, feeling or idea to be communicated, the process of **encoding** takes place, which expresses the sender's intended meaning. The sender may carefully select from a mental list of words the ones that best describe the message to be communicated. In addition, special emphasis or intonation may be used to underscore the importance of what is verbalized. The difficult part of encoding is to structure messages in a form that others can easily understand.

Transmission of Message

Once the sender has identified the thought, feeling or idea to be communicated and has encoded it into a message containing the intended meaning,

Figure 2.1
The Communication Process

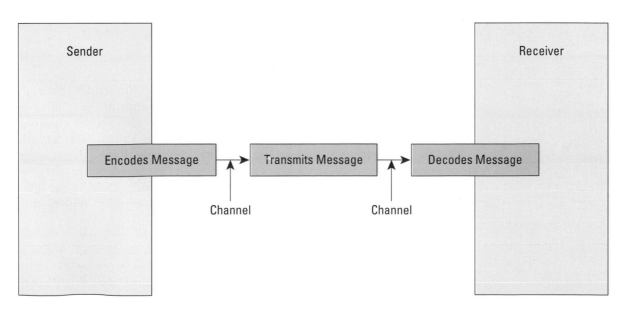

transmission takes place. Think of transmission as the process of sending a message to another person. Of course, messages can be sent in a variety of ways. You could speak to someone face to face or talk to that person over the telephone. You might use a fax machine or write a letter. These ways of transmission are some of the many **channels** you can use to transmit messages to other people.

Message Decoding

When a message is received by another person, **decoding** takes place. The receiver of the message automatically tries to make sense of the message that has been sent. Words and symbols are decoded back into thoughts, feelings and ideas that mean something to the receiver. In other words, receivers bring to interpersonal communications their own understandings, prior experiences, emotions, ideas and beliefs. They call upon these things to make sense of what they hear, see and read.

Receiver

The **receiver** in the communication process is the recipient or target of the message transmitted by the sender. No two receivers are identical because people bring to any interaction their unique personal histories, subjective feelings, thoughts, preferences and particular dispositions. It is important, therefore, to keep the receiver in mind when constructing messages for communication. If the receiver does not grasp the intended meaning of the sender's message, miscommunication, instead of communication, has taken place. Of course, if the receiver chooses to respond to the sender, the entire communication process takes place again. The only difference is that the sender and receiver exchange roles.

 ## INFLUENCE OF TYPE ON COMMUNICATION

As I've suggested, receivers may not always "get" what the sender transmits in communication. This fact underscores the importance of the human dimension in the communication process. Senders and receivers are not abstract entities, but real people. They have personal histories, values, interests and goals, as well as varying ethnic and racial backgrounds that no doubt affect communication. As well, we know from research that people differ from one another in terms of psychological type. In this section, I would like to illustrate how type theory can provide us with a richer and fuller understanding of the communication process (see Figure 2.2).

The notion of **type** takes into account psychological variables we can use to encode and decode messages more effectively. Remember, words in themselves do not carry meaning. Meanings are found in people, who in turn lend words the meaning they convey—intended or unintended. What a consideration of type does in the context of communication is provide us with

Embedded in every conversation we have is an underlying process of communication.

Figure 2.2

Type Dimension Added to the Communication Process

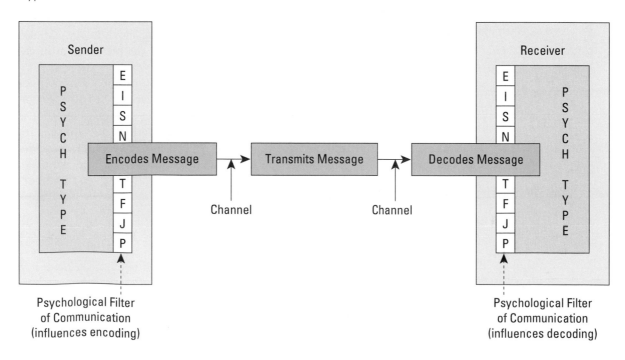

Personality differences can often strain communications.

> When we see men of a contrary character, we should turn inwards and examine ourselves.
>
> Confucius

strategies we can use to vary messages to suit the psychological preferences of target receivers. Type theory can also help us to understand where other people's communications originate, psychologically speaking.

It is important to recall that communication involves **interpretation.** We possess a great capacity to edit, select, omit, rearrange, judge and interpret any message that is sent to us. This process of interpretation (decoding) is influenced by our attitudinal preferences (introversion/extraversion), our preferred modes of information gathering (sensing/intuition), the way we make decisions (thinking/feeling) and how we orient toward life (judging/perceiving). Let's see how exactly.

PREFERRED TYPES OF COMMUNICATION

Corresponding to each psychological type are different **styles of communication.** Extraverts, for example, tend to communicate differently from introverts, and intuitives structure their messages somewhat differently from sensors. However, this difference does not suggest that extraverts cannot communicate with introverts or that intuitives and sensors are destined to a lifetime of miscommunication. As mentioned in the preceding chapter, outnumbered introverts may adapt to the majority world of the extravert very well. They may become good at "extraverted" communication, maybe even better than some extraverts. Sensors can also encode messages to suit intuitives and vice versa. In principle, any type can communicate according to opposite type preferences. However, being asked to use communication styles contrary to your own can be psychologically draining. The optimistic point is that everybody can learn to communicate effectively with all psychological types, even if we find some forms of communication less natural and more taxing than others.

APPLICATION EXERCISE 2.1

2.4

When Extraverts and Introverts Meet

1. Use the results obtained from Self-Diagnostic 1.1 (p. 6) to divide the class into two groups: introverts and extraverts.

2. Randomly pair each introvert with an extravert.

3. Ask extraverts to begin a brief discussion by describing to introverts
   a. their general impressions of introverts
   b. what they like about talking to introverts
   c. what they find difficult or challenging about talking to introverts.

4. Ask introverts to continue the discussion by describing to extraverts
   a. their general impressions of extraverts
   b. what they like about talking to extraverts
   c. what they find difficult or challenging about talking to extraverts.

5. After the pairs discussion, have someone (instructor or student) draw a chart on the blackboard like the one following. Then, have students share with the rest of the class their observations about communicating with their opposite type. The student or instructor may fill in the blackboard chart for the benefit of the class. This chart will serve as a summary of what each pair learned. You may also wish to record important observations in your textbook chart for future reference.

Introvert's Perspective

What I like about talking to extraverts.	What I find challenging about talking to extraverts.

Extravert's Perspective

What I like about talking to introverts.	What I find challenging about talking to introverts.

6. Finally, have the class list things to keep in mind for communicating with introverts and/or extraverts. Record some suggestions for personal application.

EXTRAVERTED AND INTROVERTED COMMUNICATION STYLES

> Knowledge of personality type is a great aid in adjusting communication style to the needs of the listener. We have to be willing to change what we say if people are to hear what we mean. Falling in love with our own favorite words can be disastrous if we really want to be understood.
>
> Martine J. Robards and Steven C. Coats

Communicating with Extraverts

The Sunny Side

As we've learned already, extraverts are individuals who draw their energy from other people. They value social interaction and like to be around others. For these reasons, striking up conversations with extraverts will not usually be very difficult. Another feature of extraverts is their enthusiasm and willingness to participate in group activities. They interact with ease, preferring face-to-face communications over more formal and distant interactions. Whether in groups or in pairs, extraverts enjoy sharing their experiences. They seem to need contact and conversation with other people. Because of their openness, extraverts don't take long to get to know. Their motto might be "What you see is what you get." Extraverts typically say what they mean and state what's on their minds.

The Shadow Side

Application Exercise 2.1 has helped you, I hope, to appreciate the **shadow side** as well as the **sunny side** of extraverted communication. It is worthwhile for you, especially if you're an extravert, to see how your communication messages could sometimes be received and interpreted (i.e., decoded) by others. Just imagine, for example, two strongly extraverted individuals who quickly and easily say what's on their minds. There may be problems for each of them getting a word in edgewise. Also, since some extraverts are inclined to speak first and think later, the potential for some insensitive communication arises. Furthermore, if extraverts are perceived as "talking butterflies," flitting from one person to another in social circumstances, there is a possibility that some people (especially introverts) will regard them as superficial and insincere. There is a danger, as well, that sociable extraverts may impose themselves on people preferring to remain quiet and alone. Well-intentioned, friendly conversation could, in other words, be judged as an intrusion, depending on the receiver of the extraverted communication messages.

On this note, I can remember an introvert at a workshop asking extraverts to leave him alone at parties. He told the story of a party he once attended. The introvert described himself as sitting quietly and observing everyone. The extraverted hostess, feeling the need to be gracious and hospitable, kept asking him if there was anything she could get for him. He was quite happy simply to sit and watch. What the introvert wanted was to be left alone. What the extraverted hostess did was intrude on his personal space. He said he left the party early because he felt so drained. In his mind, there was nothing he needed, nothing he lacked, and nothing was wrong. The hostess kept reacting to him as if there were. In short, even the best intentions may result in problems and miscommunication if psychological type is not taken into account. I'm sure the hostess did not intend to offend, but because she wasn't tuned-in to introverted preferences, her interpersonal communications suffered. The introvert could appreciate the hostess's generosity; he just preferred she were generous toward someone else. See Figure 2.3 for a graphic illustration of the sunny and shadow sides of communication.

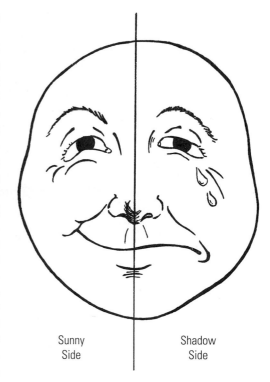

Sunny Side

Shadow Side

Figure 2.3
The Face of Communication

Communicating with Introverts

The Sunny Side

Introverts are very different from extraverts. They represent a minority in the population (three extraverts for every introvert) and are probably more commonly misunderstood. Communication strategies should be adjusted to accommodate introverted preferences if you wish to improve the effectiveness of your social interactions with this psychological minority.

As you know by now, introverts are people who are energized from within and make decisions based on personal reflection. Therefore, their need to communicate publicly with others is far less than for extraverts. Introverts, who are naturally inclined to avoid crowds and prefer independent activities, place a high value on solitude and personal space. When introverts choose to spend a lot of time alone, we should not conclude that there is something wrong. Their nonverbal communication may tell us more about their psychological preferences than about any personal or interpersonal problems. If you are communicating with someone you suspect may be highly introverted, it is prudent to avoid unnecessary interactions. Dropping in to socialize, simply for the sake of small talk, may be considered wasteful or

Man and His Shadow

There was a man
who was so disturbed
by the sight of his own shadow
and so displeased with his own footsteps
that he determined to get rid of both.
The method he hit upon was to run away from them.
So he got up and ran.
But every time he put his foot down
there was another step,
while his shadow kept up with him
without the slightest difficulty.
He attributed his failure
to the fact that he was not running fast enough.
So he ran faster and faster, without stopping,
until he finally dropped dead.
He failed to realize that if he merely stepped into the shade, his
shadow would vanish,
and if he sat down and stayed still, there would be no more footsteps.

Chuang Tzu

Source: From pp. 65-66 from *Personality and Personal Growth*, 2/e, by Robert Frager and James Fadiman. Copyright 1984 by Robert Frager and James Fadiman. Reprinted by permission of HarperCollins Publishers, Inc.

experienced as emotionally exhausting. It's probably a good idea to schedule appointments or to give advance notice to introverts that you're dropping in. If people just keep popping in without notice, introverts are likely to get "peopled out." They may become annoyed by your friendliness.

It is also more difficult to get to know introverts. They tend to be reserved and share personal information only with a few others whom they have come to love or trust over time. Instead of having many acquaintances and superficial friendships, introverts generally choose to have a small number of deep and meaningful relationships. Getting into the inner world of introverts will therefore be difficult.

In view of what has been said, don't be surprised if some of the most sociable and communicative people you've ever met turn out to be "closet introverts." Remember, anybody can learn to use psychological processes and functions that are less preferred. Nothing prevents introverts from becoming great social communicators or from behaving in sociable and gregarious ways. However, when they do, they are likely to feel the strain. Also, I cannot emphasize enough that preferences do not reflect ability or accomplishment. Your social skills may be good or bad regardless of psychological preferences. Introverts and extraverts both can interact socially; the latter may do so gladly, but poorly, and the former very well, but with greater expenditure of energy.

The Shadow Side

I mentioned earlier that extraverts tend to outnumber introverts by about three to one. The larger number of extraverts contributes to a social value system that often raises extraverted preferences to a level of virtue. Introverted preferences, on the other hand, may be regarded as weaknesses or flaws. For instance, introverts who value solitude very highly may not be seen as private or independent, in a positive sense, but as antisocial. Some people may regard the "lone wolf" attitude of the introvert as something to be corrected or adjusted, especially in contexts where teamwork and group cooperation are required. The reserved and private disposition of introverts may also be interpreted as arrogance or condescension. People may sometimes project onto quiet introverts their own fears and insecurities. They may attribute to introverts intentions and thoughts not held by them. Furthermore, since introverts avoid unnecessary interaction and because they share their most private feelings only with those very close to them, others may occasionally feel excluded, and judge introverts to be unfriendly. Valuing privacy and limited intimacy is like a glass either half empty or half full. How you choose to describe it will depend on your psychological preferences. If we are to respect all individuals, we should be careful not to consider any one set of preferences as "better" than any other.

Helpful Hints for Improving Communications

Tips for Introverts (Communicating with Extraverts)

- **Look alive** Some extraverts are frustrated by the speed at which introverts tend to respond. Try to be quicker in your responses and more spontaneous. Display a more lively, upbeat attitude.

- **Be expressive** For extraverts, you are part of the external world. Since they feed off your energy, make an attempt to show interest, emotion and involvement. Keep in mind that there's nothing wrong with enthusiasm. Just because you don't always show your feelings doesn't mean you don't have them.

- **Initiate contact** Rather than waiting for people to start conversations with you, you could start conversations yourself. Don't always leave it up to extraverts to get things going socially.

- **Provide feedback** Save others the guesswork of trying to figure out what you're silently thinking. Publicly state your agreements and disagreements. Provide information on where you stand on particular issues. After all, "Nobody can appreciate your music if they can't hear the tune you're playing."

- **Change your nonverbal communication** If you're strongly introverted, you probably look very serious to others. Try to look more relaxed and try to smile more. Assume inviting physical postures. Appear open. Don't withdraw.

- **Practise "non-productive" conversation** Learn to appreciate the value of social interaction for its own sake. Chit-chatting can be fun. The quality of ideas exchanged needn't always be a priority. Spending time in "idle conversation" has worth. It builds morale and positive relations.

Tips for Extraverts (Communicating with Introverts)

- **Respect privacy** If you're highly extraverted, you may not mind living your life as an open book to others. You may think that you have nothing to hide. You may also feel comfortable with a lot of self-disclosure. Understand that introverts generally have a greater need for privacy. Try, therefore, not to invade their private psychological territory. Don't ask them embarrassing questions or put introverts on the psychological hot seat.

Can you guess which person is introverted and which person is extraverted?

- **Take time to listen** Introverts tend to be less spontaneous than extraverts. Their response time is also slower. Make an effort to allow introverts time to reflect before acting or responding to you. Do not make surprise demands on introverts for quick actions or immediate responses. Such demands are not usually welcome.

- **Foster trust** Make sure you guard as secret what you've been told by introverts in confidence. The sphere of private information is probably larger for the introvert than it is for you, the extravert. Be sure not to make public what others consider private.

- **Don't overpower** Introverts may sometimes perceive your enthusiasm and energy as frivolous. Your excitement may not be appreciated. You may wish to think about toning down your efforts, in order not to overwhelm others. They may not be impressed by your strident nature or expressions.

- **Don't judge** Be careful not to evaluate the more methodical and quieter introvert as less able and more dull. Preferences of one type should not be used as a standard of evaluation for other types. All preferences have their advantages.

SENSING AND INTUITIVE COMMUNICATION STYLES

Communicating with Sensors

The Sunny Side

Sensors are down-to-earth individuals. As realists, they like to focus their discussions on practical issues and factual considerations. In conversation, you will often find sensors talking about details, feasibility and usefulness in a detached matter-of-fact style (Robards and Coats, 1988). Concerns about time, cost, profit and procedure will typically be very much on their minds. When it comes to public speaking presentations, sensors will usually be quite orderly and proceed in a step-by-step fashion (Hirsh and Kummerow, 1989). They will also display a high level of precision, referring to specific examples when making their points. In my own experiences as a professor and workshop leader, I have found that sensors (especially SJs) like to stick to agendas and schedules. I remember once having my presentation interrupted by a sensor who was irritated that I was running three minutes late on my scheduled activities. Other sensors might have been more forgiving, but in general it can be said that following schedules precisely is a greater concern to sensors than to intuitives.

The Shadow Side

Any strength, if it is taken to an extreme, can become a liability. In this case, the strong elements of sensing communication can become problematic if carried too far. For example, if sensors are overly preoccupied with facts and details, some may regard their messages as "nit-picking." Receivers of their messages may not take them seriously and simply tune them out. Messages may go in one ear and out the other.

Because sensors like to focus on practicalities and feasibility, they may sometimes dwell on the problems and logistical difficulties associated with any proposal or project. Consequently, there is a danger that sensors could be perceived as pessimists or cynics, "knowing the cost of everything" and "appreciating the value of nothing." Since sensors like to rely on concrete experience to illustrate points and justify arguments, there is the danger that generalizations might be based on limited information (e.g., the past experience of one individual sensor). The personal experience of one may confirm what the experience of another thousand could dispute. While experience is often helpful, it doesn't provide absolute guarantees.

Sensors who are highly pragmatic may have some difficulty communicating with possibility thinkers, visionaries and futurists. They may become impatient talking about hypotheticals or things that may never happen. In this event, messages from others about what "might be" could be blocked or possibly dismissed as frivolous. Surely, not listening to others impedes effective communication. Insistence on exclusively factual communication is limiting. The fact is that the future will arrive tomorrow, and that what isn't soon shall be.

Communicating with Intuitives

The Sunny Side

In contrast to sensors, intuitives have a lesser need to communicate accurately about specific facts and details (Hirsh and Kummerow, 1989). Intuitives generally adopt a more global and imaginative approach to life. Rather than focus discussions on evidence and experience, intuitives like to begin with insights, concepts and ideas. While sensors prefer to talk about facts, intuitives enjoy going beyond the facts to possibilities that the facts present. Intuitives often rely on their personal imaginations and hunches to support their views. Their arguments, then, are frequently not factually based.

With intuitives you'll also discover greater tolerance for anything novel or unusual. Speech patterns and presentation strategies may be less sequential and more roundabout. Typically, intuitives like to keep discussions at a general conceptual level, abstracting from factual evidence. Intuitives also usually don't mind deviating from schedules and agendas, especially when these interfere with productive meetings. In terms of linguistic style, you will note that intuitive language tends to be quite colourful, often filled with metaphors and analogies. The sensor's matter-of-fact, literal mode of expression is less preferred.

> You see things; and you say, "Why?" But I dream things that never were and I say, "Why not?".
>
> George Bernard Shaw

The Shadow Side

From the vantage point of opposite type individuals, intuitives' communication may frequently seem vague and incomprehensible. Talking in terms of hypotheticals, future possibilities and conceptual abstractions may be mildly or extremely irritating to practical-minded people. Scepticism on the part of others may also arise if the intuitive uses only personal hunches and imagination to support debatable points. The intuitive's fascination for the novel and unusual may lead to communications that seem like a waste of time to those receiving the messages of a perceived "unrealistic dreamer." Confusion and impatience in interpersonal communication could also result if intuitives are too roundabout in their presentations or if their metaphors and analogies become too colourful and abstract. Metaphors and analogies that are used in verbal explanations may sometimes get in the way of clarity and precision.

2.6 *Helpful Hints for Improving Communications*

Tips for Sensors (Communicating with Intuitives)

- **Don't overgeneralize or state absolutes** Personal experience may give sensing realists confidence in their opinions and conclusions, but it does not guarantee necessity or truth. You can be quite certain and confident but still be wrong. Understand that factual information is always incomplete and that your concrete experience is the experience of one. Not everybody experiences life the same way you do. Furthermore, experience cannot guarantee that something has been learned. "Experience is a great teacher; unfortunately not everybody understands the lesson."

- **Allow time for considering possibilities** Sensors prefer realism. The result is that you focus more on what "is" and less on what "could be." It's important not to limit your options by a limited imagination. Show greater tolerance toward idealistic thinking and intuitives who may have what you consider to be an unrealistic future orientation. Possibility thinking has real(istic) advantages.

- **Broaden your perspective** Try to display greater tolerance for broader-based conceptual thinking. Overreliance on facts and figures may get in the way of being productive or achieving longer-term goals. Preoccupation with details could lead intuitives to perceive you as petty.

- **Look for meanings and relationships** When communicating with intuitives, understand that they are less concerned with what the facts *are* and more concerned with what they *mean*. Expressing factual information outside any meaningful context will be less effective with intuitives. For intuitives, facts need to be interpreted and related to something. Allow time for this interpretation. Put your communication in a more global context.

- **Find new ways of expressing information** Intuitives appreciate novelty, unusual modes of expression and challenges. Straightforward, matter-of-fact presentations could be experienced as boring and uninteresting. Try to perk up your communication with some delightful differences. Instead of merely informing intuitives, you could try to "inspire" them. Dispirited communications are not appreciated.

Tips for Intuitives (Communicating with Sensors)

- **Focus on the here and now** You will make much more sense to the sensor if you adopt a present time orientation. Talk about future scenarios and long-term possibilities may be regarded as "intellectual masturbation" by hard-core realists concerned about today's problems. Such talk may be pleasurable for you, but for the sensor it is probably unproductive.

- **Base your opinions and suggestions on factual information** You can gain the confidence of sensors by keeping both feet on the ground. Try to relate your opinions and suggestions to facts, figures, surveys and empirical evidence. Your gut-level intuitions may carry little persuasive weight for the sensing realist.

- **Be more direct in your communication** If you wish to communicate more effectively with practical, matter-of-fact kinds of people, try to speak more directly. Metaphors and analogies may sound poetic to you, but they may serve as obstructions to individuals who prefer to be economical in their language. Why say in many words what can be said in few? Why say indirectly what can be said directly? Be a "word economist." Save words and enjoy the dividends!

- **Appear more level-headed and businesslike** Your natural enthusiasm, idealism, genius and inspiration as an intuitive can sometimes be perceived as "flaky" by the sensor. For the sensor, your enthusiasm should be based on substance, your idealism tempered by practicality, your genius founded on hard work, and your inspiration led by discipline. Without a realistic basis to support your insightful and long-term propositions, you could be seen as flighty. It's hard to put confidence in people whose heads seem to be in the clouds.

- **Respect traditional ways of doing things** Remember that old ways of doing things are not always wrong ways. For many, past procedures, rules and regulations offer stability and direction. They are not regarded as outdated or boring. Appreciate the sensor's preference for established, systematic approaches. Routine may make you restless, but it is reassuring to many sensors.

THINKING AND FEELING COMMUNICATION STYLES

Communicating with Thinkers

The Sunny Side

As a thinker (my type is INTJ), I am particularly sensitive to this type's needs in verbal and interpersonal communication. Thinkers just love discussing ideas. Often you'll find them engaged in theoretical arguments and debates. Usually, idea-oriented discussions are not seen as opportunities to express personal feelings, but as occasions for impersonal, emotionally detached critique and analysis. In fact, thinkers tend to downplay feelings in the context of debates, seeing them as inappropriate, especially when matters of ethics and fairness are involved. Thinkers decide with their heads more often than with their hearts. They prefer objectivity over subjectivity. This preference does not suggest that thinkers are void of emotion. (I would be very upset if a feeler suggested this idea!) Archetypal thinkers you find on television are Mr. Spock and Data from the television series *Star Trek* and *Star Trek: The Next Generation*. (By the way, this little distinction was made for sensors who probably would have noticed that Spock and Data come from two different versions of the same show. Intuitives, who leap over details, may have gotten the point without caring much about the distinction.) In any case, thinkers approach their communications with others in the rational mode. They like to consider advantages and disadvantages of alternative options and opportunities. Finally, thinkers tend to be goal oriented and therefore prefer their communications with others to be brief and concise. Time is not to be wasted in "unproductive" socializing.

The Shadow Side

Because of their brief and concise communications, thinkers can be perceived as cold, especially by feelers. For people who care less about what is said and more about how it's said, the emotionally detached presentation style of the thinker may be unappealing.

Thinkers may have a tendency to "T-off" other people. I can remember participating in a workshop once and asking typical T-type questions. My questions focused on abstract ideas and relations among them in some theoretical context. Well, of course, many of the sensors went bonkers because they couldn't see the practical point of my questioning. They were also irritated because my questions were taking too long, thereby disrupting the scheduled activities for the day. Furthermore, many of the F-types could not see what "human" value there was in pursuing the questions I posed. (I could tell by the clock watching, eye rolling and groaning!) In short, thinking-type communication can sometimes appear useless and unappealing to those with differing preferences.

Another danger in using a thinking-style rational approach to communication is that not everyone is persuaded by impersonal logic. Try, for example, to convince a devout fundamentalist Christian that God does not

The fictional detective Sherlock Holmes is a master thinker who uses deductive logic to solve crime mysteries.

exist, using irrefutable logic alone. Chances are pretty good that you will fail in your efforts. Some beliefs are not based on logic, and therefore a purely logical treatment of such beliefs should be reconsidered as a communication strategy. Logic is limited and sometimes limiting in human interaction. It may be that Spock and Data are interesting, but would you want them as best friends? (I don't know, but I sure would like them to be around in any confrontation with the Romulans!)

Communicating with Feelers

The Sunny Side

In contrast to thinkers, who like impersonal and objective communication, feelers prefer personal and subjective modes of expression. Feelers are likely to be more receptive to others in communication. They enjoy getting involved in friendly and sociable conversation, even if it is "unproductive" and unnecessarily time consuming from the thinker's vantage point. As well, feelers see others' positive points more easily. This difference makes talking with feelers a warm and inviting experience. When decisions are made, feelers' justifications tend to be expressed in terms of personal values and effects on people's lives.

When communicating with feelers, you'll probably notice that they tend to express more empathy and appreciation than their thinking counterparts. When they try to win arguments or persuade others, they will more often appeal to personally meaningful information than to impersonal facts or logical deductive reasoning. Their presentation style is also likely to be more enthusiastic. This idea does not suggest that feelers can't think; they just don't put great emphasis on pure thought and logical analysis. A good reason for not always communicating rationally comes from a children's movie about dinosaurs in a "land before time." To paraphrase, a mother dinosaur says in the movie to her offspring, "Child, some things you see with your eyes; other things you see with your heart." The point is that the heart enables you to appreciate things in life beyond the rational understanding of the mind. There are aspects to life that are nonrational, paradoxical, emotional and nonmaterial. The heart can show you what rational perception cannot.

The Shadow Side

One problem with feeling-type communication is that it can cause other people to become impatient. For some, taking time to be sociable and friendly, especially if it is done consistently and with everybody, could be perceived as a waste of time. Task-oriented individuals are frequently too busy getting the job done to want to share personal feelings and values. Such things may be seen as irrelevant to the task being addressed.

Feeling communicators also may have a tendency to be swept away by their own enthusiasm when delivering information or when trying to persuade others. As a result, they may pay too little attention to facts and logic in their presentations. In addition, by presenting points of agreement and focusing on social pleasantries, feelers may give too little consideration to differences and competing goals. When feeling is taken to an extreme, objectivity suffers in favour of subjectivity (i.e., the desire to be liked and to get along).

Because of their compassionate and caring side, feeling types could experience difficulties in presenting bad news or unpleasant information to others. Since feelers are less inclined to detach themselves emotionally and cognitively, as compared with their more objective and rational thinking-type counterparts, they may take negative messages more personally. Receiving and sending bad news may be more heartfelt and psychologically upsetting.

Helpful Hints for Improving Communications

Tips for Thinkers (Communicating with Feelers)

- **Make communications personally relevant and meaningful** If you're a thinking-type person, you should consider making your ideas more personally relevant and meaningful to the receivers of your messages. A theory or idea may be exciting to you and others sharing your preferences, but it can be boring, useless and irrelevant for people of the opposite type.

- **Be more appreciative of others' comments** Thinking-type individuals are likely to consider their rationality and objectivity as virtues, and in many ways they are. The problem with cool objectivity, however, is that it can be perceived as callousness. Having an intellectual evaluation and analysis for just about everything could get the thinking type labelled a terminal critic or someone who argues simply for the sake of argument, regardless of the issue or effects on people's emotions. Before attacking points made by others, take time to understand and appreciate what they mean. Paraphrase others' comments. Explore what they think and feel. Then, go on to express your point of view. Take time to really hear what is said.

- **Expand your communication messages** As a thinking-type person you may take great pride in the clarity, precision and conciseness of your communications with others. However, a terse manner of expression is sometimes perceived as unfriendly and cold. If talking to you is like talking to a computer, you may wish to consider expanding your monosyllabic responses when answering others' questions. Perhaps you could elaborate on what you mean.

- **Make room for the nonrational and paradoxical** A helpful suggestion for you, the thinker, is to believe less that "life is a problem to be solved." See it more as a "mystery to be lived." In other words, accept the proposition that not everything in life has a rational explanation or logical justification. Logic may be limited by whatever is mystical, ironic or paradoxical in life. Religious beliefs, for instance, may not be based on logic, but on faith. Such beliefs may lie beyond the domain of rational thought. Don't take rationality as the sole standard of truth.

Tips for Feelers (Communicating with Thinkers)

- **Get to the point** While other feelers like yourself may appreciate time-consuming communication, thinkers will probably not. Try to incorporate brevity in your messages to thinkers. Attempting to be friendly and to make small talk could be perceived as a waste of time.

- **Be more objective** Try to reduce your naturally subjective orientation when communicating with thinkers. Your personal values and feelings about things may not be appreciated or regarded as very important. The thinker is more impersonal and objective than you are. If you would have others listen and be persuaded, you must speak their language.

- **See both sides** There is absolutely nothing wrong with appreciating others. However, if personal likes and feelings get in the way of seeing flaws and difficulties, then problems can arise. Practise evaluating the pros and cons of different ideas, situations and alternatives.

- **Focus on content** If you're a high-level feeling type, process is probably more important to you than content. Chances are that you like experiential exercises and activities because of the personal involvement required. Remember that such process-oriented activities are less preferred by thinking types. In fact, some thinking types may greatly dislike "touchy-feely" communications. Be careful not to irritate or offend, especially in the case of introverted thinkers. Your personal approach may be perceived as a violation of privacy and inappropriate to the content being discussed.

JUDGING AND PERCEIVING COMMUNICATION STYLES

2.5

Communicating with Judgers

The Sunny Side

I can begin to explain the preferred elements of judging communication by using myself as an example. Several years ago I attended a meeting where people were trying to decide on activities and speakers for a faculty professional development day. One subgroup at the meeting informed everybody that it had a theatrical surprise in mind, but that, like the rest of the faculty, we would have to wait and see what the surprise was going to be. Some members of the larger group were quite excited about the surprise. I wasn't. In fact, I asked if it was appropriate to leave our planning committee in the dark. I understood the subgroup's intention, but I didn't think the planned activity should be kept secret from the larger group ultimately responsible for planning the professional development day. Someone at the table commented, "Tony, your personality type is showing!" In retrospect, I guess it was. As a judger, I dislike the kind of surprise described and prefer advance warnings. Sure, judgers like myself love Christmas and birthday surprises, but surprises where work tasks are involved are far less enjoyable. For someone like me, serious tasks should not involve the element of surprise. If you too are a judger, rest assured that you're not necessarily a "party pooper." You just like to know things ahead of time.

It should be no surprise that judgers like to discuss schedules and timetables. They prefer to set realistic deadlines and try to meet them. As well, judging types display a need for closure. In their communications, you can frequently observe them bringing their thoughts to conclusions. By nature they are convergent thinkers. Thus, their approach to communication is very purposeful and clear. They like to focus on relevant content and do not appreciate digressions and side discussions at meetings.

The Shadow Side

As is always true in the context of type preferences, what is positive from one psychological perspective may be perceived as negative from another. So, while J-types may be impressed with people who follow schedules, P-types may consider this approach to life rigid and inflexible. Talk about structure and closure may be impressive to the judger, but constricting and depressing for the perceiver.

Thus, the judger's preference for convergence in communication may lead to confusion and bewilderment when interacting with open-ended perceiving types. Of course, there is the ever-present danger that we all will evaluate negatively that which we don't like and don't understand. While open-endedness may seem like a virtue to perceivers, the judger is likely to respond to it adversely, possibly with frustration. Rather than recognize the limitations of J-preferences, the judger may negatively evaluate open-endedness as "wishy-washiness"—a form of communication that accomplishes little, if anything at all. The judging type's need for structure and advance warning may also interfere with spontaneity in communication. If everything must be scheduled, decided,

These two judging-type people refuse to display perceiving-type flexibility.

closed and warned in advance, there's not much time for excitement and surprise. Communicating with the J-type can therefore become overly serious and businesslike.

The J-type's need for closure can sometimes lead to premature decisions. Conclusions may be stated before all the facts are in and before all the alternatives have been considered. So while J-types usually experience few difficulties making decisions, quick decisions may result in unsound judgments. It's sometimes the case that the need for closure influences judgers to ignore counter-evidence or to downplay information that works against their premature conclusions. These decisions certainly undermine objectivity and effectiveness.

Structure and closure give judging types not only a sense of direction, but one of control. The problem is that the need for control can become a controlling obsession. Obsessions are problems in just about any context, but those dealing with control could be particularly dangerous in leadership and managerial roles. Be careful not to let control become an obsession. Others will not like it and your communications with them will suffer.

Communicating with Perceivers

2.5

The Sunny Side

Interactions with perceiving types are likely to be very different from those you have with judging types. For example, since perceivers pay less attention to schedules and timetables, they do not usually mind getting sidetracked during activities. They also like to talk about flexibility issues and enjoy discussing process-related matters. Negotiating "how" something should be done may be preferred over debating "what" should be done and "by whom."

Perceivers tend to be more tentative in their communications. By disposition, they are information gatherers who wish to remain open and flexible. Their stated positions are therefore commonly subject to change. As Hirsh and Kummerow (1989) point out, perceivers orient their communications toward options and contingencies. They anticipate the need for accommodation and change in light of new facts. Leaving meetings without any final decisions having been made is not particularly distressing for them, as it might be for the closure-oriented judging type.

Perceivers are also more likely to enjoy surprises and unforeseen circumstances. Since perceivers are adaptable to last-minute change, they may regard unexpected problems as opportunities or challenges. Thus, when things go wrong, perceivers are less likely to become upset and irritated. Rather than complain and judge, they are more likely to respond and adapt.

The Shadow Side

If you are a perceiving type, your dislike for schedules may contribute to lateness on your written assignments and communications. For you, it may not matter much if you respond to others an hour or a day late, as long as the work gets done, but to those whose time orientation is rigidly geared to schedules and deadlines, your preference for flexible time frames may be considered irresponsible or unprofessional. Timing is not trivial if you're a J-type.

If you are a perceiver, you probably think of your adaptability as a virtue. Taken to an extreme, however, overreliance on adaptability may make you appear disorganized and ill-prepared. While you may be ready to respond to last-minute difficulties, others may not appreciate having to react to the problems and crises that could have been prevented by better organization. Forcing others to adapt to your flexible approach may cause another crisis for which you have no adequate response—a crisis of confidence. If people communicating with you cannot be guaranteed responses on time and if they experience unexpected and unwanted surprises from you, then relationships will suffer. Few people like inconvenience and uncertainty, things that perceiving preferences, taken to an extreme, can present to others.

Another potential problem with perceiving-type preferences revolves around indecision. While it is prudent to look at alternative possibilities and examine the facts of any situation before making a decision, choices must eventually be made. The danger is that the perceiving type may compulsively research the facts and options without ever achieving closure on the matter at hand. Indecision as a problem may be compounded by insecurity. The perceiver may often not feel very confident that all the necessary information has been obtained to make appropriate decisions. The result may be perceived as inaction and ineffectiveness. If you believe you are communicating with someone guilty of past inaction and ineffectiveness or if that person consistently displays tentativeness, lateness and procrastination, you are not likely to have very much trust in that person's ability.

Helpful Hints for Improving Communications

> ### Tips for Judgers (Communicating with Perceivers)
>
> - **Open up to the unexpected** Disruptions to your schedule need not necessarily be upsetting. Begin to see them as occasions to "stop and smell the roses." Some interruptions may even provide you with information and insights that can be used to reconsider your plans. Don't make other people who cause unexpected changes feel unwanted.
>
> - **Build flexibility into your lifestyle** When organizing yourself, make sure you allow for "downtime." Make unforeseen circumstances foreseeable. In other words, expect the unexpected. Being psychologically prepared can help to reduce stress and frustration. Stressed and frustrated people are not usually pleasant to communicate with. Do everyone, including yourself, a favour, and "go with the flow."

- **Don't jump to conclusions** As a judger, your preference is to close matters as soon as possible. Note that your desire for closure may cause you to make decisions prematurely. Evaluations you make of people, situations and events may therefore be unjustified or ill-informed. If your stated conclusions are to be sound, they should be based on carefully considered information.

- **Listen to the other side** Counter-evidence to your own thinking may be uncomfortable to accept. Be careful not to repress or deny that which contradicts your personal beliefs, values, principles or ideas. Effective communication necessitates that you listen well, respect the viewpoints of others, and respond intelligently and sensitively to ideas contrary to your own.

- **Harness your need for control** Most J-types love to feel in control of situations. Plans, schedules, time frames and strategies of action provide a sense of personal power. While this may be good, caution yourself not to become overpowering. If you are controlled psychologically by your *need* to control, then you may become offensive to others. Most people do not like to feel dominated by others. If you wish to improve your communications as a judger, you may plan to relinquish some control and thereby "empower" others. Try this action as an experiment and witness how others begin to respond to you. If things get done and done well, but not according to your plans and schedules, what does it matter? Try not to communicate judgmentally with those having other styles of doing things.

Tips for Perceivers (Communicating with Judgers)

- **Be less vague** As a perceiver, you probably like to keep your options open. Perhaps you tend to make your decisions at the very last moment. Understand that for judgers, this tendency of yours is a bit like "holding out." The constant weighing of possibilities can represent for judgers vagueness or lack of preparation on your part. They may not be able to determine where you stand on particular issues. They have a greater need for quick confirmation. Tell judgers explicitly what considerations you are taking into account and what issues you need to resolve before coming to your final conclusions. If you can clearly articulate reasons for your indecision or inaction, then at least you provide the organized J-type with an explanation for what's holding you up. This information will likely be appreciated.

- **Be more decisive** This tip is related to the one above. As a perceiver, you have a natural tendency to gather as much information as you can. Make sure that this information-gathering process does not get in the way of making necessary and timely decisions. Tentativeness about making decisions may be perceived as insecurity or incompetence. It will be difficult for you to persuade others and to sell your ideas if you cannot gain their confidence.

- **Watch your use of "yeah, but"** Since you are keenly aware of contingencies, possibilities and alternatives, you can no doubt frequently offer "yeah, but" objections, as I call them, to almost any proposal or suggestion. Don't let your "yeah, but" get in the way of productive dialogue. Ensure that your concerns are real. Always protesting on the basis of highly improbable scenarios, for example, will lead others to take your comments less seriously.

- **Ensure your communications are on time** J-types like to operate according to schedule. While submitting a request or delivering a memo a day late may mean little for you, it may mean a lot for them. It is helpful, therefore, if you plan ahead for your pondering and procrastination. Having things well thought out in advance and allowing yourself lots of time for a consideration of possibilities will enable you to be more prepared and decisive. For example, at meetings you won't need to scramble and squirm at the last moment about where you stand on particular issues or policies. Appearing unclear and unprepared is not in your best interest, especially if you wish to be heard and respected for your point of view.

SELF-DIAGNOSTIC

2.1

2.7

My Communication Style

This self-diagnostic will help you identify the communication style preferences you display as a product of your personality type. This measure will also help you to formulate strategies for improving future communications with opposite type individuals.

Instructions: First, fill in your personality type where indicated. Use the four-letter format (e.g., ISFP). In Part A, take one letter of your personality type at a time to help you arrive at your communication style preferences. The first letter will be either E or I, the second S or N, the third T or F, and the fourth J or P. If, for example, you are an E (extraverted), ask how your extraverted psychological attitude translates into communication. What do you like, prefer, and/or need when communicating with others? Ask these same kinds of questions regarding your information-gathering preferences (S or N), your decision-making preferences (T or F), and your orientation toward the external world (J or P).

In Part B, consider the shadow side of your communication style and the differing preferences of opposite type individuals. What could you do to reduce the liabilities and potential dangers of your preferred style? What could you do to cater to the preferences of opposite type individuals?

For both Parts A and B, feel free to refer back to the chapter material for assistance.

My personality type is ____ ____ ____ ____

Part A

The first letter of my personality type (E or I) suggests the following about my communication style:

1. I like...
2. I prefer...
3. I need...

The second letter of my personality type (S or N) suggests the following about my communication style:

1.
2.
3.

The third letter of my personality type (T or F) suggests the following about my communication style:

1.
2.
3.

The fourth letter of my personality type (J or P) suggests the following about my communication style:

1.
2.
3.

Part B

Given my introversion/extraversion, I need to

1.
2.
3.

Given my sensing/intuiting, I need to

1.
2.
3.

Given my thinking/feeling, I need to

1.
2.
3.

Given my perceiving/judging, I need to

1.
2.
3.

Self-Reflection: To what extent do I communicate in ways true to my type? How strong are my preferences when it comes to type-related communication styles? Have I learned to communicate well in my "wrong hand," so to speak? Why or why not?

Optional Group Activity: After completing this self-diagnostic, students may wish to share insights and feelings with other class members. Possible questions for discussion include the following:

1. What did you already know about your communication style that was reinforced in your mind?
2. What new insights did you gain?
3. What specifically will you now do in order to improve your interpersonal communications?

Discussion of these questions can be conducted in small groups or together as a class.

APPLICATION EXERCISE 2.2

2.8

"ENTJ" *Spoken Here*

Instructions: Divide the class into small groups. Ask each group to select a spokesperson. The same person or another may act as the secretary for the group. Once organized, have someone read the case study below. Discuss and answer the questions that follow.

After small group discussions have taken place, the instructor may facilitate a discussion for the entire class. Have each subgroup share with the larger class its observations and analysis of the case study.

Case Study

Jill is a 22-year-old college graduate. She has just arrived at her first job interview and has seated herself in front of the prospective boss's desk. Jill notices a decorative Myers-Briggs plaque on it that reads: "ENTJ" Spoken Here. Jill's preferences are ISFJ.

Questions

1. In general terms, how does Jill's type compare with the ENTJ boss's type? In what respects do they differ? How are they alike?
2. If Jill chooses to communicate exclusively in her own "psychological type language," what difficulties in communication could arise? Be specific.
3. What communication strategies could Jill use to maximize her effectiveness in communicating with her prospective employer?
4. If Jill's prospective boss didn't have a decorative plaque, then what could she have said or asked to help determine the boss's psychological preferences? What could she have looked and listened for?

Structuring Psych-Smart Presentations

APPLICATION EXERCISE 2.3

2.9

This exercise will help you prepare more effective presentations that are type sensitive to the needs of your target audiences.

Instructions: This exercise can be done individually or in small groups. First, pick a topic for class presentation and then prepare a one- or two-page introduction for it. When finished, return to the Instructions. **READ NO FURTHER AT THIS POINT.**

Now that you have completed the introduction, suggest ways you could change it to make it more appealing to

- Introverts
- Extraverts
- Sensors
- Intuitives
- Thinkers
- Feelers
- Judgers
- Perceivers

Now discuss the likely effectiveness of your proposed introduction strategies.

Optional: Rewrite the original introduction incorporating your psych-type suggestions. Compare the original with the revised version. Which is likely to be more effective? Why?

S T U D Y   G U I D E

Key Terms

communication (32)	channels (34)	styles of
sender (33)	decoding (34)	communication
message (33)	receiver (34)	(36)
encoding (33)	type (34)	shadow side (38)
transmission (34)	interpretation (36)	sunny side (38)

PROGRESS CHECK 2.1 ✔

Fill-in-the-Blank Questions

Instructions: Fill in each blank with the appropriate answer from the list below.

spontaneity	alternatives
psychological type	encoded
communication style	misunderstood
speak	sequential
receiver	nitpicky
think	facts
global	sender
metaphors	channels
objective	logic
cold	present
values	experiences
closure	surprises
indecisive	heart

1. In the communication process, the person who delivers the message is called the _____.
2. The person who decodes the message in communication is called the _____.
3. Before ideas or thoughts are transmitted as messages, they must be _____.
4. Messages can be sent by many _____.
5. More effective encoding of messages can be achieved by taking into account the receiver's _____.
6. Information about personality type can serve as a great aid in adjusting _____ to the needs of the listener.
7. Extraverts generally enjoy sharing their _____.
8. Extraverts are sometimes perceived as insensitive partly due to their tendency to _____ first and think later.

9. Because introverts are outnumbered in the general population, they are often _____.

10. Introverts are sometimes perceived as hesitant because of their tendency to _____ first and speak later.

11. Sensors prefer to be factual and _____ in their communications.

12. Sensors' needs to be detailed and explicit sometimes lead others to regard them as _____.

13. The time orientation of the sensor is primarily fixed on the _____.

14. Intuitives describe their experience in more _____ terms than do sensors.

15. Intuitives love to use _____ in their speech.

16. Intuitives often propose great-sounding innovations but they tend to overlook important _____ and details.

17. Thinking types frame their communications in _____ terms.

18. Because of their concise and impersonal communication style, thinkers can sometimes be perceived as _____ and unfriendly.

19. Feeling types like to communicate in terms of personal _____.

20. Feelers tend to make decisions more with their _____ than with their heads.

21. When debating or discussing issues, feeling types often pay too little attention to _____.

22. Judging types don't like _____.

23. If you are a judger, you like to achieve _____ at meetings and discussions.

24. Perceivers remain open-ended, discussing _____ and other options.

25. Perceivers can sometimes be regarded as _____ by others.

True/False Questions

Instructions: Circle the appropriate letter next to each statement.

T F 1. An understanding of psychological diversity is important for more effective interpersonal communication.

T F 2. The person who decodes messages in the communication process is called the sender.

T F 3. Letter and telephone are two channels of communication.

T F 4. If a message is clear and concise, all receivers will decode it in exactly the same way.

T F 5. Your preferred mode of information gathering will influence how you interpret messages.

T F 6. Introverts are always less able than extraverts when it comes to interpersonal communication.

T F 7. For extraverts, there is usually the danger that they will think too long before speaking.

T F 8. Deep, silent introverts are always brighter than extraverts.

T F 9. Introverts outnumber extraverts in the general population.

T F   10. Sensors are more interested in sensory observation than in intuiting possibilities.

T F   11. Intuitives are completely unrealistic.

T F   12. Intuitives look for meanings and relationships.

T F   13. Thinkers are always unfriendly people because of their overly intellectual approach to life.

T F   14. Thinking types are smarter than feeling types.

T F   15. Thinkers are more inclined to decide with their heads than with their hearts.

T F   16. Feelers tend to be warmer than thinkers in their communications.

T F   17. Feelers' objectivity can sometimes be swept away by personal enthusiasm.

T F   18. Judgers usually make positive judgments on surprise scenarios.

T F   19. Judgers are divergent in their thinking, while perceivers are convergent.

T F   20. Perceiving types are indecisive.

T F   21. Perceivers have difficulty perceiving things clearly when circumstances change at the last second.

T F   22. Perceiving types like to consider many alternatives before making a decision.

Focus Questions

1. Why is communication important?

2. What is involved in the process of communication?

3. What does psychological type theory add to our understanding of the communication process?

4. How do communication patterns of introverts and extraverts differ?

5. What's meant by saying that communication styles have "sunny" and "shadow" sides?

6. Can you list a few "sunny" and "shadow" elements for each of the communication style preferences?

Summary

1. Why is communication important?
   - we use it to express our feelings and thoughts
   - we need it to achieve our goals
   - it enables us to understand and respond to others
   - it is a major component of personal and professional success

2. What is the process of communication?
   - it has these basic elements: sender, receiver, message, channel, transmission, encoding and decoding

- the sender has a thought or feeling to express
- the sender encodes a message
- the sender selects a channel to transmit the message
- the message is transmitted
- the receiver gets the message
- the message is decoded
- the one-way communication process is complete

3. What is the influence of type on communication?
   - senders and receivers encode and decode messages through their psychological type filters
   - we edit, select, omit, rearrange, judge and interpret messages in accordance with our preferences (i.e., our attitudes, modes of gathering information, decision-making strategies and orientations to life)
   - miscommunications can result from type differences

4. What can be said generally about type communications?
   - each style of communication has a "sunny side" and a "shadow side"
   - any strength or preference taken to an extreme can become a liability to effective communication

5. What are the sunny and shadow sides of each communication preference?

Extraverted Communication — Sunny Side
- extraverts engage easily in conversation
- they are enthusiastic and open
- they are willing to participate
- they interact with ease
- they share experiences

Extraverted Communication — Shadow Side
- extraverts may monopolize conversations
- they sometimes make insensitive comments
- their communication can be perceived as insincere and superficial
- they are psychologically intrusive with questions

Introverted Communication — Sunny Side
- introverts limit their deep meaningful communications to a few trustworthy listeners
- they think before speaking
- they limit unproductive small talk
- they like advance notice and scheduled appointments for meetings
- they are reserved and conservative in speech
- they like written communications
- introverts can learn extraverted communication skills

Introverted Communication — Shadow Side
- introverts can be misunderstood due to reserved nature
- they can be undervalued in society dominated by extraverts
- they can be regarded as antisocial or socially inept
- they may become targets of psychological projection
- they sometimes send out negative messages of exclusion to people outside the "boundaries of intimacy" with whom personal matters are not discussed

Sensing Communication — Sunny Side
- sensors like to discuss practical issues
- their communication is grounded in reality
- they present information in an orderly and sequential fashion
- they are precise and concise
- they focus on the present

Sensing Communication — Shadow Side
- sensors can become irritating "nitpickers"
- their preoccupation with details may limit innovative thought and discussion
- they may display undue confidence in personal experience to justify claims and arguments
- they can alienate visionaries and futurists

Intuitive Communication — Sunny Side
- intuitives are imaginative and act globally
- they are insightful
- they are future oriented
- they rely on their hunches
- they are novel and unusual people
- they use colourful metaphors and analogies in their speech

Intuitive Communication — Shadow Side
- intuitives can be vague and incomprehensible
- they can be perceived as impractical
- their arguments may have little basis in fact
- their proposals may seem unrealistic

Thinking Communication — Sunny Side
- thinkers enjoy theoretical issues
- they are objective
- they are critical and analytical
- they are fair, rational, concise
- they are goal oriented

Thinking Communication — Shadow Side
- thinkers can be cold and impersonal
- they can be tedious to others
- their ideas may be impractical or useless
- they may be too critical
- their logical side can be limiting

Feeling Communication — Sunny Side
- feelers' interactions with others are personal and subjective
- they are friendly
- they consider values and effects on people's lives
- they are empathetic
- they are emotionally persuasive
- they are receptive to others
- they are inviting

Feeling Communication — Shadow Side
- feelers can be time wasters
- they can lack objectivity
- they can become overwhelmed by enthusiasm or emotion
- they have difficulty expressing negative emotions

Judging Communication — Sunny Side
- judgers are prepared in advance
- they are oriented to schedules and timetables
- they are structured and organized
- their mind-set is based on closure
- they are purposeful and task oriented
- they limit digressions

Judging Communication — Shadow Side
- judgers can be rigid and inflexible
- they can be constricting and lack spontaneity
- they may have less fun because they leave no room for surprise
- they can be too serious and businesslike
- they can be guilty of premature decision making

Perceiving Communication — Sunny Side
- perceivers are flexible and accommodating
- they are cautious about stating conclusions
- they are oriented to options and contingencies
- they are responsive and adaptable

Perceiving Communication — Shadow Side
- perceivers can have a slow response time
- they can be disorganized and ill-prepared
- they can be indecisive
- they can be ineffective
- they may undermine their own confidence

Related Readings

Benfari, Robert and Jean Knox (1991). *Understanding Your Management Style*. Lexington, MA: Lexington Books.

Hammer, Allen (1996) (Ed.). *MBTI Applications–A Decade of Research on the Myers-Briggs Type Indicator*. Palo Alto, CA: Consulting Psychologists Press.

Hirsh, Sandra Krebs. *Using the Myers-Briggs Type Indicator in Organizations: A Resource Book* (1985). Palo Alto, CA: Consulting Psychologists Press.

Isachsen, Olaf and Linda V. Berens (1988). *Working Together: A Personality Centered Approach to Management*. Coronado, CA: Neworld Management Press.

Kroeger, Otto and Janet M. Thuesen (1988). *Type Talk*. New York: Dell Publishing.

Weblinks

1. Personal communication styles
   www.cics.bsu.edu/cox/ics602/verbal/index.htm

   Find out if you're noble, Socratic, reflective or something else when it comes to communication style.

2. Communication styles
   www.luxline.com/personality/comm.html

   Learn more on how communication styles can either open doors for you or provoke conflict.

3. Power-packed communication skills
   www.polk.cc.fl.us/coned/corpclas/commune.htm

   Understand why some people tend to come to a decision logically while others seem noncommittal until enough information has been gathered.

4. Speaking in business
   www.dist.maricopa.edu/eddev/artic/96/ind/ind/33.html

   Learn about using assertive, nonassertive and aggressive communication styles appropriate for the business setting.

CHAPTER 3

The lady doth protest too much methinks.

–William Shakespeare

PSYCHO-LOGICAL DEFENSIVENESS

CHAPTER OVERVIEW

LEARNING OUTCOMES

After successfully completing this chapter, you will be able to

3.1 Identify the psychological defences you use to ward off anxiety

3.2 Provide a working definition of defensiveness

3.3 Explain the psychodynamics of defensiveness and illustrate how they serve as obstacles to effective human relations

3.4 Engage in some preliminary dream analysis to help uncover repressed sources of anxiety giving rise to defensiveness

3.5 Identify defensiveness in everyday behaviour

3.6 Deal more effectively with defensiveness in yourself and others

3.7 Explain the general nature and purpose of logical fallacies

3.8 Outline and describe specific forms of fallacious reasoning

3.9 Identify fallacies in everyday arguments and conversations

"PSYCHO-LOGICAL" DEFENSIVENESS CAN BE OFFENSIVE TO OTHERS

In Chapter 1 of this book, we sought to build a solid foundation for our future human relations development. We began with a period of self-analysis through an examination of personality type theory. By increasing our self-insight, we worked toward a better appreciation and understanding of what we, as individuals, bring to our human interactions. In Chapter 2, we learned how our psychological insights, gleaned from the work of Myers, Briggs and Jung, could be applied to interpersonal relationships and how they could help to make our communications with others "psych-smart." By applying type theory concepts to the communication process, we also made efforts to become more sensitive to psychological diversity.

Now, in what follows, we will examine a few of the "psycho-logical" obstacles that interfere with productive dialogue and harmonious relations with others. Theorists often refer to these obstacles as "**noise**" in the communication process. By the way, note that I have purposely hyphenated the title of this chapter to read *"Psycho-Logical" Defensiveness*. I have done this to underscore the point that there are both **unconscious influences** (the psycho part) and **irrational thought processes** (the logical part) that hinder our ability to get along with others and to communicate effectively with them. By identifying and exposing these unconscious influences, and also by learning to make our irrational thought processes more rational, we can gain better control of our lives and reduce the amount of "nonsense" in our dealings with people. Let us begin, then, by exploring the nature and extent of our defensiveness by doing Self-Diagnostic 3.1.

How Defensive Am I?

Aim: The purpose of this self-diagnostic is simply to get you thinking about the degree to which you display defensiveness in your personal life. Results are not scientific, but merely suggestive. They are just a first step to help you determine how defensive you become in response to stress, conflict and anxiety-provoking situations.

Instructions: For each of the statements below, indicate how true each is for you. Be honest. Failure to be so is highly defensive!

1 = Never true
2 = Almost never true
3 = Sometimes true
4 = Usually true
5 = Almost always true

Score

_____ 1. When I get sexually aroused, I start thinking about something else.

_____ 2. Whenever I experience anger, I keep it inside, choosing not to express it.

_____ 3. I can offer explanations very easily and often for why I commit acts I recognize deep down as being wrong.

_____ 4. I put things off, reasoning that I can start tomorrow or make up then what I should have done today.

_____ 5. I misread people by attributing to them thoughts, feelings and intentions that are not their own.

_____ 6. I feel threatened when I'm in the presence of people I don't like.

_____ 7. I am very polite and courteous to adversaries when I would rather attack.

_____ 8. When I feel afraid or insecure, I pretend I'm happy-go-lucky, joking around and laughing.

_____ 9. When I have a bad day at school or work, I unload my frustrations on younger or less powerful people in my circle of family, friends and acquaintances.

_____ 10. I've been known to attack, both verbally or emotionally, defenceless people for no good reason.

_____ 11. I am a hero worshipper—imitating sports stars, musical artists or others of high repute.

_____ 12. If I didn't belong to a clique or in-group of some kind, I would feel left out, naked or exposed.

_____ 13. When I get upset, I either go drinking and partying or just start acting silly.

_____ 14. When mad, I pout and refuse to talk about what upsets me.

_____ 15. On days when things are not going well, I dream about better times in the future.

_____ 16. I often replay and win arguments in my mind well after they have finished.

_____ 17. I like to find theories and explanations for my unacceptable behaviours, thoughts and feelings.

_____ 18. I don't believe mistreatment directed at me should be taken too seriously. I maintain that sociological, psychological and economic factors cause people to do what they do.

_____ 19. I refuse to admit publicly that family and friends do things that are wrong and personally embarrassing.

_____ 20. I pretend not to hear things or see things I don't like.

_____ 21. I try to transform my undesirable impulses into actions that are socially acceptable.

_____ 22. I use creative or constructive outlets (e.g., painting, jogging) to vent my frustrations.

How to Score

All the above statements reflect defensive acts or tendencies. Add all the numbers that you placed in the Score column. Divide by 22. Round your score, if necessary. This method of calculation will give you your average score. An average score of 1 suggests that you are almost never defensive or possibly that you are unaware of your defensiveness. A score of 2 means that you are rarely defensive. A score of 3 indicates occasional defensiveness. A score of 4 reflects strong defensive tendencies, while a score of 5 could mean that you are defensive almost all the time.

Remember that your results are tentative and need to be verified. You may wish to discuss your results with someone you trust and know well. Note that statements are grouped in pairs, each relating to a particular defence mechanism that you'll learn about in this chapter. Which defences did you score highest on?

Questions	Defence Mechanism Reflected
1 and 2	Repression
3 and 4	Rationalization
5 and 6	Projection
7 and 8	Reaction Formation
9 and 10	Displacement
11 and 12	Identification
13 and 14	Regression
15 and 16	Fantasy Formation
17 and 18	Intellectualization/Isolation
19 and 20	Denial
21 and 22	Sublimation

UNCONSCIOUS AND IRRATIONAL DEFENSIVENESS

> The poets and philosophers before me discovered the unconscious. What I discovered was the scientific method by which the unconscious can be studied.
>
> Sigmund Freud

Defensiveness is something we should all try to reduce in our psychological and interpersonal lives. For our immediate purposes, it can be defined simply as the psyche's unconscious effort to protect the self from disquieting **anxiety**, either through **diversionary** and **intimidation tactics** or by **distortions of reality**. As you'll soon see, defensiveness takes on many forms, but whatever the form, you can probably already appreciate how irritating it can be to be around people who unwittingly try to reduce anxiety by twisting things, by constantly attacking others, or by making efforts to justify themselves by rationalizing their actions. Such people tend to be insecure and abrasive. For reasons we don't always understand, they seem to take things too personally. Being around defensive people can lead to conversations that are very one-sided and uninteresting, making interactions with them emotionally draining.Thus, as the title of this section suggests,being defensive can be offensive to others. It is important, therefore, that you learn more about defensiveness so that you can reduce it in yourself. You probably don't want your own defensiveness to get in the way of positive and fruitful relationship building; nor do you want it to alienate others and prevent you from achieving your goals. Understanding your own defensiveness, then, reducing it in yourself, and working productively with it when found in others, can be enormously helpful.

> They defend their errors as if they were defending their inheritance.
>
> Edmund Burke

Sigmund Freud was the founder of psycho-analysis.

In advance of our discussion of the "psycho" part of psycho-logical defensiveness, it is only fitting to make brief reference to the work of **Sigmund Freud**. His pioneering work in **psychoanalysis**, developed and furthered by daughter Anna, has helped us to understand the unconscious dimensions of life and how we often twist reality in order to feel better about ourselves. According to Freud, not all psychological experience takes place at a **conscious** level. Some things are found at the **preconscious** level and others are deeply buried in the **unconscious**. What is conscious is what we are currently experiencing with respect to our feelings, thoughts and sensations. What is preconscious is that which we can call up at will. For instance, if now asked, you could no doubt give someone your birthdate or telephone number—things that were probably not occupying your conscious mind just a moment ago. However, what is unconscious is currently unavailable to self-awareness. The fact that there are things happening in the unconscious mind is important to remember. Frequently, in response to underlying fears and anxiety-provoking situations, we unwittingly resort to the use of psychic defences that allow us to cope. These defences reduce unpleasant feelings or shield them from conscious awareness.

Unfortunately, an overreliance on unconscious defensiveness as a **coping mechanism** can lead to gross distortions of reality. A failure to appreciate the role played by unconscious defensiveness in your life can also prevent you from functioning in healthy and autonomous ways. Buried fears and anxieties may dictate your actions and thoughts in ways you don't recognize. By learning more about defensiveness and by reducing it in ourselves, we can free ourselves from unconscious debilitating forces and we can learn to perceive situations and other people with less anxiety-based distortion.

> We wouldn't worry about what other people thought of us if we knew how seldom they did.
>
> Anonymous

Figure 3.1
A Glossary of Freudian Terms

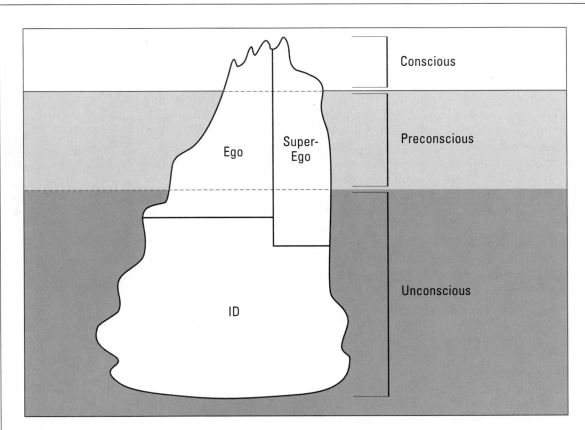

Levels of Consciousness

Conscious: Includes thoughts, feelings, sensations and experiences that we are aware of at any moment in time.

Preconscious: Lies just below the level of conscious awareness. Contents of preconscious can be called into conscious awareness with a minimum of effort.

Unconscious: Comprises drives and instincts outside the realm of conscious experience. Access to it can be gained indirectly by free association, dream analysis and so on.

Structure of Personality

ID: Refers to the biological components of personality (e.g., sex drive). It operates on the pleasure principle and is irrational and impulsive. The ID makes up the largest part of the psyche; it is most influential in determining behaviour.

Superego: Houses our moral conscience and ego ideals. It is instrumental in making value judgments and helping us to distinguish between right and wrong. It operates on the perfection principle.

Ego: The rational part of personality. It operates on the reality principle. It serves to balance all parts of the personality to minimize anxiety.

Dream Work

3.4

Background: Sigmund Freud believed that mental activity is largely unconscious. He also argued that access to the unconscious (where defensiveness originates) must be indirect. Interpreting dreams is one indirect approach to the mind that can help you to understand better its unconscious workings. Dream analysis can enable you to locate sources of anxiety against which you unconsciously defend yourself. Of course, dream analysis is best done with the assistance of professionally trained experts. Our less-than-expert efforts here are for preliminary consideration only. Sweet dreams!

Instructions

1. Before going to sleep, place a pad of paper and a writing instrument next to your bed. You could also have a tape recorder handy, if available.
2. Tell yourself that you will remember your dreams for the night. Everybody dreams but we don't always remember what we've dreamt. (I've found that telling myself to remember is helpful.)
3. Immediately after waking up, record any dreams you had on paper or tape. You may wish to fill in details about your dream later on in the day.
4. Analyse your dreams by asking yourself the following questions:
   a. Are my dreams all over the place or is there a sequence to them?
   b. What parts of my dreams reflect the activities of the previous day? Is this significant?
   c. How do my dreams reflect my personal wants or attitudes toward others?
   d. What meaning could I give to my dreams?
   e. Do this dream work for several weeks. Continue your analysis and interpretation. Look for any recurring themes and patterns. They may help you to uncover repressed material.
   f. Record your personal insights in journal form.

Source: This activity is a variation of "Dream Journal" by Frager and Fadiman, found in *Personality and Personal Growth*.

PSYCHO-*logical* DEFENCE MECHANISMS

Since anxiety is inherently unpleasant, human beings have developed strategies to reduce its intensity. One strategy requires us to confront or run away from the threats that face us. We thereby eliminate difficulties, lower the chance of their future occurrence, or decrease the prospects of additional anxiety in the future.

A second strategy for coping with anxiety is to employ **PSYCHO-logical defence mechanisms**. They include repression, rationalization, projection, reaction formation, displacement, identification, regression, fantasy formation, intellectualization/isolation, denial and sublimation. As mentioned before, defence mechanisms operate on an unconscious level. This explains why defensive people are usually unaware of their defensiveness. Also recall that defence mechanisms distort the reality of anxiety-provoking situations that give rise to the defence mechanisms in the first place. When we use defence mechanisms, then, we unconsciously seek to protect ourselves against any real or perceived threat by falsifying the nature of the threat. That part of the psyche which actually uses psychological defence mechanisms, Freud calls the **ego**.

You should note that everybody uses defence mechanisms. If we didn't, we could all be overwhelmed by anxiety. The danger for us comes from an overreliance on the mechanisms. If we become too dependent on them, they could cause gross distortions of reality and we could begin to lose touch with what's really going on. People displaying great amounts of defensiveness often show symptoms of neurosis (Frager and Fadiman, 1984). It is important, therefore, to learn about the defence mechanisms discussed below and to become sensitive to your reliance upon them.

Repression

Repression is a primary ego defence that makes all other psychological defensiveness possible. It is the central mechanism used by the ego to prevent anxiety-provoking thoughts from entering the conscious level of awareness. These thoughts may originate in our biological instincts or from painful events experienced during our lifetime. Unacceptable sexual desires, for instance, may be repressed to the unconscious as could childhood traumas. It is important to emphasize that "repressed" people are not aware of their own anxiety-provoking conflicts in the psyche, nor do they consciously remember the emotionally traumatic past events now buried in the unconscious recesses of the mind. As Freud (1915: 147) put it, "The essence of repression lies simply in turning something away and keeping it at a distance from the consciousness."

Despite its very real potential for harm, the use of repression helps us cope with everyday problems. Let's suppose, for example, that a friend said something spiteful to us. We might conveniently forget what was said in order to maintain the relationship. Then, we might also "forget" to show up at the friend's pool party to which we were invited shortly after the remarks were made. In both such cases, repression would have a role to play.

Repression can also act as a temporary coping mechanism in response to conflict and pain stemming from our individual histories. Unpleasant things may have happened to us that are too horrible to bear consciously. Distancing ourselves psychologically for a time may help us to survive, even if we are emotionally wounded. On this note, I might add that a lot of the "inner child" work done these days by therapists and social workers aims to *unrepress* forgotten traumatic episodes in the lives of emotionally hurting individuals. Bringing to consciousness painful memories and learning to deal with them can have a healing, therapeutic effect.

Obstacles

On the negative side, repressed memories, conflicts, thoughts, feelings and impulses do not just disappear when repressed. They remain active in the unconscious. Psychic energy is continually spent to prevent their emergence into conscious awareness. This strain drains much of the ego's resources and, therefore, less energy is available for more constructive, self-enhancing and creative behaviours (Hjelle and Ziegler, 1981). After all, "It's hard to expand your horizons when you're busy defending your borders."

As well as draining your creative energies, repression has the negative effect of precluding any possible resolutions to conflicts still buried in the unconscious. If you don't know what's disturbing you, it's difficult to make the appropriate adjustments in your life. Affected by anxiety, the true source of which is not understood, repressed people tend toward rigidity, lack of spontaneity and an inability to meet the challenges of life head-on. They may consequently seem awfully "stiff" or overly reserved to those communicating with them.

Even more serious, highly repressed people may, over long periods of time, develop other unhealthy psychological and physical symptoms. Phobias (e.g., fear of snakes) are derivative of repressed feelings as are hysterical reactions. Psychosomatic illnesses (e.g., ulcers, asthma and arthritis) may also be linked to repressed anxiety (Frager and Fadiman, 1984). Psychosexual disorders (impotence and frigidity) probably have a basis in repression as well.

In his treatment of patients, Freud discovered that repressed impulses find outlets in dreams, slips of the tongue and in other manifestations of what he described as the "psychopathology of everyday life" (Hjelle and Ziegler, 1981). You might wish to engage in some dream analysis yourself to uncover any personal repressions. What are your nighttime fantasies or daydreams all about? What could the themes indicate? Also, try to catch yourself in the act of "changing the subject," "pretending that you didn't understand" or making it appear that you "didn't hear what someone said." That which was changed, not understood or not heard may give you some insights into yourself and the workings of your mind. You may be able to uncover some fears and anxieties that you never consciously knew you had.

> "The dream is the royal road to the unconscious."
>
> Sigmund Freud

Rationalization

A defence mechanism many people rely on heavily is **rationalization**. In this case, the ego enlists the powers of reason to attempt to cope with disquieting anxiety. In order to protect the self, unacceptable thoughts, actions, mistakes, poor judgments and failures must somehow be explained away. What the ego self does in its own defence is provide "reasonable," but dishonest, explanations and justifications to support behaviours recognized at an unconscious level as wrong or undesirable. To recognize consciously and admit our failures, wrongdoings or unacceptable cravings could be too painful to bear. Instead, the ego disguises our true motives, distorts the reality of situations and makes things look more morally acceptable than they are. This self-deception helps us to cope with immediate anxiety; however, it is not productive to the extent that it shields us from recognizing the real reasons behind our behaviours, attitudes, thoughts and feelings. We provide ethical-sounding rationales for things that arise from other less commendable motivating forces.

Two "fruitful" examples of rationalization are "sour grapes" and "sweet lemons." Using the sour grapes rationalization, we try to minimize something to which we've aspired but failed. Simply, we wanted something, but after discovering the impossibility of getting it, we undercut its value. Aesop's fable serves us well here. Remember the fox who wanted to eat the grapes? When the fox discovered they couldn't be reached, he decided that they were probably sour anyway. It's emotionally easier to cope with the fact that something *undesirable* is out of reach than something much sought after. Failing to get what we want produces frustration and anxiety.

Using the sweet lemon rationalization, people glorify something later on that was not considered very attractive or desirable in the first place. For example, people may be forced to do unwanted tasks only to react later by praising the benefits of doing them. In truth, there may be little to be gained, but believing there is a benefit allows people to cope with unpleasant situations.

Obstacles

One negative result of rationalization is impaired judgment. If we see life as a collection of sweet lemons and sour grapes, we may end up with a basket

Source: Reprinted by permission of UFS, Inc.

of rotten fruit. Describing objects of our desire as less desirable simply because of personal frustration or making undesirable objects sound more desirable than they really are just because of personal necessity may help us to feel better temporarily, but it certainly won't enable us to see clearly, impartially and objectively. As rationalizing people, our judgments will be more reflections of our wants and frustrations than accurate evaluations of objects in the external world. Impaired judgment, like impaired driving, is dangerous and may get you into a lot of trouble. This idea takes us to the ethical problems associated with rationalization.

If we rely on rationalization whenever we violate social norms or personal standards of conduct, then we cease to function as moral people. Rationalizing helps us to justify unjustifiable acts in our own minds. It helps us to get off the hook of moral responsibility for all wrongdoing. Heavy reliance on rationalization spares us from guilt and self-blame. From the vantage point of others, however, refusing to accept responsibility for our wrongdoing can be perceived as immature, if not immoral. No doubt, appearing immature and immoral is not in your personal self-interest. These qualities are not likely to endear you to others. It is important, therefore, that you minimize rationalization in your efforts to reduce anxiety in your life and improve your interpersonal effectiveness.

Projection

3.3

Projection is the unconscious act of attributing to others one's own feelings, thoughts and intentions. Through the process of projection, undesirable aspects of one's own personality can be displaced from within onto the external environment of people, animals or objects. By externalizing what is in fact internal, people can deal with anxiety-provoking thoughts and intentions without having to admit or be aware of the fact that these disturbing thoughts are their own (Frager and Fadiman, 1984). Projection offers temporary relief from anxiety as it allows people to blame someone or something else for their own personal shortcomings (Hjelle and Ziegler, 1981). Projection thus seems to come in handy whenever the ego or self-esteem is threatened. See Figure 3.2 for an example of projection.

The danger with projection is that it may become too intense and habitual. If this occurs, then gross distortions of reality can result. People could even become psychologically ill or disturbed. They might, for example, become paranoid and attribute aggressive thoughts to others that originate within themselves. On a less serious note, projections could cause people to evade responsibility or to perform at less than optimum levels. Students who don't study for tests and who don't wish consciously to admit their irresponsibility might unfairly criticize their professor for being unprepared in class. The next time you criticize anyone about anything, it could be insightful for you to ask, "To what extent is my criticism an accurate reflection of reality?" or "What does my criticism of another tell me about myself?"

Figure 3.2
Projection

Obstacles

The use of projection could have negative social consequences for people relying on it too frequently. If you unconsciously attribute to others your own hostile or aggressive urges and impulses, you may develop unwarranted suspicions. You won't be very trusting as an individual. This will surely make it difficult to establish close relationships (Barocas, Reichman and Schwebel, 1983).

Excessive projection could also make you fall prey to social prejudice and scapegoating. Ethnic and racial groups provide convenient targets for the attribution of your own negative personal characteristics to others (Adorno, Frenkel-Brunswick, Levinson and Sanford, 1950, cited in Hjelle and Ziegler, 1981). For instance, people who feel inferior may project their inferiority onto selected racial, ethnic or religious groups. Ambitious types may blame the "system" or some stereotyped elitist group for their difficulties in achieving success. Projection deflects attention away from ourselves and helps us to feel better about our personal shortcomings. Unfortunately, these better feelings come at the expense of others.

Finally, I should add here that projection can have negative career consequences. If you display an inability to judge other people's motives, you may suffer from poor work adjustment. When trying to read others (i.e., their wants, goals and preferences) you may simply be projecting and perceiving yourself externalized in someone else. Misjudgment of people is surely a liability in the professional world. Vaillant (1977) discovered in a longitudinal study of sophomores that those who used projection to a significant degree "had the worst career adjustments." Also, we learn from research that people with above-average relationships apparently do not significantly use projection. For interpersonal and professional success, then, a reduction of projection is indicated.

Reaction Formation

Reaction formation is used by the ego to control the expression of forbidden impulses. This mechanism works in two ways. First, unacceptable impulses are repressed in the unconscious. Second, opposites to the impulses are expressed on a conscious level (Hjelle and Ziegler, 1981). For example, people who are threatened by their own sexual urges or libidinal impulses may become crusaders against pornography and liberal laws on sexual conduct. Others who are highly anxious about their violent tendencies may become "peace-niks" or advocates of animal rights. In a letter to Masserman, a famous psychologist who did work on alcoholism in cats, an antivivisectionist's moral crusade "covers up" the person's apparent violent tendencies. Notice in the following letter the lack of love and compassion for the drunkard and the personal assault on Masserman.

> I read [a magazine article...on your work on alcoholism]....I am surprised that anyone who is as well educated as you must be to hold the position that you do would stoop to such a depth as to torture helpless little cats in the pursuit of a cure for alcoholics....A drunkard does not want to be cured—a drunkard is just a weak minded idiot who belongs in the gutter and should be left there. Instead of torturing helpless little cats why not torture drunks or better still exert your would-be noble effort toward getting a bill passed to exterminate the drunks. They are not any good to anyone or themselves and are just a drain on the public, having to pull them off the street, jail them, then they have to be fed while there and it's against the law to feed them arsenic so there they are....If people are such weaklings the world is better off without them....

> My greatest wish is that you have brought home to you a torture that will be a thousand fold greater than what you have, and are doing to the little animals....If you are an example of what a noted psychiatrist should be I'm glad I am just an ordinary human being without letters after my name. I'd rather be myself with a clear conscience, knowing that I have not hurt any living creature, and can sleep without seeing frightened, terrified dying cats—because I know they must die after you have finished with them. No punishment is too great for you and I hope I live to read about your mangled body and long suffering before you finally die—and I'll laugh long and loud. (Masserman, 1961: 35)

Of course, not all advocates of peace or animal rights display reaction formation defensiveness. Many, if not most, have genuine and legitimate ethical disagreements with war and the destruction of animals. The clue in determining the difference between true feelings and defensiveness is found in the degree to which the feelings are emphasized (Hergenhahn, 1993). Reaction formations have a tendency to be more intense and extravagant in their expression. There may be something compulsive or exaggerated in the feelings communicated. The threatening urge (e.g., sexual or aggressive) to be repressed must be obscured again, again and again (Frager and Fadiman, 1984). Unconsciously, there is the fear that the unacceptable urge or impulse will break through if repeated attacks on it or denials of it do not continue.

Obstacles

There are negative social consequences to using reaction formation. Relationships may be crippled by the defensive person's rigidity. Reaction formation contributes to building an "all or nothing" attitude toward life that makes the defensive person unyielding and inflexible. Little compromise may be possible with those whose strong feelings about something are merely a cover-up for unconscious fears and anxieties. Reasoning with unconsciously defensive people may sometimes seem next to impossible. Try, for example, to debate rationally the issue of pornography with a person whose moral zeal is based on personal guilt and insecurity. Not much will be accomplished.

Displacement

Like other defence mechanisms, **displacement** is an unconscious process. It too has much to do with our primitive and instinctual impulses. Whenever we feel the urge to meet the demands of the **id** (a term used by Freud to designate the part of the personality directed at biological need satisfaction), we invest **psychic energy** in need-satisfying objects. When objects that would directly satisfy the impulses of the id are not available, or when they include some threat or unpleasantness, we may shift our impulses onto other objects. This substitution is called displacement (Engler, 1985). Sigmund Freud used the term **cathexis** to describe the investment of psychic energy in objects that satisfy needs (Hergenhahn, 1993). If need-satisfying objects are not available, an intense longing may manifest itself in the form of thoughts, images and fantasies. Such thoughts persist until needs are satisfied. When needs are finally satisfied, psychic energy dissipates to become available for other cathexes.

If the structure of personality contained only impulses of the biological id and conscious ego functioning, society would probably degenerate into some form of animalistic existence (Hergenhahn, 1993). Instinctual needs from the id would arise and these needs would continue to create tension within individuals until satisfied. Unbridled sexual and aggressive impulses, for exam-

A Poison Tree

I was angry with my friend;
I told my wrath, my wrath did end.
I was angry with my foe;
I told it not, my wrath did grow.
And I watered it in fears,
Night and morning with my tears.
And I sunned it with smiles,
And with soft deceitful wiles.
And it grew both day and night,
Till it bore an apple bright.
And my foe beheld it shine,
And he knew that it was mine.
And into my garden stole,
When the night had veil'd the pole;
In the morning glad I see;
My foe outstretched beneath the tree.

William Blake

Source: Courtesy of Jeremy Tarcher Publishers, Inc.

ple, could be directed at target objects for rape and assault. Furthermore, with only an ego to serve the needs of the id, there would be no regard for the welfare of other people and no distinctions made between acceptable and nonacceptable objects of need satisfaction.

Fortunately, the human psyche has developed a moral superego that functions to inhibit primitive urges, instincts and desires. This inhibition requires energy to be spent on preventing unacceptable cathexes. Energy that is used to prevent unacceptable cathexes is called **anticathexis** (Hergenhahn, 1993). If an unacceptable cathexis were allowed to emerge, the superego would ensure that anxiety would result. To reduce anxiety, the ego and the **superego** (a term used by Freud to capture the notion of moral conscience) combine their efforts to create an anticathexis that is sufficiently strong to inhibit the primitive cathexes of the id. Note that the original needs of the id do not vanish. Rather, the original cathexis is displaced onto other safer objects and activities. This displacement is illustrated in Figure 3.3, where dancing becomes a non-anxiety-provoking substitute (displacement) for sex, which causes significant anxiety through guilt.

In general terms, we can say displacement occurs whenever an instinctual impulse is redirected from a more threatening activity, person or object to a less threatening one (Hjelle and Ziegler, 1981). As a student angered by the comments of one of your instructors, you might swear at a roommate or sibling. If you are upset because your parents won't let you have the car this weekend, you might kick your pet in frustration. Both examples illustrate how primitive impulses (of anger) find their targets in innocent and less threatening objects. Swearing or kicking a pet is no doubt less morally desirable than dancing with someone to displace the unsatisfied need for sex, but I suppose it could be argued it is better than physically

Figure 3.3

An Example of Displacement

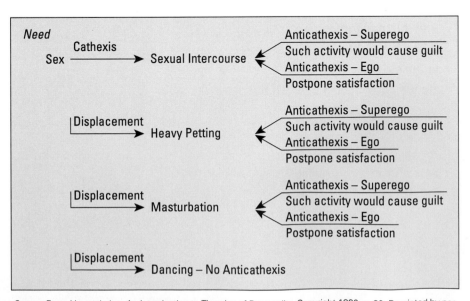

Source: From Hergenhahn, *An Introduction to Theories of Personality*, Copyright 1990, p. 32. Reprinted by permission of Prentice-Hall, Inc., Englewood Cliffs, NJ.

assaulting your parents or killing your cat. It's unfortunate that innocent objects often unjustifiably suffer from the anxiety-induced displacements of others. By increasing awareness of this unconscious defence mechanism, perhaps we can reduce the injury and suffering of all.

A less common form of displacement involves "turning against the self" (Hjelle and Ziegler, 1981). In this case, hostile impulses toward other people are redirected at one's own person. The result can be depression and self-deprecation. If other innocent and less threatening objects are unavailable for displacement, the self can become its own target.

Obstacles

Social and interpersonal manifestations of displacement can be rather unpleasant. First of all, innocent people are attacked, criticized, abused and hurt. They suffer merely by virtue of their relatively nonthreatening natures. Unjustified

> To understand all is to forgive all.
>
> French proverb

psychological assault can be destructive to interpersonal relationships. Second, people unconsciously relying on displacement tend to exhibit hypersensitivity to minor annoyances (Hjelle and Ziegler, 1981). For example, people criticized by overdemanding bosses may react violently to the slightest provocation from a spouse or friend. Target objects of hostility are simply substitutes for the boss who cannot be attacked. The boss has too much power and is therefore too threatening. If some "little comment" you innocently made once was met with undue anger or hostility, perhaps you witnessed displacement; you might also have become the target object of someone's defensiveness designated to reduce that person's own level of anxiety. The benefit of knowing this is that you can increase your compassion for others experiencing psychological pain. You needn't take their outbursts and attacks personally. Through understanding, you might be able to help. At the same time, forgiveness becomes a real possibility. It's probably easier to forgive people you see as suffering than those you see simply as attackers launching unjustifiable assaults on you and others.

Identification ✓

3.3

Identification is a psychological defence mechanism unconsciously used to decrease anxiety by increasing feelings of self-worth. It involves taking on the characteristics of someone admired or considered successful (Hergenhahn, 1990). An obvious example of identification is hero worship as exhibited by school-age boys and girls (Barocas, Reichman and Schwebel, 1983). Typical heroes are rock stars and athletes. Young people are very motivated to find out everything they can about their heroes. They join fan clubs, purchase tapes and CDs, buy sports cards and memorize statistics and facts about those whom they worship. Identification is clearly present when they adopt their favourite hero's hairstyle and dress or when they begin to imitate the hero's behavioural traits and speech patterns. Sometimes people identify with sports celebrities by "feeling part of the team" (e.g., the Vancouver

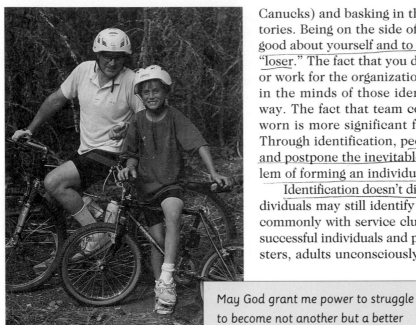

A child's identification with a parent helps to minimize anxiety and build self-esteem.

May God grant me power to struggle to become not another but a better man.

Samuel Taylor Coleridge

Canucks) and basking in the sunshine of its glorious victories. Being on the side of the winner is one way to feel good about yourself and to convince yourself you're not a "loser." The fact that you don't actually play on the team or work for the organization may be unimportant details in the minds of those identifying themselves in such a way. The fact that team colours and sweaters are being worn is more significant for purposes of identification. Through identification, people temporarily gain security and postpone the inevitable confrontation with the problem of forming an individual identity.

Identification doesn't disappear in adulthood. Older individuals may still identify with athletic teams, but more commonly with service clubs, professional organizations, successful individuals and political leaders. As with youngsters, adults unconsciously attempt to bolster feelings of self-worth through identification and thereby protect themselves from anxieties related to the self. Of course, identifications can fail in their hidden purpose by creating a certain vulnerability. If, for example, a political party suffers an humiliating defeat, any individual who is overidentified with that party may suffer a depression that reflects loss of self-esteem (Barocas, Reichman and Schwebel, 1983).

It is important to remember that the purpose of identification is to reduce anxiety. By assuming the characteristics of models who appear to us to be highly successful in gratifying their needs, we can come to believe that we also possess their attributes (Engler, 1985). On this note, permit me to offer a personal example of my own defensiveness to help illustrate identification.

When I was 19, I made arrangements to take my girlfriend to a fancy restaurant for her birthday. Up until this occasion, I had never eaten in an expensive dining room. Pizza joints and "greasy spoons" were my usual places to frequent. In any case, I felt a little nervous about impressing my date. I wasn't quite sure how to act or what to say to the maitre d', my table waiter or to the host of people who kept filling our water and wine glasses. In addition, I was anxious about what to do with the multiple spoons and forks and knives surrounding my plate, which was complete with a decorative pewter cover. I can remember being very worried about exposing my ignorance about fine-dining etiquette. My ego was on the line and I felt it. In my anxiety, I kept looking around the restaurant to see what others were doing. I recall focusing on a distinguished gentleman nearby. He looked very confident. He appeared to have a good grasp of the situation and, unlike me, was actually enjoying his meal. Upon reflection, I now know that I unconsciously chose to imitate the behaviour of this man. In fact, after watching him take a closer look at a painting on the wall of the restaurant, I did likewise—after he left, of course! I guess I wanted to appear cultured and sophisticated like him. Now that considerable time has passed and my self-esteem remains more or less intact, I look back on my teenage defensiveness as a bittersweet memory. I see it as one young man's desperate attempt to feel good about himself by impressing his girlfriend. (By the way, the meal was terrible and the food was cold. I told the waiter that everything was fine and left a big tip to show my date I was a big spender!)

Apart from helping us to cope with anxiety, identification also has an important role to play in the formation of personality. When, as children, we identified with our parents and caretakers, we came to accept their values. This identification enabled us to limit or eliminate punishments that would otherwise come from expressing contrary and conflicting values. Therefore, this acceptance and internalization of parental values not only reduces the fear of retribution, but also helps to form the superego. Later on in life we further superego development by internalizing society's values and norms.

Obstacles

Ironically, overuse of identification can contribute to problems of personal identity. If you're always trying to be like someone else, then you're not spending much time being yourself. This can lead to inauthenticity. You can't really know yourself or express who you are if you're always trying to imitate others. Emulating your heroes may give rise to playing roles and behaving in unnatural ways. It could also lead to certain pretences. Your attraction to others and emulation of them may erroneously lead you to conclude that you share their qualities and personal characteristics. Being a hard-core fan of somebody does not make you that somebody, just as hanging around intelligent people doesn't make you smart.

> This above all: to thine own self be true,
> And it must follow as the night the day,
> Thou canst not then be false to any man.
>
> William Shakespeare

Another potential problem related to identification is ostracism or separation from others. If you choose to be loyal to certain groups, you may have to reject others. They may have different values, norms and principles of conduct. Furthermore, strong identification with any group or person may make you a target for opponents of that person or group. If you wish to be a neo-Nazi skinhead, for example, don't be surprised if you're shunned by mainstream society. You may be stereotyped as much as you stereotype those outside your identified group.

I emphasize again that identification is a defence against anxiety. In this case, anxiety results from an unclear sense of self. While identification may temporarily relieve insecurity, it is not the final answer to the question of who you are; it is not the final answer to the question of your identity. Identification is merely a diversion from mental pain. Finding your true self is therefore not some kind of frivolous philosophical pursuit, but an important life task. Failure to find yourself may relegate you to a life of anxiety and inauthenticity.

3.3 → *Regression*

Like other defence mechanisms, **regression** is used to defend against the conscious experience of anxiety. By means of it we revert to an earlier, more childlike stage of development. This "going back" enables us to alleviate anxiety by retreating to a previous period in life that was experienced as being more secure and pleasant. At this earlier stage, there were fewer responsibilities and more parental/caretaker attention. Security came from being cared for and having one's gratification assured (Barocas, Reichman and Schwebel, 1983). Calvin Hall (1954: 95–96) offers us a list of regression examples below.

> *Even healthy, well-adjusted people make regressions from time to time in order to reduce anxiety, or, as they say, to blow off steam. They smoke, get drunk, eat too much, lose their tempers, bite their nails, pick their noses, break laws, talk baby talk, destroy property, masturbate, read mystery stories, go to the movies, engage in unusual sexual practices, chew gum and tobacco, dress up as children, drive fast and recklessly, believe in good and evil spirits, take naps, fight and kill one another, bet on the horses, daydream, rebel against or submit to authority, gamble, preen before the mirror, act out their impulses, pick on scapegoats, and do a thousand and one other childish things. Some of these regressions are so commonplace that they are taken to be signs of maturity. Actually they are all forms of regression used by adults.*

Source: Reprinted by permission of HarperCollins Publishers, Inc.

As with any defence mechanism, regression only temporarily relieves the experience of anxiety. It leaves the cause unaddressed (Hjelle and Ziegler, 1981). Hence, anxiety-producing conflicts and situations are not truly re-

Source: "Cathy" by Cathy Guisewite. Reprinted by permission of Universal Press Syndicate.

solved by regression, only obscured from conscious awareness. In cases of severely disturbed individuals, we may witness significant regression to early infantile states. People may begin to babble like babies or assume childlike appearances. Less serious examples of regression can be found in people who are fatigued or ill. When sick, people often increase the need to be pampered and cared for. Exhausted adults may become easily irritated and throw tantrums like overtired children. On this note, you might notice that even precocious children may revert to thumb sucking just before bedtime or when stressed. A classic example of childhood regression is bedwetting just before starting kindergarten. Unconsciously, the child may think, "If I bedwet, then I won't have to go to school because I'm too young and immature."

Obstacles

Regression obviously interferes with human communication. Someone reduced to babbling will not send coherent messages. Also, if highly anxious individuals display regressive symptoms of raging and tantruming, then it will be difficult to conduct level-headed conversations. Furthermore, if regressed people are preoccupied with the need to be cared for, they will appear very narcissistic or selfish to others. It is difficult to develop intimate relationships with those who only wish to take from others in order to satisfy their own security needs. Some people are simply put off by the immaturity of regressive behaviour. People displaying this behaviour may be avoided.

Fantasy Formation

3.3

Fantasy formation is a defence that involves "gratifying frustrated desires by thinking about imaginary achievements and satisfactions" (Weiten, Lloyd and Lashley, 1996). Through fantasy formation, we become what we're not, we have what we don't own, we accomplish what we've never done and we visit places to which we've never been. Fantasy formation provides yet another way of helping us to cope with anxiety. Let's suppose you just failed a test; dreaming about the day you graduate may help you to deal with the temporary setback. Or, think of somebody you particularly dislike; expressing your hostile feelings in fantasy is much better than physically or verbally assaulting the target of your aggression. In short, creative use of fantasy can sometimes be the key to dealing effectively with negative emotions and periodic frustrations.

Most obvious examples of fantasy are found with children. Often powerless to control others, they create imaginary playmates or animals who obey them (Barocas, Reichman and Schwebel, 1983). If threatened by guilt, they may conjure up monsters in their minds. Such fantasizing prepares children for reality and for the need to relieve pain.

Obstacles

Extended use of fantasy formation can transport people psychologically away from real problems and real situations. Presented with the threat of anxiety, some people may use fantasy as a way of retreating from relationships of all kinds (Barocas, Reichman and Schwebel, 1983). In this case, problems and people are not directly faced. Avoidance and illusion are used to sweep the dirt of anxiety under the carpet of conscious awareness. Personal and interpersonal problems go unnoticed.

People relying heavily on fantasy formation as a defence mechanism may be difficult to communicate with. Their perceptions of reality may be highly unrealistic. Living in a future dream of success, they may overlook their current failures. Imagining how things could be, they may be blind to how things actually are. Pragmatic discussions, for example, ones that are based on facts and reality, may be difficult to hold with those living in a fantasy world.

Intellectualization/Isolation

Intellectualization (or **isolation**) is a way of suppressing unpleasant emotions by engaging in detached analyses of threatening problems (Weiten, Lloyd and Lashley, 1996). This defence mechanism enables us unconsciously to "isolate" anxiety, separating parts of a situation from the rest of the psyche. Through this act of partitioning, little or no emotional reaction to the situation or event is consciously experienced (Frager and Fadiman, 1984). By isolating problems and conflicts from the rest of the personality, events can be recounted with no feeling. The emotional detachment makes it seem like the situation or event involves a third party, not the one doing the isolating. By withdrawing more and more into the world of ideas, intellectualizing people need less and less to deal with the reality of their own feelings (Frager and Fadiman, 1984). Of course, there is nothing wrong in analysing situations or intellectualizing them. This problem occurs only when isolation is being used unconsciously to protect the ego from acknowledging anxiety-provoking aspects of situations, events or interpersonal relationships. Thinking, in itself, is not necessarily a diversion from emotional experience.

The quotation below provides an illustration of intellectualization. In it, a person named Alan presents many great ideas about threatening matters (e.g., sex) but does not possess the feelings that normally accompany them. Let's see how.

> *Alan offers a perfect example. At eighteen, one of his chief delights is to discuss philosophic ideas on love, politics, and death. But he thinks very little about his daily life. His lofty views on love in no way prevent him from being childish and callous with women. He wittily criticizes the middle-class marriage for its imperfections and hypocrisies. But he cannot move past the most obvious clichés in his own relationships.*
>
> *Perhaps most striking is the way Alan handles sex. He talks about it and reads books, including marriage manuals and*

intellectual histories translated from the French. When he is attracted to a woman, he tends to involve her in long discussions about the philosophic implications of sexual freedom and commitment. What Alan does is to intellectualize, or connect his feelings with abstract theories, with the result that he seldom experiences his feelings at all.
(Barocas, Reichman and Schwebel, 1983: 118)

While overdependence on intellectualization can become a general pattern of maladjustment, this defence is useful to the extent to which it enables the ego to become stronger and more mature. It can help to make later defensiveness unnecessary. Some have pointed out that intellectualization is developmentally appropriate in adolescence, but that it becomes less and less useful as the individual matures (Barocas, Reichman and Schwebel, 1983).

Obstacles

Intellectualization can cause problems for effective interpersonal communication. For example, if people are not in touch with their real feelings, they will not be able to share them with others. Also, if individuals persist in analysing and intellectualizing their lives, intimacy may suffer. Conversations may begin to sound more like abstract theoretical discussions. This need not be frustrating in itself; however, sensitive receivers of "intellectualized" defensive messages may become frustrated because they cannot make personal contact with the defensive people involved or appreciate what they are truly experiencing. Intellectualizing can create psychological distance.

Denial

3.3

The defence mechanism of **denial** blocks from the ego threatening events or facts found in external social reality (Atwater, 1999). Not accepting the fact that your ex-fiancée is having a sexual relationship with your best friend would be a case of denial. Here, threatening thoughts would surface in your conscious mind, but you would refuse to believe them. There would be a conscious effort to suppress what you'd experience as unpleasant.

Sigmund Freud did not claim to discover denial (Frager and Fadiman, 1984). Awareness of denial was enhanced by Darwin and Nietzsche's (a German philosopher) earlier observations about themselves. Darwin (cited in Frager and Fadiman, 1984: 25) wrote in his autobiography:

I had during years followed a golden rule, namely, whenever I came across a published fact, a new observation or idea, which ran counter to my general results, I made a memorandum of it without fail and at once; for I had found by experience that such facts and ideas were far more apt to slip the memory than favorable ones.

Along the same vein, Nietzsche wrote the following:

> *"I have done that," says my memory. "It is impossible that*
> *I should have done it," says my pride, and it remains in-*
> *exorable [incapable of being moved]. Finally my memory*
> *yields. (25)*

As a defence mechanism, denial does offer certain adaptive advantages. In certain situations it can effectively reduce stress (Atwater, 1999). It can also enable people to live through difficult times and unbearable situations. For example, two psychiatrists at the Massachusetts General Hospital found that "major deniers" of heart trouble had better survival rates than those people who only partially or minimally denied.

Obstacles

Overreliance on denial may indicate that mature problem-solving methods of dealing with life have not been learned and that some degree of maladjustment may be present (Barocas, Reichman and Schwebel, 1983). For instance, alcoholics who deny they drink too much are not doing themselves any favours. Physical symptoms can arise and social relationships can begin to suffer. People who eat too much and then deny it by blaming their weight on metabolism are probably not doing much in the long run to improve their self-esteem. In short, some painful realities have to be faced before they can be overcome. Not facing up to them probably doesn't help others and in most cases probably doesn't help you.

 # Sublimation

Sublimation is the only defensive strategy used by the ego to divert instinctual impulses into something advantageous to society (Hjelle and Ziegler, 1981; Hergenhahn, 1993). Freud (1930) argued that sublimation "is an especially conspicuous feature of cultural development; it is what makes it possible for higher psychical activities, scientific, artistic or ideological, to play such an important part in civilized life" (cited in Hergenhahn, 1993: 35). An example here would be the young person whose hostility toward a parent finds a productive outlet in legal struggles for the disadvantaged (Barocas, Reichman and Schwebel, 1983).

Another way of understanding sublimation is to see it as an "adaptive" use of the displacement defence mechanism, which was discussed earlier. By using displacement, aggressive or sexual impulses may be diverted from one object to another that is less threatening. Anger diverted from a parent or authority figure onto a younger, smaller or more innocent target may help to reduce the anxiety in the angry person, but such diversion does little for the new targeted object. By contrast, anger transformed into something socially useful (e.g., a crusade against violence) can be said to be sublimated.

Sublimation is not a defence mechanism that is called into action to protect a temporarily weak ego responding to crisis (Barocas, Reichman and Schwebel, 1983). Rather, it involves a life-long defence against our broader realization that we cannot satisfy our urges and impulses in order to get what we want. Through sublimation, we give up primitive satisfaction in favour of an investment in society. We find culturally sanctioned channels to express our basic needs.

Obstacles

As mentioned above, sublimation is the most adaptive and advantageous of all defence mechanisms. If there is a downside to sublimation, perhaps it comes from the possibility that we could lose touch with the primitive, biological side of ourselves. We may lose sight of our instincts and urges, forgetting that we are physical, as well as social, beings. At worst, our zealous efforts to contribute culturally or socially could merely become a self-deception. What we are fighting or doing may be only a substitution for what we unconsciously want.

Instinctual impulses can be sublimated into artistic and creative pursuits.

DEFENCE MECHANISMS IN SUMMARY

In summary to this section, it should be repeated that psychological defence mechanisms help us to reduce anxiety by distorting our perceptions of reality. They protect the psyche from internal imbalances and external tensions.

> *The defences avoid reality (repression), exclude reality (denial), redefine reality (rationalization), or reverse reality (reaction formation). They place inner feelings on the outer world (projection), partition reality (isolation), or withdraw from reality (regression). (Frager and Fadiman, 1984: 29)*

Defence mechanisms not only help us to deal with unacceptable anxiety-provoking instinctual impulses, they also help us to master a variety of life conflicts. For instance, they can help us to contain ourselves emotionally when confronted with sudden life crises (e.g., a serious illness). They can help us to fashion changes in our self-image when required (e.g., after a demotion). Defences enable us to cope with unresolvable conflicts with significant others as well as to survive major conflicts of conscience stemming from our (mis)treatment of other people (Vaillant, 1977).

The danger of defensiveness arises when reality distortions become too great and too frequent. They diminish strength and rob energy from more creative and productive psychological functioning. As isolated responses to temporarily weakened egos, defence mechanisms have their usefulness. However, if they are unconsciously adopted as general strategies to deal with life, they are potentially unproductive and detrimental to personal well-being. They certainly can get in the way of effective interpersonal relations. See Table 3.1 for typical defences used in various kinds of anxiety-provoking situations.

Table 3.1   Defensive Response Patterns

Anxiety-Provoking Stimulus	Commonly Used Defences
Prohibited sexual urges or behaviour	Sublimation, repression, rationalization and projection
Feelings of inferiority	Fantasy, identification and regression
Guilt	Rationalization and projection
Failure	Intellectualization/isolation, projection and rationalization
Hostility	Sublimation, displacement, reaction formation, repression and fantasy
Disappointment	Intellectualization, fantasy and rationalization
Personal limitations	Denial, fantasy and regression

Source: Adapted from Coleman, James C. and Constance Hammen (1974). *Contemporary Psychology and Effective Behavior.* Glenview, IL: Scott Foresman and Company.

APPLICATION EXERCISE 3.2

Name the Defence Mechanism

Aim: This exercise will help you identify defensiveness in everyday behaviour. It should help you notice defensiveness in others and become more aware of it in yourself. This exercise can be done individually or in small groups. Allow time for discussion. Explanations should be offered for each selection.

   a. Repression
   b. Rationalization
   c. Projection
   d. Reaction formation
   e. Displacement
   f. Identification
   g. Regression
   h. Fantasy formation
   i. Intellectualization/Isolation
   j. Denial
   k. Sublimation

Instructions: Place the correct letter next to each example of defensiveness. Letters correspond to the defence mechanisms listed above.

_____ 1. Michael always teases his sisters after his parents discipline him.

_____ 2. Mary's parents both died when she was young. When I asked her what it was like growing up with no parents, she said she couldn't remember. Years of her life seem to be a blank.

_____ 3. When the police officer told Mr. Boudreau that his son was found in possession of cocaine, he responded, "There must be some mistake! My boy does not do cocaine, never has, and never will. You simply don't have the right person."

_____ 4. Why do you keep saying I'm mad at you when I'm not?

_____ 5. I can't believe how friendly Kristine behaves toward Katherine face to face. She told me long ago how much she hates Katherine.

_____ 6. Person A: I can't believe you cheated on the exam. How could you do such a thing?

Person B: Everybody else was doing it.

_____ 7. Did you hear about Gloria? Can you believe that someone who had so many sexual partners herself is now a nun doing personal counselling with sex addicts?

_____ 8. Ever since Bill broke up with Angela, he's been drinking and playing poker with the boys every night.

_____ 9. Jim recently went to listen to a lecture given by the Maharesi Mahesh Yogi. He has now decided to grow his hair long and wear sandals and East Indian clothing.

_____ 10. Jennifer is experiencing great difficulties with her academic studies. She is failing every subject but one. She tells me that she manages to cope by picturing graduation in her mind and the great job she anticipates getting once her degree is in hand.

_____ 11. Whenever John is upset about anything, he always goes and finds a psychology textbook that explains his thoughts and emotions. Quoting chapter and page, he tries to illustrate the universal psychodynamics behind his unpleasant experiences.

Answer Key: 1. e, 2. a, 3. j, 4. c, 5. d, 6. b, 7. k, 8. g, 9. f, 10. h, 11. i

APPLICATION EXERCISE

3.3

3.6

Dealing with Defensiveness

Aim: The purpose of this activity is to help you deal more effectively with defensiveness in yourself and others.

Instructions: Get into small groups. Next to each defence mechanism listed, provide an example to illustrate its workings. The example can be real or hypothetical. Choose what feels comfortable. For each example, brainstorm ways you could deal with the defensiveness. First, see yourself as the one being defensive in the example. Second, see yourself as the one witnessing the defensiveness in another. What could you do to help yourself? What could you do to help another person?

Defence Mechanism	Example/ Illustration	Effective Handling (Yourself and Others)
1. Repression		
2. Rationalization		
3. Projection		
4. Reaction formation		
5. Displacement		
6. Identification		
7. Regression		
8. Fantasy formation		
9. Intellectualization/Isolation		
10. Denial		
11. Sublimation		

THINKING STRAIGHT CAN HELP YOU RELATE

In the preceding discussion, we looked at the "psycho" side of psycho-logical defence mechanisms. We saw how unconscious mental processes function to protect the conscious ego from disquieting anxiety. In the rest of this chapter, we'll be looking at the "logical" side of psycho-logical defensiveness. As you'll soon discover, however, the logical side is not always so logical and the rational processes of thought used to protect and defend oneself or one's viewpoint can sometimes be irrational and lead to unjustifiable conclusions.

Much **miscommunication**, or communication that does not send an effective message, arises from the faulty use of logic. Sometimes our conclusions

Faced with the choice between changing one's mind and proving there is no need to do so, almost everyone gets busy on the proof.

John Kenneth Galbraith, Canadian-born Harvard economist

do not follow from preceding premises, while, at other times, our assumptions are unfounded or unjustifiable. Often, we fail to communicate effectively, solve problems or make good choices because the "facts" are in dispute.

Treatments of logical and rational thinking have traditionally been reserved for philosophy and critical reasoning courses. This is unfortunate, however, because thinking is part of life. It is an important element behind human action and social interaction. What we think, and how we think, frequently determine what we see, feel and do, and therefore, how well we get along with others. For our purposes here, I plan to have you look at a number of **logical fallacies**. These are irrational thought processes that interfere with productive interpersonal communications. By learning to clean up our "logical acts," we can increase clarity and understanding, as well as improve our chances to share differing viewpoints in constructive ways. By knowing the differences between good and bad reasoning, we can defend ourselves against illogical attacks and irrational attempts to manipulate our feelings, thoughts and actions. Good thinking has a personal and social payoff.

SELF-DIAGNOSTIC 3.2

How Reasonable Am I?

Developing good reasoning skills can improve interpersonal communications. Good sense often makes for good relations. On the other hand, the use of bad logic in everyday interactions can contribute to irreconcilable differences, hurt feelings, personal attacks, dishonest and diversionary maneuvers, as well as gross distortions of reality. In what follows, you will be presented with several examples of logical thinking that may or may not be rationally acceptable. Circle "A" next to examples that are acceptable and "U" next to those that are unacceptable. To find out if you can spot "sleazy logic" when you hear it, check your responses against the Answer Key that follows the examples.

A U 1. We shouldn't accept Professor Knowitall's argument that drinking coffee causes cancer. He's just a greedy and vain researcher trying to make a name for himself.

A U 2. Don't believe anything Mr. DeNile says. I know his relatives and they're all liars.

A U 3. If Wayne Gretzky, the greatest hockey player that ever lived, says that you must only play to win, then it must be so.

A U 4. You ought to be opposed to legalized gambling. Once you permit it, prostitution will necessarily follow. After that will come organized crime. In the end, legalized gambling will make our city streets less safe than before.

A U 5. Listen, I dislike cheating as much as you do. But when everybody else cheats, you have to cheat in order to survive.

Answer Key

All the examples above present different forms of unacceptable reasoning. They each contain an informal logical fallacy.

1. U *ad hominem* fallacy
2. U fallacy of guilt by association
3. U fallacy of appealing to authority
4. U slippery slope fallacy
5. U two-wrongs fallacy

Note: To learn more about each fallacy, read the following section in this chapter entitled Fallacies and Psycho-LOGICAL Defensiveness.

FALLACIES AND Psycho-LOGICAL DEFENSIVENESS

> A great many people think they are thinking when they are merely rearranging their prejudices.
>
> William James

People often feel threatened when their viewpoints are challenged. If there has been a lot of ego investment in a particular viewpoint or a deep involvement of personal feelings, improper forms of reasoning called logical fallacies may be used to perform the emotional rescue of the threatened self. Fallacies are irrational. They involve thinking processes that lead to **unsound conclusions** and unacceptable positions. Fallacies are designed to persuade us emotionally and psychologically, not rationally (Johnson and Blair, 1993). People who use them try to divert attention from the real issues and arguments under discussion to something more favourable to themselves. Fallacies can also be used as forms of **intimidation**. Defensive people, worried about being wrong, may respond aggressively toward others. Putting someone else on the defensive requires you to be less defensive about yourself. Essentially, fallacies work through **diversion** and **attack**. As instruments of persuasion and rhetoric, they are unfortunately sometimes very effective. However, as ways of thinking, they are always wrong. Let's now look at some common fallacies you'll need to avoid or guard against in efforts to be more reasonable in your dealings with people.

> We find comfort among those who agree with us, growth among those who don't.
>
> Frank Clarke

> Men stumble over the truth from time to time, but most pick themselves up and hurry off as if nothing happened.
>
> Winston Churchill

Ad Hominem *Fallacy*

When you disagree with someone, the proper response is to criticize your opponent's position. If instead of debating the issues involved, you attack your opponent personally, your actions are based on the **ad hominem fallacy**. For example, a wasteful person who resents the inconvenience brought about by recycling might refuse to support ideas and arguments presented by Pollution Probe on the grounds that all environmentalists are "60s' losers." Of course, the merits of an idea should not be judged by what generation the person advocating it comes from. Recycling is either good or bad in itself, regardless of its advocates' birthdates. To better understand how *ad hominem* reasoning works, see Figure 3.4.

Despite the ill logic it contains, *ad hominem* reasoning is very common in everyday discussion and debate. This type of thinking process can be

Figure 3.4

Ad Hominem Fallacy

Step I

Sender —transmits→ Message (e.g., argument) —to→ Receiver

Step II

Receiver —ignores→ Original Message ← Sender

• Receiver attacks sender   • Attack is not relevant
• Attack diverts attention   • It intimidates sender

Step III

Receiver —rejects→ Sender's Message (argument)

• Message or argument never addressed
• Message rejected but never criticized

Politicians may use fallacious reasoning in efforts to win arguments in the House of Commons.

emotionally satisfying, insofar as it belittles or puts down people with whom we disagree. We find it unsettling to be forced to concede that an individual we dislike has made a valid point. Also, if we are highly committed to the viewpoint that's being attacked by another, we may erroneously perceive such an attack as a personal attack. In reflex fashion, we may counterattack with an *ad hominem* verbal barrage against the perceived threat. When we do, we allow irrationality, hostility and aggression to interfere with productive communication. Our own defensiveness becomes an offensive act targeted at others. Look for *ad hominem* attacks whenever people's personalities, characters, ethnic/racial backgrounds, underlying motives, or special interests are criticized in response to messages perceived to be threatening. Also, don't allow yourself to be sidetracked when presenting your own viewpoints by defending yourself in response to others' *ad hominem* attacks on you. Stick to the issues.

Straw Man Fallacy

3.8

When communicating with others, we don't always like what we hear. In response, we may misrepresent what others have said in order to make their arguments clearly unacceptable. We may then proceed to argue against the unsatisfying version to reject the original, but unaddressed arguments. Our action is based on the **straw man fallacy**. The process of straw man reasoning is illustrated in Figure 3.5.

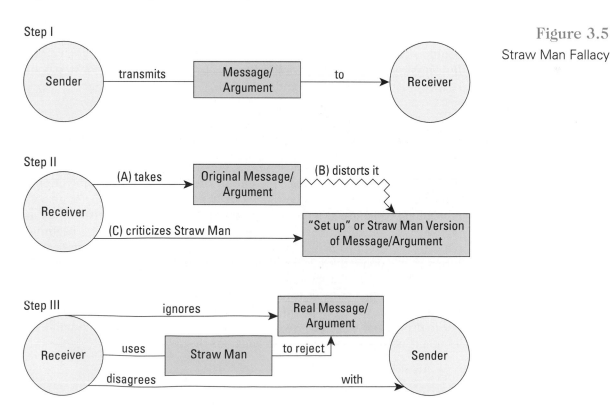

Figure 3.5

Straw Man Fallacy

A caution might be in order here. Occasionally recipients of messages honestly do not understand what was intended by the message conveyed. They may then respond to what was never said. This kind of honest mistake may reflect a problem of listening, decoding or comprehension. It is unlike the straw man fallacy, in which one person is deliberately misrepresenting the viewpoints of another. I guess we get into foggy territory when misrepresentations occur unconsciously in psychological efforts to reduce anxiety. Conscious or unconscious, however, straw man fallacies are irrational distortions of the truth.

Suppose that a new provincial premier has just been elected to office. She supports tax increases for middle-income earners. In response someone says, "This doesn't surprise me! She's always been against working people belonging to unions and this is just another measure designed to undermine their interests. If we allow unions to crumble, democracy in this country will be threatened!" Notice that in the critic's reply, democracy, unions and working people are brought to our attention, not the rationale behind the tax increases. Presumably it is easier to argue for democracy and union people than it is to argue against unwanted tax increases. By diverting attention to what we do like or want and criticizing from that vantage point what we don't want (i.e., increased taxes), the original position supporting tax increases is rejected, though never properly addressed.

Since you can probably appreciate how annoying it is when others criticize what you never said, be sure to ask questions for clarification before criticizing others' arguments or viewpoints. Your criticisms are only valuable if they relate to what was actually intended and said. Conversely, before allowing others to criticize *your* arguments and viewpoints, you could ask others to repeat in their own terms what they think you've said. If necessary, clarifications could be made. In the end, this extra step could reduce miscommunication and save time.

 ## Circular Reasoning/Begging the Question

Have you ever been in arguments that seem to go nowhere but around in circles? If you have, perhaps someone in the argument was using **circular reasoning**, also known as the **fallacy of begging the question**. In circular reasoning people use as a premise of their argument the conclusion they are trying to establish. In other words, people assume as true in the beginning what they intend to prove logically at the conclusion of their argument. When this is done, there is pre-judgment (prejudice) on the issue being debated. The "logical" argument doesn't take you anywhere except back to what was assumed to be true at the outset. For this reason, begging the question is circular, taking us around and around. What we assume is what we set out to prove, and what we prove is what we originally assumed. Circular reasoning is perhaps most evident in religious discussions.

I. M. Agnostic: How do you know God exists?

B. Lever: Because it says so in the Bible.

Premise M

Conclusion X

M is
acceptable
only if X has
already been
accepted

M is used
to support X

Figure 3.6
Circular Reasoning

I. M. Agnostic: How do you know the Bible is telling you the truth?

B. Lever: Because it's the inspired word of God.

In the example above, B. Lever uses the Bible to prove the existence of God. The authority of the Bible is based on the premise that God inspired it. Therefore, it's assumed that God actually does exist (the point under debate). But if B. Lever assumes to be true at the beginning what he is trying to prove at the end, nothing has been proven and we've just gone around in a circle. I don't mean to say that rational proofs cannot be given for God's existence, only that circular arguments don't work. Look at Figure 3.6 to better appreciate the process of circular reasoning.

Two-Wrongs Fallacy

Arguing based on the **two-wrongs fallacy** involves defending a particular wrongdoing by drawing attention to another instance of the same behaviour that apparently went unchallenged and was therefore accepted by implication. For instance, I remember that there were traditional initiation rituals for the University of Toronto "frosh" (first-year students) that required minor acts of vandalism (e.g., painting a certain statue in Queen's Park). Once confronted about the justifiability of such acts, a student (guess who?) responded by saying that the frosh had been doing it for years. Apparently for him, the previous year's vandalism served as a justification for his wrongdoing.

Highway speeders also provide us with an example of two-wrongs fallacious reasoning. When stopped for speeding, those charged often argue with the officer that they were just keeping up with traffic. In other words, they were

Figure 3.7
Two-Wrongs Fallacy

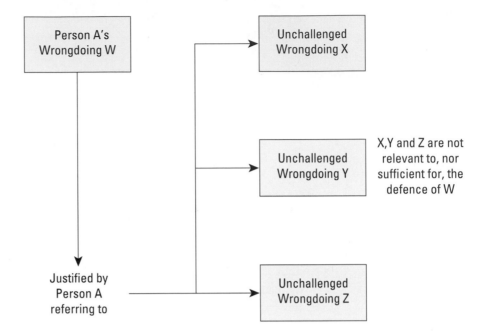

doing nothing other than breaking the law just like everybody else. As you may have already learned from experience, most police officers will not accept this line of reasoning. The two-wrongs fallacy is illustrated in Figure 3.7.

 ## *Slippery Slope Fallacy*

People who rely on the **slippery slope fallacy** display this form of ill logic when they object to something because they incorrectly assume that it will necessarily lead to other undesirable consequences. For example, you may object to smoking marijuana. You could reason that such behaviour will surely lead to harder drug usage, addiction and eventually to a life of crime. Since crime is unwanted, you conclude that smoking marijuana is therefore wrong.

Notice that in this hypothetical example the major objection is to crime, the presumed eventual result of smoking marijuana. However, the conclusion drawn here is not inevitable. After experimenting once, you may choose to avoid it in the future. Or you might decide to use it only occasionally in recreational ways. After smoking it, you could become a crusader against mood-altering drugs. The point is that smoking marijuana is a separate and distinct act from harder drug use, addiction and crime. Each must be considered independently and evaluated on its own terms. While it may be that many criminals and addicts begin their lives of crime by smoking marijuana, not everybody who smokes marijuana becomes a criminal addict. Many law-abiding, non-addicted people have experimented with marijuana. Therefore, there is no necessary **causal connection** between marijuana and criminality.

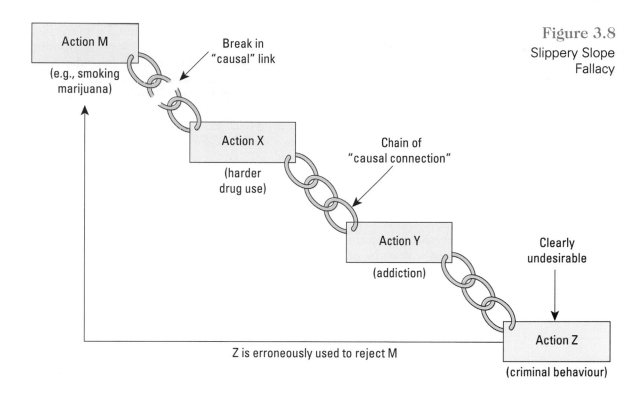

Figure 3.8
Slippery Slope
Fallacy

To say this means that there is no cause-and-effect relationship. One does not have to lead to the other. If you can find a break in the causal chain that presumably links two unrelated acts, you uncover the presence of a slippery slope. See Figure 3.8.

Fallacy of Appealing to Authority

When people get into arguments, they frequently rely on the **fallacy of appealing to authority** to justify their positions. Some appeals to authority are proper, while others are not. Proper appeals can be made to support factual claims within larger arguments. If in the previous example about marijuana, someone had wanted to condemn its use on medical grounds, scientific and empirical research data could have been presented to support claims about marijuana's adverse physical effects. As long as the data presented were based on the recognized contributions of medical researchers in the field and accepted after peer review and evaluation, such data could have been justifiably used to support factual claims imbedded in the broader argument. Of course, recognized researchers do not always agree amongst themselves; that's the reason scientific method cannot yield "absolute" proof. Even when citing

> Man is a credulous animal and tends to believe what he is told. Historically, philosophers...have taken great pains to point out that authority is at least as important a source of error as it is of knowledge.
>
> Joseph Brennan

scientific data, then, it is important to exercise some caution. To appreciate why, just ask what current scientific studies say about the effects of drinking coffee, for example. Some studies suggest caffeine is harmful, while others disagree. In such cases, it is prudent to go with the weight of the evidence. Ask, "What do most studies suggest?" or "Is there overwhelming evidence one way or another?" When the data are highly suggestive one way or another, at least references to them go beyond personal opinion to a recognized body of knowledge. Authoritative appeals can best be made in the hard sciences. Statements made in these disciplines can be verified in principle and hypotheses can be tested. There are clear public standards to test the validity of claims made.

When questions of value are at issue, it is much more difficult, and usually unjustifiable, to make authoritative appeals. Normative assumptions and principles (for example, people should always behave in their own self-interest) cannot be proven true or false by empirical observation or scientific experiment. Whether or not people actually behave in their own self-interest cannot tell us whether or not they should. Where matters of value are concerned, authoritative appeals cannot be made in rationally acceptable ways. This idea also applies where interpretation and personal preferences play a role or where the boundaries of subject matter are in dispute. Where experts have no empirical means or scientific procedures to settle disputes, authoritative appeals should be avoided. Such disputes must be settled by reason and argument. The next time you get into an argument, you should ask yourself what kind of claim is being made. Is the claim factual in nature? If so, where can you obtain legitimate support? If the claim is normative or value-related, how should you proceed to justify your position or criticize that of another?

One improper appeal to authority involves the notion of popularity or democracy. In this case, a conclusion is supported by an appeal to numbers. If a majority of people supports something, then that something is necessarily good, right or praiseworthy. Of course, numbers guarantee nothing. Historically speaking, majorities have been proven wrong. The fact that a majority of people in the southern United States once favoured slavery does not justify it. Reference to the will of the majority proves nothing. The moral status of slavery must be considered independently from its supporters. If 51 percent of the people in Lunenburg, Nova Scotia, are in favour of cheating Revenue Canada on their income taxes, this fact alone does not make it right. The next time you think about trying to convince your parents, friends or spouse that you should be allowed to do something "just because *everybody else* says it's OK," reflect on the fallacy of appealing to authority. Could you give other reasons to support what you want to do?

Appeals to traditional wisdom are also fallacious. In this case, actions are justified by saying, "This is the way it's always been done." Other actions are rejected by saying, "We've never done things this way before." However, actions that are justified by reference to past conventions (i.e., socially accepted ways of doing things) are not necessarily justified at all. For instance, suppose someone said, "We should never have allowed a woman, especially Kim Campbell, to become prime minister of Canada because we never had a woman occupy that office before." Obviously, a history of gender bias and discrimination cannot properly serve as a justification for continuing this practice. While tradition often gives us many valuable insights, it can also present its own moral problems. In itself, traditional wisdom is not unconditionally valid. Be careful, though, not to throw the "traditional baby" out with the "dirty bathwater." Tradition does have its legitimate place in the human family.

A final criticism of authoritative appeals is directed at the fact that authorities often disagree among themselves when matters of value are at issue. If authorities cannot reach a consensus, we cannot rely on authoritative judgments to settle disputes. Maybe you could look for an authority over authorities, but even this would be a problem. Your ultimate authority (e.g., God) may not be accepted by others (e.g., atheists). In a tolerant, democratic, multicultural society, it is usually improper to use your chosen authority figure as a reference point for judgment when dealing with others. Commitments to your own beliefs should not violate the rights of others. The rules and regulations of your religious, political or military authorities, for example, may contain little rational moral force when applied to those who have different commitments. To put the danger of authoritative appeals into perspective, suppose someone's supreme authority were Luc Jouret, leader of the Solar Temple cult in Quebec. You will recall that his cult took part in a mass murder-suicide in 1994, with incidents in both Canada and Switzerland. Nobody knows all the details of what happened, but let's speculate for an instant that Jouret ordered his followers to kill themselves. Would this action, in itself, justify their actions? Rational thinking requires that we say no. In fact, many philosophers have often argued that suicide is inherently irrational and therefore unjustified. Trying to justify murder-suicide by reference to Jouret's authority would involve the use of fallacious reasoning. Refer to Figure 3.9 for a visual depiction of the fallacy of appealing to authority.

Figure 3.9
Fallacy of Appealing
to Authority

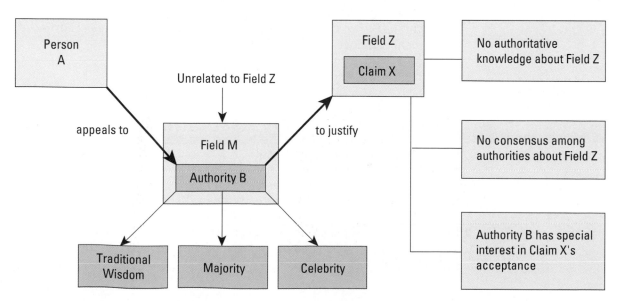

Red Herring Fallacy

The **red herring fallacy** is another favourite form of ill logic used by rationally dishonest or unconsciously irrational individuals. The name of this fallacy comes from the sport of fox hunting. In this sport, hunters on horseback follow a pack of hounds tracking a fox's scent. In order to save the fox in the end, dried and salted red herring is drawn across the fox's tracks ahead of the pack. The herring is then pulled in a direction away from that which the fox took. The dogs are diverted by the stronger and fresher scent of the herring. The fox is left alone.

In the red herring fallacy a controversial claim or position is defended by taking the offensive. This defence involves setting up a new issue that has only a weak or tenuous connection with the original one. Since this original position is weak, the defender proceeds to argue for the new issue or position that is more supportable. In other words, attention is deflected from the original position to a new one, which is probably less open to question and debate. Below is an example of red herring reasoning. Notice what the patriotic bartender does when he perceives his country is under attack. He diverts attention from the Canadian's allegations of crime, violence, discrimination and influence peddling to space technology, universities and military might. The latter can more easily support his claim that "America is the greatest." The Canadian's critical comments make such a claim highly questionable.

Detroit Bartender: The United States is the best country in the world.

Canadian Tourist: You must be kidding. The U.S. is falling apart at the seams. Murders are committed by the thousands every year. Women and minorities are discriminated against and lobby groups have too much power in Washington. On top of this, fear of being victimized by criminals in the streets frightens people from walking outdoors in the evening. Face it, your nation is in decline.

Detroit Bartender: What are you talking about? We have the most military might in the world. We have the best universities and the most advanced space technology. America is the greatest.

The red herring fallacy is illustrated in Figure 3.10.

Fallacy of Guilt by Association

This form of ill logic is generally used in adversarial situations in an attempt to discredit an opponent or that opponent's arguments, claims and positions; it draws attention to an alleged association that the opponent has with some group or individual that has already been discredited. The attempt to discredit is not direct as in typical *ad hominem* arguments, but indirect. The guilt of the discredited individual or group is transferred to the opponent.

Let us suppose that someone refused to vote "socialist" in the next elec-

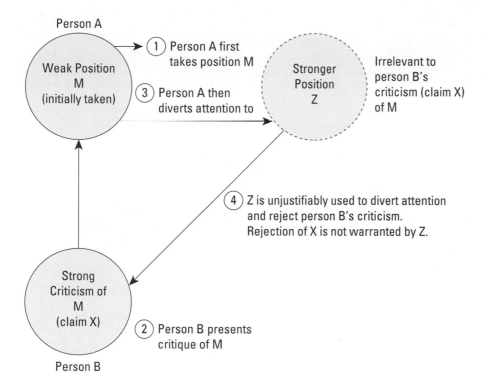

Figure 3.10

Red Herring Fallacy

tion. His reason is that the "socialists almost sent England and France into bankruptcy." The unspoken claim is that if elected here, they will bankrupt this country too. Apparently, for this voter, socialist mismanagement across the ocean is enough to convict socialists here of incompetence. They are found guilty prior to doing anything wrong. It is possible, in principle, that a socialist government could mismanage our country—some argue that liberals and conservatives have been doing so for years! But in any case, actions and policies of foreign socialist governments alone cannot serve as an adequate basis of judgment on domestic socialism. Our socialism may be different in significant ways. Our socialists may have learned from the mistakes of their European counterparts. Perhaps contemporary North American socialism has evolved into something more akin to capitalism? There could be almost no political communication between the two socialist groups named. Who knows? Simply put, you can't pin incompetence on Canadian socialists because of what foreign socialists have done. To do so is to argue based on the **fallacy of guilt by association**. Nonetheless, by using this diversion tactic, fear can be created in the minds of unreflective voters and it may work as a means of persuasion. Creating fear is not very rational, but against people lacking the skills of logical self-defence, it often works. The fallacy of guilt by association is illustrated in Figure 3.11. See also Table 3.2 for some helpful hints on what to do (and avoid) during an argument.

Figure 3.11
Fallacy of Guilt by Association

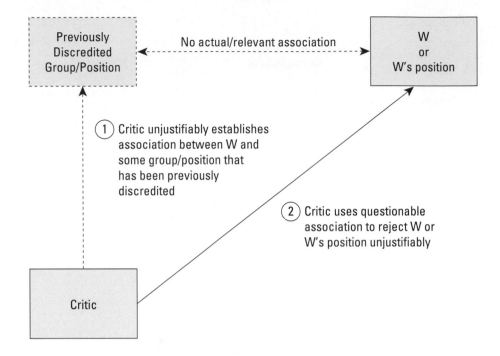

Table 3.2   Some Dos and Don'ts for Argument's Sake

Don't	Do
Attack or intimidate	Remain rational and emotionally detached
Divert attention from the real issues	Stay objective
Base arguments on emotional or psychological appeals	Listen to opposing viewpoints with openness
Build false or questionable claims into your argument	Analyse conflicting positions fairly and impartially
Take disagreements personally	Examine the logical thinking behind particular conclusions
Appeal to authorities unjustifiably	Look for fallacious reasoning
Attribute to others what they didn't say	Stick to the issues
Make illegitimate associations	Base your positions on sound arguments
Contradict yourself	
Change the subject when challenged	
Be inconsistent	
Use faulty causal reasoning	
Justify one wrongdoing with another	
Be diverted or intimidated by fallacious reasoning	

3.9

Identify the Fallacy

This exercise will give you an opportunity to apply your knowledge and understanding of fallacious reasoning. Being able to identify fallacious reasoning will protect you against illogical attacks and irrational attempts to manipulate your thinking. Recognizing fallacies will also help you to minimize them in your own communication.

Instructions: Below are examples of fallacious reasoning. Identify which fallacies are present by placing the appropriate letter next to the example. This exercise can be done individually or in groups. For classroom discussion purposes, be prepared to provide explanations for each identification.

a. *ad hominem* fallacy
b. straw man fallacy
c. circular reasoning
d. fallacy of two wrongs

e. slippery slope fallacy
f. fallacy of appealing to authority
g. red herring fallacy
h. fallacy of guilt by association

_____ 1. You shouldn't accept the premier's arguments in favour of Sunday shopping. After all, he's a godless communist.

_____ 2. I can't believe you're in favour of having premarital sex. It's obviously wrong. The Pope says so.

_____ 3. Two students were having a disagreement about cars. Curtis said, "I can prove to you that a Nissan 240 is faster than a Toyota Camry. John owns a Nissan and he told me that he has beaten every Camry he has ever raced on the highway." Michael asked, "How do you know John is telling the truth?" Curtis replied, "Someone who drives the fastest car wouldn't have to lie."

_____ 4. We can't allow marijuana to be legalized. If we did, sooner or later everyone would become addicted to harder drugs and after that the crime rate would surely rise.

_____ 5. It's perfectly all right to go through stop signs on quiet streets; everybody else in town does it.

_____ 6. The consultant recommended that the company switch to voice mail as a way of receiving and sending internal messages. He claims that this change will make our operation more efficient. I can't believe this guy. He thinks every problem in the world has an electronic solution. Computers and telephones can't improve the economy or morale at work. I think we should reject his recommendation.

_____ 7. You don't seriously believe what André Cousineau says about promoting national unity. Remember, he's from Quebec and related to the leader of the Parti Quebecois. That party wants Quebec to separate from the rest of Canada. We should reject anything he suggests.

_____ 8. What do you mean I'm not making sense? Did you hear your own nonsense yesterday when you said that you had an encounter with an alien? I think your credibility needs to be reexamined.

Answer Key: 1. a, 2. f, 3. c, 4. e, 5. d, 6. b, 7. h, 8. g

STUDY GUIDE

Key Terms

noise (70)
psycho-logical defen-
siveness (70)
unconscious influ-
ences (70)
irrational thought
processes (70)
defensiveness (72)
anxiety (72)
diversionary and in-
timidation tactics
(72)
distortions of reality
(72)
Sigmund Freud (73)
psychoanalysis (73)
conscious (73)
preconscious (73)
unconscious (73)
coping mechanism
(73)
psychological defence
mechanisms (76)
ego (76)

repression (76)
rationalization (77)
projection (79)
reaction formation
(81)
displacement (82)
id (82)
psychic energy (82)
cathexis (82)
anticathexis (84)
superego (84)
identification (85)
regression (88)
fantasy formation (89)
intellectualization/iso-
lation (90)
denial (91)
sublimation (92)
miscommunication
(96)
logical fallacies (97)
unsound conclusions
(99)
intimidation (99)

diversion (99)
attack (99)
ad hominem fallacy
(99)
straw man fallacy
(101)
circular
reasoning/beg-
ging the question
(102)
two-wrongs fallacy
(103)
slippery slope fallacy
(104)
causal connection
(104)
fallacy of appealing to
authority (105)
red herring fallacy
(108)
fallacy of guilt by as-
sociation (109)

Fill-in-the-Blank Questions

Instructions: Fill in each blank with the appropriate response from the list below.

repression	projection
fantasy formation	two-wrongs
circular reasoning	regression
reaction formation	rationalization
straw man	denial
identification	*ad hominem*
red herring	displacement
intellectualization/isolation	

1. People who behave in ways exactly opposite to their true feelings display _____.

2. Keeping disturbing or anxiety-provoking thoughts buried in the unconscious is called _____.

3. Reverting to immature patterns of behaviour in response to problems and difficulties is called _____.

4. Diverting strong negative emotions from a threatening target to a less threatening substitute is called _____.

5. Attributing your own thoughts, feelings and motives to another is labelled _____.

6. Imagining a pleasurable future as a way of escaping harsh current realities indicates _____.

7. Refusing to accept the facts as they present themselves is evidence of _____.

8. The act of objectifying emotions and dealing with them in detached, theoretical ways is called _____.

9. Individuals who enhance their self-esteem by forming real or imaginary alliances with groups and organizations exhibit _____.

10. The act of creating false but plausible excuses in order to justify unacceptable behaviour is called _____.

11. To assume as true at the beginning of an argument what you are setting out to conclude is to argue based on the fallacy of _____.

12. Taking someone's argument, changing it into something less acceptable, and then criticizing this less acceptable version as a way of rejecting the original is relying on the _____ fallacy.

13. Attacking an individual personally, rather than responding to that person's argument, is evidence of the _____ fallacy.

14. Trying to justify your wrong actions by referring to similar unpunished wrong acts performed by others is to fall prey to the _____ fallacy.

15. If you change the subject to something more defensible when someone criticizes your original viewpoint, then you are using the _____ fallacy.

True/False Questions

Instructions: Circle the appropriate letter next to each statement.

T F   1. Anxiety is caused by defence mechanisms.

T F   2. Sigmund Freud discovered the unconscious.

T F   3. Psychological defence mechanisms are used unconsciously.

T F   4. Repression enables us to bury anxiety-provoking conflicts and memories in the unconscious.

T F   5. Isolation is another term for rationalization.

T F   6. Hero worship is an example of identification.

T F   7. Breaking down in tears in response to news of a death in the family is an example of reaction formation.

T F   8. Displacement occurs when individuals forget why they are anxious.

T F   9. Fallacious reasoning is sometimes designed to intimidate.

T F 10. Winning arguments by making emotional appeals should be encouraged in rational debate.

T F 11. Attacking the person whose argument you find threatening is an example of using the slippery slope fallacy.

T F 12. Some arguments are better, or more rational, than others.

T F 13. To say that watching violence on TV necessarily leads to insensitivity, increased aggression and eventually to murder in the streets is to rely on the slippery slope fallacy.

T F 14. In the straw man fallacy, the sender of a message/argument tries to change it in response to criticism without others noticing.

T F 15. Appeals to authority in rational argument are permitted when matters of value and ethical principle are in dispute.

Focus Questions

1. What is defensiveness? What kinds are there?

2. What is the purpose of defensiveness?

3. Is human consciousness completely transparent to itself? What implications does this have in understanding defensiveness?

4. What are some PSYCHO-logical defence mechanisms? Which one(s) do you see most in your daily interactions with other people?

5. What is fallacious reasoning? What is its impact on interpersonal communication?

6. What are some examples of fallacious reasoning? Can you give any personal illustrations not found in the text?

Summary

1. What is defensiveness?
   - psyche's unconscious effort to protect the self from disturbing anxiety either through diversionary and intimidation tactics or by distortions of reality
   - a coping mechanism used by the ego

2. Why is defensiveness undesirable?
   - it creates "noise" in the communication process
   - it adds to "nonsense" in our dealings with people
   - it's irritating and offensive to others
   - it blocks awareness of what really troubles us
   - it leaves us blind and insensitive to others' needs

3. How many levels of consciousness are there? At what level does defensiveness occur?
   - Sigmund Freud has identified three levels: conscious, preconscious and unconscious
   - defensiveness occurs at the unconscious level.

4. What defence mechanisms were covered in this chapter?
   - repression
   - rationalization
   - projection
   - reaction formation
   - displacement
   - sublimation
   - identification
   - regression
   - fantasy formation
   - intellectualization/isolation
   - denial

5. How does each of the defence mechanisms function? What obstacles does each present to personal growth and interpersonal communication?

Repression
Function: to keep anxiety-provoking thoughts buried in the unconscious
Obstacles:
   - unconscious repressions prevent psychological conflict resolution
   - the ego's resources are diverted from more self-enhancing and creative behaviours
   - relationships suffer due to rigidity, lack of spontaneity and inability to deal with challenges
   - phobias, hysterical reactions and psychosomatic illnesses

Rationalization
Function: to cope with anxiety by offering plausible but false explanations and justifications for unacceptable behaviours

Obstacles:
- impaired judgment
- reduction in objectivity
- potential ethical problems (excuses for wrongdoing)
- may contribute to immaturity (flight from responsibility)

Projection
Function: to attribute to others negative feelings, thoughts and intentions that actually originate in oneself
Obstacles:
- unwarranted suspicions of others may develop
- trust will diminish
- social prejudice and scapegoating
- ethnic and racial stereotyping
- inability to judge other people's motives
- career adjustment suffers

Reaction Formation
Function: to reduce anxiety by behaving in a way that is opposite to how one really feels
Obstacles:
- rigidity and an "all or nothing" attitude develops
- little compromise with others offering different viewpoints
- lose touch with true feelings

Displacement
Function: to divert emotional energy (e.g., anger) from an original threatening object to a less threatening substitute object
Obstacles:
- innocent people are victimized, attacked, criticized, abused and hurt
- hypersensitivity to minor annoyances

Identification
Function: to increase feelings of self-worth and decrease anxiety by taking on the characteristics of someone or some group that is admired or considered successful
Obstacles:
- problems of personal identity
- unnaturalness, pretenses
- separation from unidentified others
- stereotypical behaviour

Regression
Function: to reduce anxiety by reverting to immature patterns of behaviour
Obstacles:
- interference with communication (e.g., babbling like a baby is incomprehensible to others)
- raging and tantruming are not productive
- narcissism

- interference with intimacy
- avoidance by others

Fantasy Formation

Function: to alleviate anxiety caused by frustrated desires through imaginary achievements and satisfactions

Obstacles:

- it is unproductive because people and problems are not faced directly
- it encourages unreality; current failures and shortcomings are overlooked
- living in the fantasy of the future or the past may prevent productive living in the present

Intellectualization/Isolation

Function: to diffuse anxiety (unpleasant emotions) by engaging in detached analyses of threatening problems

Obstacles:

- lose touch with real feelings
- intimacy suffers, personal contact becomes difficult

Denial

Function: to protect the self from anxiety by refusing to perceive unpleasant reality

Obstacles:

- lack of mature response to problem solving
- contributes to poor adjustment (e.g., an alcoholic denying alcoholism)
- physical symptoms (e.g., obesity from denial that one eats too much)

Sublimation

Function: to divert instinctual impulses into something socially acceptable or advantageous to society

Obstacles:

- lose touch with the primitive, biological side of personality
- self-deception (diversion from what we really want)

Related Readings

Adler, Ronald and Neil Towne (1996). *Looking out, Looking In*, 8th edition. Fort Worth, TX: Holt, Rinehart and Winston.

Falikowski, Anthony (1998). *Moral Philosophy for Modern Life*. Scarborough: Prentice Hall Allyn and Bacon Canada.

Freud, Anna (1971) [1936]. *The Writings of Anna Freud*, Volume II. "The Ego and the Mechanisms of Defense," revised edition. New York: International Universities Press, Inc.

Hergenhahn, B.R. (1993). *An Introduction to Theories of Personality*, 4th edition. Upper Saddle River, NJ: Prentice Hall.

Johnson, R.H. and J.A. Blair (1993). *Logical Self-Defense*, 3rd edition. Toronto: McGraw-Hill Ryerson Ltd.

Weblinks

1. Defeating defensiveness
www.mbsnet.com/padefense.htm

   Learn how to "work around" staff members with a defensiveness and attitude problem.

2. Defensiveness at work
www.srg.co.uk/defensive.html

   Do you ever…repackage your blunders so you won't look so bad…Blame circumstances, luck, the weather or others when things don't go your way? If so, then check out this web site.

3. Tactile defensiveness
www.schdist42.bc.ca/projectinfo/access95/tactiledefensive.html

   Visit this site for more information on tactile defensiveness and the visually impaired.

4. American Psychoanalytic Association
apsa.org/links.htm

   To learn more about psychological defensiveness and its theoretical underpinnings, visit the site of the American Psychoanalytic Association. It provides links to other web sites on psychoanalysis, the theoretical basis for explanations of defensiveness.

5. The Center for Critical Thinking
www.sonoma.edu/cthink/

   This centre offers a collection of articles focused on the background and theory of critical thinking. It can help you to avoid irrationality and fallacious reasoning. The centre offers an archive of the critical thinking e-mail discussion group, and information on critical seminars and in-service training.

They are playing a game.
They are playing at not playing a
game. If I show them I see they are
playing a game, I shall break the
rules and they will punish me. I
must play the game of not seeing
that I play the game.

—R.D. Laing

GAMES PEOPLE PLAY: BETTER RELATIONSHIPS THROUGH TRANSACTIONAL ANALYSIS

CHAPTER OVERVIEW

LEARNING OUTCOMES

After successfully completing this chapter, you will be able to

4.1 Provide a definition of, and an historical background for, transactional analysis

4.2 Identify your dominant ego state as revealed by your personal egogram

4.3 Outline the basic features of the child, adult and parent ego states

4.4 Associate typical behaviours with each ego state

4.5 Analyse and describe types of communication transactions

4.6 Explain the nature and types of strokes, as well as their importance to healthy psychological development

4.7 Describe four basic life positions by which people orient to others in the world

4.8 Give examples of psychological games and explain why they are counterproductive

4.9 Discuss the roles played in psychological games

4.10 Break up psychological game playing

4.11 Write more effective memoranda that are ego-state sensitive

4.12 Identify ego-state reactions in others

TRANSACTIONAL ANALYSIS

In the preceding two chapters you learned much about defensiveness and how it can disrupt interpersonal communications. You were introduced to some of the irrational and unconscious ways people try to "twist" reality in order to protect themselves when they feel threatened by other people. Further insights into the communication process will now be gained by turning to the theory of **transactional analysis**. T.A., as it's known, can help us to identify many of the games and conflictual transactions that interfere with healthy relationships and effective social communication. This identification can in turn help us to respond to games and conflicts in useful and productive ways.

Transactional analysis is a "broad theory of personality and interpersonal relations that emphasizes patterns of communication" (Weiten, Lloyd and Lashley, 1991: 265). Originally conceived by Canadian-born and educated psychiatrist Eric Berne (1910–1970) during the 1950s, it underwent numerous changes and refinements over the years. While initially developed for research purposes and therapeutic applications, T.A. gained widespread acceptance in the general population. Well-known books based on transactional analysis include *Games People Play* (Berne, 1964), *I'm OK—You're OK* (Harris, 1967) and *Born to Win* (James and Jongeward, 1971). In recent

SHOWCASE PROFILE

Eric Berne

Eric Berne (born Eric Lennard Bernstein) was born on May 10, 1910, at his family home in Montreal, Quebec. The descendant of Polish immigrants, he earned his bachelor's degree, his medical degree and his Master of Surgery degree by the age of 25 from McGill University. In 1936, Berne started a psychiatric residency at the Psychiatric Clinic of Yale University School of Medicine. In 1941, he accepted the position of Clinical Assistant in Psychiatry at Mt. Zion Hospital in New York City. Also in that year, he began his training in psychoanalysis under the famous Erik Erikson at the New York Psychoanalytic Institute. From 1943 to 1946, Berne served in the U.S. Army Medical Corps, where there was a great need for psychiatrists during World War II. After serving with the army, Berne moved to California where the early de- velopments of transactional analysis began. In 1964, Berne established the International Transactional Analysis Association, a body that still exists today with chapters in Canada and throughout the world. Years after the introduction of transactional analysis, many practitioners from the fields of psychiatry, business, education and social work continue to apply its principles in their personal and professional lives.

years, transactional analysis has lost some of its popularity. Nevertheless, it is still used by many human service practitioners who continue to see its practical value. Let's now discover how transactional analysis can help us to master human relations.

Ego States

Have you ever resented being talked down to? When frustrated or upset, have you ever responded childishly by pouting or throwing an adult version of a temper tantrum? Perhaps you like to use the word "should" a lot, using the pointed index finger for authoritarian emphasis. Maybe your general pattern of communication is to speak matter-of-factly about whatever is being discussed. The important point to note here is that what we say and how we respond to what others say originate in what Eric Berne (1961) refers to as **ego states**. By learning more about ego states, we can better understand where communication messages are coming from, psychologically speaking. We can modify our own message delivery, if necessary, and make intelligent decisions about how to respond to others. Recognizing that social communication does not occur in a psychological vacuum will also help us very shortly to better understand the nature of crossed and ulterior communications as well as the unfortunate games people play when interacting with one another. Before learning more about ego states, you are now invited to do Self-Diagnostic 4.1.

SELF-DIAGNOSTIC 4.1

4.2

What's My Dominant Ego State?

This instrument will increase your self-awareness and self-understanding. Results suggest which ego state is likely dominant in your life at this time. Scores will help you to identify areas for self-improvement. They will also help you to establish behavioural strategies for enhancing interpersonal relations. Your dominant ego state will be the one from which much of your communication originates and the one from which you often respond to others when interacting socially. The notion of ego state can be understood as the operating psychological structure that organizes your perceptions, processes information and reacts to the world. In truth, we function in a variety of ego states; however, we sometimes tend to rely on one more than the others. This reliance has important social consequences, as you will soon see.

Instructions: Described below are five situations with different possible reactions to each. Next to each reaction, indicate how likely it would be for you to respond in that fashion or in one similar to it. When finished, complete the scoring.

1 = I would not react in this way or in any similar way

2 = I might react in this way or in a similar way

3 = I would be likely to react in this way or in a similar way

4 = I would almost surely react in this way or in a similar fashion

1. Your Human Relations instructor doesn't show up for the appointment you scheduled to discuss your term paper. What would you say to yourself?

_____ a. It's O.K. that she forgot about the meeting. The instructor has been under a lot of stress lately and probably needed a break.

_____ b. Not showing up is totally irresponsible! Lazy teachers these days can't even keep simple appointments.

_____ c. I wonder if the instructor misplaced her appointment book? Perhaps car trouble caused the missed appointment? I'll check it out.

_____ d. Great, the instructor didn't show up. Now I've got an extra hour to do whatever I want.

_____ e. OK, fine! See if I show up for our next scheduled appointment!

2. Your brand new computer breaks down. What do you think?

_____ a. I hate garbage clones. Wait until I give that salesperson who sold it to me a blast.

_____ b. Wow! Can you believe it? My computer is already *kaput*. It always amazes me how these things work anyway.

_____ c. I guess I'll call the service department this afternoon for repairs.

_____ d. I think the manufacturer of these clones should be notified that they don't work as advertised. They probably use cheap components to maximize profits. It's wrong to sacrifice quality for profit.

_____ e. Well, I guess technology isn't perfect. Mistakes are sometimes made. I'll see if I can help the computer store identify the problems.

3. Rumour has it that the grade results on the first term test are very low. What would you do?

_____ a. Attend the next class to find out what happened.

_____ b. Plan to justify your belief that the test was unfair.

_____ c. Go to class because you're curious how others will react once the tests are handed back.

_____ d. Tell the instructor how to construct better tests in the future.

_____ e. Go to class in order to raise hell about the results.

4. You are not accepted into the college program of study for which you applied. How would you respond?

_____ a. I would either get very angry and upset or perhaps I would get depressed and cry.

_____ b. I would ask the admissions committee the rationale behind my non-acceptance and then take steps to increase my chances next time.

_____ c. I would forget about the refusal very quickly and get excited about other possibilities.

_____ d. I would criticize the selection process.

_____ e. I would console other friends and acquaintances who were not accepted either.

5. You and a few others have just been laid off from your part-time jobs. What would you probably say to yourself?

_____ a. This job stinks, anyway!

_____ b. I guess I have some new financial problems to deal with.

_____ c. Money and work—easy come, easy go! Isn't life so unpredictable? Time for a pastry!

_____ d. They should at least have given us some warning.

_____ e. Maybe I should have the others who've been laid off over to my place for a farewell party. This might make everyone feel better.

Scoring: Each situation above has five possible reactions (a to e). Next to each possible reaction you placed a number indicating the chances you would respond in that way or in a similar fashion. Record your values below.

Add the columns to obtain your ego state scores. After referring to the model egogram on the next page, plot your scores on My Personal Egogram (Figure 4.1) to create a similar bar graph.

1.	a. _____	b. _____	c. _____	d. _____	e. _____
2.	e. _____	d. _____	c. _____	b. _____	a. _____
3.	d. _____	b. _____	a. _____	c. _____	e. _____
4.	e. _____	d. _____	b. _____	c. _____	a. _____
5.	e. _____	d. _____	b. _____	c. _____	a. _____
Total	_____	_____	_____	_____	_____
	Nurturing Parent (NP)	Critical Parent (CP)	Adult Ego State (A)	Natural Child (NC)	Adapted Child (AC)

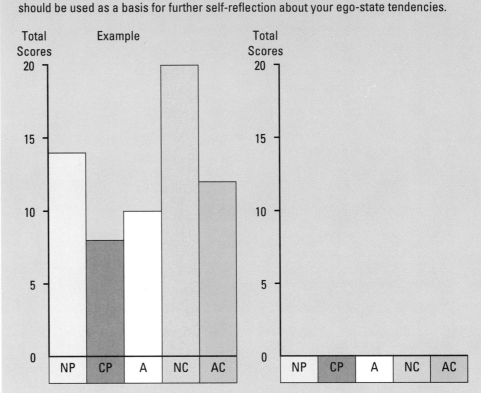

Plot your score below to create a bar graph of your personal egogram. Your results should be used as a basis for further self-reflection about your ego-state tendencies.

Figure 4.1

My Personal Egogram

Complete Personality

Parent Ego State

Adult Ego State

Child Ego State

According to transactional analysis, the personality of a fully grown person is something like a psychological trinity. It comprises three unique aspects, or ego states as Berne (1964) calls them. They include the Child ego state, the Adult ego state and the Parent ego state. As you will learn shortly, the Child and Parent both have sub-states that are reflected in your personal egogram. With respect to the basic three ego states, each one develops in a consistent, predictable sequence (Gilliland, James and Bowman, 1989). Ego states function like three distinct beings within each one of us (Levin, 1988). For example, the Parent within us judges, the Adult figures out solutions, while the Child expresses feelings and needs. Let's now look at each of the three ego states in a bit more detail. It is important to understand their nature before we go on to examine their influence on interpersonal communication. See Figure 4.2.

Figure 4.2

The Three Ego States Forming Personality

The Child Ego State

The **Child ego state** is the first structural element formed within our personalities. This state has its own inner sequence of development. At first, we see its rudimentary beginnings in observable behaviours such as crying, sucking and gurgling. These behaviours reflect the earliest substructure of the fully formed Child. It is called the Early or Somatic Child (see C_1 in Figure 4.3).

Whenever you find people behaving like crybabies, they are likely behaving that way as a function of their Early Child ego state (Gilliland, James and Bowman, 1989). In time, infants begin to explore themselves and their environments. They start to form that aspect of the Child ego state labelled the Early Adult or "Little Professor" (A_1 in Figure 4.3). The Little Professor processes information on a preverbal level and makes decisions based on it. Young children display an intelligence of action that they cannot express in words. It's fascinating to watch children solve problems with their hands. The Little Professor possesses both creative and intuitive potential. However, it is possible that this Little Professor may sometimes record faulty information and choose to act on incorrect data.

The third substructure of the Child ego state is the Early Parent (P_1 in Figure 4.3). This aspect of the Child is formed by children's early perceptions of parental behaviours and feelings before the development of language. The Early Parent contains nurturing or negative messages that the child interprets and internalizes (Goulding and Goulding, 1979).

In the formation of the Child ego state, we find a permanent record of events during early development. It's as if the Child ego state has **taped events** of what the child's parents or caretakers said and did. Using scientific evidence obtained from Wilder Penfield's neurological studies on epilepsy at McGill University in Montreal, transactional analysts claim that early childhood memories are stored in their natural forms as ego states (see the Showcase Profile on Wilder Penfield). When grown individuals are put into situations similar to those encountered in childhood, taped events of feelings are recorded in the brain and replayed in the present. Someone's current dislike of being told what to do, for example, may reflect earlier negative feelings toward parental authority. In the Child ego state we find the "recordings of the child's early experiences, responses, and the 'positions' taken about self and others" (James and Jongeward, 1971: 18).

How your Child ego state functions in interaction with others and the world can be better explained by making a functional distinction between the Free Child (FC) or Natural Child (NC) and the Adapted Child (AC). See Figure 4.4. Also refer back to your personal egogram.

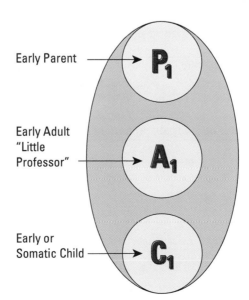

Early Parent → P_1

Early Adult "Little Professor" → A_1

Early or Somatic Child → C_1

Figure 4.3

Substructures of the Child Ego State

Figure 4.4

Functional Distinctions in
the Child Ego State

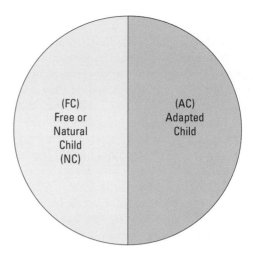

| (FC) Free or Natural Child (NC) | (AC) Adapted Child |

SHOWCASE PROFILE

Wilder Graves Penfield

Wilder Graves Penfield (1891–1976) was the American-Canadian neurosurgeon who devised a surgical method of treating epilepsy. Born in Spokane, Wash., on Jan. 26, 1891, he graduated from Princeton University in 1913. As a Rhodes Scholar at Oxford, he was greatly influenced by Sir William Osler and was introduced to the study of the brain by Sir Charles Sherrington, who pioneered in neurological studies of decerebrate animals. He received his medical degree from Johns Hopkins in 1918 and spent a year's internship under Harvey Cushing at Peter Bent Brigham Hospital in Boston before returning to Oxford to study neurophysiology.

For seven years Penfield practised neurosurgery in New York City before being named in 1928 as professor of neurology and neurosurgery at McGill University, where he taught until 1954. In 1934 he established, with the aid of the Rockefeller Foundation, the Montreal Neurological Institute, which stressed a multidisciplinary approach to the nervous system. He served as its director until 1960. Penfield died on April 5, 1976, in Montreal.

Penfield was one of the first neurosurgeons to apply neurophysiological techniques to the study of the human brain. Through his innovative work on the development of surgical techniques for the removal of scar tissue from the brains of epileptics, he employed electrical stimulation of the exposed cerebral cortex of patients undergoing surgery. He used this procedure both to minimize surgical damage and to map out the anatomy of the brain and locate such functional areas as the motor, sensory, and speech centres.

His career-long interest in identifying the neural substrates of consciousness led him to propose a "centrenecephalic" system to explain consciousness. This system stressed the role of the upper brain stem as opposed to the cortical areas, in the integration of higher functions, although the system was controversial at the time of its proposal, current opinion generally supports this explanation.

Like the children in the picture above, the natural child in all of us enjoys fun and excitement.

When we function with our **Free** or **Natural Child** in control, we tend to display curiosity, or a need for intimacy, fun, joyfulness, fantasy and impulsivity (Lussier, 1990). A liability of staying in our Free Child too much or for too long is that others may begin to perceive us as irresponsible or out of control. In contrast to the Free Child, the **Adapted Child** may be whiny, defiant or placating. The Adapted Child may appear pouty, sad or display an innocence marked by a closed, tight posture. Thus, when we behave in our Adapted Child state we are either compliant or rebellious. We may look ashamed or exhibit a demanding attitude. If you have ever seen anyone who appears guilty, depressed and robot-like, or if you witness someone having a tantrum, you are observing the Adapted Child at work.

Adult Ego State

The operation of our **Adult ego state** makes us behave in rational and thoughtful ways. We gather and store information. We engage in factual inquiry and we do so in an objective, emotionally detached fashion. The Adult in us reasons things out and evaluates probabilities (Lussier, 1990). The Adult also acts as referee between the demands of the Parent ego state and the wants of the Child ego state. As Gilliland, James and Bowman (1989: 115) put it, the

Adult ego state "provides the 'how to' for the personality by asking 'why' questions and considering consequences." Harris (1969) says that by means of the Adult we can begin to tell the differences between life as it was taught and demonstrated to us (Parent), life as we felt it, wished it or fantasized about it (Child), and life as we figure it out for ourselves (Adult). It might be helpful to see the Adult as a data-processing computer. It makes decisions after computing information from all three ego state sources. The updating function of the Adult examines the data in our Parent to see whether they are sound and applicable today. Then the data are accepted, rejected or modified accordingly. Lessons we were taught as youngsters may be counterproductive, unhealthy or downright wrong today. The Adult ego also appraises the Child to see whether or not the feelings located there are appropriate to current circumstances (Harris, 1969).

The Parent Ego State

The **Parent ego state** contains all the rules we've learned concerning how things should and shouldn't be. This ego state houses our morals and manners. The Parent ego state defines for us what is important. It gives us instructions about what we should know and do in order to survive and function successfully in our culture. Whenever we talk about values that are important to us or when we discuss matters of principle, the Parent ego state is at work.

Like the Child ego state, the Parent can be broken up into two functional elements. These two elements are called the **Nurturing Parent** (NP) and the **Critical** or **Controlling Parent** (CP). When people operate in their Nurturing Parent ego state, they behave in a caring, concerned and protective manner. By contrast, the Critical Parent may have us present ourselves as oppressive, prejudiced, powerful, intimidating or controlling (Gilliland et al., 1989). The Critical Parent in us distrusts our own thinking. It calls upon external authority to enforce its demands.

With respect to its structure, the Parent ego state can be subdivided into three parts. As the Parent develops we incorporate into this ego state messages from caretakers and parental figures that reflect Child, Adult and Parent type responses. When operating in our Parent ego state we may copy our parents' and caretakers' functioning in their Parent state (Pp), their Adult state (Ap) or their Child state (Cp). For instance, imagine someone scolding another as his mother used to do in her Critical Parent state or scolding that other as the mother did in her frustrated Child state (Gilliland et al., 1989). The scolding in both cases comes from the Parent ego state. Differences in the way the scolding occurs depend on what was recorded and internalized from the parent. See Figure 4.5 below for both a structural and functional depiction of the three ego states. Also look at Table 4.1 for a summary of typical behaviours associated with each ego state, including the Parent.

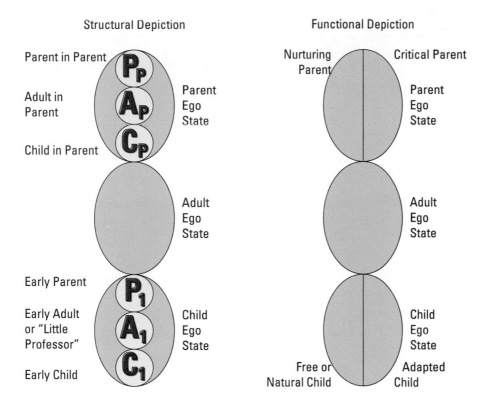

Structural Depiction

Parent in Parent

Adult in
Parent

Child in Parent

Early Parent

Early Adult
or "Little
Professor"

Early Child

Parent
Ego
State

Adult
Ego
State

Child
Ego
State

Functional Depiction

Nurturing
Parent

Critical Parent

Free or
Natural Child

Adapted
Child

Parent
Ego
State

Adult
Ego
State

Child
Ego
State

Figure 4.5

Structural and
Functional
Depictions of Ego
States

Table 4.1   Typical Behaviours Associated with Each Ego State

Ego States	Common Verbal Expressions	Characteristic Voice Patterns	Body Language Clues
Critical Parent	That's nice, bad	Judgmental	Points or wags finger
	That's cute, good	Admonishing	Frowns, squints
	You should	Critical	Feet apart, hands on hips
	You ought	Condescending	Slaps, spanks
	You never	Loud	Serious looking
	Be quiet, good	Disgusted, sneering	Arms crossed, closed posture
	Don't you	Scheming	Foot tapping
	Ridiculous	Comparing	Looks up in disgust
	You must	Demanding	Pounds table

Table 4.1 (continued)

Ego States	Common Verbal Expressions	Characterisic Voice Patterns	Body Language Clues
Nurturing Parent	Uses Words that are		
	Reassuring	Soft	Arms open
	Comforting	Concerned	Palm outward
	Consoling	Soothing	Holds hands
	Loving	Encouraging	Hugs, holds, kisses
	Supporting	Sympathetic	Cradles
	Nonjudgmental		Smiles, touches, strokes, nods approvingly
Adult	Asks questions:		
	How	Modulated	Relaxed
	What	Appropriate	Stroking the chin
	Where	Corresponds to feelings	Finger pointing to head area
	Who	Controlled, calm	Looks up (as if in search of answers)
	Why	Straight	Brow wrinkles when thinking
	It seems to me	Confident	
	Let's see what we find		Supporting head with hands
	The solution is		Attentive
	I wonder		
Natural Child	I wish	Loud or quiet, depending on mood	Showing off
	I want	Laughs	Rolls, tumbles
	I hope	Cries	Walks freely, easily
	I can't	Rages	Posture open, ready to swing into action
	I won't	Giggles	Flops easily and comfortably on chair or floor
	Wow		Skips
	Gee		
	Whoopee		
Adapted Child	*Compliant words:*		
	Yes, OK, You're right	Annoying	Showing off
	I'll do it, I'm wrong	Repetitive	Pouting
	Defiant, rebellious words:	Sweet	Fights aggressively
		Placating	or
	No, Make me	Angry	Withdraws timidly
	I won't, You're wrong, I don't care	Defiant	Chip on shoulder
		Loud or soft	or
	Other expressions:	Total silence	Passive conformity
	Help me, It's your fault, You'll be sorry		Teary eyed
			Looks innocent

Source: Hamachek, Don. *Encounters with the Self,* 3rd edition. Holt, Rinehart and Winston.

Exploring Your Ego States

This activity is designed to help you get in touch with the three basic ego states that make up your psychological self. They've been there for a long time, so it's time you got to know them. By experiencing and recognizing them in yourself, you'll begin to see them in others.

Instructions: Bring to mind an important decision you need to make. Use this decision to fill in the blanks below.

1. We can hear the voice of our Child ego state when it talks about feelings, wants and needs. For example, it might say, "I *feel* happy, sad, mad, glad, frightened or delighted," "I *want* more money, a vacation, a fancy car and a promotion at work" or "I *need* to eat better, sleep more, get more exercise and have more fun."

Now fill in the blanks below (with respect to the decision to be taken).

My Child feels

_____

_____

My Child wants

_____

_____

My Child needs

_____

_____

2. The voice of the Adult ego state sounds like a computer. It calculates, measures, predicts, reasons and reports our thinking. For example, it might say that 7+5=12, the meteor shower will occur August 11 and the roads are wet and slippery.

Now fill in the blank below (with respect to the decision to be taken).

My Adult thinks

_____

_____

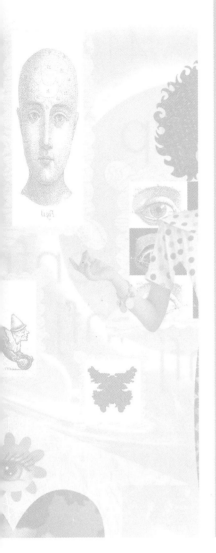

3. The voice of the Parent ego state addresses values and moral considerations. For example, it might say, "I should do my homework, arrive to work on time, look after my personal hygiene, go to church and never commit murder."

Now fill in the blank below (with respect to the decision to be taken).

My Parent says I should

_____

_____

4. Now that you have heard your Child, Adult and Parent speak on the important decision to be made, listen carefully again to uncover any conflicts among the three parts of your self. What, if any, conflict is contained?

What does your Child need or feel?

_____

What does your Adult think?

_____

What does your Parent demand or prohibit?

_____

What will you do?

_____

Source: This exercise is a variation of one found in Pamela Levin, *Becoming the Way We Are*, pp. 5-6.

TYPES OF TRANSACTIONS

Now that we are familiar with all three ego states, we can move on and examine communication patterns that involve them. Berne writes that when people verbally communicate with each other, **transactions** take place.

> *The unit of social intercourse is called a transaction. If two or more people encounter each other...sooner or later one of them will speak, or give some other indication of acknowledging the presence of others. This is called the transactional stimulus. Another person will then say or*

do something which is in some way related to the stimulus,
and that is called the transactional response. (Berne, cited
in Harris, 1969: 33)

It is important to note that transactional stimuli and transactional responses arise from ego states. Our job and the task of transactional analysts is to appraise "which ego state implemented the transactional stimulus and which executed the transactional response" (Berne, 1964: 29). There are several types of transactions, depending on how ego states interact and what was really intended by the messages transmitted. Here we'll look at complementary transactions, crossed transactions and ulterior transactions.

Complementary Transactions

There are two types of **complementary transactions**. In the first type, the receiver of a message responds to it from the same ego state the sender used in transmitting the message. For example, the sender sends a Parent message and the receiver responds in the Parent mode. Complementary transactions of this sort can also take place at the level of Adult and Child. See Figure 4.6 below.

A second type of complementary transaction is based on unequal relationships. For instance, the transaction could be from Parent to Child or vice versa. It might also be from Child to Adult or Adult to Child. In all unequal complementary transactions, the lines of communication are still parallel. Whether transactions are equal or unequal, the first rule of T.A. is that when source stimulus and receiver response occur in a parallel fashion, transactions are complementary and can go on indefinitely (Harris, 1969). For an illustration of unequal complementary transactions, see Figure 4.7.

In his book *I'm OK—You're OK*, Harris provides an example of a com-

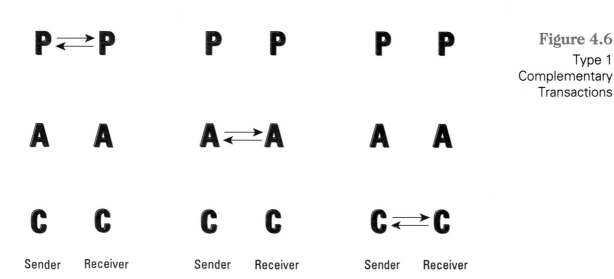

Figure 4.6
Type 1
Complementary
Transactions

Figure 4.7

Type 2 Unequal
Complementary
Transactions

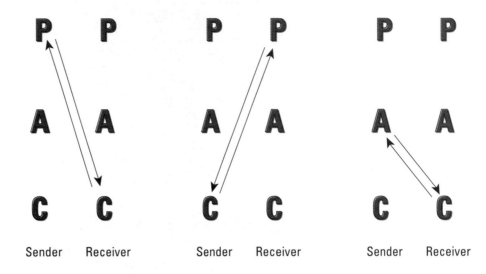

plementary transaction occurring between two women complaining to each other about how their bus is going to arrive late at its destination. This transaction occurs in a parallel fashion at the Parent ego state level. A paraphrase of Harris's example is found below.

Elvira: While glancing at her watch, mumbling to herself and catching the eye of the female passenger next to her, she sighs wearily.

Lilith: Sighs back in response; adjusts herself and looks at her watch.

Elvira: We're going to be late again.

Lilith: It always happens.

Elvira: Have you ever seen this bus arrive on time?

Lilith: Never have.

Elvira: Just like I was saying to my husband yesterday—you just don't get quality service like you used to.

Lilith: You're absolutely right. I don't know what's wrong with people today.

Elvira: They still like to take your money, though, don't they?

In the example above, both passengers engage in a judgmental exchange about service. They seem to enjoy complaining to each other. Communicating Parent to Parent, they could go on forever. Harris (1969: 94–95) says:

> *When we blame and find fault, we replay the early blaming and fault-finding which is recorded in the Parent, and this makes us feel OK, because the Parent is OK, and we are coming on Parent. Finding someone to agree with you, and play the game, produces a feeling well-nigh omnipotent.*

Source: Reprinted by permission of HarperCollins Publishers.

Crossed Transactions

In **crossed transactions**, the lines of communication are not parallel. Rather, they cross or intersect each other at some point. Instead of promoting further communication, crossed transactions disrupt it. Thus, a second rule of T.A. "...is that communication is broken off when a crossed transaction occurs" (Berne, 1964: 30). Crossed transactions come in two types. A Type 1 crossed transaction is illustrated in Figure 4.8.

In a Type 1 crossed transaction the message stimulus is Adult-to-Adult. In the example below, an appropriate response would have been something like "No, I don't" or "The last time I saw it, it was on your desk in class." Instead, what we have is a receiver who flares up and responds in a Child-to-Parent fashion. As Figure 4.8 shows, the two vectors of communication cross. Communication is thereby broken off. If communication is to resume, either the sender must become Parental to complement the receiver's Child or the receiver's Adult ego state must be activated as a complement to the sender's Adult.

In a Type 2 crossed transaction, an Adult-to-Adult stimulus message is answered with a Parent-to-Child response. Let's modify the example about the textbook to illustrate the point. See Figure 4.9.

In both Type 1 and Type 2 crossed transactions, communication about the book stops. Either a digression must be made about who got blamed for what or talk must resume about who's acting like a child. The location of the book becomes a dead issue. See Figure 4.10 for additional illustrations of crossed transactions.

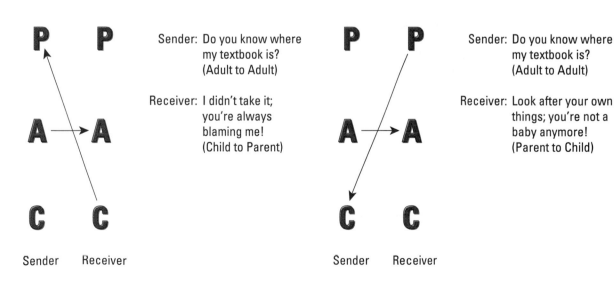

Sender: Do you know where my textbook is? (Adult to Adult)

Receiver: I didn't take it; you're always blaming me! (Child to Parent)

Sender Receiver

Sender: Do you know where my textbook is? (Adult to Adult)

Receiver: Look after your own things; you're not a baby anymore! (Parent to Child)

Sender Receiver

Figure 4.8
Type 1 Crossed Transaction

Figure 4.9
Type 2 Crossed Transaction

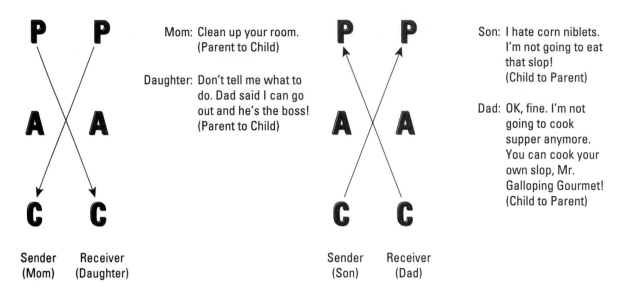

Mom: Clean up your room.
(Parent to Child)

Daughter: Don't tell me what to
do. Dad said I can go
out and he's the boss!
(Parent to Child)

Son: I hate corn niblets.
I'm not going to eat
that slop!
(Child to Parent)

Dad: OK, fine. I'm not
going to cook
supper anymore.
You can cook your
own slop, Mr.
Galloping Gourmet!
(Child to Parent)

Sender (Mom)   Receiver (Daughter)

Sender (Son)   Receiver (Dad)

Figure 4.10
More Crossed Transactions

Ulterior Transactions

Ulterior transactions are complementary transactions that include **hidden messages** intended to serve **ulterior motives** (Weiten, Lloyd and Lashley, 1991). Ulterior transactions use more than two ego states simultaneously (Berne, 1964). When observing ulterior transactions we discover surface level and subsurface level messages being communicated at the same time. At the obvious surface level, there is the manifest content of the message. Below the surface occurs the latent, but more meaningful exchange (Weiten, Lloyd and Lashley, 1991). In ulterior transactions, Adult-to-Adult surface communication patterns, for example, may be adopted for the sake of appearances. Underneath appearances, however, another totally different sort of communication may be taking place.

Ulterior transactions may be angular or duplex. Angular ulterior transactions involve three ego states. Berne (1964) uses the example of a salesman to illustrate this point. See Figure 4.11 for an adaptation. Duplex ulterior transactions involve four ego states (Berne, 1964). We commonly find them in flirtation games. Again, in this instance, there is the obvious message at the social level of communication as well as the latent message at the subsurface psychological level. Berne's example of the cowboy is useful here. See Figure 4.12.

We see that at the social level an Adult conversation about barns is taking place. At the psychological level we find a Child conversation involving innocent foreplay. It would appear that the more interesting interaction is taking place at the hidden or subsurface level.

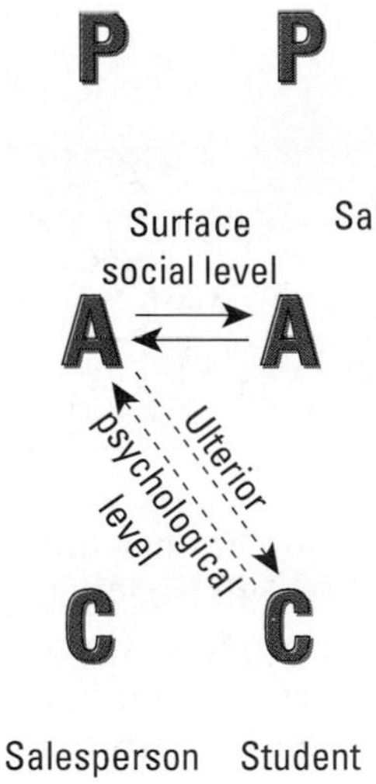

P P

Surface
social level

A ⇄ A

Ulterior
psychological
level

C C

Salesperson   Student

Surface Level
Transaction
Adult to Adult

Salesperson: This compact
disc player is
better but you
probably can't
afford it.

Student: That's the one
I'll take.

Subsurface Level
Ulterior Transaction
Adult to Child
Child to Adult

Salesperson: I'll appeal to his
real wants and
act a little
condescending.

Student: Just because I'm a
student doesn't
mean I'm not as
good as any of her
other customers.

Figure 4.11
Angular Ulterior
Transactions

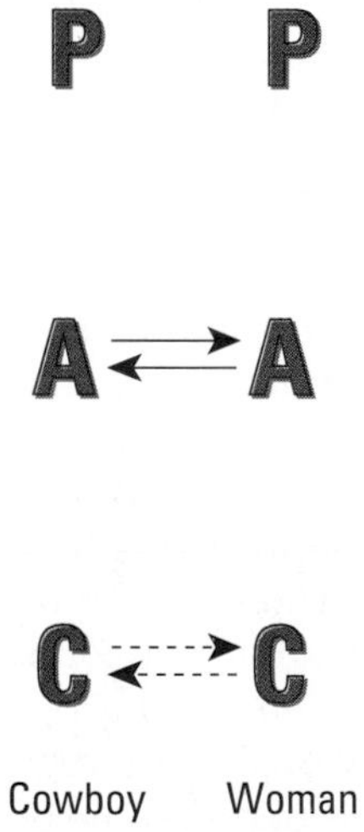

P P

A ⇄ A

C ⇠⇠⇢ C

Cowboy   Woman

Surface Level
Transaction
Adult to Adult
Adult to Adult

Cowboy: I can show you
the barn.

Woman: I've always
loved barns. Can
we go now to
see it?

Subsurface Level
Ulterior Transaction
Child to Child
Child to Child

Cowboy: Wow! I like you.

Woman: I like you too.
Let's play!

Figure 4.12
Duplex Ulterior
Transactions

STROKES

4.6

Whatever the nature of people's communication transactions (complementary, crossed, ulterior), the basic motivation behind the social interaction is the need for **strokes** (Dusay and Dusay, 1979: 377). All three ego states require stroking for optimal development. The Parent might need strokes for being a good listener, caretaker, advice giver or character model. The Child may crave stroking for displaying creativity and curiosity or for being fun-loving and spontaneous. The Adult might need strokes for being a good thinker and decision maker (Gilliland et al., 1989).

The idea that we all have a basic need for strokes comes from research

If you touch me soft and gentle
If you look at me and smile at me
If you listen to me talk sometimes before you talk
I will grow, really grow.

Bradly (age 9)
(Source: James and Jongeward, 1978)

in infant development. Studies indicate that touch is important. For instance, it stimulates an infant's chemistry for mental and physical growth (see Spitz, 1945: 53–74). "Infants who are neglected, ignored, or for any reason do not experience enough touch, suffer mental and physical deteriorization even to the point of death" (James and Jongeward, 1978). Their spinal cords tend to shrivel and deteriorate. This condition is known as **marasmus** (see Freed and Freed, 1973). If you ever have a chance to visit a neonatal ward in a hospital, take note of the nurses, parents and volunteers who are instructed to physically "stroke" premature infants for about 15 to 20 minutes daily. This stroking helps them to thrive. Without stroking, premature infants develop more slowly and, with extreme neglect, may not survive.

Transactional analysts claim that the need for strokes does not end with infancy. As ego states develop, the Parent, Adult and Child in us all require stroking for healthy growth and development. A gentle and caring touch continues to be a positive stroke for us throughout our lifespan. As we emerge from infancy, however, we begin to experience strokes often on a more subtle and symbolic level (Gilliland et al., 1989). Whenever we enter the awareness of another person and express the message verbally or nonverbally that "I know you're there and I recognize you," we provide a life-sustaining stroke (Gilliland et al., 1989). While this stroke could be a nonverbal touch, it could also be a wish or letter. It could come in the form of a thank-you, an effort to remember a name, or it might be delivered as a specific verbal reinforcer (Harris and Harris, 1985). Listening in an attentive fashion is perhaps one of the finest strokes you can give to another person (James and Jongeward, 1971). We all like to be listened to and taken seriously. It's annoying to speak with people who aren't paying attention, who are preoccupied or who look right through us. Such things **discount** the importance of what we're saying. They can also discount us personally.

Strokes come in different forms and are delivered under varying sets of circumstances. Some strokes come as freebies, some are earned and still others are requested (Freed and Freed, 1973). The freebies are the best. You get these strokes from people for just being you. **Freebie strokes** don't require you to impress anybody or to do anything. A second kind of stroke is an earned one. **Earned strokes** are obtained by getting good grades, for instance, or by winning or doing things for people. Strokes can also be gained by simply asking for them. Children frequently ask their parents, "Do you love me?" When parents respond, "Of course we love you. You're very special to

From infancy onward we all have a basic need for strokes; that is, a need to be held, cuddled, touched and cared for.

us," a stroke is delivered. When you ask professors what they think of your work, your aim is **requested strokes**. There is nothing wrong with this method; strokes leave us feeling happy and contented. In T.A. jargon, these feelings are referred to as **warm fuzzies**.

In contrast to warm fuzzies, which are pleasant, some strokes can be unpleasant. These are referred to as **cold pricklies** (Steiner, 1977). Such strokes, though negative, at least make us feel alive. If we can't get the warm fuzzies we need, we'll do what it takes to get cold pricklies. As Freed and Freed said, "Any stroke is better than no stroke" (1973: 12). This point can be illustrated by the individual who'd rather be hated than not be noticed at all. The overlooked child may act up to get parental attention, even if punishment follows.

LIFE POSITIONS

The nature and frequency of the strokes we receive from early infancy onward establish for us our **life positions** in relation to the world. Our personal life position results from the decisions made in response to how parents and caretakers reacted to our initial expressions of feelings and needs. We either got warm fuzzies (positive strokes), cold pricklies (negative strokes) or nothing at all (abandonment or lack of response). Our stroking history, then, contributes significantly to the formation of four possible life positions.

I'm Not OK—You're OK

During early development, children are at the mercy of others. They are small, weak and incapable. By comparison, adults are big and strong, possessing what seems to the child like infinite abilities. Since they deliver the strokes children need, adults are OK. If children's needs are not met, they may decide that the lack in their lives is their fault. In this case, this conclusion is drawn: I'm not OK.

In adulthood, the I'm Not OK—You're OK life position may be lived out by withdrawal (Harris, 1969). People in this position may find it too painful to be around OK people, especially since they don't perceive themselves to be OK. They may also live in a world of fantasy, saying to themselves that life will be good "if I..." or "when I...." They may provoke people so that others turn on them. Resulting negative stroking reinforces the I'm Not OK life position. (Remember, negative strokes are better than no strokes at all.)

Individuals adopting the I'm Not OK—You're OK stance in life frequently seek out friends and associates with a big Parent (Harris, 1969). Not-OK people are typically eager and willing to comply with the demands of others. As Harris (1969) puts it, "Some of our best people are where they are because of these efforts to gain approval." Unfortunately, the approval-seeking Not-OK person is committed to a lifetime of endless mountain climbing. After reaching the summit of one mountain, another mountain presents itself. The Not-OK position can never provide lasting satisfaction because "No matter what I do, I'm still Not-OK" (Harris, 1969).

I'm Not OK—You're Not OK

Infants who receive relatively little stroking sometimes find that as they get a bit older and mobile, the stroking all but disappears. "If this state of abandonment and difficulty continues without relief through the second year of life, the child concludes I'm Not OK—You're Not OK (Harris, 1969). After reaching this conclusion, the Adult stops developing. It ceases to grow since its primary function of getting strokes is frustrated. There is no source of stroking to be found.

People in the I'm Not OK—You're Not OK position tend to give up on life. They may lose hope. They may barely survive or display symptoms of extreme withdrawal, ending up in mental institutions. They may also show regressive behaviour patterns that point to a longing to get back to very early infancy where at least some minimal stroking occurred.

I'm OK—You're Not OK

If children are mistreated, they may decide unconsciously that others are Not-OK. The conclusion that they (i.e., the children) are OK themselves probably comes from **self-stroking** (Harris, 1969). Commenting on how battered children, for example, stroke themselves, Harris (1969:72) writes:

> *I believe this self-stroking does in fact occur during the time that a little person is healing from major, painful injuries such as are inflicted on a youngster who has come to be known as "the battered child"....I believe that it is while this little individual is healing, in a sense "lying there licking his wounds," that he experiences a sense of comfort alone and by himself, if for no other reason than his improvement is in such contrast to the gross pain he has just experienced. It is as if he senses, "I'll be all right if you leave me alone. I'm OK by myself."*

Source: Reprinted by permission of HarperCollins Publishers.

People adopting the I'm OK—You're Not OK life position could be described as **survivors**. Unfortunately, such survivors may wish to "strike back" at the cruel world later in life. They have witnessed toughness and know very well how to be tough themselves. Deep-seated hatred may become a life-sustaining force, even though it is masked by politeness or social etiquette. Underscoring the energizing power of hatred, Caryl Chessman said, "There is nothing that sustains you like hate; it is better to be anything than afraid" (cited in Harris, 1969: 73). The hatred that sustains this position is often found in incorrigible criminals. Described as people lacking a moral sense of right and wrong, they are convinced that they are always OK, regardless of what they do. Where fault is to be found, it is always found in others.

A serious problem that arises when people adopt this life position is that they set themselves up for **stroke deprivation**. If it is true that a stroke is only as good as the stroker, and if there are no OK people, it follows that there are no OK strokes (Harris, 1969). If people in the I'm OK—You're Not OK position gather together an entourage of praising and stroking "yes men," even then the strokes delivered are not accepted at face value. In fact, the more the "yes men" stroke, the more they may be despised. The attitudinal stance toward others is nicely captured by the saying "Come close so I can let you have it" (Harris, 1969: 73).

I'm OK—You're OK

This life position offers us considerable hope. While the first three positions form unconsciously as a product of our stroking histories, the fourth is a product of conscious decision. It is "based on thought, faith, and the wager of action" (Harris, 1969: 74). Harris describes the adoption of the I'm OK—You're OK position as a conversion experience. It includes not yet experienced possibilities as well as the abstractions of philosophy and religion. In this life position, OK-ness is not bound by personal experience. We can transcend our histories and circumstances to make life OK for us and OK for everyone else. This does not mean that we can simply discard our pasts by choosing this position. Harris (1969: 76) points out that

> *[t]he not OK recordings in the Child are not erased by a decision in the present. The task at hand is how to start a*

*collection of recordings which play OK outcomes to trans-
actions, successes in terms of correct probability estimating, successes in terms of integrated actions which make
sense, which are programmed by the Adult, and not by the
Parent or Child, successes based on an ethic which can be
supported rationally. If we now wish to work toward adopting the "I'm OK—You're OK" position, we should be forewarned that instant OK feelings cannot be guaranteed. We
must acknowledge the presence of "old tapes" playing in
our memories. What we can try to do is turn unpleasant
tapes off when they threaten to undermine the faith we have
placed in our new ways of thinking. In time, the gradual
growth and development of the Adult will result in a new
happiness and a more satisfying way of life.*

Source: Reprinted by permission of HarperCollins Publishers.

 ## GAMES

In order to get necessary life-sustaining strokes to feel OK, people sometimes get involved in "game playing." The game playing referred to here is not
fun. The intent is serious and the playing field is found on the level of the unconscious. We're playing for keeps, only we don't know we're in the game.

Games involve recognizable patterns of human communication. Eric
Berne describes game playing below (1976: 69).

*A game is an ongoing series of complementary ulterior
transactions progressing to a well-defined predictable outcome. Descriptively it is a recurring set of transactions,
often repetitious, superficially plausible, with a concealed
motivation; or, more colloquially, a series of moves with a
snare, or "gimmick." Games are clearly differentiated from
procedures, rituals, and pastimes by two chief characteristics: (1) their ulterior quality and (2) the payoff. Procedures may be successful, rituals effective, and pastimes
profitable, but all of them are by definition candid; they
may involve contest, but not conflict, and the ending may
be sensational, but it is not dramatic. Every game, on the
other hand, is basically dishonest and the outcome has a
dramatic, as distinct from merely exciting, quality.*

For Berne, people become involved in game playing because there is
precious little opportunity for intimacy in daily life. Intimacy may simply
not be available for some people or perhaps it is psychologically impossible
for particular individuals. The result is that people can spend a great deal of
their social life seriously playing games. In fact, game playing may become necessary for maintaining mental health. Psychic stability may be so precari-

ous and life positions so tenuously maintained that to deprive some people of their games may be to plunge them into irreversible despair (Berne, 1964).

Transactional analysis has identified a variety of games. Berne (1964) classifies games under the following headings: life games, marital games, party games, sexual games, underworld games, consulting room games and good games. Ken Ernst (1972) has paid special attention to games that students and teachers play. He calls them troublemaker games, put-down games, tempter games, I-know-best games, helping games and close-to-student games. If you wish to master a detailed knowledge of games, I suggest you read Ernst and Berne in the original. For our purposes here, we'll look at a few of the more popular, commonly played games that interfere with honest and productive communication.

If It Weren't for You (IFWY)

If It Weren't for You is classified by Berne as a marital game, one frequently played by marriage partners. It can also be played between children and parents or between boyfriends and girlfriends. In all cases, there is typically a long-term established relationship.

When playing this game, one person charges another with restricting his or her behaviour. Let's suppose, for example, that a wife mentions the fact that a high school friend is about to graduate from medical school. In response, the husband says, "That's wonderful." This response sets the stage for the wife to assert with anger and frustration, "If it weren't for you, I could be a doctor today." (While her husband is barely surviving as a guitar player in a failing band, the wife has been working as a waitress to pay the rent and buy groceries). With her response, the wife brings up an old source of bitterness and conflict between them.

When people play games, there are psychological payoffs. Remember, too, there is dishonesty. In this example, the wife is actually afraid of going back to school. She unconsciously fears the challenge is too great. The result is that she engages in self-deception to suppress hidden insecurities and maintain her self-esteem. Dishonestly blaming her husband for her own missed opportunities can also provide the game-playing wife with a bargaining advantage in future communication transactions.

As Berne (1964) points out, many men and women select domineering partners who restrict their behaviour so that they can play a lifetime of If It Weren't for You/Him/Her. In fact, the person allegedly doing the restricting is doing the game player a kind of service. The domineering person who forbids or somehow prevents the other from doing something actually feared helps the game player suppress awareness of that fear. However, if the domineering partner ceases to restrict behaviour and allows the game player to do whatever she wants, then the game is over and the underlying fears and phobias are uncovered. The game player can no longer attack the dominant partner. The sources of fear must then be confronted face to face. Since it is easier to blame others than to face your own fears, IFWY is a favourite game people play.

Blemish: A Put-Down Party Game

Like other games, Blemish is played in an unconscious and dishonest fashion. Unfortunately, it causes a lot of petty discord in everyday life (Berne, 1964). This game is played from the vantage point of the depressive Child ("I am no good" or "I'm not OK") that is protectively transformed into the Parental position ("They are no good" or "They are Not OK"). The task for the game player here is to prove the thesis of the second position.

Blemish game players are often perfectionists. They may be looking for the "perfect knight in shining armour" or the "flawless and radiant princess" of their dreams. Before perfectionistic Blemish players get too close to anyone, they look for flaws in that person, either physical or psychological (Ernst, 1972). Since Blemish players are not OK in their own minds, they do not feel comfortable unless they are around others who are at least as Not OK as they are. When it comes to intimacy, "Closer relations are first encouraged, but when the person comes closer the Parent panic-button is pushed and the 'Blemish' is used as ammunition" (Ernst, 1972: 61). In other words, the fault is found and distance is created.

Creative players of this game can use almost anything about a person as a blemish. They can criticize and distance people because of their social status, education, colour, ethnicity, acne pimples or hair style. I guess transactional theory supports folk-wisdom here: "People who criticize others usually don't like themselves." This is certainly true with Blemish players. The advantage of Blemish is that it wards off depression about being Not OK. It also has the psychological payoff of avoiding intimacy that could expose the game player's own blemishes. According to Berne (1976), this game is usually based on sexual insecurity and its aim is reassurance.

"Why Don't You"—"Yes, But" (YDYB)

"Why Don't You"—"Yes, But" is also a party game that can be played at all kinds of occasions. Of all games, this one is best understood by transactional analysts (Berne, 1964). It was the first game to be identified for analysis. Personally speaking, before I ever learned anything about T.A., I knew a YDYB player who was a very good friend of mine. I'm amused to remember how he would always say "yeah, but" whenever suggestions were made about solving his problems. In response to almost any recommendation, he would shout out "Yeah, but...yeah, but" until he could get the person's attention. Below is an example of someone playing this game.

Farquar: My sister always insists on having Christmas dinner at her place, but she always messes up the meal and usually most of the food ends up tasting terrible.

Skivington: Why doesn't she take a cooking class?

Farquar: Yes, but she doesn't have time.

Skivington: Why don't you buy her a cookbook?

Farquar: Yes, but she probably wouldn't read it.

Skivington: Why don't you suggest a catering service provide this year's Christmas dinner?

Farquar: Yes, but that would cost too much.

Skivington: Why don't you lighten up on your sister's main course; bring your own dessert, and fill up on that?

Farquar: Yes, but that would hurt her feelings.

Typically, an exchange between a "yes, but" player and another ends in silence (Berne, 1964). The silence may be broken, in this case, by a comment like, "Well, I guess some people just can't cook!" Berne (1964: 116–117) says the following about this game:

> YDYB can be played by any number. The agent presents a problem. The others start to present solutions, each beginning with "Why don't you…?" To each of these White [the game player] objects with a "Yes, but…." A good player can stand off the others indefinitely until they all give up, whereupon White [the game player] wins. In many situations she [or he] might have to handle a dozen or more solutions to engineer the crestfallen silence which signifies her [or his] victory….

Since YDYB players reject, with rare exceptions, all solutions to their problems, the game must have some kind of ulterior purpose. The game is not really played as an Adult search for solutions and information, but rather as a means of gaining reassurance and gratification for the Child. This is the payoff. The manifest transaction may sound Adult-to-Adult in nature, but in truth game players present themselves as a Child too incapable or inadequate to meet the demands of problem situations. Others are transformed into wise Parents anxious to dispense wisdom for the benefit of the game player. Figure 4.13 depicts both social and psychological levels of YDYB transactions. Note that a "Why don't you…" comment acts as a Parent-to-Child stimulus that elicits the Child-to-Parent response, "Yes, but…" (both at the ulterior level).

In playing YDYB, both participants are usually unconscious of the ulterior transactions. The initiator of the game gains pleasure in rejecting all suggestions. The larger payoff doesn't come, however, until after all others have racked their brains and failed to find acceptable solutions. The resulting silence confirms for the game player that others are inadequate; they are unable to solve his problem. When this is "proven," the YDYB player "wins."

Response: Why don't you…?

Stimulus: Yes, but…

Game Initiator   Other(s)

Figure 4.13
Social and Psychological Levels of YDYB Transactions

Rapo

Berne (1964) classifies Rapo as a sexual game. According to him, it is a form of flirtation carried out between men and women. (In principle, this kind of flirtation game could also be played by homosexuals.) Other possible names for this game are Kiss Off, or Indignation. A fairly harmless form of this game is often played at social gatherings. It is made up of mild flirtation. Players signal their availability and take pleasure from the pursuit of others. As soon as those others commit themselves, the game is over. Polite Rapo players may say to their pursuers something like, "I appreciate your compliment and thank you very much," while moving on to the next conquest (Berne, 1964: 26).

In another more serious variation of Rapo, the initiating game player gets only secondary satisfaction from the advances of others. The primary satisfaction comes from delivering the rejection. A woman might say to a man, for example, "Buzz off, buster!" A man may, after some flirtation, say, "Take a hike, honey!" The Rapo player gets the other person into a much more serious commitment and then enjoys observing the discomfort created by the rejection.

See What You Made Me Do (SWYMD)

Another form of dishonest game playing in interpersonal relations is See What You Made Me Do. In its classical form, it is very much a marital game, though it can also be played between parents and children or between workers and bosses. When used in work contexts, SWYMD is classified as a life game (Berne, 1964).

As with Rapo, there are degrees of seriousness exhibited by SWYMD game players. First-degree players begin by wanting something, such as privacy. Someone else frustrates this want by interrupting. At the same time, the initiating game player makes a mistake in his work and conveniently blames the interrupting player for the mistake, even though the interruption actually has little or nothing to do with the error. By blaming the other person, the initiator discourages future interruptions and gets what's wanted, namely, privacy.

Second-degree SWYMD players use this game as more than an occasional protective mechanism. SWYMD becomes for them a way of life. Their strategy is to defer decisions and responsibilities to others. If things work out well, there is a payoff. The initiator enjoys the results of good decisions and related actions. If things don't turn out well, there's still a payoff because someone else can be blamed for what went wrong. Eric Berne (1964) does not regard this game as an end in itself. For the second-degree player, it merely offers passing satisfaction on the way to "I told you so" or "See what you've done now."

The game of SWYMD is often found in real-life work situations. For example, bosses may ask their subordinates for suggestions on improving productivity or performance. On the surface, they may appear to be good managers who operate democratically. Beneath the surface appearance, however, these game-playing bosses use employee suggestions to terrorize those beneath them. Mistakes are used against those who tried to be helpful. People may be criticized or harshly dealt with. In this case, bosses use the guise of democratic management to relieve themselves of personal responsibility. When things go wrong, it's not their fault, but the fault of others. That's the payoff.

Third-degree SWYMD is very serious. It may be played by paranoid individuals against people rash enough to give them advice. The paranoid may use the advice given to them in order to combine a second game with the first. The second game is called You Got Me into This (UGMIT). The SWYMD-UGMIT combination is a wickedly effective game as far as psychological dishonesty is concerned. In this combined game, blame and condemnation of others is combined with fear and paranoia. The serious third-degree player probably needs professional help.

High and Proud

Before concluding this section on games, I thought it might be interesting to look at one that you might observe in your college or university classrooms. In his classic work, *Games Students Play*, Ken Ernst (1972) draws our attention to High and Proud, a nifty little game used by students to gain the moral high ground above recognized authorities. In this game, students provoke situations of conflict in which the evidence for wrongdoing on the part of the enemy (i.e., the authoritarian professor or educational administrator) is beyond question. Confrontations are so designed and manipulated that any reasonable observer of the dispute would be aroused by the enemy authority's overreaction. Gaining support of a "reasonable public" enables the High and Proud player to win.

High and Proud is illustrated in the following example of fraternity president Stu Dent, and professor of administrivia Dr. Dic Tator. First of all, Stu Dent arrives at his first class with skinhead and satanic tattoos proudly displayed. He's wearing torn jeans and a ripped T-shirt. Stu refuses to follow the dress code at his exclusive private college. He will not wear a jacket and tie as required by school regulations. Within minutes of arriving, he invites a number of his classmates to smoke marijuana after class. His language is foul and he seems to enjoy breaking all the rules laid down by administration. By his combination of all these actions, Stu is well equipped to bait school authorities.

Dr. Dic Tator, on the other hand, is obligated to enforce the rules of his educational institution. He is required by his Parent ego state or the Parent rules of the school to respond punitively to Stu, who is flagrantly violating authority. Of course, objective evaluation clearly indicates that being a skinhead does not interfere with learning. Also, scientific evidence suggests that smoking marijuana isn't more harmful than smoking cigarettes. Four-letter words are only offensive to those who choose to be offended by them. With all this information ready to access and present as a defence, Stu Dent causes Dic Tator to overreact. Stu becomes the martyr and Tator becomes the villain. The stronger the overreaction by Tator and school authorities, the better for Stu. "This type of reaction demonstrates that there is something wrong with the Parent-type person" (Ernst, 1972: 82). Ernst classifies High and Proud as belonging to the "tempter variety" of games.

Some students get strokes playing High and Proud when they're feeling low and ashamed.

ROLES PLAYED IN PSYCHOLOGICAL GAMES

Now that you are aware of some of the psychological games people play, you need to understand that people adopt particular **roles** when they get involved. For example, do you know someone who always seems to get picked on by others? Perhaps you know people who spend a lot of time themselves picking on others or putting them down. You may also know a person who typically intervenes when other people are having problems. If you have met or seen individuals such as those described above, you've quite likely witnessed game players in action. When getting into a game, people can adopt the role of **persecutor**, **victim** or **rescuer**. Of course, some people are truly persecuted (e.g., due to race); others are truly victimized (e.g., by sexual abuse); still others really function heroically as rescuers (e.g., from physical danger). These people are not playing games. What is also true, however, is that people sometimes assume illegitimate roles they can act out as part of their psychological game playing. Illegitimate or phony roles are outlined below by James and Jongeward (1975: 114).

Persecutors: People who set unnecessarily strict limits on behaviour; who enforce rules with sadistic brutality; who make others suffer because they are weaker.

Victims: People who do *not* qualify for a job but falsely claim they are denied it because of race, sex or religion. People who feel continually put upon.

Rescuers: People who, in the guise of being helpful, keep others dependent upon them, don't really help them and in fact may resent helping. Phony roles are always part of a game.

HOW TO BREAK UP PSYCHOLOGICAL GAMES

In *The People Book*, James and Jongeward (1975: 139) offer us some helpful suggestions for breaking up games. They are listed and briefly explained below.

- **Use the Adult ego state to break up games**   Use your Adult to understand the nature and purpose of games. Consider your own favourite game role. Examine how the game roles of others complement yours. Try to discover how the games you get involved in produce bad feelings in the end. Use your Adult to figure out other options besides game playing. Try out new patterns of behaviour.

- **Stop playing the complementary hand. Cross transactions instead**   You can stop playing someone else's game by refusing to play the complementary hand. If someone else is playing "Yes, but," that person wants you to give advice that will be rejected for purposes of the game. Either don't give the advice or put the problem back on the shoulders of the would-be game player. You could answer, for example, "I really don't know what I'd do" or "What do you think is best?" These responses will cause a crossed transaction and end unproductive communication.

- **Don't play the victim, persecutor or rescuer**   To end game playing, stop seeing yourself as a victim, acting helpless and dependent when, in fact, you are able to support yourself. Second, don't play the illegitimate role of persecutor, criticizing those who don't need or deserve it. Furthermore, don't reinforce your role as rescuer, giving help to those who don't need it. Don't help someone if you'll resent giving assistance.

- **Stop exaggerating**   Game players exaggerate the strengths and weaknesses of others as well as themselves. You can help stop game playing by quitting the exaggeration. For example, if you are constantly putting yourself down (e.g., "How stupid of me!") and blaming yourself inappropriately, you're probably playing an illegitimate role in some psychological game. Stop it. This exaggeration doesn't help yourself or others.

- **Don't misuse time**   If you choose to give up your psychological game playing, you'll find you have much more time to do other productive things. You might develop a new skill, exercise your talents, form new friendships or spend more time in leisure activities.

- **Stop collecting negative strokes**   If you are a game player, you must learn to get more positive strokes. If someone else you know is playing games, you can refuse to deliver the negative strokes they want and find ways of giving positive strokes. The danger is that all strokes might disappear when game playing ceases. Remember negative strokes are better than no strokes at all.

- **To get positive strokes, be more generous in giving them**   Positive stroke givers attract positive strokes from other people. Mutual positive stroking can help to create and sustain long-lasting relationships. "To have friends, a person must learn how to be a friend."

APPLICATION EXERCISE

4.2

4.11

Ego States and the Effective Memorandum

Whatever you eventually do for a living, you will probably be required at some time to communicate with others in writing. One such format is the memorandum. It is commonly used in all kinds of organizations and institutions.

Memoranda are not always well received. Sometimes people object to the tone of a particular memo as much as they do to its content. The tone of a memorandum likely has something to do with the "voice" of the ego state used to create it. It is important, therefore, that you recognize the ego states imbedded in your written communications. It is also important that you activate the desired ego states in your readers in order to make your memos more effective.

Instructions: Read the memorandum below. Then identify
1. The ego state from which the memo was written.
2. The ego state likely activated in the reader.
3. The probable effectiveness of the memo.

"Do Your Part" **Memo**

To: All Parents and Teachers at Sunnybrook Cooperative Daycare

From: The President of Sunnybrook

This memo is to remind you to get excited about our Christmas fund-raising auction. I expect all parents and co-op teachers to encourage their neighbours, friends and relatives to come out to the auction and support our fund-raising efforts.

As long as you keep bringing in money, you needn't worry about Sunnybrook closing. Good daycare is hard to come by, so it's in your interest to work hard.

As a member of this cooperative, it's your duty to keep us financially afloat. Make sure to do your part!

After personal reading and analysis of the memo, form small groups to discuss your answers. When group discussion on the memo is completed, have everyone work together to rewrite the memo in a way that makes it more effective. Be prepared to discuss your group's improvements in "ego state" language.

Events and Ego-State Reactions

APPLICATION EXERCISE 4.3

4.12

Part A

Any one situation or stimulus event can elicit three possible ego state reactions. Under each situation listed below are different responses. Your job is to identify each as either Parent, Adult or Child in nature. You will have to imagine the tone of voice used and the gestures that accompany each response.

1. A 19-year-old son loses an important application.

   _____ a. "What's wrong with you? Why can't you keep track of things for which you are responsible?"

   _____ b. "You could telephone the college's lost and found to see if anybody turned it in."

   _____ c. "I don't know where your stupid application is! I didn't take it. Why do you always blame me?"

2. A ride to school doesn't show up on the day of a big test.

   _____ a. "I'm not going to give you gas money for this week's rides."

   _____ b. "Why didn't you show up?"

   _____ c. "I can't count on you for anything! You've elevated irresponsibility to an art form."

3. Someone you thought was your friend ignores you in the hallway.

   _____ a. "Were you busy thinking about the assignment tomorrow?"

   _____ b. "What's the matter? Aren't I good enough for you?"

   _____ c. "I really think you should be more courteous to your friends if you wish to keep them."

Part B

Your task here is to create three situations of your own. For each situation, provide a Parent, Adult and Child response. Your responses to each situation could be read out in class. For a bit of fun and learning, have others identify them.

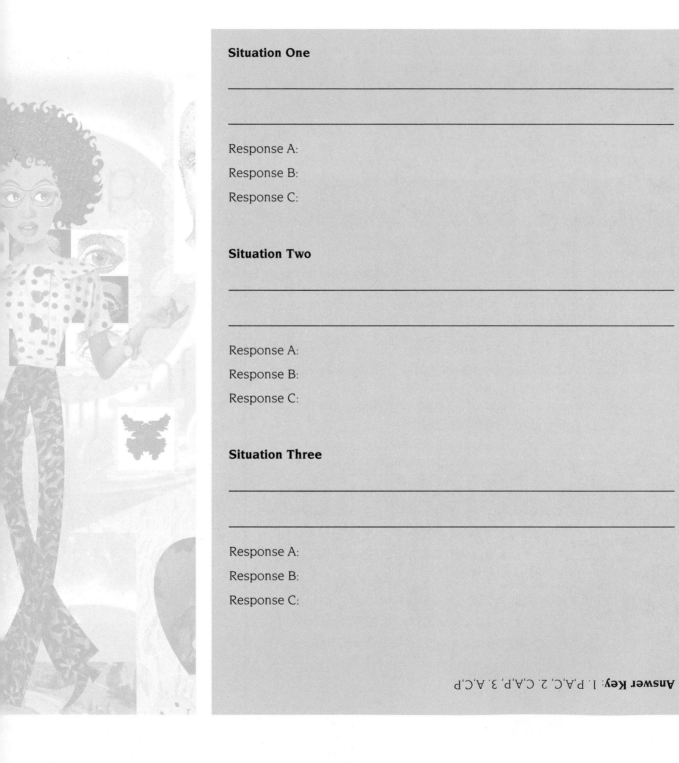

Situation One

_____

_____

Response A:

Response B:

Response C:

Situation Two

_____

_____

Response A:

Response B:

Response C:

Situation Three

_____

_____

Response A:

Response B:

Response C:

Answer Key: 1. P,A,C. 2. C,A,P. 3. A,C,P.

S T U D Y   G U I D E

Key Terms

transactional analysis (122)
ego states (123)
Child ego state (127)
taped events (127)
Free Child/Natural Child (129)
Adapted Child (129)
Adult ego state (129)
Parent ego state (130)
Nurturing Parent (130)
Critical Parent/ Controlling Parent (130)
transactions (134)

complementary transactions (135)
crossed transactions (137)
ulterior transactions (138)
hidden messages (138)
ulterior motives (138)
strokes (139)
marasmus (140)
discount (140)
freebie strokes (140)
earned strokes (140)

requested strokes (141)
warm fuzzies (141)
cold pricklies (141)
life positions (141)
self-stroking (142)
survivors (143)
stroke deprivation (143)
games (144)
roles (150)
persecutor (150)
victim (150)
rescuer (150)

Fill-in-the-Blank Questions

PROGRESS CHECK 4.1 ✔

Instructions: Fill in each blank with the appropriate answer from the list below.

child
parent
transactions
life position
game playing
adult
persecutor
intimacy
self-stroking
complementary

ulterior
strokes
marasmus
transactional analysis
rational
victim
crossed transactions
unequal relationships
ego states
crossed

1. _____ is a broad theory of personality and interpersonal relations that emphasizes patterns of communication.
2. According to transactional analysis, personality comprises three _____.
3. The "Little Professor" belongs to the _____ ego state.
4. The Adult ego state is _____.

5. The _____ ego state is like a data-processing computer.

6. The caregiver who gives support and concern to another is functioning in the role of Nurturing _____.

7. According to Eric Berne, the Canadian-born psychiatrist, communication can be analysed in terms of _____.

8. When lines of communication are not parallel, we can describe them as _____ transactions.

9. Transactions that include hidden messages can be described as _____ transactions.

10. Parallel communications are _____.

11. The basic motivation behind any social interaction is the need for _____.

12. The belief that I'm OK—You're Not OK is a _____.

13. Infants who fail to prosper and sometimes die due to lack of strokes suffer from _____.

14. People with an I'm OK—You're Not OK life orientation often engage in _____.

15. In order to get life-sustaining strokes, people sometimes get involved in _____.

16. People who illegitimately claim to be discriminated against play the role of _____.

17. Demanding that other people adhere to your unrealistic and demanding rules places you in the role of _____.

18. _____ can help you to put an end to psychological game playing.

19. People get involved in game playing because they often lack _____ in their lives.

20. It is possible to have complementary transactions in _____.

True/False Questions

Instructions: Circle the appropriate letter next to each statement.

T F   1. Interpersonal communication occurs in a psychological vacuum.

T F   2. According to T.A., we should try to mature and go beyond our Child ego state.

T F   3. Functionally speaking, the Child ego state can be separated into two elements: the Natural Child and the Adapted Child.

T F   4. The Adult ego state serves as referee between the demands of the Parent ego state and the wants of the Child ego state.

T F   5. When operating in our Parent ego state, we are always punitive and judgmental.

T F   6. Complementary transactions are impossible in unequal relationships.

T F   7. When two people complain to each other about others, they are communicating Parent to Parent.

T F   8. Ulterior transactions include hidden messages.

T F   9. Ulterior transactions are always negative or hurtful.

T F   10. Negative strokes are better than no strokes at all.

T F   11. Marasmus is a form of hypnosis used in persuasion.

T F   12. You can give a positive stroke to another by listening carefully to what that person says.

T F   13. The strokes we do or don't get in childhood help to establish our life positions.

T F   14. People adopting the I'm OK—You're Not OK position can be described as survivors.

T F   15. A psychological game is an ongoing series of complementary ulterior transactions progressing to a well-defined predictable outcome.

T F   16. Once game playing starts, there's no way to end it.

T F   17. If It Weren't for You is a game that helps people divert attention from their own fears and insecurities by blaming others.

T F   18. Blemish is a game played by people from the vantage point of the I'm Not OK life position.

T F   19. "Why Don't You"—"Yes, But" players sincerely want your advice to help them solve problems.

T F   20. First-degree Rapo is a form of mild flirtation.

T F   21. See What You Made Me Do is a game sometimes played to get privacy.

T F   22. High and Proud is a game used to make others look unreasonable by baiting them and taking the moral high ground.

T F   23. In the context of game playing, we can be truly helpful to victims by adopting the role of rescuer.

T F   24. Psychological games help to promote healthy relationships.

T F   25. People are always aware of the games they play.

Focus Questions

1. What is an ego state? What kinds of ego states are there? Can you describe each?

2. How do ego states function? How do they influence interpersonal communication?

3. What are some common verbal expressions, voice patterns and body language cues associated with each of the ego states?

4. What is a transaction? What kinds of transactions are there? Can you explain them?

5. Which kinds of transactions lead to good communication? Which do not? Why?

6. What are strokes? What kinds are there? Why do we need them?

7. What are life positions? Can you name and explain each? How do life positions develop?

8. What are games? Can you name some? How and why are they played?

Summary

1. What is transactional analysis?
   - it is a broad theory of personality and interpersonal relations that emphasizes patterns of communication

2. What are the three ego states?
   - Parent (Critical and Nurturing)
   - Adult
   - Child (Adapted and Natural)

3. How do each of the ego states function?
   - the Adult calculates, referees, decides and figures out solutions
   - the Parent judges, gives instructions, cares and nurtures, and criticizes
   - the Child responds spontaneously and displays curiosity, joyfulness and rebelliousness

4. What kinds of communication transactions are there?
   - *complementary:* sender and receiver communicate from the same ego state, or messages are parallel though originating from different ego states
   - *crossed:* messages intersect and cause a break in communication
   - *ulterior:* hidden messages serve ulterior motives; they are latent messages, but provide a more meaningful exchange

5. Why are strokes important?
   - they are required for healthy growth and development
   - infants who do not experience strokes can develop a condition known as marasmus
   - some examples are a touch, wink, letter, thank-you, an effort to remember someone's name, and listening attentively

6. What kinds of strokes are there?
   - *freebies:* you get these strokes for just being you
   - *earned:* you obtain these for doing something
   - *requested:* these strokes are asked for
   - *warm fuzzies:* these strokes leave us feeling good
   - *cold pricklies:* although they are negative strokes, they make us feel alive

7. What life positions can we take in relating to the world?
   - I'm Not OK—You're OK
   - I'm Not OK—You're Not OK
   - I'm OK—You're Not OK
   - I'm OK—You're OK

8. What are games? Can you give examples?
   - they are unconscious, serious and deceptive ways of getting life-sustaining strokes

- games have an ulterior quality and a payoff
- examples are If It Weren't for You, Blemish, "Why Don't You"—"Yes, But," Rapo, See What You Made Me Do, and High and Proud

9. What roles are played in psychological games?
   - *victim:* the person wrongly feels put down or put upon
   - *persecutor:* the person sets unrealistic standards and rules to justify punitive behaviour
   - *rescuer:* the person keeps others dependent by helping them

10. How can you break up psychological games?
    - use your Adult ego state
    - cross your transactions and stop playing complementary roles
    - don't play victim, persecutor or rescuer
    - stop exaggerating
    - don't misuse time
    - stop collecting negative strokes; instead, be more generous giving positive strokes

Related Readings

Bennett, Dudley (1980). *Successful Team Building Through T.A.* New York: Amacom.

Harris, A.B. and T.A. Harris (1985). *Staying OK.* New York: Harper & Row Publishers.

Keepers, Terry and Dorothy Babcock (1986). *Raising Kids OK.* Menlo Park, CA: Menalto Press.

Wagner, Abe (1981). *The Transactional Manager: How to Solve Problems with Transactional Analysis.* New York: Prentice Hall Press.

Weblinks

1. United States of America Transactional Analysis Association
   www.usataa.org

   Visit this web site to learn about this organization's mission statement, member benefits, directory, events and articles relating to transactional analysis.

2. International Transactional Analysis Association
   www.itaa-net.org

   ITAA is a professional organization of psychotherapists, organizational consultants, educators and government personnel in approximately 65 countries. It offers certification and training in various clinical and special fields categories.

3. The Berne Institute: Training in Psychotherapy and Counselling
   www.theberne.u-net.com

   Offers ongoing professional training and supervision in psychotherapy and counselling plus a varied program of workshops, seminars and other training events. The core model is transactional analysis.

4. Transactional Analysis Journal
   www.itaa-net.org/taj.htm

   Visit this site to learn more about the official professional journal of the International Transactional Analysis Association.

"Come to the edge," he said.
They said, "We are afraid."
"Come to the edge," he said.
They came.
He pushed them
And they flew.

–Guillaume Apollinaire

LEADERSHIP PERSPECTIVES

CHAPTER OVERVIEW

LEARNING OUTCOMES

After successfully completing this chapter, you will be able to

5.1 Define leadership

5.2 Distinguish between leadership and management

5.3 List the functions of management

5.4 Outline and describe six approaches to leadership

5.5 Decide on the best form of situational leadership to use in a case study example

5.6 Assess your leadership temperament

5.7 Modify leadership appreciation strategies to fit psychological temperament types

LIFE AND LEADERSHIP

Experience suggests that no matter who you are or what you do for a living, chances are pretty good that you will be required to assume a leadership role at some time in your life. You may become a leader among your friends, a class leader at college, a neighbourhood organizer, the head of a family, or someone expected to provide direction at work or in some civic organization operating within your local community. Given the likelihood that leadership demands will be placed upon you in the future, if not right now, you are well advised to develop an understanding of the nature and process of leadership. It is important that you prepare yourself for carrying out leadership roles in order to maximize your effectiveness. This preparation may indeed turn out to be instrumental to your personal and professional success.

Defining Leadership

Leadership is one of those vague concepts that everyone seems to understand intuitively, but which few can define precisely. Over the years, many models and approaches to leadership have been developed. In this chapter, we'll be looking at a few of them, but before we begin, it will be helpful to provide a simple working definition of leadership.

Leadership involves the ability to influence the actions of others (Benton and Halloran, 1991). People displaying leadership can cause others to work toward common goals in social, institutional and organizational settings. Leaders can get others to do things that they otherwise wouldn't do. Examples of great Canadian leaders include Pierre Elliot Trudeau (former prime minister), Wayne Gretzky (team captain and hockey player extraordinaire) and Nellie McClung (political activist who helped win women the vote in Alberta in 1916).

Leadership versus Management

Common sense might seem to dictate that leadership has something to do with management functions. You may be inclined to think that departmental managers, institutional directors, presidents of corporations and assembly-line bosses are typical examples of people who act as leaders in our society. Higher authority and greater levels of responsibility could appear to make someone a leader. Yet some writers and researchers on the subject of leadership would take issue with such a notion. They would not accept the idea that managers are destined to become leaders simply by virtue of their institutional or organizational roles (Barr and Barr, 1989). While it may be true that some managers function as effective leaders, other managers may manage but fail to lead. You may also have individuals in your group, neighbourhood or class who hold no special title, no au-

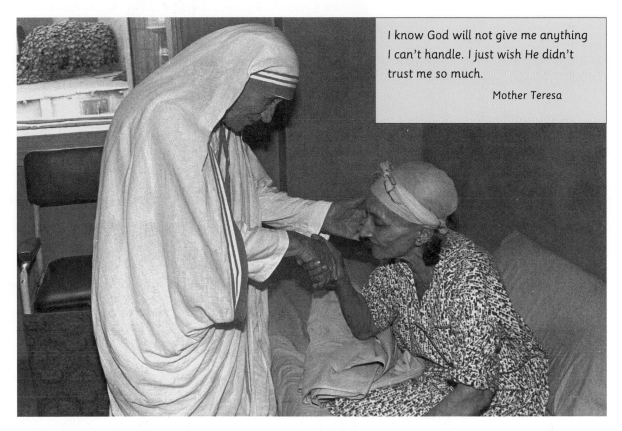

I know God will not give me anything I can't handle. I just wish He didn't trust me so much.

Mother Teresa

A leader herself, the late Mother Teresa followed instructions from an even "higher authority."

thority or no formal responsibility—in short, people who are not charged with the task of managing anyone or anything—but who are still recognized as leaders. Furthermore, you may know people who have both management and leadership abilities, but no opportunity to use them. Thus, given the possibilities, we have

1. Individuals who manage, but do not lead.
2. Individuals who lead, but do not manage.
3. Individuals who both lead and manage.
4. Individuals who have both leadership and management abilities, but no people who follow them.

In Figure 5.1 you can see the four categories of individuals depicted graphically. In case you're still a little unclear about the differences between management and leadership, here is a quote from Lee and Norma Barr (1989: 9): "**Management** affects work; leadership affects people. Management maintains orderly work systems; leadership maintains an enlivening, unfolding, dynamic development of people. They work well together, but they are not the same."

Figure 5.1
Leadership, Management and People

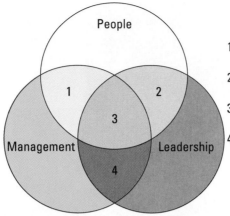

1 = Individuals who manage, but do not lead

2 = Individuals who lead, but do not manage

3 = Individuals who both lead and manage

4 = Individuals who can lead and manage, but have no people to follow them

APPLICATION EXERCISE 5.1

Take Me to Your Leader

Pretend that you are taking me to meet the leader you admire most. How would you describe this leader? What is it about him or her that makes this person your favourite? What does the person do? What does that person say? What emotions does the person elicit? How does your favourite leader get people to do things they otherwise wouldn't do?

Would you be willing to make any generalizations about great leaders based on your individual favourite? If so, what general statements would you be willing to make? Jot down your answers on a piece of paper and share them with others in the class. Are there any personal leadership qualities commonly identified in the favourites selected by your classmates? If so, what are they? Why are these qualities important?

> Leadership is the process of influencing people to give their energies, use their potential, release their determination, and go beyond their comfort zones to accomplish goals. Leadership is a dynamic process. It affects, risks, drives, inspires, threatens, supports, and leads. Leadership draws trust, acknowledgment, risk, and loyalty from the led.
>
> Lee and Norma Barr

THE BEST AND WORST LEADERS
A leader is best
When people barely know he exists,
Not so good when people obey and acclaim him,
Worse when they despise him.
But of a good leader, who talks little,
When his work is done, his aim fulfilled,
They will say:
We did it ourselves.

Lao-Tzu

GETTING THE JOB DONE
The Story of Everybody, Somebody, Anybody and Nobody

There was an important job to be done.
EVERYBODY was asked to do it.
EVERYBODY was sure that SOMEBODY would do it.
ANYBODY could have done it, but NOBODY did it.
SOMEBODY got angry about that because it was EVERYBODY'S job.
EVERYBODY thought that ANYBODY could do it, but NOBODY realized that
EVERYBODY wouldn't do it.
It ended up that EVERYBODY blamed SOMEBODY when NOBODY did what
ANYBODY could have done.

Anonymous

Now, before examining the leadership of people more closely, let us briefly look at some managerial functions for purposes of contrast and comparison. One function of management is **planning**. This could be short or long term. The manager involved with short-term planning decides what needs to be done, where it will be done, who will assume responsibility for doing it, the time frame within which the work will be done, how required tasks will be performed, and which resources will be needed to complete them. Long-term planning requires managers to ask questions about the general direction to be taken by the organization, future needs, resource development and financial matters (Barr & Barr, 1989).

Managers are also charged with the responsibility of **organizing**. They must provide structures within which to

If a person wants to lead somebody, he must first lead himself.

Anonymous

implement their plans. They may have to list priorities, establish procedures, and set performance guidelines.

Once matters are planned and organized, managers perform their next duty through **implementation**. They may have to delegate tasks, assign necessary responsibilities, and convey practical instructions to get plans moving in the right direction. Implementation requires managers to function as consultants and guides (Barr and Barr, 1989).

Of course managers must continually **communicate** while performing their functions. Information must be transmitted and ideas must be exchanged. By means of communication, managers "assign work, correct performance, negotiate differences, present ideas and confront non-productive behaviour." (ibid.: 8).

Managers also **control** and **evaluate**. They must ensure that goals and plans are achieved and that quality is maintained. When goals are not being met or when substandard performance is at issue, then managers must take corrective action.

On the subject of management proper, Lee and Norma Barr (1989: 8) make a second interesting distinction between **managerial functions** and **managerial skills**. They say: "Managerial functions [like those discussed] are inherent in the work; managerial skills are within the person." For them, excellence in managerial functioning is not enough in today's world. While getting things done efficiently is important and desirable, it is no longer enough if one is to gain the competitive edge or to achieve the highest quality in performance or product. Renewed emphasis must be placed on people skills and human resource development. All the plans, organizational structures, standards and performance appraisals in the world will not work if the human side of leadership is ignored. The efficient manager must therefore master human relations skills to be an effective leader.

 ## APPROACHES TO LEADERSHIP

> From the moment of their birth, some are marked for subjugation and others for command.
>
> Aristotle

> Leadership is the ability to decide what is to be done, and then to get others to want to do it.
>
> Dwight D. Eisenhower

As someone preparing to assume a leadership role in society, you may at this point in your life be somewhat uncertain about the best way to go about performing your anticipated function. While learning by trial and error can provide you with much valuable experience, you should rest assured that there's no need to repeat others' mistakes or to "reinvent the wheel," so to speak. For decades now, extensive research on leadership has been conducted and valuable insights have been fashioned into various models of leadership. It is helpful and time saving to review some of the major models here. By examining different conceptions of leadership, you'll be able to extract what's personally useful as you begin to develop your own approach.

Trait Leadership Theory

Historically, many efforts have been made to identify personal characteristics that make someone an effective leader. The practical benefits of such efforts are clear. If you can find the common traits of successful leaders, then you can select individuals who would do a good job functioning in leadership roles.

According to **trait leadership theory**, leaders are born, not made. They possess certain distinctive physical and psychological characteristics that contribute largely to their leadership effectiveness. Traits such as persuasiveness, self-reliance, appearance and dominance have been analysed and considered important to leadership.

Unfortunately, after decades of effort and hundreds of trait studies, findings about the importance of traits to leadership remain inconclusive (Lussier, 1990). Nobody has been able to arrive at a universal list of traits that all effective leaders possess. While "height" was once singled out as an identifiable trait of leaders, it has been noted that Napoleon was short. Add the more recent leadership of Ross Perot (1993 U.S. presidential candidate)—a diminutive man—and you can see that height does not prevent short people from becoming successful leaders. Furthermore, when lists of leadership traits were compiled, it was found that many people who possessed all of them were not necessarily successful in leadership roles (Lussier, 1990). The importance of traits also became suspect when people were found to be successful in one leadership position, but not in another. This suggested that something other than traits was influencing leadership effectiveness.

In 1971, Edwin Ghiselli published his results from a study of more than 300 managers from 90 different businesses. He concluded that there are

Source: Reprinted with permission of King Features Syndicate.

traits that tend to be important to effective leadership, though not all are prerequisites for success. Traits deemed by Ghiselli to be significant are listed below in order of importance.

1. **Supervisory ability**   Effective leaders complete tasks through others. They are able to perform management functions well.

2. **Need for occupational achievement**   Good leaders typically seek responsibility. They are motivated to work hard and succeed.

3. **Intelligence**   Effective leadership usually results from good judgment and from sound reasoning and thinking abilities.

4. **Decisiveness**   Successful leaders display good problem-solving skills and competence in decision making.

5. **Self-assurance**   Effective leadership is associated with self-assurance, i.e., feeling confident that one is able to cope with problems and display self-confidence to others.

6. **Initiative**   Good leaders tend to be self-starters. They work with a minimum of supervision.

> In Aristotelian terms, the good leader must have ethos, pathos and logos. The ethos is his moral character, the source of his ability to persuade. The pathos is his ability to touch feelings, to move people emotionally. The logos is his ability to give solid reasons for an action, to move people intellectually.
>
> Anonymous

Behavioural Leadership: Theory X and Theory Y

In a classic work entitled *The Human Side of Enterprise*, Douglas McGregor (1960) suggested that all managerial decisions and actions are ultimately based on fundamental assumptions about human nature and human behaviour. In other words, managerial leaders operate according to certain psychological principles, beliefs about people, and understandings of what makes human beings tick. Such principles, beliefs and understandings are grouped under the headings **theory X** and **theory Y**. Let's now look briefly at each.

Theory X: The Traditional Autocratic Approach

- People have an inherent or natural dislike of work and will avoid it if they can.

- Because of people's aversion to work, they must be coerced, controlled, directed and threatened; otherwise, they will not put forth sufficient effort to achieve organizational goals.
- People typically prefer to be directed, to avoid responsibility, to show little ambition, and to seek security above all else.

In general terms, a theory X approach to managerial leadership is built upon the assumption of the "mediocrity of the masses" (McGregor, 1960: 34). While managers and leaders may pay lip service to the ideal that all human beings have equal worth and are deserving of respect, those adhering to theory X assumptions actually adopt a **paternalistic attitude** toward subordinates. For them, democratic treatment of individuals often results in permissiveness and inefficiency. Authoritarian control, sometimes disguised as benevolent paternalism and direction, is preferable. People need to be told what to do and how to do it. Add threat to the business of control and the job will get done. According to McGregor, theory X is by no means a defunct managerial philosophy. Though it may sound harsh to those holding contemporary social values, theory X management continues to be practised today.

Theory X could be described as traditional autocratic management. The traditional leader uses rewards, promises, incentives, threats and other coercive devices to achieve organizational and institutional goals. McGregor points out that the "carrot and stick" understanding of human motivation, which underlies theory X, works fairly well when people are struggling to satisfy lower level needs for safety and survival. However, it "...does not work at all once man has reached an adequate subsistence level and is motivated primarily by higher needs." (McGregor, 1960: 41). When people have their basic needs met, leaders are well-advised to adopt a different set of behavioural assumptions—those falling under theory Y.

Theory Y: A Participative Approach

Affluence, as well as an established sense of safety and security in the minds of followers, requires that managerial leaders shift their motivational emphasis to the social and psychological ego needs of those with whom they work. These needs relate to self-esteem, self-respect, autonomy, achievement, knowledge, status, recognition, association, appreciation and self-fulfillment (McGregor, 1960: 38). If managers fail to satisfy these higher-order needs, people will feel deprived and their deprivation will be reflected in diminished personal performance. Organizational goals may not be met; quality may suffer. Under conditions of higher-need deprivation, rewards and punishments, related to survival and physiological needs, are not likely to be effective. The alternative assumptions of theory Y, which would probably be more effective, are listed below:

- Mental and physical work are as natural as play, given favourable conditions.
- People will exercise personal initiative and self-control when there is commitment to organizational or institutional goals.

- Under suitable conditions, people can learn not only to accept, but actually to seek out responsibility.
- The capacity for creative problem solving within organizations is widely—not narrowly— distributed throughout the population.
- Under current conditions of modern life, the potentialities of people are only partially realized. They have much more to offer given the chance.

From our brief overview of theory X and theory Y, we can appreciate how the behavioural and motivational assumptions that leaders make about people affect the ways in which they behave. Theory X and theory Y assumptions give rise to differing attitudes and predispositions toward people. It's not necessary, however, that theory X managers come across as "dictators." They may be very friendly in their paternalism. Also, don't assume theory Y management will always produce the best results. People often fail to live up to their potential (Paul R. Timm and Brent D. Peterson, 1982). In any case, it's probably rare to find somebody who operates strictly by theory X or theory Y assumptions. Most people probably fall somewhere on a continuum between the two (Callahan and Fleenor, 1988).

APPLICATION EXERCISE 5.2

Boss-Behaviour Analysis

Probably by now in your life, you've had at least one part-time job. Maybe you've worked in the retail industry as a salesperson, in the restaurant business as a server, cook or dishwasher, or maybe you've had a temporary seasonal job such as one selling tickets at the Calgary Stampede or the Canadian National Exhibition in Toronto. Regardless of your particular job, if you've worked for someone else, then you've had a boss—or "leader," if you will. Think about that boss now. Did that person operate on theory X or theory Y assumptions about people? Explain and illustrate. Was your boss's leadership style effective? Why or why not?

Three-Factor Theory

Recognizing that most leaders probably operate on principles falling somewhere between theory X and theory Y, Robert Tannenbaum and Warren Schmidt (1973) developed a three-factor leadership continuum model identifying five points between the two extremes of boss-centred leadership (theory X) and subordinate-centred leadership (theory Y). See Figure 5.2.

According to Tannenbaum and Schmidt, a wide range of factors determines whether autocratic leadership, participative leadership or something in between is most effective. These factors are listed next.

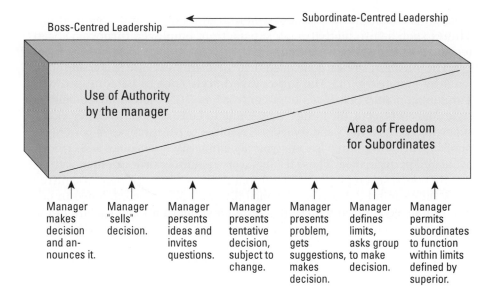

Figure 5.2

A Continuum of
Leadership Tactics

- **Manager factors**   Personal values, levels of security/insecurity, individual leadership tendencies, confidence in subordinates.
- **Subordinate factors**   Need for independence, willingness to take on responsibility and make decisions, tolerance for ambiguity, interest in problem solving, comprehension of and commitment to departmental, institutional/organizational goals, relevant knowledge and experience, as well as expectations.
- **Situation Factors**   Time constraints, group effectiveness, organizational type, and nature of the problem.

As a potential leader, these factors can be useful for you to consider. You can use them to analyse and assess situations to determine which styles of leadership will work best. If something must be done in a hurry, for example, then a directive or autocratic style could be the most appropriate. There may be little or no time for consultation. As we can see, then, time constraints on decision making can be an important factor to consider in determining preferred leadership styles.

The University of Michigan Studies

Job-Centred versus Employee-Centred Styles of Leadership

In the 1940s, the University of Michigan conducted a large-scale research program dealing with problems of administration. Under the direction of Rensis Likert (1961), researchers wanted to discover the principles and methods of managerial leadership that resulted in optimum performance. The research compared styles of leadership with specific performance variables in the best and worst departmental units of several organizations. Things such as productivity, job satisfaction, employee turnover, absenteeism, cost and waste were examined.

The Michigan studies concluded that there are two basic leadership styles used by managers: (1) The **job-centred style** (not to be confused with Tannenbaum and Schmidt's boss-centred) and (2) the **employee-centred style**. Managers using the former were found to be very directive. They closely supervised their workers and sometimes resorted to negative uses of power (e.g., punishment). Job-centred leaders typically emphasized schedules and critically evaluated performance. These leaders were definitely **task-oriented**.

By contrast, employee-centred managers were more person-centred. They didn't mind delegating responsibility and placing confidence in others. Employee-centred managers showed a concern for the welfare of employees, individual needs, advancement and personal growth. While job-centred leaders tended to make assumptions about people falling in line with theory X, employee-centred managers were much more likely to accept theory Y assumptions.

The Michigan studies suggest that employee-centred leadership is preferable to job-centred leadership. Work units headed by employee-centred leaders tend to be more productive than those headed by job-centred leaders. No guarantees are possible, however. One-third of the employee-centred units were low in performance, while one out of eight job-centred units was high in performance. The conclusion we derive from this research is that variables apart from leadership are probably involved in performance.

Situational Leadership

If no one leadership style can guarantee success or optimal performance, then perhaps the effectiveness of any particular style depends on the situation. This is exactly the position taken by Paul Hersey and Kenneth H. Blanchard (1982). For them, effective leadership requires a leader to select the right style that depends on the followers' "**maturity**." Maturity is a technical term that will be explained in a moment. The point is that in the leadership equation, followers cannot be ignored. It is they who either accept or reject the leader. "Regardless of what the leader does, effectiveness depends on the actions of his or her followers. This is an important dimension that has been overlooked or underemphasized in most leadership theories" (Robbins, 1993).

According to Hersey and Blanchard (1982), we can choose appropriate leadership styles in particular situations by first establishing the maturity levels of the individuals and groups who will perform specific tasks and functions. Note that the term "maturity" refers to *task-relevant* maturity. Situational leaders ask: "How mature is the person or group relative to the function, goal or objective assigned?" Maturity takes the following into account:

- **Achievement Motivation**   Ask: Does the individual or group set high, but attainable goals?
- **Responsibility**   Ask: Do the people involved show a willingness to as-

sume responsibility? To what extent are individuals and groups committed to take on specific tasks? (a question of psychological maturity)

- **Ability** Ask: What level of relevant knowledge or skill and ability does this individual or group bring to this particular task? (a question of job maturity)
- **Education and Experience** Ask: Does the individual or group have the education or experience necessary to complete the task?

Maturity is a useful concept. It can help leaders determine the appropriate mixture of **relationship building** and **task directing** when it comes to increasing the probability of effectiveness (Timm and Peterson, 1982). As maturity varies from task to task, and from this individual and group to that individual or group, so too will preferred leadership styles and associated communication patterns. An important objective of leadership in this context is to move people toward ever-increasing levels of maturity—both psychological and job-related.

There are four levels of maturity (M1, M2, M3, M4). Read what follows to learn more about what each displays.

M1 At this low level, individuals or groups are both unable and unwilling to assume responsibility for performing a function. They are neither confident, nor competent.

M2 At this low to moderate level, people are unable but nonetheless willing to do necessary job tasks. They are motivated, but lack necessary skills.

M3 At moderate to high levels of ability and willingness, individuals are able but unwilling to do what the leader requests.

M4 At high levels of maturity, people are both able and willing to do what is asked of them. They are intrinsically motivated.

According to the situational model, there are four basic styles of leadership, i.e., telling, selling, participating and delegating. Appropriate matches should be made between any one style and the maturity of the followers, given the specific task or function to be performed. Brief descriptions follow. While reading, remember that each style differs in terms of supportive and directive behaviour. Also, each has its own predominant communication pattern.

Situational Leadership Styles

1. **Telling (high task/low relationship behaviour)**

   This leadership style is essentially autocratic. People are told what to do, how to do it, when it should be done and where it's supposed to be done. Little relational support is provided. Directive behaviour is emphasized. The major focus is on providing specific instructions and supervising closely.

2. **Selling (high task/high relationship behaviour)**

Leaders using this style display both directive and supportive behaviours. They explain decisions taken and provide opportunities for clarification. While this style involves issuing many instructions and directions, significant support and reassurance are offered.

3. **Participating (low task/high relationship behaviour)**

In this case, leaders provide much support, but show relatively little directive behaviour. Increasing maturity requires less direction. Using this style, leaders share ideas and facilitate decision making.

4. **Delegating (low task/low relationship)**

Leaders who delegate show the least amount of directive and supportive behaviour. Since job maturity and psychological maturity are very high, followers can function independently with minimum supervision. All

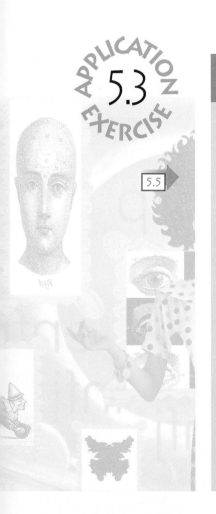

APPLICATION EXERCISE 5.3

5.5

Following the Leader at Camp Athabasca

Task: Given the information and details of the case study provided below, your task is to analyse it using Hersey and Blanchard's model of situational leadership. Determine which leadership strategy is most appropriate. Explain why. This task may be completed individually or in groups.

Mary had been a leader at Camp Athabasca for the past three years. This particular year, and without any notice or job competition being posted, she was surprisingly selected by the owners of the camp to supervise all the other camp leaders. Mary was quite happy about her selection, but others were not. Some felt that they, not Mary, were more deserving of the supervisory position. They resented not having had a chance to apply for Mary's new position. As a consequence, they showed a reluctance to cooperate with her in any way. On top of this, Mary was asked by the owners of the camp to implement a whole new program of games and activities for the children who were about to attend the summer session at the lake. None of the camp leaders was familiar with these new games and activities. They seemed confused when trying to master the skills that they were supposed to teach the children soon to arrive. Necessary equipment and props required to do the new activities and games were constantly not put away, mishandled, and often misplaced.

Question: If you were in Mary's situation, which leadership approach would be best to use in the process of training and supervising your staff? Explain why. What specifically would you do?

that is needed is to make them aware of the tasks and objectives for which they are responsible.

To help us decide on the most appropriate leadership style to use, given the particular situation, Hersey and Blanchard have combined a maturity scale with a leadership matrix that contains four quadrants, labelled according to the four types of leadership just described. (See Figure 5.3.) First determine the maturity of the follower(s) in the situation. Mark this with an "X" on the continuum. Next, draw a vertical line upward from the "X" until it hits the bell-shaped curve. The line will meet the curve in one of the quadrants (either S1, S2, S3 or S4). The quadrant where line and curve meet indicates the most appropriate leadership style to use. If, for example, followers are high in maturity, then "delegating" becomes the style of choice. By contrast, if job and psychological maturity are low, then "telling" should become the predominate communication pattern for leadership behaviour.

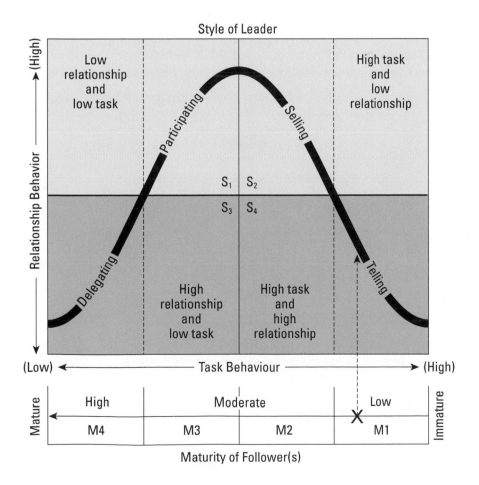

Figure 5.3

Situational Leadership Model

SELF-DIAGNOSTIC 5.1

Assessing Your Leadership Temperament

Background: This instrument will help you to start thinking about your personal leadership style, which is highly influenced by psychological temperament. The notion of **temperament**, as used here, refers to observable patterns of behaviour. It describes differences in people that have been witnessed and recorded by civilizations throughout history. There are four basic temperaments, which include the preferences of all 16 personality types identified by the Myers-Briggs Type Indicator (see Chapter 1). Reducing 16 personality types to four temperaments for purposes of analysing leadership style simplifies matters. This instrument is a practical application based on the writing and research of Sandra Hirsh (1985: 13–16) and incorporates the insights of David Keirsey and Marilyn Bates (1984).

Instructions: Below you will find 11 incomplete statements. Your task is to look at the four possible ways of completing each statement and decide on your preference. Each option *must* be given a numerical value (i.e., 1=1st or most preferred choice, 2=2nd choice, 3=3rd choice, and 4=4th or least preferred choice). Note that no answers are necessarily right or wrong. Please be accurate and honest with your replies. Answer in ways that indicate *your* true preferences, not others' expectations.

1. People occupying formal leadership roles should pay attention to
   ___ a. the immediate practical needs of the organization
   ___ b. the philosophy and systems of the organization
   ___ c. the organization's hierarchy
   ___ d. the future growth needs of the organization

2. As a leader, I am/would be best able to
   ___ a. use my charisma to facilitate participation and group decision making
   ___ b. build conceptual frameworks and develop models
   ___ c. respond immediately and realistically to problems in an open and flexible way
   ___ d. establish rules and policies while at the same time bringing projects to completion

3. As a leader of others, I am inclined to ask questions like
   ___ a. How will this affect people's morale? Who should be informed? What is most important to people?
   ___ b. What's the immediate need? Where is the problem? What are the risks and benefits? How soon can we get started to resolve the matter?
   ___ c. What's involved? Who possesses the power or authority? What's the system? What's the strategy?
   ___ d. What's my responsibility? What's the proper sequence? Why should we change? Can this be justified?

4. My personal belief is that leaders
   ___ a. should run an organization/group/institution to meet current needs
   ___ b. should run an organization using solid and reliable information
   ___ c. should help organizations and institutions to operate according to their missions
   ___ d. must use their followers' talents and potentials to maximize the strength of the group or organization

5. In functioning as a leader of people, I (would) value
   ___ a. cooperative effort and good interpersonal relations
   ___ b. an environment that encourages flexibility and risk taking
   ___ c. ability and intelligence, complexity and principles
   ___ d. caution, care and accuracy

6. At work, I (would) orient to
   ___ a. things that affect current needs
   ___ b. things that meet or don't meet standards
   ___ c. planned change for the future
   ___ d. motivating others to get the best from them

7. What I appreciate in myself as a (potential) leader is
   ___ a. my active nature, cleverness and great sense of timing
   ___ b. my high energy level, the unique contributions I can make, as well as my ability to value others
   ___ c. my sense of responsibility, loyalty and industry
   ___ d. my genius, thinking ability and idea production

8. As a leader, I need others to
   ___ a. respond to me
   ___ b. appreciate me as an individual
   ___ c. recognize my talents and abilities
   ___ d. approve of my efforts

9. I would be irritated at work
   ___ a. if people criticized me and treated me impersonally
   ___ b. by silly mistakes, stupidity, ill logic and unnecessary duplication
   ___ c. by ignored deadlines, rule violations and violations of standard operating procedures
   ___ d. by having limits imposed, being told what to do and having to do things conventionally

10. I irritate others by
    ___ a. lack of follow through, careless haste and ill preparation
    ___ b. my sarcasm, seriousness or by my critical, pessimistic attitudes
    ___ c. hurting their feelings, nitpicking, my scepticism and by taking others for granted

____ d. getting emotional, moralizing, overextending myself and creating dependencies

11. My liabilities as a leader arise from the fact that I
   ____ a. often ignore problems and sweep difficulties under the rug while playing favourites and trying to please
   ____ b. am impatient with human concerns, escalating standards and lack of personal execution after designing something
   ____ c. am impatient about project delays, I make hasty decisions, I am preoccupied with negative outcomes and I believe long and hard work is the way to succeed
   ____ d. am unpredictable, impatient with theoretical abstractions, tactless, and unconcerned with the past or its implications for the future

Scoring: Next to each lettered sentence completion above you indicated your preference for it. Now record those preferences below. Once all statement preferences have been recorded, add up the columns: SP, SJ, NT and NF.

Score Calculation

Styles

	SP	SJ	NT	NF
1. Attention	a. ____	b. ____	c. ____	d. ____
2. Abilities	c. ____	d. ____	b. ____	a. ____
3. Questions asked	b. ____	d. ____	c. ____	a. ____
4. Personal beliefs	a. ____	b. ____	c. ____	d. ____
5. Personal values	b. ____	d. ____	c. ____	a. ____
6. Orientation	a. ____	b. ____	c. ____	d. ____
7. Appreciates in self	a, ____	c. ____	d. ____	b. ____
8. Needs	a. ____	b. ____	c. ____	d. ____
9. Sources of irritation	d. ____	c. ____	b. ____	a ____
10. Irritates others by	a. ____	b. ____	c. ____	d. ____
11. Liabilities as leader	d. ____	c. ____	b. ____	a. ____
Totals	____	____	____	____

Preference Values

Strong Preference	11–17
Moderate Preference	18–26
Low Preference	27–35
Little or No Preference	35–44

Note: A low score means a high preference and a high score means a low preference. Your lowest score reflects your dominant **leadership style**; your second lowest score indicates your back-up style; your third lowest score points to a leadership style you use only occasionally; your highest score points to your least preferred leadership style.

Results Suggest the Following about My Leadership Style

	Dominant Style	Back-up Style	Supportive Style	Least Used Style
Style Score				

Leadership Styles

SP = The Troubleshooter
SJ = The Traditionalist
NT = The Visionary
NF = The Catalyst

Summary Descriptions of Leadership Styles

The Troubleshooter (SP)

As a **troubleshooter,** you see yourself as a negotiator or "fire fighter." When problems arise, you like finding clever solutions for dealing with them. You have a laid-back, flexible style with people. Your sensing orientation makes you realistic and clearly focused on the here and now. You enjoy teamwork and fraternity among your colleagues. Your flexibility contributes to your willingness to take risks.

The Traditionalist (SJ)

As a **traditionalist**, you are a stabilizing force. You enjoy working according to established policies and procedures. You pay close attention to detail and display caution and care in whatever you do. Working hard, showing loyalty and displaying responsibility are important for you. Such actions help you to consolidate your working environment.

The Visionary (NT)

As a **visionary**, you see yourself as the master builder or architect of systems. You love to develop prototypes, conceptual frameworks, models and plans. You place great importance on logic and ingenuity in what you do. You orient yourself toward the future. Your primary focus is on the mission and systems of the organization or institution in which you find yourself.

The Catalyst (NF)

As a **catalyst** of an organization, you address its growth needs. Your personal charismatic nature helps you to energize others into participating and group decision making. Your concern is with morale, people and what they need to know. You believe that effective leadership requires all workers, subordinates and followers to use their talents.

Character is fate.

Heraclitus

It's hard to work in a group when you're omnipotent.

Q, Star Trek: The Next Generation

Leadership by Temperament Style: Keirsey and Bates

The final leadership theory we will cover in this chapter has to do with the notion of temperament. This theory was developed by David Keirsey and Marilyn Bates. According to Keirsey and Bates (1984), temperament is a unifying principle of personality. It provides the overall colouration of someone's character. Temperament "is that which places a signature or thumbprint on each of one's actions, making it recognizably one's own" (1984: 27). Temperament can also be viewed as that which makes actions consistent—a consistency that can be observed from a very early age. While experience gives "content" to living, temperament is the "form" that gives experience its quality and texture.

Keirsey and Bates (1984) maintain that leaders have stable temperaments, as do followers and subordinates. In any situation where you have people leading and following, there will necessarily be an interaction of temperament types. It is important to recognize this idea if effective leadership is to emerge. There is a human dimension to leadership that affects how well a person leads and to what extent people follow. We can become more effective leaders if we learn to work with temperamental differences.

The temperament approach to leadership is based on the assumption that we all are social creatures who wish to please (or displease) those who have authority over us. We cannot be indifferent. We may or may not wish to learn for our professor, win for the coach, or mature as responsible persons for our parents. Even highly independent people who function quite well apart from others desire a thank-you for their efforts. In short, "We all want appreciation, and we want it from the person in charge" (Keirsey and Bates, 1984: 129). People usually want the appreciation expressed to be proportional to their achievement. The greater the achievement, the greater the hunger for appreciation. Thus, if you're a high achiever, you probably have more appetite for appreciation than do low achievers. The importance of appreciation in leadership is nicely summarized by Keirsey and Bates (1984: 130) as follows:

> Since leadership is getting people to do what the leader wants them to because the leader wants them to, and since achievement creates a hunger for appreciation by the leader, then it follows that the primary job of the leader is appreciation. Other tasks the leader may have must be regarded as trivial in comparison to this. The leader has got to learn how to notice achievement and thereupon to thank the follower for his gift.

Source: Reprinted by permission of the Board of Prometheus Nemesis Book Co.

If we are to function as effective leaders, we must become aware of and sensitive to differing temperaments, both our own and those of our charges. If, as leaders, we are not self-conscious with regard to our own tempera-

Student employees are more likely to do a good job if they feel appreciated by their boss.

ments, *we* will be unconsciously predisposed to acknowledge only those things we value and remain oblivious to achievements valued by other temperaments. So even if we try to appreciate others who follow, we could botch things up by unwittingly imposing our own style onto subordinates. We may thank them for doing things they consider irrelevant or trivial.

Your preparatory task as a leader, then, is to learn more about your own temperament to see how it influences your perceptions, judgments and actions. It is also your task to develop an understanding of other temperament types so that you can learn to tailor your efforts to appreciate in ways that fit the values, priorities and preferences of subordinate others. Self-Diagnostic 5.1 allowed you to gain some preliminary insight into your leadership temperament. Let's now look at all temperament types in a little bit more detail.

Keirsey and Bates (1984) have identified four basic temperaments. Each is named after a Greek figure who, in myth, displays a distinctive style and spirit of character. The four are listed below.

- **The Dionysian Temperament** (named after Dionysus, the god of wild nature and wine)
- **The Epimethean Temperament** (named after Epimetheus, who was loyal and long suffering)
- **The Promethean Temperament** (named after Prometheus, the Titan pioneer of civilization)
- **The Apollonian Temperament** (named after Apollo, god of manly beauty, poetry, music and wisdom of oracles)

These temperament types can be superimposed on the Myers-Briggs table of psychological types (see Table 5.1). SP types are Dionysian in temperament, SJs are Epimetheans, NFs are Apollonians and NTs are Prometheans.

The Dionysian Troubleshooter

5.7

Leaders with a **Dionysian temperament** negotiate with great facility. Realists at heart, they love to deal with practical problems and relish occasions when they can unsnarl messes. Troubleshooters display an attitude of sureness and a knack for gaining cooperation from others. Leadership strengths include practicality, adaptability and informed awareness. Rather than fight the system, troubleshooters use it to solve problems. The Dionysian temperament contributes to the leaders' ability to respond easily to others, if presented ideas are concrete. Their flexibility and patience makes them easy to get along with. The Dionysian leader will often encourage risk taking, not bothered much by the possibility of failure. Dionysians try not to judge others, but rather accept their behaviour as matters of fact. Approval and appreciation are easily and often expressed.

Table 5.1   Keirsey-Bates Temperaments Superimposed on Myers-Briggs Personality Types

ISTJ EPIMETHEAN	ISFJ EPIMETHEAN	INFJ APOLLONIAN	INTJ PROMETHEAN
ISTP DIONYSIAN	ISFP DIONYSIAN	INFP APOLLONIAN	INTP PROMETHEAN
ESTP DIONYSIAN	ESFP DIONYSIAN	ENFP APOLLONIAN	ENTP PROMETHEAN
ESTJ EPIMETHEAN	ESFJ EPIMETHEAN	ENFJ APOLLONIAN	ENTJ PROMETHEAN

Psychological Type	Temperament Type	Leadership Style
SP	Dionysian	Troubleshooter
SJ	Epimethean	Traditionalist
NT	Promethean	Visionary
NF	Apollonian	Catalyst

On the downside, Dionysians may become impatient with abstract and theoretical ideas. They prefer to avoid the unfamiliar. A present-day orientation may occasionally interfere with past decisions and commitments.

How to Appreciate Dionysian Followers

- Recognize the clever ways in which they do their work. Notice the way something is done, not just what is done. The SP individual is process oriented, not product oriented.
- Provide companionship for celebrating successful results.
- Offer encouragement and support when things don't work out.
- Applaud Dionysian boldness, stamina, cleverness, adaptability and timing.
- Allow freedom for how tasks can be done.
- If possible, try not to let standard operating procedures interfere with the SP individual's preferred ways of doing things.

The Epimethean Traditionalist

5.7

Leaders displaying an **Epimethean temperament** could be called traditionalists as well as stabilizers or consolidators. These "company people" focus on the organization. SJ leaders' abilities are found in establishing policies, procedures, rules, schedules, routines, regulations and hierarchies. They are very capable when forming lines of communication and following through with actions. Loyal to the company, institution or organization in which they work, traditionalist Epimetheans conduct their affairs in an orderly way, and thereby bring stability with them. Epimetheans possess a strong sense of social responsibility. They seek to learn their duties and then get busy doing them. Epimetheans are industrious indeed. Decisiveness is a distinctive strength of SJ leaders. They enjoy the decision-making process. Once decisions are made, they will patiently and steadily work, persevering through any hardships. Thorough in approach, Epimetheans tend to run efficient meetings with well-ordered agendas.

The dark side of the Epimethean temperament reveals possible leadership weaknesses. Decisions may be made too quickly or prematurely. SJs' concern with tradition and stability may cause them to defend outdated and questionable rules and regulations. The traditionalist leader may also not be responsive enough to the changing needs of an organization—especially during times of great transition. SJs also tend to see worst-case scenarios first. They may expend significant energy worrying about things that never happen. When making evaluations, Epimetheans tend toward black-and-white thinking. Unfortunately, evaluations of actions as either good or bad sometimes get transferred onto people. When this occurs, Epimethean traditionalists cause tensions by their blaming and negativity.

How to Appreciate Epimethean Followers

- Since SJs are product oriented, comment on how things produced conform to established standards.

- Reward their responsibility, loyalty and hard work.
- Show an abundance of appreciation, even if pleasure is not shown.
- Pay attention to the caution, carefulness and thoroughness displayed and valued by the Epimethean.

The Promethean Visionary

In contrast to troubleshooters who enjoy putting out fires and traditionalists who like to set up rules and regulations, people who display the **Promethean temperament** need to conceptualize. They are intuitive-thinking visionaries who are designers by nature. They are inspired and energized when asked to build, engineer or serve as conceptual architects. Prometheans pride themselves on their technical knowledge. They enjoy using intellect to sort out complexities, develop models or respond to design challenges. Since visionaries tend to focus on the future, they typically function well as agents of change. Since they perceive things globally, they find it easy to fit parts into total systems. Interworkings of systems are appreciated in terms of their short- and long-term implications.

However, Promethean visionaries also have their weaknesses. Focused on principles, they are often unaware of others' feelings. They often fail to appreciate the joys and hurts of others. As a result, visionaries may present themselves as distant and cold. Others may not feel comfortable in their presence and find it difficult to carry on a casual conversation, which is not good for morale and team building. The intellectual probing nature of visionaries may make them appear as terminal sceptics, hair-splitters of the worst kind. Failure to notice feelings and an inclination to take practical contributions for granted are not things that endear visionaries to others. Troubleshooters and traditionalists should not be ignored or offended by the visionaries. They are needed to execute and implement in practical terms those models and plans envisioned by the Promethean.

How to Appreciate Promethean Followers

- Acknowledge their ideas.
- Present yourself as an intelligent listener.
- Avoid comments of a personal nature; respond by recognizing capabilities.
- Don't offend NTs by complimenting them on routine tasks well done; they may become suspicious.
- Try not to let rules, traditions and standard operating procedures get in the way of maximizing the NT's productivity.
- Comment on good uses of logic, reasoning and principle.

The Apollonian Catalyst

Leaders with an **Apollonian temperament** are very personable. They are "people people." Focusing on the growth needs of organizations, they are capable of drawing out the best in others. What you'll find is that Apollonians can easily become committed to the progress of those around them. NF catalysts are sensitive to possibilities for people, both in terms of career development and personal growth. Catalysts have a way of bringing out latent potentials in those with whom they work.

Interest in, and sensitivity to, people makes catalysts natural democratic leaders who instinctively prefer participatory processes and cooperative ways of doing things. NF leaders are born appreciators, in fact, always searching for the best in others. Catalysts are good listeners and when communicating, typically display verbal fluency. Catalysts have the ability to act as enthusiastic spokespeople for their organizations. They are charismatic, "superbly empathic, and have a flair for dramatizing the mundane events of living into something special" (Keirsey and Bates, 1984: 149). Probably the finest leadership ability possessed by Apollonian catalysts is their talent for turning any liability into an asset. A positive and productive outlook greets any problem or obstacle. For catalysts, problems always offer opportunities.

Negatively speaking, NFs may use up too much of their energy responding to others. Overly generous with their time, they may neglect obligations and necessary regenerating recreational time may be lost. Without time for self-renewal, energies can be drained to the point where catalysts find themselves immobilized and unproductive. Also, when NFs provide empathic sensitivity to opposing groups and individuals, commitments to help both sides may leave them torn apart. NFs may be so in tune with the feelings and emotions of others that they find themselves wanting to please all of the people all of the time—and we know this is impossible. Finally, concern for others and willingness to help may foster "dependency relationships." People may inappropriately lean for support on NFs when more responsible independent action is called for.

How to Appreciate Apollonian Followers

- Express your appreciation of NFs in personal terms. See them as unique individuals making unique contributions.
- Provide constant approval and positive feedback. Negative criticism is likely to discourage and immobilize the NF.
- Encourage personal growth and development. Allow for autonomy and individual expression.
- Try to understand the NF's feelings as well as her ideas.
- Avoid impersonal treatment.

When subjects do not get what they want from their rulers, the rulers cannot get what they seek from their subjects either. What rulers and subjects give each other is motivated by reciprocity, for which subjects will exert themselves to the full and lay down their lives in the interests of their rulers, while rulers will grant honours for the benefit of their subjects.

Lesson from *The Masters of Huainan*

Source: Reprinted by permission of Shambhala Publications, Inc.

In this chapter we've addressed the importance of leadership for mastering human relations. We've contrasted leadership with management and examined more closely the influence of temperament on leadership. With the aid of Self-Diagnostic 5.1, you started to reflect on your own leadership temperament style. An outline of Keirsey and Bates's work has helped you to see how, according to their theoretical model, there are four basic temperament styles in leadership, each having its own distinctive strengths and weaknesses. By now you've learned how to appreciate, according to temperament type, people under your management, authority or control.

If leadership really does depend on appreciating others, as Keirsey and Bates claim, we are now much better prepared to move forward in our lives and assume leadership roles. We know something about our own temperament, what *we* need to feel appreciated, what we tend to appreciate in others, and finally, what *others* need *from us* to feel appreciated. Given that temperaments differ, it's virtually inevitable that conflicts will arise. Certainly, there are many other reasons for conflict, but differing temperaments is surely one. Whatever the cause, a generic skill useful for leaders and non-leaders alike is the ability to handle conflict effectively. Let's look now at the nature of conflict and ways in which it can be resolved. Your efforts to master leadership, certainly for professional purposes, must address the issue of managing people and their differences.

STUDY GUIDE

Key Terms

leadership (164)
management (165)
planning (167)
organizing (167)
implementation (168)
communicate (168)
control (168)
evaluate (168)
managerial functions (168)
managerial skills (168)
trait leadership theory (169)
supervisory ability (170)

need for occupational achievement (170)
intelligence (170)
decisiveness (170)
self-assurance (170)
initiative (170)
behavioural leadership (170)
theory X (170)
theory Y (170)
traditional autocratic approach (170)
paternalistic attitude (171)

three-factor theory (172)
The Michigan Studies (173)
job-centred style (174)
employee-centred style (174)
task-oriented (174)
situational leadership (174)
maturity (174)
achievement motivation (174)
responsibility (174)
ability (175)

education and experience (175)	temperament (178) leadership style (180)	Epimethean temperament (185)
relationship building (175)	troubleshooter (181) traditionalist (181)	Promethean temperament (186)
task directing (175) telling (175)	visionary (181) catalyst (181)	Apollonian temperament (186)
selling (176) participating (176) delegating (176)	Dionysian temperament (184)	

Fill-in-the-Blank Questions

PROGRESS CHECK 5.1 ✔

Instructions: Fill in each blank with the appropriate word from the list below.

maturity	Epimethean
appreciation	planning
trait theory	leadership
Dionysian	theory Y
three-factor theory	Apollonian
work	situational leadership theory
theory X	task-oriented
Promethean	

1. _____ is the ability to cause people to work toward common goals.
2. _____ is what puts a thumbprint on each of our actions, making it recognizably our own.
3. According to Keirsey and Bates, we are all social creatures who need_____.
4. Loyal and persevering workers probably possess a(n) _____ temperament.
5. One function of managers is short- and long-term _____.
6. According to _____, leaders are born, not made.
7. If you think that people essentially dislike work and therefore must be coerced into performing, then you probably buy into the _____ conception of behavioural leadership.
8. _____ takes the position that mental and physical work are as natural as play, given favourable conditions.
9. Tannenbaum and Schmidt's _____ identifies five points between the two extremes of boss-centred and subordinate-centred leadership.
10. Job-centred leaders can be generally described as _____.
11. _____ holds that the effectiveness of any particular leadership style depends on the situation.

12. According to Paul Hersey and Kenneth Blanchard, follower _____ largely determines which leadership style should be used.

13. Leaders who function as realistic troubleshooters possess a(n) _____ temperament.

14. Visionary leaders, who love to conceptualize systems, possess a(n) _____ temperament.

15. People-sensitive leaders, who serve organizations well as catalysts, display a(n) _____ temperament.

True/False Questions

Instructions: Circle the appropriate letter next to each statement.

T F   1. Most people will never become leaders.

T F   2. Leadership is something that comes automatically with managerial authority.

T F   3. Management and leadership are virtually identical.

T F   4. The Promethean temperament reflects the preferences of the NT (intuitive-thinking type).

T F   5. The Dionysian leader is a troubleshooter.

T F   6. Individuals with Apollonian temperaments serve well as catalysts, fostering growth and development for people and organizations.

T F   7. Managers don't have to learn how to communicate well with people because they mostly plan and organize.

T F   8. The idea that tall people should be the preferred leaders in any group or organization is consistent with trait leadership theory.

T F   9. Leadership based on theory X assumptions about people reflects the traditional autocratic approach.

T F   10. Leadership based on theory Y assumptions should be practised when followers' basic needs have not been met.

T F   11. Tannenbaum and Schmidt's three-factor theory identifies several styles of leadership that fall somewhere between theory X and theory Y.

T F   12. The Michigan studies suggest that employee-centred leadership is preferable to job-centred leadership, though no performance guarantees are possible.

T F   13. Hersey and Blanchard's notion of task-relevant "maturity" entails achievement motivation, responsibility, ability, education and experience.

T F   14. Edwin Ghiselli deemed the following traits to be important to leadership: supervisory ability, need for occupational achievement, intelligence, decisiveness and initiative.

T F   15. Theory Y leadership will always work better than a leadership style based on theory X assumptions.

Focus Questions

1. Why is the study of leadership important to the mastery of human relations?
2. How can leadership be defined? How is it related to management?
3. Is there more than one way to lead people? How so?
4. What are some of the behavioural assumptions leaders make about their followers? Which assumptions would *you* make about people?
5. Which leadership theory do you like best? Would your preference be most effective? Explain why.

Summary

1. What is leadership?
   - the ability to influence the actions of others
   - the ability to cause others to work toward common goals within social, institutional or organizational settings
   - a dynamic process
   - it draws trust, acknowledgment, risk and loyalty from followers

2. How does leadership relate to management?
   - they are not equivalent
   - leadership is but one management function
   - leadership can be found outside formal managerial settings
   - someone can lead but not manage

3. What are some management functions?
   - planning: short and long term
   - organizing: listing priorities and establishing procedures and guidelines
   - implementation: delegating tasks and issuing responsibilities
   - communication: transmitting information, exchanging ideas
   - evaluation and control: maintaining quality, achieving goals

4. What are some approaches to leadership?

   Trait Leadership Theory:
   - personal characteristics define an effective leader; leaders are born, not made; important traits include supervisory ability, need for occupational achievement, intelligence, decisiveness, self-assurance, initiative

   Behavioural Leadership (Theory X and Theory Y)
   - leadership/management decisions based on fundamental assumptions about human nature and human behaviour; according to theory X, people dislike work and need to be directed; according to theory Y, work is as natural as play and people will exercise personal initiative and self-control with commitment

   Three-Factor Theory (Tannenbaum and Schmidt)
   - a continuum model identifying five points between two extremes of

boss-centred leadership (theory X) and subordinate-centred leadership (theory Y)

The Michigan Studies: Job-Centred versus Employee-Centred Leadership

- job-centred is very task oriented, directive and uses power, as well as sanctions
- employee-centred is people oriented; there is concern for employees' welfare; there is much delegation; studies suggest employee-centred leadership is better.

Situational Leadership (Paul Hersey and Kenneth Blanchard)

- effective leadership must take into account the "maturity" of the followers, i.e., their achievement motivation, responsibility, ability, education and experience; followers cannot be ignored in the leadership equation; there are four styles of situational leadership: telling, selling, participating and delegating.

Keirsey and Bates Temperament Style Approach

- effective leaders work with temperamental differences; good leaders achieve goals by learning to appreciate the efforts of subordinates; temperaments identified are the Dionysian, Epimethean, Promethean, and Apollonian.

Related Readings

Fiedler, Fred A. (1967). *Theory of Leadership Effectiveness*. New York: McGraw-Hill.

Fitzgerald, Catherine and Linda Kirby, (eds.) (1996). *Developing Leaders: Research and Applications in Psychological Type and Leadership Development*. Palo Alto, CA: Consulting Psychologists Press.

Gordon, Thomas (1975). *P.E.T.: Parent Effectiveness Training*. New York: New American Library.

———— (1980). *The Essentials of Situational Leadership: An Approach for Increasing Managerial Effectiveness*. Escondido, CA: Leadership Studies Productions Inc.

Hirsh, Sandra (1985). *Using the Myers-Briggs Type Indicator in Organizations: A Resource Book*. Palo Alto, CA: Consulting Psychologists Press, Inc.

Keirsey, David (1987). *Portraits of Temperament*, 2nd edition. Del Mar, Ca: Prometheus Nemesis Book Company.

Weblinks

1. American Management Association
   www.tregistry.com/ama.htm.

   The AMA offers courses and conferences on managing change and removing barriers to creative problem solving and decision making.

2. Human Synergistics/Center for Applied Research
   www.hscar.com/us.html

   This site offers for sale diagnostic tools assessing leadership and organizational effectiveness. Materials and programs focus on human resource management, conflict management, ethical decision making, as well as thinking strategies and skills.

3. National Outdoor Leadership School
   www.nols.edu/

   NOLS is a wilderness-based, nonprofit school teaching leadership skills with a strong conservation focus.

4. Achievement Corporation
   www.acorp.co.uk

   Provides high-quality and cost-effective human resource services to businesses and organizations of all sizes. It is dedicated to improving the success of companies and their employees.

People who think they know it all are especially annoying to those of us who do.

—Anonymous

CONFLICT

CHAPTER OVERVIEW

LEARNING OUTCOMES

After successfully completing this chapter, you will be able to

6.1 Provide a definition of conflict

6.2 Outline the various types of conflict

6.3 State the benefits of conflict

6.4 Explain and give three examples of psychological orientations to conflict

6.5 Provide descriptive outlines of five conflict management styles

6.6 Identify your dominant and back-up conflict management styles

6.7 Go through the steps to arrive at win-win conflict resolutions

6.8 Use psychological type insights for purposes of conflict resolution

THE EXPERIENCE OF CONFLICT

Situation One

Sigmund: It's my turn!

Samuel: No, it's *my* turn!

Sigmund: But you went first last time!

Samuel: No, I didn't. *I'm* going first this time!

Situation Two

Husband: I think we should invest our bingo winnings in a new stereo system.

Wife: I think we should use the money to pay down our personal line of credit at the bank which, by the way, is "maxed out."

Husband: No way! This is bonus money to be spent on fun things.

Wife: You can't have fun if you can't afford it.

Someone once said that there are two unavoidable things in life: death and taxes. I'd like to offer a third necessity, namely **conflict.** As we can gather from the situations above, people do not always agree with one another. Talk to any person on the street about what's good or bad, useless or worthwhile, and you'll almost certainly find differences of opinion. At social gatherings, where politics or religion are the issue, disputes can rarely be avoided. Amazingly, even family discussions about next year's vacation destination can sometimes flare up into screaming matches. One person may insist on going to the Rockies, while the other demands to go to the east coast. Our everyday experience would seem to suggest, then, that conflict is something that cannot be escaped in our interactions with others. Conflict is a common occurrence.

In Chapter 3, we looked at a number of psycho-logical defence mechanisms people often employ when conflicts and strong disagreements lead to anxiety and other unpleasant emotions. We learned how people do things such as twist reality, divert attention or intimidate others when involved in disputes or confrontations of egos. In this chapter, what we'll do is look more carefully at the nature of conflict itself. We'll see how theorists have conceptualized conflict, how people adopt different psychological orientations toward it, and how there are different methods and styles of conflict resolution. By understanding such things, we'll be better able to manage conflict and to deal with it in our personal and professional lives, as well as in our informal interactions with friends, relatives and neighbours.

THE NATURE OF CONFLICT

Though commonplace, conflict is not something that permits precise and easy definition. *The New Webster's Encyclopedic Dictionary of the English Language* defines it as "a fighting or struggle for mastery." It is also defined

The Six Men of Indostan

It was six men of Indostan
    To learning much inclined,
Who went to see the elephant
    Though all of them were blind
That each by observation
    Might satisfy his mind.

The first approached the elephant
    And, happening to fall
Against the broad and sturdy side,
    At once began to bawl:
"Why, bless me! But the elephant
    Is very much like a wall!"

The second, feeling of the tusk
    Cried: "Ho! What have we here
So very round and smooth and sharp?
    To me, 'tis very clear,
This wonder of an elephant
    Is very like a spear!"

The third approached the animal,
    And, happening to take
The squirming trunk within his hands
    Thus boldly up he spake:
"I see," quoth he, "the elephant
    Is very like a snake!"

The fourth reached out his eager hand
    And felt about the knee:
"What most this wondrous beast is like
    Is very plain," quoth he:
"'Tis clear enough the elephant
    Is very like a tree!"

The fifth who chanced to touch the ear
    Said: "E'en the blindest man
Can tell what this resembles most—
    Deny the fact who can:
This marvel of an elephant
    Is very like a fan!"

The sixth no sooner had begun
    About the beast to grope
Than, seizing on the swinging tail
    That fell within his scope,
"I see," quoth he, "the elephant
    Is very like a rope!"

And so these men of Indostan
    Disputed loud and long,
Each in his own opinion
    Exceeding stiff and strong,
Though each was partly in the right,
    And all were in the wrong.

John G. Saxe

Figure 6.1
The Six Men of
Indostan

Source: Saxe, John G. from *The Hokusai Sketchbooks* by James A. Michener. Charles E. Tuttle, Publisher. Copyright James A. Michener.

> *Conflict is the gadfly of thought. It stirs us to observation and memory. It instigates to invention. It shocks us out of sheeplike passivity, and sets us at noting and contriving.*
>
> John Dewey

as "combat, a striving to oppose or overcome; active opposition; contention; strife." As a verb, to conflict means "to meet in opposition or hostility; to contend; to strive or struggle; to be in opposition; to be contrary; to be incompatible or at variance." From this definition, we get the general idea that conflict somehow involves opposing forces and differing objectives. Let us now explore in a bit more detail what this variance, opposition and struggle is all about.

TYPES OF CONFLICT

Psychological

Perhaps the best place to start our explorations is with the individual. Some conflict that occurs in life happens internally. We call this **psychological conflict**. This type of conflict could be going on within you right now with nobody else around even noticing. For example, you may be having erotic fantasies about someone in the class, but be experiencing guilt because such fantasies violate your religious values and beliefs. In this case, your biological sexual instincts may be at odds with your moral standards. This kind of psycho-sexual conflict is captured nicely in the New Testament of the Christian Bible. In St. Paul's letter to the Galatians 5:16 in the *Good News Bible*, it is written, "For what our human nature wants is opposed to what the spirit wants, and what the spirit wants is opposed to what our human nature wants. These two are enemies, and this means you cannot do what you want to do." To express the same Christian insight in Freudian psychoanalytic terms, the "id is in conflict with the superego" (see Chapter 3). For Freud, life itself is a continuing saga of conflict. The conscious rational ego must balance the opposing parts of the psyche and reconcile primitive biological urges with the demands presented by civilized society. According to Freud, our personalities are always in conflict to some degree.

> *No conflict is so severe as his who labours to subdue himself.*
>
> Thomas à Kempis
>
> *I am never upset for the reason I think.*
>
> A Course in Miracles

Social

As you can no doubt readily appreciate, some conflictual experience in life occurs between or among people, not strictly within them. You and your siblings may, for example, be strong rivals, always fighting over things like who gets the telephone next or who gets the bigger bedroom in the new house. This *me against you* type of conflict involving two different individuals can be described as **interpersonal**.

> My idea of an agreeable person is a person who agrees with me.
>
> Benjamin Disraeli

Sometimes the conflicts we face are not me against you, but rather *us against them*. This type of social or interpersonal conflict entails intergroup struggles and disputes. Land developers may be at odds with residence groups, or business associations may be at war with community planners about proposed changes to the downtown core of a city.

Still another variation of social conflict is *me or you versus them*. In this case, there's an individual opposing a group of some sort. Let's say that you're doing a group project. Everyone, but you, is willing to do the least possible work to complete only the minimal requirements of an assignment. For them, grades don't matter. On the other hand, grades do matter to you and you want to do the best possible job by exceeding the instructor's expectations. In this situation, different wants create the oppositional forces.

Sometimes, all group members agree on their wants and goals, but they still cannot agree on how best to achieve them. Let's say that as a member of the student union, you and some members of your governing council wish to affect change at your school immediately; others belonging to the union desire the same change, but wish to proceed more slowly. Your faction is militant and extreme, while the other faction within the group is more moderate. In other words, you all want the same thing, but differ on strategies to get it. This type of opposition can be described as **intragroup conflict**. See it as the social equivalent of **intrapsychic conflict**, where the disequilibrium is all inside.

Approach-Avoidance

Whether conflict is social or psychological in nature, some people have found it useful to think of it in terms of desirable and undesirable characteristics or **approach-avoidance** features. In this light, conflict can be described as approach-approach, avoidance-avoidance or approach-avoidance. See Figure 6.2 for an illustration.

Let's consider **approach-approach conflict** first. Suppose you want to go out on a date with a special somebody, for example, but you also want to go skiing with other friends at the same time. We'll assume that taking your date skiing is not possible. In this case, two desirable things are wanted, but only one option can be chosen.

When we face two equally unattractive alternatives, we face **avoidance-avoidance conflict**. You may not wish to study for an exam or mow your lawn. Nonetheless, you are asked by your parents to do one or the other (some choice, eh!), or you won't be allowed to use the family car.

A third kind is **approach-avoidance conflict**, which you may experience, for example, if you wish to change college or university programs because of

Figure 6.2

Types of Conflict

Approach — Approach
"I want this" but "I also want that"

Avoidance — Avoidance
"I don't want this" and "I don't want that"

Approach — Avoidance
"I want this" but "I don't want what this entails"

what you've heard about another; the problem is that you're insecure about setting off on a whole new course (no pun intended). Obviously, there are attractive and unattractive aspects to either choice. If you stay put, you will continue to be dissatisfied, though confident. If you move on, you'll be energized and enthusiastic, though insecure. In some respects, "you're damned if you do and damned if you don't." If you're at all worried about how others may react to your conflict-related decisions, you may wish to take comfort in the anonymous poem that I've entitled "Conflict Resolutions for Life."

Functional versus Dysfunctional Conflict

Because conflict is often associated with disruptions and unpleasant feelings, many people try to avoid it as much as possible. Common experience tells us that conflict can frequently be counterproductive. This kind of **dysfunctional conflict** hinders group performance and upsets personal psychological functioning. If you're "torn apart" inside by conflict, you may not be able to concentrate on your studies or do your job at work. If there is great animosity between individuals in an organizational department, differences between them may become irreconcilable. Productive teamwork and cooperative efforts may become next to impossible to achieve.

By contrast, writers and researchers have noted that there also exists **functional conflict** (Robbins, 1993). Some companies, such as IBM, see such conflict from an **interactionist perspective**. At IBM, conflict is encouraged, "...on the grounds that a harmonious, peaceful, tranquil, and cooperative group is prone to becoming static, apathetic, and nonresponsive to the needs for innovation" (ibid.: 446). From this view, a small and optimum level of conflict can

> If, in an organization, two people always agree with one another, then one of them should be let go!
>
> Tonee Balonee

Conflict Resolutions for Life

People are unreasonable, illogical and self-centred.
Love them anyway.
If you do good, people may accuse you of selfish motives.
Do good anyway.
If you are successful, you may win false friends and true enemies.
Succeed anyway.
The good you do today may be forgotten tomorrow.
Do good anyway.
Honesty and transparency make you vulnerable.
Be honest and transparent anyway.
What you spend years building may be destroyed overnight.
Build anyway.
People who really want help may attack you if you help them.
Help them anyway.
Give the world the best you have and you may get hurt.
Give the world your best anyway.
The world is full of conflict.
Choose peace of mind anyway.

Anonymous

help to keep groups viable, self-critical and creative. To determine whether a (social) conflict is functional or dysfunctional, it is helpful to look at group performance. If the conflict serves to achieve group objectives in the end, then it is functional. If it gets in the way and undermines group performance, then it is dysfunctional.

 ## BENEFITS OF CONFLICT

> What sort of thing would life really be with your qualities ready for a tussle with it, if it only brought fair weather and gave those higher faculties of yours no scope?
>
> William James
>
> The gem cannot be polished without friction—nor a man without trials.
>
> Chinese Proverb

By making a distinction between functional and dysfunctional conflict, the idea is captured that not all conflict is necessarily bad. Optimistically speaking, conflict needn't be destructive at all in some cases. When handled properly, it can be an occasion for growth and development. Conflict, like argument, should be seen as an opportunity, not an obstacle. On this note, David Johnson (1990: 216-217) has listed the benefits of conflict, when skilfully managed. They are paraphrased in what follows.

1. Conflicts enable us to become aware of problems within relationships.

2. Conflicts serve as a catalyst for positive change. Maybe we need to experiment and do things a little differently (for our good and the good of others).

3. Conflicts are energizing and can motivate us to deal with immediate problems.

4. Conflicts add spice to life. They stimulate interest and curiosity.

5. Conflicts can be cathartic. A good argument may relieve minor tensions associated with interacting with other people. (Isn't it enjoyable to make up after a good "fight"?)

6. Conflicts can cause decisions to be made more carefully and thoughtfully.

7. Conflicts promote self-knowledge. For example, they heighten aware-

ness concerning what angers us, what frightens us and what is important to us.

8. Conflicts are potentially energizing and fun, if not taken too seriously. Competitive games and sports can be enjoyable when conflict is involved.

9. Conflicts can improve relationships in the long term. People learn that relationships can hold up under stress. Conflicts can clear the air of unexpressed resentments.

I don't have a warm personal enemy left. They've all died off. I miss them terribly because they helped define me.

Claire Booth Luce

He that wrestles with us strengthens our nerves, and sharpens our skill. Our antagonist is our helper.

Burke (1729–1797)

PSYCHOLOGICAL ORIENTATIONS TO CONFLICT

 6.4

Whether or not people see value in conflict will largely depend on their psychological orientations toward it. Clayton Lafferty and Ronald Phillips (1990) at Human Synergistics in Plymouth, Michigan, have identified 12 individual styles of approaching conflict, which they group into three basic orientations. Before we examine each one in turn, however, let us first spell out what is meant by the notion of **orientation** itself.

For our purposes here, it will be helpful to conceptualize a **conflict orientation** as something psychological. When faced with conflict, we all display certain **predispositions**. Some of us are inclined to approach people with whom we disagree, while others are more inclined to withdraw or attack those who choose to dispute with us. The notion of psychological orientation also involves one's **beliefs** and **perceptions**. There are those who see opportunity and challenge in conflict, whereas others believe that it is something essentially destructive and undesirable. Furthermore, when faced with conflict, some of us wish to resolve differences and get on with things. By contrast, others apparently have a real need to win or come out on top. In other words, people have different **motivations** in their dealings with conflict. **Intentions** vary as do corresponding **behaviours**. A psychological orientation to conflict can be defined, then, by our perceptions, motivations and predispositions, as well as by our beliefs and intentions.

Figure 6.3

Psychological
Orientations to Conflict

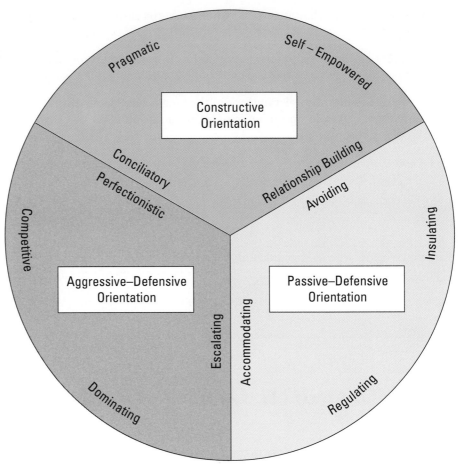

It's worth noting at this point that no one's psychological orientation to conflict is carved in stone. It is possible to change from one orientation to another. For example, if you've fallen into some bad habits where conflict is concerned—say, stomping away in anger—you can learn new behavioural patterns and effect necessary attitude adjustments to more productively handle conflictual situations in the future.

Constructive Orientation to Conflict

Since we've already had a chance to consider the potential benefits of conflict and because we're on the topic of handling conflict productively, perhaps it's best to start with the constructive orientation to conflict resolution. From this vantage point, conflict is regarded as something normal and commonplace. It is viewed as useful for achieving longer-term interests. People with a constructive orientation are **realistic**, using their analytical abilities to clarify and discuss issues. The **pragmatic approach** adopted means that feelings are expressed in honest and direct ways. The pragmatism also means that those adopting this orientation dissociate their self-worth from any results arising from the dispute. Not getting one's own way is not a blow to self-esteem or a slight against one's ego.

Another important characteristic about people choosing a constructive orientation is that they are **self-empowered**. This means they are "**internally centred**," so to speak. They recognize that their power comes from inside themselves and not from associations with others, wealth or expertise. Self-empowered individuals respect their opponents in conflictual situations, refusing to become hostile and defensive toward them. They tend to address differences with sensitivity and patience.

Constructively oriented people are **conciliatory**. They assume that people are basically well-intentioned and that they prefer to work through differences in a **fair** and **reasonable** fashion. Instead of being offended by caustic behaviour, these individuals look for the underlying needs and desires motivating it. An insult, for instance, would not be taken at face value, but appreciated in terms of what's going on inside the person who issued it. By standing back from the unpleasantness often associated with conflict, constructive people maintain an **objective perspective**. They make efforts to diffuse passions and facilitate negotiations by refusing to be diverted by irrelevant side issues. Finally, constructively oriented people place great value on loyalty to the relationship. For them, few issues are important enough to break the bonds of a friendship.

Passive-Defensive Orientation to Conflict

A less than constructive psychological approach to conflict is the **passive-defensive orientation**. Rather than seeing conflict as normal and possibility-generating, people with this orientation view conflict as threatening. They avoid getting involved and make efforts to "calm troubled waters." The belief is held that conflict is unnecessary and destructive.

People with a passive-defensive orientation are **accommodating**. With an aim to maintain a climate of perpetual harmony, they have a tendency to passively acquiesce and do what others expect. They are upset by conflict and believe that little good comes from it. For accommodating individuals, self-worth is measured by others' acceptance and approval.

Passive-defensive individuals try to **insulate** themselves from controversies and disputes. Conflict is regarded as a power struggle in which they are powerless to defend their own interests. Insulating persons often feel frightened and helpless and, as a result, try to remain unnoticed and inconsequential. Passive-defensive people are always "hiding out," so to speak. This fact points to the notion that passive-defensives are **avoiders**, frequently withdrawing from conflict or denying that it exists. Since conflict is seen as unnecessary and destructive, they flee from it whenever possible. Others are allowed to handle disputes. The passive-defender **regulates** things by staying in the background, trying to shame antagonists into more cooperative

Individuals with a constructive conflict orientation work together to resolve differences.

behaviour. Seldom, then, will you find passive-defensive individuals balking at authority. Instead, you're more likely to find them behaving as loyal, law-abiding employees or citizens, seeking out dependent relationships with those more powerful than they are.

To increase the probability of constructive conflict outcomes, passive-defensive individuals need to do the following:

- Recognize that conflicts can be useful
- State their interests clearly and forcefully
- Stand up for themselves and for what's important
- Recognize that power can be given away
- Stop believing that others will necessarily protect their interests
- Accept that conflict does indeed exist, if others say it does

Aggressive-Defensive Orientation to Conflict

In stark contrast to the passive-defensive orientation that minimizes conflict, the **aggressive-defensive orientation** intensifies or **escalates** it. Aggressive-defensive individuals believe that competence—particularly intellectual prowess—is the key to their acceptance by others. We see in escalators a desire to **aggrandize** themselves at their opponent's expense. The primary strategy here is to camouflage their own inadequacies by highlighting those of others. You can tell when you're around escalating, aggressive-defensive types, for they tend to create a highly adversarial climate of attack and counterattack.

Another variation of this orientation is found in the **dominator**. Dominators seek the high ground of **power** and **authority**. They attempt to dictate the terms of their relationships. High-level dominators take every opportunity to attack the power of opponents either directly or by indirect means. Dominating aggressive types live by the ethic "Might makes Right," using **force** to manipulate others.

From the vantage point of the aggressive-defensive orientation, conflict is about **competition**. Conflict becomes a context in which people either gain or lose status. When involved in any conflictual situation, the primary motivation is to gain recognition and the admiration of others. Winning is important for it is associated with self-worth. According to the competitive aggressive-defensive type, there is no such thing as a win/win solution.

Finally, some individuals express their aggressive-defensive orientation through **perfectionism**. They set unrealistic standards and demand the impossible from others. No outcome is ever accepted as good enough, while the belief is held that an ideal solution to conflict is indeed possible. By explicitly or implicitly communicating that others have failed or fallen short, a position of (dishonest) superiority can be maintained. Because perfectionistic

> *Whoever is dissatisfied with himself is continually ready for revenge.*
>
> Friedrich Nietzsche

Some athletes break the rules of the game in competitive struggles.

individuals make unrealistic demands on themselves too, they never feel good enough and, hence, suffer from low self-esteem. In their minds, it is better to have others feel inadequate than to feel inadequate oneself.

Things aggressive-defensive people can do to achieve more constructive resolutions to conflict include the following:

- Don't confuse force with power. "...[T]he more force used to assert your interests, the less power you have to sustain them."
- Separate your personal worth from the outcome of a conflict.
- Apply standards of fair conduct
- Explore differences rather than force win/lose settlements.
- Be willing to accept less than perfect solutions.
- Respect the interests of others.
- Learn to accept feelings as facts.

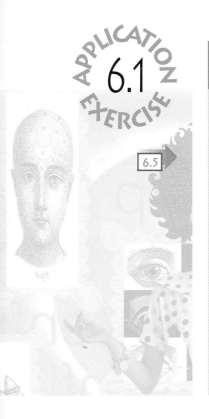

APPLICATION EXERCISE

6.1

6.5

My Personal Experience of Conflict

Your task in this exercise is to bring to mind a memorable conflict that you've experienced sometime in your life. This is a conflict you're willing to comment on and share with others in the class. (You needn't get too personal or too detailed!) Answer the following questions:

1. What was the conflict about?
2. How did you feel? What were your thoughts? What did you do? How did you act?
3. What type of conflict were you involved in? Was it functional or dysfunctional, psychological or interpersonal, approach-avoidance or something else?
4. Were there any benefits arising from the conflict? If so, explain. Was the conflict destructive? Why?
5. What sort of psychological orientation did you assume in the conflictual situation? If others were involved, what attitudinal stance did they adopt? How did these orientations facilitate or hinder conflict resolution?

 6.6

CONFLICT MANAGEMENT STYLES

In view of the fact that people display different psychological orientations to conflict and differing behavioural tendencies either to approach, attack or withdraw from others who are involved, it is perhaps not surprising that different conflict management styles have been identified. (see Lafferty and Phillips, 1990; David Johnson, 1984; Stephen Robbins, 1993; and M.A. Rahim,

1983.) To identify your own personal conflict management style, do Self-Diagnostic 6.1.

Self-Diagnostic 6.1 has helped you to begin identifying your dominant and back-up **conflict management styles**. Here, we'll look at each of your preferred styles as well as others to promote further self-understanding. We'll exam-

> *Wise people seek solutions;*
> *The ignorant only cast blame.*
>
> Lao Tzu

> *If we could read the secret history of our "enemies" we should find in each man and woman's life sorrow enough to disarm all hostility.*
>
> Henry Wadsworth Longfellow

What's My Conflict Management Style?

SELF-DIAGNOSTIC 6.1

6.6

Instructions: Listed below are 15 statements. Each statement provides a possible strategy for dealing with conflict. Give each statement a numerical value (i.e., 1=Always, 2=Very often, 3=Sometimes, 4=Not very often, 5=Rarely, if ever) depending on how often you rely on it. Don't answer as you think you should; answer as you actually behave.

_____ a. I argue my case with peers, colleagues and coworkers to demonstrate the merits of the position I take.

_____ b. I try to reach compromises through negotiation.

_____ c. I attempt to meet the expectations of others.

_____ d. I seek to investigate issues with others in order to find solutions that are mutually acceptable.

_____ e. I am firm in resolve when it comes to defending my side of an issue.

_____ f. I try to avoid being singled out, keeping conflict with others to myself.

_____ g. I uphold my solutions to problems.

_____ h. I compromise in order to reach solutions.

_____ i. I trade important information with others so that problems can be solved together.

_____ j. I avoid discussing my differences with others.

_____ k. I try to accommodate the wishes of my peers and colleagues.

_____ l. I seek to bring everyone's concerns out into the open in order to resolve disputes in the best possible way.

_____ m. I put forward middle positions in efforts to break deadlocks.

_____ n. I accept the recommendations of colleagues, peers and coworkers.

_____ o. I avoid hard feelings by keeping my disagreements with others to myself.

Scoring: The 15 statements you just read are listed below under five categories. Each category contains the letters of three statements. Record the number you placed next to each lettered statement. Calculate the total under each category.

				TOTALS
Forcing Shark	a. ____	e. ____	g. ____	____
Collaborating Owl	d. ____	i. ____	l. ____	____
Avoiding Turtle	f. ____	j. ____	o. ____	____
Accommodating Teddy Bear	c. ____	k. ____	n. ____	____
Compromising Fox	b. ____	h. ____	m. ____	____

Results: My dominant style is _____ (lowest score) and my back-up style is _____ (Second lowest score).

Interpretation of Results: Read the section of the text entitled "The Conflict-Management Menagerie," on p. 212–14.

Source: Based on the work of David Johnson (1984), Stephen Robbins (1993) and M.A. Rahim (1983).

ine the basic features of each style, the ego states energized by each style, the types of situations created by the different conflict resolution approaches, the advantages and disadvantages of each style, and suggestions about when each style could best be used. (If you wish, refer back to Chapter 4 to refresh your memory with regard to psychological ego states.)

Writers and researchers in the field of human relations have identified at least five different conflict management styles (Lussier, 1990; Johnson, 1990):

1. Forcing (or competing)

2. Avoiding (or withdrawing)

3. Accommodating (or smoothing)

4. Compromising

5. Collaborating (or problem confronting)

Each of these styles takes into account the two major concerns people have when they get into conflict: **goals** and **relationships**. When you experience interpersonal conflict, you typically have a goal that is at odds with another person's goal. Your goal may or may not be highly important to you. As well, when you are in conflict, you're usually required to take into account relationship considerations. Either the relationship in the conflict situation is, or is not, important to you. Looking at the importance of goals in light of the importance of relationships allows us to identify the five conflict management styles listed. Johnson (1990) has associated, in a playful and creative way, different animals with each one. (No offence to the animals intended!) See Figure 6.4.

According to Johnson, the particular conflict strategy you should use in any given situation depends on how important goals and relationships are to you. For him, each conflict management style has its proper place. It's probably not well-advised to behave in the same fashion in every conflict you encounter. Johnson says, "To be truly skilled in conflict management, you need to be competent in all five strategies and be able to vary your behaviour according to the person and the situation. You do not want to be an over-specialized dinosaur who can deal with conflict in only one way" (1990: 248). An important point to note here is that you have choice. Conflict resolution styles are not inborn or innate, but learned. If you have learned only one and rely too heavily on it, it's probably best that you familiarize yourself with the others and practise them when appropriate. Although Self-Diagnostic 6.1 has helped you to identify your two most preferred styles, nothing prevents you from using others.

Figure 6.4
A Menagerie of Conflict Management Styles

Source: Johnson, David, *Reaching Out.* Copyright 1990 by Allyn and Bacon. Reprinted by permission.

The Conflict Management Menagerie

The Competing Shark

Sharks use a **forcing** (or **competing**) conflict management style. They are highly goal-oriented people where conflicts are concerned. Relationships take on a much lower priority for them. Sharks do not hesitate to use aggressive behaviour in order to resolve conflicts. They try to achieve their goals at all costs. Unconcerned with the feelings and needs of others, they are uncooperative, autocratic or authoritarian. They can also be very threatening and intimidating. They seek to force resolutions onto problems. Sharks have a need to win and for them this means that others must lose; in other words, Sharks create win-lose situations in their dealings with conflict. They do so by employing the Critical Parent and Adapted Child ego states. This is where the aggression comes from, as well as the need to satisfy their own wants at the expense of others, if required (Lussier, 1990).

One advantage of this conflict style is that better decisions can be made (assuming the Shark is right) as compared with less effective compromised decisions. A deterrent to using this style is that it may breed resentment and hostility toward the person (leader) using it. The forcing style is appropriate to use when

- The conflict involves personal differences that are difficult to change.
- Fostering intimate or supportive relationships is not critical.
- Others are likely to take advantage of noncompetitive behaviour.
- Conflict resolution is urgent, in emergency situations, or when decisive action is vital.
- Unpopular decisions need to be implemented.

The Avoiding Turtle

Turtles adopt an **avoiding** (or **withdrawing**) conflict management style. They try to ignore conflicts rather than resolve them. Metaphorically speaking, they withdraw into their shells. Turtles' need to avoid or delay confrontation usually leaves them uncooperative and unassertive. Since they stay away from contentious issues, they give up their personal goals and relationships; they do this while displaying the passive behaviour of the Adapted Child or Nurturing Parent ego state. By leaving conflicts alone, they create lose-lose situations.

One advantage of Turtle avoidance is that it may help to maintain relationships that would be hurt by efforts at conflict resolution (Lussier, 1990). On the downside, conflicts remain unresolved. Furthermore, Turtles overusing this style may find that people are walking all over them. Leaders who don't face the fact that subordinates are breaking the rules must live with the consequences of their inaction. Turtle avoidance can appropriately be used when

- The personal stakes are not high or the issue is trivial.
- Confrontation will hurt a working relationship.
- There's little chance of satisfying your wants.
- Disruption outweighs the benefits of conflict resolution.

- Gathering information is more important than an immediate decision.
- Others can more effectively resolve the conflict.
- Time constraints demand a delay.

The Accommodating Teddy Bear

Teddy Bears use an **accommodating** (or **smoothing**) conflict management style. They place a great deal of importance on human relationships. However, their own goals are of little importance. The Teddy Bear tries to resolve conflicts by giving in to others. Anyone using this style of conflict resolution operates passively in the Adapted Child or the Nurturing Parent ego state. The general approach is unassertive and cooperative. The result of this approach is a win-lose situation. The Teddy Bear loses, but the other party involved in the conflict wins.

As with the other conflict management styles already discussed, there are advantages and disadvantages associated with this one. On the upside, accommodating helps to maintain relationships. On the downside, giving in to another in conflict may not be productive. The Teddy Bear may need a better solution. Overreliance on accommodation may lead others to take advantage of Teddy Bears, which is certainly not in their personal best interest.

Lussier (1990) and Thomas (1977) offer us suggestions as to when accommodating is the best conflict style to use.

- When maintaining a relationship far outweighs the importance of all other considerations.
- When suggestions and changes are not important to the accommodator.
- When trying to minimize losses in situations where you are outmatched and losing.
- When time is limited.
- When harmony and stability are valued.

The Compromising Fox

Foxes use a **compromising** conflict management style because they are concerned with both goals and relationships. They try to resolve interpersonal conflicts through concessions. They are willing to forfeit some of their goals while persuading the other person in conflict to give up part of his. Conflicts are resolved by both sides getting something. Foxes will accept sacrifice in order to achieve agreement.

This process of compromise elicits both assertive and cooperative Adult ego-state behaviours. Win-lose or lose-lose situations may be created by the compromises found. When both parties give up what they want and get what they don't want, a lose-lose compromise results. In this case, nobody is really satisfied with the resolution. When each party gets some of what's wanted and loses some, you could say a win-lose situation results.

Compromise, as a conflict resolution strategy, is beneficial because relationships are maintained and conflicts are removed relatively quickly. The problem is that compromise sometimes creates less than ideal outcomes.

Game playing may also result. Understanding that things will have to be given up, people may make exaggerated and unrealistic demands, hoping to get what they really want. Use compromise when

- Important and complex issues leave no clear and simple solutions.
- All conflicting people are equal in power and have strong interests in different solutions.
- There are time constraints.

The Collaborating Owl

Owls adopt a **collaborating** (or **problem confronting**) conflict management system and they value both their goals and relationships. Owls view conflicts as problems to be solved. Collaborators try to resolve disputes by finding solutions agreeable to all parties. They use their Adult ego state to find win-win situations. They believe that a conflict is not settled until people get what they want and all tensions and negative feelings have been extinguished. The disadvantage is that solving every conflict consumes a great deal of time and effort. Collaboration is useful when

- Maintaining relationships is important.
- Time is not a concern.
- Peer conflict is involved.
- Trying to gain commitment through consensus building.
- Learning and trying to merge differing perspectives.

For a summary statement of conflict management styles, associated ego states, resulting situations, and occasions when indicated, see Table 6.1.

Table 6.1   Conflict Management Styles

Conflict Management Style	Associated Ego States	Resulting Situations	When Indicated	Pros and Cons
Competing Shark	Critical Parent Adapted Child	Win-Lose	High Goal–Low Relationship Concerns	Pro: Better Decisions Con: Resentment and Hostility
Avoiding Turtle	Adapted Child Nurturing Parent	Lose-Lose	Low Goal–Low Relationship Concerns	Pro: Relationship Maintenance Con: Unresolved Conflict
Accommodating Teddy Bear	Nurturing Parent Adapted Child	Win-Lose	Low Goal–High Relationship Concerns	Pro: Preserves Relationship Con: Exploitation of Accommodator
Compromising Fox	Adult Ego State	Win-Lose Lose-Lose	Moderate Goal–Moderate Relationship Concerns	Pro: Conflict Resolution, Relationships Maintained Con: Less than Ideal Outcomes, Game Playing
Collaborating Owl	Adult Ego State	Win-Win	High Goal–High Relationship Concerns	Pro: Best Resolutions Con: Required Time and Effort

Pick the Most Appropriate Conflict Resolution Style

Your task in this exercise is to analyse the following case study in light of what you've learned on the subject of conflict and conflict management. What sort of conflict or conflicts are we dealing with? Explain, given the facts, which conflict management style is the best one to use. What led you to your conclusion?

> Mr. Wonderful is the teacher of your general education elective in philosophy offered by the computer studies department. Try as he might, his class is not going very well by mid-term. Mr. Wonderful has noticed that several students in the class always sit close to each other and disrupt proceedings by their rude behaviour and sarcastic questions intended not to clarify matters, but to embarrass the instructor and others. On top of this, students in the elective class don't get along well together. They come from various streams of study within the computer studies department. Some students are fresh out of high school, while others are direct entry, meaning that they already possess either a diploma or degree at the time of course enrollment. Still others are "mature students" who qualified for admission to computer studies by virtue of their age and experience. Often, you can hear arguments among the students who group themselves according to stream. In fact, physical fights have even broken out in the hallways. Mr. Wonderful wishes the conflict would end, that a civilized environment for learning could be reestablished and that everybody would get back to their schoolwork.

In your own words, describe the conflict situation. What should Mr. Wonderful do? What conflict management style would be reflected by these suggested actions? Why do you favour this style in this case?

WIN-WIN CONFLICT RESOLUTIONS

The ideal resolution to conflict is **win-win**. In this case, everybody benefits and nobody loses. Of course, unequal power relationships, time constraints and other concerns sometimes make win-win resolutions to conflicts difficult to manage. But when conflicting parties are peers or colleagues with essentially equal power, and when they have a desire to achieve mutually beneficial outcomes, the collaborating or problem confronting style of conflict management is to be preferred; this style makes win-win outcomes most probable.

David Johnson (1990) has done an excellent job of explaining the steps involved in using the win-win confronting/collaborating style of conflict resolution. The step-by-step discussion that follows draws heavily from his work.

Seven Steps to Constructive Conflict Resolution Using the Collaborative Style

1. Confront the opposing party.

2. Define the conflict together.

3. Communicate personal positions and feelings.

4. Express cooperative intentions.

5. Understand the conflict from the other party's viewpoint.

6. Be motivated to resolve the conflict and to negotiate in good faith.

7. Reach an agreement.

Step 1: Confront the Opposing Party

If you're going to resolve any conflict constructively using the collaborative strategy, the first thing you have to do is to let the other person(s) know that a conflict exists. If the other party doesn't know that you're bothered or upset about something, then from that person's perspective, there is no conflict and nothing is wrong. When you properly confront another person, what you must do is express your view of the conflictual situation and relate your feelings about it, while inviting the other party to do the same.

Of course, whether you choose to confront depends on the quality of relationship, the importance you place on it, and how the person is likely to respond to the confrontation. As a general rule, the stronger or more solid the relationship, the more forceful the confrontation may be. As Johnson (1990: 238) points out, however, if the other party in the conflict displays high anxiety and a low motivation for change, or if the confrontation will not be used as an invitation for self-examination, then confrontation should be avoided. "Whether you decide to open your mouth or button your lips depends on the other person and the situation" (Johnson, 1990: 239).

Step 2: Define the Conflict Together

After you have confronted the other person, your second task is to define the conflict in a mutually agreeable fashion. Both of you must agree on what the problem, in fact, is. This must be done fairly and objectively and in a way that doesn't make anyone feel defensive.

When you try to arrive at a common definition of the problem, make efforts to avoid insults, veiled statements and negative value judgments. Personal attacks and prejudgments on the issues are not likely to take you very far down the road of constructive conflict resolution. Furthermore, when defining the conflict, try to be as clear and specific as possible. Leaving things vague or implicit may lead to misunderstandings and crossed communications. As part of defining the conflict situation, accurately describe your feelings and, for purposes of verification, reflect back to the other person her feelings as you experience and understand them. Try as well to control your passions as you describe your own actions and the actions of the other person that contribute to the conflict as you see it.

Step 3: Communicate Personal Positions and Feelings

During the process of conflict resolution, positions taken on issues may change, as may feelings on them. It is important, therefore, to keep the lines of communication open. If you're going to disagree with another person's position, you must know what that position is. The same is true if you wish to suggest changes to that position or if you wish to criticize it. If you don't understand how the other person's thoughts, feelings, wants and goals differ from your own, then the chances of reconciling your differences are jeopardized. Similarly, if the other person doesn't properly appreciate where you stand, or how your stand has changed, finding satisfactory solutions to the conflict will be much more difficult.

While exploring your positions in a conflict situation, seek to uncover precisely what your differences are. Also look for commonalities and points of agreement. Identify which behaviours, on both sides of the conflict, parties find objectionable. Explore possible solutions to the expressed conflict that would prove satisfying to all parties concerned. Think about the things both you and the other person need to do to resolve the conflict.

Step 4: Express Your Cooperative Intentions

If you're going to adopt a constructive orientation to conflict resolution in dealings with people whom you value, then you don't want differences to terminate or somehow undermine your relationships with them. It's a good idea, therefore, to make it clear to others that you don't wish to threaten friendships and ongoing associations. Make it known that you want to work together to reach a settlement that is agreeable to all. Show optimism and confidence that the conflict can eventually be resolved with the net effect of strengthening the bonds you have already established.

Step 5: Understand the Conflict from the Other Party's Viewpoint

Problems with conflict resolution sometimes arise because people remain **"cognitively egocentric"**; that is, they tend to see problems and conflicts only from their own psychological standpoint. They have difficulties "decentring" from their own point of view to see things more objectively, from different angles and from other perspectives. I suspect that the more emotionally invested a person is in his own position, the more difficult it is for that individual to appreciate things from alternative vantage points. Certainly, if you wish to constructively resolve conflicts, you cannot ignore, fail to recognize or discount the perspectives of others. Such actions would violate the spirit of mutually respectful win-win negotiations.

Step 6: Be Motivated to Negotiate in Good Faith

It is important in win-win negotiations not to use dishonesty, deception or misrepresentation. Trying to fool people into believing they have gotten what they wanted, when you know this isn't true, is bargaining in **bad faith**. Healthy and long-lasting relationships cannot be based on lies, half-truths and broken promises. It is important, therefore, to be motivated by **honourable intentions**. Also, ask yourself if you really want to perpetuate the conflict. What would you gain by ending the conflict? What would the other person gain? What would you and the other person lose if you prolonged the dispute? Are the losses worth it? Are you both motivated, then, to come out as winners? Understand that people's motivations to terminate conflicts can change. If you can increase the gains for resolving conflict or show how the costs of continuing the conflict are likely to increase, you might be able to motivate conflicting parties to make quicker changes that would lead to a settlement of the conflict.

Step 7: Reach an Agreement

Once you have defined and confronted the problem, communicated personal positions and associated feelings, expressed cooperative intentions,

People who use appropriate conflict management techniques can enhance their interpersonal effectiveness.

understood the problem from alternative vantage points, negotiated in good faith, and shown your resolve to reach a solution, then it is time to finalize an agreement. A win-win agreement requires that everyone be satisfied and that they be committed to abide by the agreement. A successful resolution specifies clearly the shared position adopted. It also specifies how people will act differently in the future and how cooperation will be restored if someone backslides and acts inappropriately. It is also advantageous if conflicting parties can agree to meet later on in order to discuss how cooperation can be strengthened.

SYMPTOMS OF INNER PEACE

Be on the lookout for symptoms of inner peace. The hearts of a great many have already been exposed to inner peace and it is possible that people everywhere could come down with it in epidemic proportions. This could pose a serious threat to what has, up to now, been a fairly stable condition of conflict in the world.

Some Signs and Symptoms of Inner Peace

- A tendency to think and act spontaneously rather than on fears based upon past experiences
- An unmistakable ability to enjoy each moment
- A loss of interest in judging other people
- A loss of interest in judging self
- A loss of interest in interpreting the actions of others
- A loss of interest in conflict
- A loss of ability to worry (a serious symptom)
- Frequent, overwhelming episodes of appreciation
- Contented feelings of connectedness with others and nature
- Frequent attacks of smiling
- An increasing tendency to let things happen rather than make them happen
- An increased susceptibility to the love extended by others as well as the uncontrollable urge to extend love to others

Caution

If you have some or all of the above symptoms, please be advised that your condition of inner peace may be so far advanced as to not be curable. If you are exposed to anyone exhibiting any of these symptoms, remain exposed only at your own risk.

6.8

Type Tips for Conflict Resolution

By this point in your efforts to master human relations you have become quite familiar with matters of psychological type, temperament and the notion of differing cognitive and behavioural preferences. This familiarity can help you to appreciate better the psychology of conflict as well as accommodate differing preferences in an effort to resolve interpersonal disputes. In *Type Talk at Work*, Otto Kroeger and Janet Thuesen say that "any conflict-resolution model that does not consider personality differences is doomed to fail" (1992: 128). This claim may be somewhat overstated; nonetheless, personality is clearly one important variable to be taken into account when trying to resolve any interpersonal conflict. In fact, sometimes personality differences are the causes of conflicts. What the thinker may interpret as simply making a case, for instance, the feeler may understand as provoking an argument.

To prevent any defensiveness here, I'd like to emphatically state that no one type has a monopoly on starting conflicts, nor does any one type excel at dealing with them. Conflict can unfortunately bring the worst out in all of us. For example, TJs (thinking-judging types) tend to become overly rigid, while extraverts can become excessively loud and needlessly aggressive (Kroeger and Thuesen, 1992). In their work, Kroeger and Theusen (1992) have identified five steps to conflict resolution. This strategy is type sensitive. The five steps are listed below. Following the steps, I've paraphrased their recommendations for all types involved in conflict resolution.

Five Steps to Conflict Resolution

1. Define the issues involved.
2. Try to put the issues into a typological framework, ideally pinpointing them to a letter preference.
3. Examine the probable cause of the conflict, in typological terms if possible.
4. Ask each party involved to identify with the other's point of view.
5. Seek compromises or contracts that can move the conflict toward resolution.

A type-sensitive strategy for resolving conflicts requires that

- **extraverts** stop to look and listen. Care must be taken to appreciate the other person's point of view.
- **introverts** express themselves. They must be heard by extraverts, who sometimes won't let them get a word in edgewise.
- **sensors** get beyond the facts. Facts are sometimes misleading or perceived differently by different people. Look to extenuating circumstances. Other issues besides the facts may need to be taken into account.
- **intuitives** address the issues; they do not cloud the issues with vague generalities. They must try to deal with the specifics that contribute to the conflict at hand.

- **thinkers** allow for the possibility of expressing emotion. They must understand that expressing emotion and dealing with it is integral to successful conflict resolution.
- **feelers** be direct and confrontative. They must say what's on their minds. They shouldn't apologize for their feelings. Rather, they should just state them. Frankness will be appreciated.
- **judgers** recognize that they're not always right. They must stop seeing life and situations in purely black-and-white terms. They must accept the fact that judgers can be wrong.
- **perceivers** must learn to take a stand. They cannot forever remain flexible and undecided. Sooner or later decisions must be made and actions must be taken.

Personal "Shoulds" for Conflict Resolution

In the spaces provided below, list the four letters of your psychological type. Next to each letter, indicate what you should do or consider when faced with conflict, given the type-sensitive suggestions listed earlier. (Refer to Chapter 1, if necessary, to find your psychological type.)

My psychological type is

____ (E or I)

____ (S or N)

____ (T or F)

____ (J or P)

When in conflict with others, I should

(What should I do about my E or I attitude?)

_____

_____

(What should I notice about my S or N perceptions?)

_____

_____

(What should I realize about my T or F decision-making tendencies?)

_____

_____

(How should I deal with my J or P orientation to the external world?)

_____

_____

STUDY GUIDE

Key Terms

conflict (196)
psychological conflict (198)
interpersonal (199)
intergroup (199)
intragroup (199)
intrapsychic (199)
approach-approach conflict (199)
avoidance-avoidance conflict (199)
approach-avoidance conflict (199)
dysfunctional conflict (200)
functional conflict (200)
interactionist perspective (200)
orientation (203)
conflict orientation (203)
predispositions (203)
beliefs (203)
perceptions (203)
motivations (203)
intentions (203)

behaviours (203)
constructive orientation to conflict (204)
realism (204)
pragmatic approach (204)
self-empowered (205)
internally centred (205)
conciliatory (205)
fair (205)
reasonable (205)
objective perspective (205)
passive-defensive orientation (205)
accommodating (205)
insulate (205)
avoiders (205)
regulates (205)
aggressive-defensive orientation to conflict (206)
escalates (206)
aggrandize (206)
dominator (207)

power (207)
authority (207)
force (207)
competition (207)
perfectionism (207)
conflict management styles (209)
goals (210)
relationships (210)
forcing/competing (212)
avoiding/withdrawing (212)
accommodating/ smoothing (213)
compromising (213)
collaborating/problem confronting (214)
win-win conflict resolutions (215)
cognitively egocentric (217)
bad faith (218)
honourable intentions (218)

PROGRESS CHECK 6.1 ✔

Fill-in-the-Blank Questions

Instructions: Fill in each blank with the appropriate response from the list below.

psychological
dysfunctional
passive-defensive
conflict management styles
wrong

self-knowledge
constructive
collaborating
win-win
aggressive-defensive

conflict orientation   intragroup
competing shark   conflict
approach-approach

1. If we oppose people, strive to overcome them or struggle for mastery over them, then we are engaged in _____.

2. The poem "The Six Men of Indostan" illustrates that people who disagree among themselves can be partly right, but all be _____ in the end.

3. Conflicts that occur inside oneself or in one's mind are _____.

4. Conflicts that arise among members of one single group can be labelled _____.

5. Having to decide between two desirable items—only one of which can be had—is the very definition of _____ conflict.

6. Conflict that interferes with a group's performance and productivity is _____.

7. Conflict can promote _____ by heightening awareness of what upsets or frightens us.

8. A _____ is defined by a person's beliefs, perceptions, motivations and behaviours toward others in situations of disagreement and dispute.

9. Somebody who is realistic, pragmatic, self-empowered, fair and conciliatory displays a _____ orientation to conflict.

10. Somebody who is accommodating and avoidant when it comes to conflict displays a(n) _____ orientation.

11. Some people intensify and escalate conflict. They often use force. These people adopt a(n) _____ orientation.

12. David Johnson has identified five _____.

13. Lafferty and Phillips's notion of the aggressive-defensive orientation is most closely related to Johnson's style of the _____.

14. The _____ conflict management style is most like the constructive orientation.

15. The ideal resolution to conflict is _____.

True/False Questions

Instructions: Circle the appropriate letter next to each statement.

T F   1. The best way to deal with conflict is simply to ignore it.

T F   2. To say that someone is "cognitively egocentric" is to suggest that the person is selfish.

T F   3. Some Myers-Briggs personality types are more likely than others to start conflicts, while other types are usually better at resolving them.

T F   4. With proper human relations training, conflict can be avoided most of the time.

T F   5. Conflict somehow involves opposing forces and differing objectives.

T F 6. Conflict always takes place between two or more individuals or groups.

T F 7. From an interactionist perspective, an optimum level of conflict can help to keep groups viable and creative.

T F 8. Conflicts can cause decisions to be made more carefully and thoughtfully.

T F 9. The behavioural tendency to attack personally people who disagree with you reflects the aggressive-defensive orientation to conflict.

T F 10. Refusing to engage in conflict and withdrawing from it reflects the constructive orientation to conflict.

T F 11. From the aggressive-defensive orientation, people try to aggrandize themselves at the expense of others.

T F 12. The compromising (fox) conflict management style is the one most likely to lead to win-win solutions.

T F 13. David Johnson believes that no one strategy is best for resolving all disputes.

T F 14. The accommodating (teddy bear) style of conflict management places a great deal of importance on human relationships.

T F 15. The collaborating (owl) style of conflict management is best to use when time is limited.

Focus Questions

1. What is the nature of conflict?

2. What types of conflict can be identified?

3. Are there any advantages to conflict? Explain and illustrate.

4. How do people orient themselves to conflict? Is there one orientation better than the others? Why?

5. Is there more than one style of managing conflict? If so, what are those styles? Can you briefly describe them?

6. What are the various components of win-win conflict resolutions.

Summary

1. What is the nature of conflict?
   • defined as combat, a striving to oppose or overcome
   • to meet in opposition or hostility
   • to be incompatible or at variance

2. What are some types of conflict?
   • psychological-intrapsychic
   • social: interpersonal, intergroup, intragroup
   • approach-approach, approach-avoidance, avoidance-avoidance
   • functional versus dysfunctional

3. What are the benefits of conflict?
- problem awareness
- change catalyst
- energizing and motivating
- stimulating and interest generating
- cathartic
- improves quality of decisions
- promotes self-knowledge
- enhances fun
- potentially improves relationships in the long run

4. What constitutes a psychological orientation to conflict?
- predispositions, beliefs, perceptions, motivations, intentions and behaviours

5. How do people psychologically orient to conflict?
- constructive orientation: realistic, pragmatic, self-empowered, conciliatory, fair, reasonable, objective
- passive-defensive orientation: accommodating, insulating, avoidant, regulating
- aggressive-defensive orientation: escalates conflict, self-aggrandizing, dominating, competitive, perfectionistic

6. What are five conflict management styles identified by David Johnson?
- forcing/competing: goal oriented, uncooperative, win-lose
- avoiding/withdrawing: ignore conflicts, sacrifice goals & relationships, lose-lose
- accommodating/smoothing: values relationships over goals, unassertive, uncooperative
- compromising: values goals and relationships, uses concessions, assertive and cooperative
- collaborating: problem confronting, works toward consensus, win-win

7. How are win-win conflict resolutions achieved?
- use the collaborating style: confront the opposing party; define the conflict together; communicate personal positions and feelings; express cooperative intentions; understand the conflict from the other party's viewpoint; be motivated to resolve the conflict and to negotiate in good faith; reach an agreement

Related Readings

Adler, Ronald B. and George Rodman (1994). *Understanding Human Communication*, 5th edition. Toronto: Harcourt Brace College Publishers.

Adler, Ronald B. and Neil Towne (1996). *Looking Out, Looking In* , 8th edition. Toronto: Harcourt Brace College Publishers.

Gordon, Thomas (1975). *P.E.T. Parent Effectiveness Training*. New York: New American Library.

Napoli, Vince and James M. Kilbride, Donald E. Tebbs (1992). *Adjustment and Growth in a Changing World*, 4th edition. St. Paul: West Publishing.

Weeks, Dudley (1992). *The Eight Essential Steps to Conflict Resolution*. New York: G.P. Putnam's Sons.

 ## *Weblinks*

1. Graduate studies in conflict resolution
   Teachers College, Columbia University
   www.tc.columbia.edu/~icccr/gradp1.htm

   Teachers College, Columbia University, offers a program of study grounded in social and organizational psychology to help people develop their conflict resolution skills.

2. Conflict Smarts
   www.mindspring.com/~dschan/ConflictSmarts.html

   Discover how interactive multimedia software has been designed to help children learn interpersonal skills to deal with conflicts without resorting to violence.

3. Professional personalized studies in how to solve and control interpersonal conflicts
   www.ludine.com/personality/index.html

   Learn to resolve interpersonal conflicts over the Internet in a way that safeguards your privacy and independence.

4. NTL Institute for Applied Behavioural Science
   www.ntl.org/gettok.now.htm

   Dedicated to personal and professional advancement through behavioural training and development, this institute helps people to foster change and resolve conflicts.

CHAPTER 7

Because their hearts are pure, the innocent defend true perception instead of defending themselves against it.

–A Course in Miracles

PERCEPTION AND THE SELF: WHAT I SEE DEPENDS ON ME

CHAPTER OVERVIEW

Perception

    The Construction of Personal and Social Reality

    Selecting

Application Exercise 7.1 May I Have the First Section, Please?

    Organizing

Interpreting

    How I See the World Is My Responsibility

Perceptual Errors

    Stereotyping

    Self-Fulfilling Prophecy

LEARNING OUTCOMES

After successfully completing this chapter, you will be able to

7.1   Provide alternative explanations of perception

7.2   Explain how personal and social reality is "constructed"

7.3   Demonstrate selective perception to yourself

7.4   Understand how perception can be a matter of personal responsibility

7.5   Describe a number of common perceptual errors

7.6   Reduce errors in your perceptions of people and situations

7.7   Articulate your self-concept based on previously completed self-diagnostics

7.8   Explain what's meant by self-concept

7.9   Increase self-awareness while promoting appropriate self- disclosure

7.10 Define and enhance personal self-esteem

7.1 ▶ *PERCEPTION*

> *What you see is what you get.*
>
> Anonymous
>
> *The world we see merely reflects our internal frame of reference — the dominant ideas, wishes and emotions in our minds. "Projection makes perception."...If we are using perception to justify our own mistakes — our anger, our impulses to attack, our lack of love in whatever form it may take — we will see a world of evil, destruction, malice, envy and despair. All this we must learn to forgive, not because we are being "good" and "charitable" but because what we are seeing is not true.*
>
> A Course in Miracles
>
> *The essence of genius is to know what to overlook.*
>
> William James

Developing an understanding of **perception** is important to mastering human relations. Perception and interpersonal communication are so intimately related that it is virtually impossible to understand one without the other. By means of perception, we become aware of our physical and social surroundings. We gather information, experience people, give meaning to situations, attribute motives and intentions to individuals, form impressions and learn about ourselves and others in the world. The window of perception enables us to see inside while looking out.

For centuries, philosophers have argued over the nature of perception in their quest for knowledge. **Empiricists**, like John Locke, have claimed that the mind is like a blank slate. For him, the mind perceives only that which experience presents. In his view, all knowledge is a product of experience and derived from it. In psychological terms, this theory means that people are essentially passive organisms and serve as stimulus receptors. Experience simply imprints itself on the mind. Perception is thus a reflection of external reality. For the empiricist, people, situations and events are "out there," so to speak. They are separate from the person perceiving them. External reality possesses a kind of independent status. Perhaps you have always been an empiricist without knowing it. If you have ever said things like "Seeing is believing" or "I know, I saw it with my own two eyes," you have probably made empiricist assumptions about perception.

According to **rationalist thinkers**, reason, not experience, is the ultimate source of all knowledge. For them, experience is something that can be deceiving. Even though the saying is "Seeing is believing," surely you have been deceived before by what you have seen. Optical illusions cause people to arrive at false conclusions. Circumstantial evidence can sometimes convict innocent people. Things are not always as they appear. In short, experience cannot provide absolute certainty. What is true today may be false tomorrow; what looks true from here may look false from there. If you are a rationalist, you may distrust your sensory experience, seeking to find greater assurance through reasoning and thought processes.

Finally, if you adopt the **interactionist theory of knowledge** of philosopher Immanuel Kant or psychologist Jean Piaget, you grant both reason and experience a place in the formation of knowledge. You recognize how the contents of experience (sensory data) are poured into the forms of rational understanding provided by the mind to produce knowledge and our perceptions of the world. This point will be explained momentarily. For purposes of the discussion that follows, you should know that we will be adopting an interactionist perspective.

> All ideas come from sensations or reflection — Let us then suppose the mind to be, as we say, white paper, void of all characters, without any ideas: — How comes it to be furnished?...Whence has it all the materials of reason and knowledge? To this I answer, in one word, from experience. In that all knowledge is founded; and from that it ultimately derives itself.
>
> John Locke

> Perceiving something clearly and distinctly is essentially a matter of perceiving certain logical relationships.
>
> Harry G. Frankfurt

> While all our knowledge begins with experience, it does not follow that it all arises out of experience.
>
> Immanuel Kant

> ...no form of knowledge, not even perceptual knowledge, constitutes a simple copy of reality, because it always includes a process of assimilation to previous structures.
>
> Jean Piaget

The Construction of Personal and Social Reality

When you understand perception in interactive terms, it becomes clear that how we see ourselves and others is more than a simple matter of passively receiving external stimuli. The perception of self and others is an active process. The experience of reality is a **construction**, not a recording. To illustrate how your mind actively constructs reality and gives meaning to it, let's look at Figures 7.1 and 7.2. Ask yourself what you see.

Do you see a triangle in Figure 7.1? If so, your mind actively linked the three dots together. Perhaps you saw the "therefore" symbol from logic and mathematics. Sensory experience provided the raw data or contents of this perception, while your mind provided the form of understanding. But what you probably did not see is what I actually intended to draw. What you "should" have seen are three unrelated dots—what I in fact presented to you.

What do you see in Figure 7.2? Nothing? A shoe? Perhaps you saw the

Figure 7.1

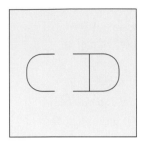

Figure 7.2

letters C and D. If so, ask yourself now what they mean. If you come from a computer background, the letters may mean "change directory." If you know something about fashion, they may stand for the designer Christian Dior. If you are a music enthusiast, they could mean "compact disc." However, if you just saw the comedy *Roxanne*, you might conclude that CD refers to the nickname of the firechief Steve Martin plays in the film. From these examples you can better appreciate the notion that reality is not completely external and independent of ourselves. We actually do something to incoming sensory information in order to make sense of the world. The next time you see somebody or perceive a situation in a certain way, remember that your mind has played a part in the construction of the experience.

The active process of perception involves the application of **categories**. Think of a category as a concept or mental structure. The categories of the mind give form to the contents of experience. They organize incoming information in ways we can assimilate or make sense of. Sometimes the demands of external reality force us to change our ways of thinking. Forms of understanding must therefore be significantly altered to accommodate novel situations to make sense of the world. To help demonstrate how mental forms give structure to experience, look at the four frames in Figure 7.3, each containing what at first glance appear to be random shapes. What do you see? (Don't read on until you've looked at the frames.)

Figure 7.3

What Do You See?

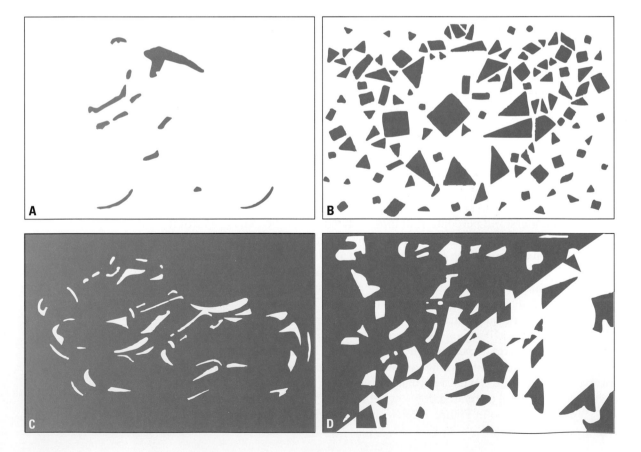

As you looked at the frames, did you notice how your "mind's eye" kept trying to arrange and rearrange the shapes in each frame to "fit" some idea or concept of what it might be? Your mind spontaneously tried to assimilate the sensory data into preexisting forms. Perhaps you were readily able to see the objects contained in each frame. Perhaps not? Now, let me give you perceptual categories that you can use in each frame in order to make sense of it. In Frame A, look for a person on a bicycle. In Frame B, look for a teapot. In Frame C, you will find three shoes, while in Frame D, there is a water faucet. I suspect now that you have been given the forms, you will begin to mentally arrange the sensory data to see what is there. Imagine, however, that you lived in a culture where running tap water did not exist, where there were no such things as bicycles, where tea was unheard of and where people walked barefoot. In that culture, would anyone "see" a bicycle, teapot, shoes or a faucet? Probably not.

Another important aspect of reality construction is that the perceptual categories we use to make sense of the world are largely a product of socialization. Some categories—such as space, time, number and causality—seem to be innate or biologically preprogrammed (according to Jean Piaget's research), but most are handed down to us by our family, culture, friends and social institutions. In some ways we see what we are conditioned to see.

Perceptual categories that organize social experience are not static. They develop and change as we grow. Furthermore, no two people have identical sets of perceptual categories. Different people in our lives, different circumstances and different experiences create different ways of looking at the world. What we in fact perceive is greatly influenced by our values, needs, goals, preferences, interests, beliefs, attitudes, expectations, wants, language and education. It is unlikely, therefore, that any two people will ever see life in exactly the same way. For example, if you have been encouraged to become an aspiring businessperson, you may see the chief executive officer of the corporation for which you work as highly admirable and successful. However, the same CEO may be seen by the radical communist student as a capitalist pig. An education in Marxism can filter perceptions very differently as compared with an education in business. Clearly, then, things such as acquired knowledge and personal value systems can influence how anyone perceives. Commenting on the role of **perceptual filtering**, Richard Weaver (1993: 76) says the following:

> *Our filtering system determines how we view the world. The world exists for us as we perceive it. We cannot "tell it like it is"; we can only tell it like we perceive it.*

See Figure 7.4 for a graphic depiction of Weaver's point.

Selecting

The process of perceptual construction involves not only an application of categories, but also selecting, organizing and interpreting (Weaver, 1993). Since we cannot possibly process all of the information that we are bombarded with on a daily basis, our minds limit the quantity of stimuli to

Figure 7.4

Appearance versus Reality

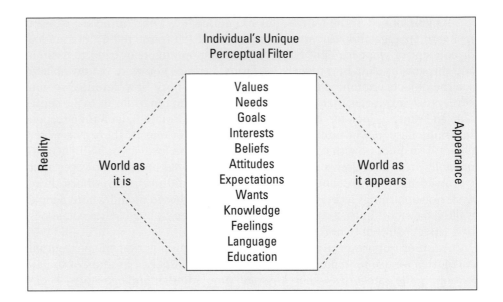

Individual's Unique
Perceptual Filter

Reality

World as
it is

Values
Needs
Goals
Interests
Beliefs
Attitudes
Expectations
Wants
Knowledge
Feelings
Language
Education

World as
it appears

Appearance

which we attribute meaning. In **selecting**, we tend to choose sensory data or communication messages we agree with and which are most meaningful to us. For instance, we tend to register positive comments made by people we like and negative or unacceptable comments made by people we don't like or don't support. The rest go largely unnoticed. Also, what we select to perceive will be influenced by personal history and past experience. If we were always taught to believe that being industrious is good, we may notice how hardworking someone is or how much effort is put forth on the playing field. If good grooming and appearance have been reinforced in our lives, we may pay attention to how people dress and style their hair. You can experience firsthand the process of selective perception by paying attention to how you read the newspaper. Do the experiential exercise below.

APPLICATION EXERCISE

7.1

7.3

May I Have the First Section, Please?

Instructions: Pick up a copy of the newspaper. Start reading and leafing through it as you normally would. If a newspaper is not readily available, recall your usual way of going through it. Answer the questions below. Discuss your answers with others in the class.

1. Which section of the newspaper did you turn to first? Why?
2. In what order did you read the remaining sections of the newspaper? Is this an order you often choose? Does this suggest anything about your interests and priorities?

3. Were there any sections or articles you opted not to read? What parts of the paper did you ignore purposely or unwittingly? What didn't you look at?

4. Have you started reading sections or articles of the newspaper recently that you used to ignore? Are you now ignoring sections that you once read? If so, what does this shift tell you about yourself? What changes in your life have taken place to influence your selection of information in the paper?

For thought: This exercise was developed to help you better understand the process of selective perception. When "reading" people and situations, what do you tend to notice first? What goes overlooked? If you don't see everything about a person or situation, then what exactly do you see? Do you notice things about people now that you never did before? What do your perceptions of others tell you about yourself?

Organizing

As mentioned, active perception involves **organizing** information. One way to organize incoming data is "to put the words we hear into a larger context so that we can understand them better" (Weaver, 1993: 81). This aspect of organization is called **enlarging**. When we enlarge, we actually look for a frame of reference in order to make sense of the received message. For example, to make sense of an ambiguous comment (one having more than one possible meaning) we might enlarge it by looking at the speaker's nonverbal communication. We might relate it to what the person said earlier, what happened before, or what the speaker's mood was when the comment was made.

A second way to organize perception is by means of **simplifying**. For example, as you read this section of the text on perception probably your mind is trying to order the incoming data so that the essential information can be recalled later on for testing purposes. You may take notes using headings or use point form to condense large amounts of material. In my college lectures I often summarize paragraphs of books by trying to capture in a nutshell what the author is trying to communicate. I try to say, in one sentence, what may be expressed in half a page. In this case I share the products of my own simplifying with students. This is hard for me, I might add, for I usually find it easier to say in a paragraph what could be said in a simple sentence.

Closing is a third aspect of perceptual organization. When we perceptually "close," we try to fill in the gaps between pieces of information (Weaver, 1993). If you saw a triangle in the three random dots illustrated in Figure 7.1, you can appreciate how you connected them to form one unified whole. Spontaneously, your mind took fragmented

> *Why say in a few words that which could be said in many?*
>
> Tonee Balonee
>
> *Simplicity is very difficult for twisted minds.*
>
> A Course in Miracles

Differing interpretations of abstract art clearly show how individual perception is an active process of construction.

bits of information and imposed closure. Other examples of closure are finishing someone else's sentence or filling in the missing parts of a conversation when only fragments of it can be overheard due to external noise.

Interpreting

In addition to selecting and organizing information, the process of perception also involves **interpreting** it. When we interpret, we give meaning to information, evaluate it, and arrive at conclusions about it. We can then respond appropriately and better predict future events and surprises (Weaver, 1993). Interpretation involves identification and evaluation. A bump in the night may be startling or somewhat frightening until it is identified as the banging water pipes in the basement. Once the noise is identified, it is spontaneously evaluated. The first question, "What's that noise?" is followed by the second, "Is it dangerous?" When we evaluate sensory information we call upon all our knowledge and previous experience. Of course, sometimes our interpretations are erroneous. We may mislabel the noise, for instance, identifying it as something it is not. The bump may have been a burglar. We may also incorrectly evaluate the danger factor. We could conclude that the situation does not need our immediate attention when it really does. While errors can be made on both counts, sensory identification is usually fairly reliable, whereas interpretation is open to greater question (Weaver, 1993).

How I See the World Is My Responsibility

When perception is understood as an active process of construction, the notion that we are largely responsible for what we see becomes intuitively clear. While it is true that our parents, caretakers and societal culture all helped to form our current perceptions, as adults we can constantly make changes. We can add to our list of perceptual categories through learning, experience and rational choice. We can also modify or reject categories we were raised with. For example, we can choose to see people as morally equal, not unequal, because of differences in skin colour. We can choose to see people however we wish. Furthermore, if we have unconsciously ignored certain kinds of sensory information in the past, we can now choose to pay attention. If we have defensively blocked out undesirable messages before, we can now opt to listen and perhaps learn from our adversaries. When planning to experience things in the future, we can decide what to look for and even prepare for experiential opportunities. Before visiting an art gallery, for instance, we can read art history books and stock up on artistic categories that will help us to appreciate the artwork on view. Whether we see a painting as a good example of French impressionism or as a better colour-contrasting accent piece for our living room ensemble depends on us. Instead of concluding that "what you see is what you get," perhaps we ought to say, "What I see depends on me."

In the context of human relations development, the perception of "self" and "others" is vitally important. If we don't like what we see in ourselves, this will affect our self-esteem, our world view, and the ways in which we communicate and respond to others. Similarly, how we see other people may determine whether we approach them, talk to them, avoid them, criticize them, trust them or ignore them. Social perception may have us attribute causes to people's behaviour, label them in certain ways, or read things into their intentions and motivations. Whether we look at ourselves or at others, it is important to know the factors that influence our perception. Let us now turn to some common **perceptual errors** that distort our vision and influence our interactions with others.

PERCEPTUAL ERRORS

Stereotyping

Existentialist philosophers have argued that individuals are as unique as their fingerprints. They support this argument with the fact that never before in the history of humanity has there been another you and never for all eternity will there be another you. Individual uniqueness is universal. Not only are we different, but so too is everyone else. In view of this individual uniqueness, a perceptual mistake we sometimes make is lumping different individuals together and wrongly attributing to them common characteristics. This perceptual error is better known as **stereotyping**.

The tendency toward stereotyping exists in the minds of many perceivers and leads us to make incorrect judgments about people, most of whom are strangers to us. For instance, we may assume that all foreign college students from Asia excel in computer science, every Quebecker is a separatist, all men lack feeling, all feminists are man-haters, or all Canadians play hockey and drink beer. How would you feel having your individual uniqueness so easily dismissed by someone else pigeonholing you into some kind of racial, ethnic, linguistic, national or gender stereotype? Chances are pretty good that you would feel violated, angry or hurt. Misrepresentations, arising out of stereotyping, then, can lead to negative feelings. They can damage interpersonal relationships.

Notwithstanding the fact that stereotyping distorts the truth about individuals and thereby causes inaccuracy in social perception, it persists. One reason is that stereotyping is functional (Weaver, 1993; Weiten, Lloyd and Lashley, 1991). This process helps us to simplify the complex information we receive about others in the external world. We may not have the capacity, patience, interest or desire to learn about the uniqueness of all those whom we encounter. Instead, we may reduce people to stereotypes in order to simplify matters. However, what we gain in (over)simplification, we lose in accuracy.

The process of **selectivity** in perception also perpetuates stereotypes. When we have a stereotype, we often unconsciously but actively look for things in others that confirm it. If you stereotype all Lutonians (a fictitious race of people created by the late comedian John Candy) as stupid, for instance, you might not hear the intelligent things they say. As singer-songwriter Paul Simon put it, "A man hears what he wants to hear and disregards the rest." Perceptions that are inconsistent with any stereotypes may be ignored, easily forgotten or denied. An intelligent comment by a Lutonian could thus be discounted as mere "book learning" or dismissed as a repetition of what someone else said before. Intelligent comments will not be received and accepted at face value.

Self-Fulfilling Prophecy

The **self-fulfilling prophecy** is another process that influences perception and social interaction. It occurs when you make a prediction about something

Source: Reprinted by permission of UFS, Inc.

or somebody that comes true, mainly because you made the prediction and behaved as if it were true. If you enter a room thinking the people there won't like you, you may act coldly and aggressively toward those present. If you do, they may respond to you in unfriendly ways. What you end up seeing are people who don't behave nicely toward you, just as you expected. What you may not see is that you actually helped cause the unfriendliness. To perceive others as unfriendly is to see only half the picture. If this is not a misperception, then it is surely an incomplete perception.

Self-fulfilling prophecies can work positively as well. In one psychological study, teachers were told that certain pupils in their classes were late bloomers, but that they were expected to do exceptionally well. In truth, children's names were drawn at random by the researchers. The results of the study indicated that selected students did in fact perform at higher academic levels compared with the students who were not named as ones possessing exceptional abilities. Given the randomness of the selection procedure, the teachers' expectations probably generated special attention to the selected students, thereby naturally affecting their performance. This widely known example of the self-fulfilling prophecy is referred to as the **Pygmalion effect.** (Rosenthal and Jacobson, 1968).

Halo Effect

The process of selective perception can sometimes lead to what's called the **halo effect**. The halo effect occurs when people form a general impression of an individual based on a single characteristic, or a limited number of characteristics attributed to that individual. For example, if you believe that a person possesses several positive qualities, you may conclude that the individual possesses certain other positive qualities. Your perception of other people may thus be filtered by an "implicit personality theory" of which you may not even be conscious (DeVito, 1993). On this note, DeVito asks how we would complete the following sentences.

> You never get a second chance to make a first impression.
>
> Shampoo commercial

John is energetic, eager and (intelligent, unintelligent).

May is bold, defiant and (extraverted, introverted).

Joe is bright, lively and (thin, fat).

Jane is attractive, intelligent and (believable, unbelievable).

As DeVito points out, some choices seem right, others wrong, depending on our implicit personality theory. "Most people's rules tell them that a person who is energetic and eager is also intelligent. Of course, there is no logical reason an unintelligent person could not be energetic and eager" (DeVito, 1993: 49). Given this notion, you may see qualities in people that are not there. You may also ignore or distort qualities and characteristics in people that do not conform to your implicit personality theory. Before you look at very many more people, it is worth reconsidering your psychological assumptions about them. You may be witnessing your assumptions, not necessarily what is true about them. Be careful, as well, not to fall victim to the **reverse halo effect**. Just because a person has a few negative qualities does not mean that the person has others. A selfish, egotistical person needn't be dishonest or emotionally abusive to others. Finally, do not jump to conclusions about people based on what you observe. Two people can do the same thing for very different reasons. Two storekeepers can return the correct change to a young customer, one because of fear that dishonesty may hurt business in the long run (an act of self-interest), the other because treating all people honestly is simply the right and virtuous thing to do (an act of morality). The storekeeper's intentions are thus more revealing than the observed actions themselves. Again, maybe the saying "Seeing is believing" should be amended this time to something like "Given what I see, what should I believe?" This brings us to another kind of perceptual error.

Attribution Errors

In the storekeeper example above, we learned that the same behaviour can be attributed to different intentions and motivations. This idea is important to note, for sometimes our attributions are incorrect. To better appreciate the nature of **attribution errors**, it is helpful to explain the kinds of attributions that we can make. When we observe someone's behaviour, it is possible to attribute to it either internal or external causes. Perhaps the person's bad mood (internal cause) led to explosive behaviour. Or maybe the individual barked at us because of something that happened at work that day (external cause). The internal-external dimension of attribution thus locates the source of behaviour as inside or outside. Internal attributions "ascribe the causes of behaviour to personal dispositions, traits, abilities, and feelings" (Weiten, Lloyd and Lashley, 1991: 130). External attributions ascribe the causes of people's behaviour to situational factors. Environmental demands, constraints and events may give rise to certain behaviour.

A second dimension relevant to attribution is stability. Some causes of behaviour (internal or external) are temporary or unstable (e.g., a weakened physical condition brought on by the flu). Others may be stable or permanent (e.g., one's temperament or the demands of a job). Understanding attribution in terms of the two dimensions discussed allows us to form a four-part grid. See Figure 7.5.

It is important to note that we can and often predictably make certain types of attributional errors when interpreting, evaluating or trying to understand people's behaviour, including our own. One good way of understanding these errors is in terms of **actor-observer differences** (Weiten, Lloyd and Lashley, 1991).

In any behavioural situation, the actor performs and the observer looks on. Research indicates that actors and observers see situations differently (Jones and Nisbett, 1971). As a result, we can find very interesting and different explanations for things like failure and success. A student who fails an exam, for instance, may find fault with the test measure, the noise in the

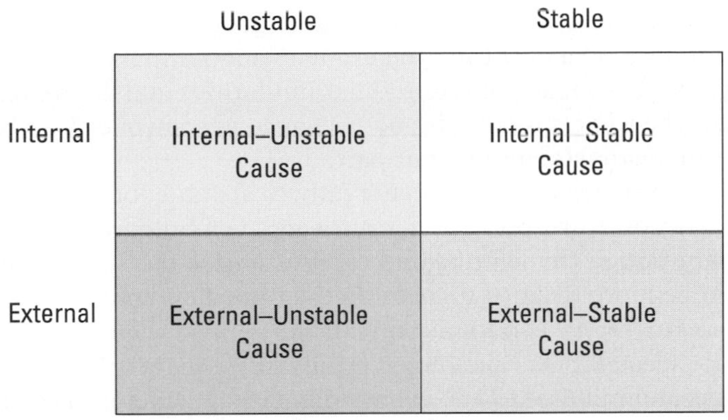

	Unstable	Stable
Internal	Internal–Unstable Cause	Internal–Stable Cause
External	External–Unstable Cause	External–Stable Cause

Figure 7.5

Types of Attributions

room during the testing or the fact that unforeseen circumstances prevented her from properly studying. As observers, we and the instructor may attribute the student's failure to poor study skills, lack of intelligence or irresponsibility. If the student was indeed prevented from studying for an exam because of a family emergency, but we attributed the student's failure to lack of intelligence, misperception would certainly occur. The wrong explanation would be given to account for the behaviour. Interestingly, when success is the issue, actor-observer perceptual tendencies become reversed. Actors are more likely to attribute personal successes to internal factors. Observers have a tendency to attribute them to external factors, such as luck. Of course, perceptual tendencies in either direction can lead to error— something to think about the next time you want to figure out why something happened to somebody and why somebody acted in a certain way. The next time you try to explain your own successes and failures, be careful not to fall prey to a **self-serving bias**.

Proximity

Proximity is another important factor that can sometimes lead to perceptual error (Weaver, 1993). Proximity can be physical or psychological. With physical proximity, distance influences our perception of people. Someone perceived as attractive from a distance may be seen as less attractive up close. Skin blemishes and other facial features that were unnoticeable from afar may become prominent when near. In this case, vision corrected by closer proximity could turn initial attraction into disinterest or repulsion. Psychological proximity deals with similarity of attitude. We tend to evaluate people who display attitudes similar to our own more positively than we do people whose attitudes are dissimilar to ours. For instance, when students and teachers are attitudinally similar, teachers get higher scores when rating things like openmindedness, personal attractiveness and teaching skills. When teachers' attitudes are largely dissimilar, their ratings are lower (Good and Good, 1973, cited in Weaver, 1993). Of course, something like a person's openmindedness does not hinge on other people's attitudes; only the perception of it does. The next time you evaluate another person's performance, it might be useful to take your attitudinal similarities and dissimilarities into account. Maybe what is required is not a change in someone else's behaviour, but an attitude adjustment on your part.

Psychological proximity refers not only to attitude, but to our readiness or predisposition to respond in certain ways. A photographer watching a movie might notice the lighting and camera angles used in filming; an actress might be more inclined to focus on the timing and physical movements of the performers; an economist might fixate on the cost of background scenery, the special effects and props. The point is that people bring their own experiences and mindset to any event or situation. Different individuals are psychologically closer to different aspects of what is perceived. Most people's psychological mindset can influence perception as much as, if not more than, the actual facts of the event witnessed (Weaver, 1993). To the extent that this idea is true, perceptions can become distorted in one direction or another. Given our current mindset, we may attribute undue importance to certain variables when describing or explaining people, situations and events when, in fact, others are more significant.

Role Definition

In society, we all play **roles**. Your role, as you read this book, is that of a student. At your full- or part-time job, your role is worker. At home, your role may be that of brother, sister, mother or father. In fact, there are many types of roles: family, gender, occupational and so on. The roles that we play affect our personal needs, our attitudes and expectations, our beliefs and the perspective we take when perceiving people and situations. For instance, if we live by traditional gender roles (e.g., those accepted by the arch-conservative Archie Bunker in the classic sitcom *All In the Family*), the same behaviour exhibited by males and females will be perceived differently.

> All the world's a stage,
> And all the men and women merely players.
>
> Shakespeare, As You Like It,
> Act 2, Scene 7

An aggressive male may be seen as self-willed and determined. An aggressive female may be perceived as domineering and bitchy. In both cases, the behaviour is the same, but when it is observed and filtered through the lenses of traditional role definition, it is perceived positively in the case of the male and negatively in the case of the female. Roles, then, influence our perceptions, and as the example above illustrates, can often lead to bias and inconsistent evaluation.

In closing, let me remind you that perceptual errors are numerous. They result from stereotyping, self-fulfilling prophecies, halo effects, attribution errors, proximity and role definition. Allow me to remind you as well that perception is largely a matter of personal responsibility. Richard Weaver (1993) has made a number of useful recommendations for minimizing your own perceptual errors. An abbreviated paraphrased list of them follows.

Canadian astronaut Roberta Bondar has helped us
to change our role-defined perceptions of women.

HOW TO REDUCE ERRORS IN PERCEPTION

1. **Avoid hasty conclusions** Don't overgeneralize. Base conclusions on strong evidence and repeated observations. Maintain a healthy balance between openness and scepticism. Expand your perceptual frame of reference by broadening your personal experience. Encourage communication to gain new evidence and to form new impressions. Guard against selective perception. Don't overlook contradictory information.

2. **Allow yourself more time** Develop more accurate perceptions of people by spending more time with them and getting closer to them. Erroneous initial impressions may change to more accurate ones with time. Temporarily suspend judgment. Show patience. Give your mind time to analyse and sift through relevant information before making judgments.

3. **Make yourself available** Be present for others both in mind and body. When you are with others, try to see things from their vantage point. Communicate in sincere and meaningful ways. Go beyond superficial niceties. Be open and honest. Attempt to connect and empathize. Show your reactions and participate in others' reactions.

4. **Commit yourself** Consciously decide to seek out as much information as possible before making a judgment or forming an opinion. More infor-

mation will probably lead to less perceptual distortion. Develop your knowledge and expand your range of experience. One-sided people do not experience life fully.

5. **Create the proper climate** Try to create a climate conducive to communication, one in which self-disclosure is likely to occur. Develop mutual trust to allow for the exchange of honest messages. Make an effort not to manipulate others, dominate them or run their lives. Avoid pretence, defence and deception.

6. **Make adjustments when necessary** Since people and situations change, be flexible and prepared to change your perception. Also, develop perceptual sensitivity. Recognize that your own perceptions will change as your interests and experiences change. Today's perception may not be accurate if based on yesterday's attitudes.

THE SELF

> In all communication the most important part is the self. Who you are and how you see yourself influences the way you respond to others.
>
> Joseph A. DeVito
>
> ...how we summarize information about other people is bound up with our own view of self.
>
> N.A. Kuiper and T.B. Rogers
>
> ...for the love of one's neighbour is not possible without love of one's self.
>
> Herman Hesse

SELF-DIAGNOSTIC

7.1

7.7 ▶

What's My Self-Concept?

Previous self-diagnostics in this text have given you many opportunities to engage in self-reflection. Hopefully, you understand more now than you did before about your personality type, psychological temperament, communication style, defensive tendencies, rationality, dominant ego states, leadership qualities and preferred ways of handling conflict. There is obviously more to self-concept than this (e.g., body image), and certainly no one paper-and-pencil measure can capture your entire self. Nonetheless, assembling and summarizing information obtained from previous self-diagnostics will be helpful when you form a clearer self-concept. Take time to consider your earlier self-reflections by answering the questions below. Refer back to completed self-diagnostics if necessary.

Process your self-revelations in private or share them with others. As you continue to paint the masterpiece portrait of yourself, what seems to be emerging?

1. What is my personality like? (See Self-Diagnostic 1.1.)

   How am I energized?

   _____

   How do I gather information about people, situations and events?

   _____

   What is my preferred way of making evaluations and judgments about what I perceive?

   _____

   How do I orient myself to the external world?

   _____

2. How do I communicate? (See Self-Diagnostic 2.1.)

   What is my communication style?

   _____

   What are the strengths of my style?

   _____

   What are the potential weaknesses or liabilities of my style?

   _____

3. How defensive am I? (See Self-Diagnostic 3.1.)

   What defence mechanisms do I often use?

   _____

   What obstacles does my defensiveness create?

   _____

4. How reasonable am I? (See Self-Diagnostic 3.2.)

   What is my command of logic?

   _____

   What uses do I make of fallacious reasoning and inappropriate rhetorical devices (e.g., emotional appeals)?

   _____

5. What is my dominant ego state? What part of myself is most strongly expressed? (See Self-Diagnostic 4.1.)

   What ego state dominates my communication and interaction with others?

   _____

   What personal behavioural tendencies are associated with my dominant ego state?

   _____

6. What leadership qualities do I possess? (See Self-Diagnostic 5.1.) How does my temperament affect my leadership contributions?

_____

7. How do I tend to handle conflicts and interpersonal disputes? (See Self-Diagnostic 6.1.)

_____

Self-Concept

> If a man wants to be of the greatest possible value to his fellow creatures let him begin the long, solitary task of perfecting himself.
>
> Robertson Davies, Canadian writer

> Perception is a selective process and the picture we have of ourselves is a vital factor in determining the richness and variety of the perceptions selected.
>
> Don Hamachek

Writers, poets and psychologists have for a very long time recognized the importance of the **self** to interpersonal relations. People with a poor self-concept, for example, can be their own worst enemy when trying to establish healthy and happy communications with others. They may fall prey to self-created self-fulfilling prophecies. People who think of themselves as unattractive and undesirable, for instance, may dress and act accordingly. They may avoid others, allow personal hygiene to slip and present themselves in unpleasant ways, thereby causing others to respond to them negatively. This negative response reinforces the initial poor self-concept. Conversely, people with positive self-concepts may expect the best, display optimism and consequently elicit support from others. See Figure 7.6 for an illustration of self-concept.

In general terms, **self-concept** refers to the overall way you see and understand yourself. It includes all of your self-referring beliefs and attitudes, as well as all of your recognized values, feelings, preferences and dispositions. Such things add up to make you who you are. The self can, in principle, be conceptualized in many different ways. Some say there is not one self, but many selves. It is possible, for instance, to talk about your private self, your social self, your work self, your leisure self, your serious self, your ideal self or your physical self. Your personal self-concept depends on what you choose to pay attention to. Of course, there are external factors influencing the formation of self-concept. In early development, parents, caretakers and significant others function as mirrors to the self. What they say to us or tell us about ourselves, how they respond to our actions, and what opportunities they provide us influence the development of self-concept. Children who were repeatedly told that they were a "mistake," for example, may struggle to develop a positive self-concept. They may try to become people they're not or experience debilitating insecurity. They may feel negative emotions and begin to see themselves as undesirable or unloved by others. Fortunately, self-concepts are not static (Atwater, 1983). They change with time and experience. Thus, it's possible to build positive self-concepts, even if negative ones were initially formed.

The significance of self to interpersonal relations can be illustrated by the fact that what you reveal about yourself affects how others respond to you. If you tell people little or nothing about yourself, you remain a mystery to them. Not knowing who you are, they may not see the real you, only a projection of their own fears and insecurities. If you do not share a part of yourself with others, they may also be reluctant to tell you about themselves, thereby creating cold and distant communications. A refusal to open up could even lead to hostility and distrust. History teaches us that people frequently become suspicious of individuals and things they don't understand. They tend to attack the unknown as a kind of psychological defence against anxiety. Thus, if you wish to make your interpersonal relations warmer and closer, you might need to engage in more self-disclosure. Of course, self-disclosure hinges largely on self-awareness. You can't consciously disclose what you don't know about yourself. Without self-awareness you may also end up unintentionally disclosing things about yourself that you wish you hadn't. In what follows, we will look a little more closely at self-awareness and self-disclosure as they pertain to human relations. We'll look at ways to increase self-awareness and provide some guidelines to help us distinguish between appropriate and inappropriate self-disclosure. We'll also consider the issue of self-esteem.

Self-Awareness

7.9

At this point in your journey to human relations mastery, you've already spent a great deal of time and effort increasing your **self-awareness**. Your completion of the self-diagnostics has enabled you to develop a working hypothesis about who you are. As you proceed through the rest of this text, additional self-diagnostics will promote even further self-awareness. Prepare yourself for a long and exciting adventure. Be forewarned, however, that your journey on the road to self-awareness may be without end. It's unlikely that people ever completely know themselves. Fortunately, trying to reach the destination is just as rewarding as achieving the destination itself.

Joseph Luft and Harry Ingham have provided one explanation of self-awareness (1955). Together they created a theoretical device called the Johari Window, a label that combines their first names. This device divides the self into four areas. Each captures aspects of the self, reflecting levels of awareness and disclosure. Taking these areas into account, a four-part grid results. See Figure 7.6.

The Open Self

In the **open self** quadrant you find things about yourself that are known both by you and others. For example, you're aware of your name, gender, skin colour and the college or university you attend. So too are others. You also know what your favourite sports teams are, as well as your preferred musical artists. This information about

Figure 7.6
The Johari Window

	Known to Self	Not known to Self
Known to Others	Open Self	Blind Self
Not known to Others	Hidden Self	Unknown Self

Source: From *Group Processes: An Introduction to Group Dynamics* by Joseph Luft, by permission of Mayfield Publishing Company. Copyright 1984 by Joseph Luft.

> Some things you know about yourself; some things you don't.
>
> Some things you'll share with others; while other things you won't.
>
> (Perhaps I'm a poet, but don't know it?)
>
> Tonee Balonee

yourself you can choose to share with others. If you do, such information becomes part of your open self. Generally speaking, all attitudes, feelings, ideas, desires and motivations that you regard as yours and that you display publicly or share with others belong to your open self.

It is important to note that the size of your open self can vary. Depending on the time and place, we may open up to others or perhaps choose to close tight (Johnson, 1990: 36–37). If people are to build deep and meaningful relations, they must be prepared to share themselves with others. If we don't let others get to know us, communication becomes very difficult. Psychological type may have an influence here. If researchers on type are correct, introverts will probably share less about themselves compared to extraverts, whose lives are sometimes lived like open books. To the extent this fact is true, introverts may be somewhat more challenged in the realm of interpersonal communications. Joseph Luft (1970) claims that the smaller the open self quadrant, the poorer the communication.

The Blind Self

When it comes to self-awareness, there are things that others can see in us but we cannot see in ourselves. This part of us is referred to as the **blind self**. For example, you may display certain peculiarities or quirks without knowing it; others may notice right away. Perhaps you play with your hair when conversing or become very polite as a reaction formation to anger. If you don't recognize these things about yourself, they belong to your blind self. It is important that you discover as much as you can about the blind self. By increasing self-awareness in this area you will be better able to manage the impressions you make on others. Other people's reactions to you will also become more understandable. When people react to aspects of your personality that you're unaware of, their behaviour may seem strange. When you know what you do and say, how you appear and what impressions you make, others' reactions can become not only more comprehensible but maybe even predictable (Weaver, 1993).

The Unknown Self

The **unknown self** is the part of you that neither you nor others know. Much of what makes up the unknown self is buried in the unconscious (DeVito, 1993). To gain greater awareness of the unknown self, you could avail yourself of certain psychotherapeutic techniques (e.g., dream analysis, hypnosis or psychological testing) or you could engage in further self-exploration with trusted family members, friends or loved ones. It is important to gain insight into your unknown self. If you don't, your untapped resources will go unused. Your full potential will never be actualized. In short, you will not become the person you *could* be (Weaver, 1993). Through interactions with others, you can discover more about yourself and reduce this portion of your self.

The Hidden Self

The **hidden self** is the part of you over which you have control. There are things about yourself that you know, but you choose not to share with others (e.g., your finances or previous relationships). The hidden self is personal and private and never needs to be disclosed. All of us establish personal boundaries that we use to protect our innermost selves. What we choose to share and withhold from others is a matter of self-disclosure.

It is worth noting that the four areas of the self are interdependent. Changes in one area affect other areas. For example, when you expand your open self by being more self-disclosing, you reduce the size of the hidden self. As you encourage others to be self-disclosing about what was once hidden but now is open for them, and as you allow them to be honest with you, your blind self also diminishes (Johnson, 1990). Let's say, for instance, that you express a radical political viewpoint that startles a listener. The reaction may come from the fact that the listener has always perceived you as a staunch conservative and has treated you accordingly. By communicating your radical politics openly, you may find yourself revealing things to others that were always hidden, or at least previously unexpressed. Now that the listener has shared with you his surprise, you realize what impression you unwittingly gave to others in the past. The impressions you gave were part of your blind self. You didn't know how you appeared. Now that it has been revealed and shared with you, the impression you give becomes a part of your open self. See Figure 7.7 for a representation of the four selves.

How to Increase Self-Awareness

1. **Adopt the perspective of others** Try to see yourself through the eyes of your friends and acquaintances.

2. **Create a list of your attitudinal, behavioural and perceptual tendencies** How do you generally orient to people? What do you look for when perceiving them? How do you act as a result?

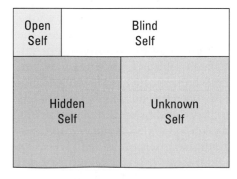

The Self Early
in a Relationship

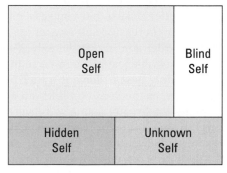

The Self in a Longer-Term
Close Relationship

Figure 7.7

Variations of the
Johari Window

3. **Pay close attention to others with whom you interact** They serve as a kind of mirror to the self. Look for any verbal and nonverbal clues that might provide new insights into yourself. Remember the advice given to us by the German poet Goethe, who suggested that if we wish to learn more about ourselves, we should look at others.

4. **Increase openness to others** The size of your blind self can be reduced if you allow others to know you better and respond to you. Through witnessing others' reactions to you and carefully listening to their responses, you can learn things about yourself that you didn't know. As others disclose their feelings and their perception of you, you increase your self-awareness.

Self-Disclosure

As you learned in the preceding discussion, the various "panes" of the Johari Window can vary in size depending on people's self-awareness and willingness to share themselves with others. In this part of the chapter we will examine a little more closely the nature of self-disclosure, its risks and benefits, as well as a few guidelines for its use. If you are going to increase the size of your open self and reduce the dimensions of your hidden, blind and unknown selves, in hopes of improving interpersonal relations, you should proceed carefully with an informed understanding.

> By letting you know me, I allow you to like me. By disclosing myself to you, I create the potential for trust, caring, commitment, growth, self-understanding and friendship.
>
> David Johnson

Self-disclosure involves the intentional act of revealing information about yourself to others. This information represents something new, not previously known by the chosen recipients of your self-disclosing. The information relayed in self-disclosure may be important or insignificant. You may choose to disclose something highly personal, or something rather trivial such as your preference in candy bars. One could argue that some self-disclosure is unconscious and, hence, unintentional. Nonverbal cues may, for instance, reveal your true feelings and falsify what you actually say to others. Those others may learn more about you through your body language and tone of voice than through what you say. Inadvertent slips of the tongue, as well, may uncover some hidden desire that you've been trying to conceal from others (DeVito, 1992). By increasing self-awareness and by making the open self larger, the blind, hidden and unknown selves—which give rise to unconscious or unwanted self-disclosure—can be reduced. If self-disclosure is going to occur, it's probably best to have it under personal control. Ideally, self-disclosure should be, as much as possible, a matter of conscious and deliberate choice. Remember, by increasing self-awareness, unwanted self-disclosure can be minimized. Since our treatment of self-awareness should help you limit unwanted self-disclosure, let us focus our attention on purposeful self-revelation.

Self-disclosure is not about emotional dumping or laying blame. Nor is it about brutal honesty and indiscriminate frankness. Self-disclosure refers to sharing parts of yourself with others in ways that respect their rights and sensitivities. Proper self-disclosure takes into account the impact it is likely to have on others. It is not surprising that people are often afraid to engage in self-disclosure. When you choose to tell others about yourself, "you expose yourself not only to a lover's balm, but also to a hater's bombs! When he knows you, he knows just where to plant them for maximum effect" (Jourard, 1971: 5). To put it more plainly, what you give away about yourself today may be used against you tomorrow. Fear of this possibility prevents many from self-disclosing. Also, people are afraid of rejection (Weaver, 1993). If we lay down our social masks and allow people to see us as we really are, they may not accept us. They may not give us the support or kind of reaction we were hoping for. What then? We may also avoid self-disclosure if we fear hurting others. Perhaps our true feelings and thoughts would emotionally wound people we care about. Instead of being honest and forthright, then, we may choose to remain private. Last, we may opt against self-disclosure because we do not wish to project an unwanted image. If I tell you about myself, you may begin to paint a picture of me that I don't like. Rather than doing that, I might prefer that you be able to paint no picture at all. In this case, little or no significant self-disclosure would be forthcoming.

Notwithstanding the risks, self-disclosure does have many potential benefits. When you choose to share things about yourself with others, you open the door for others to do the same. When mutual self-disclosure takes place, people get to know and understand one another better. The scene is thus set for closeness and greater intimacy. Without self-disclosure it would be difficult, if not impossible, to establish and maintain friendships. Liking someone and being liked entails caring and sharing. It is difficult to help a friend, empathize with that person or share useful feedback if that person refuses to self-disclose. Likewise, how can anyone help you or respond appropriately if you are hiding your true self? We learned from the Johari Window that self-disclosure helps to reduce the size of the blind self. By sharing ourselves with others, we afford them an opportunity to respond to us. We discover much about ourselves by noticing how others react to us. As we reduce the size of our blind self, we grow in self-awareness and assume greater control of our lives.

Finally, researchers have found some interesting correlations between self-disclosure and personal well-being. For instance, people who display good mental health typically exhibit high disclosure to a few significant others and medium disclosure to others in a social environment (Cozby, 1973, cited in DeVito, 1992: 117). Also, people who self-disclose have been found to have more effective immune systems than those who do not (Pennebacker, 1991, cited in DeVito, 1992: 118). They can then ward off illnesses more effectively. If you want to be healthier and happier, you might consider the importance of self-disclosure.

Guidelines for Self-Disclosure

By emphasizing the benefits of self-disclosure to personal well-being and interpersonal relations, I have not suggested in any way that you should go

Appropriate self-disclosure forms a solid basis for friendship and intimate relations.

out and spill your guts to every stranger on the street. Self-disclosure is something you ought to think about seriously. When decisions are finally made to self-disclose, you ought to proceed with caution. Some helpful guidelines for self-disclosing are provided below. See Table 7.1 on p. 253 for tips on listening and responding to other people's self-disclosures.

1. **Examine and evaluate your intentions** Before you begin self-disclosing your feelings, thoughts, values, behaviours or your past, ask yourself this question: "What's motivating me?" Are you self-disclosing to enhance a relationship? Or are you telling someone about some "good dirt" in your past that will likely cause hurt? When self-disclosures have hurtful intentions, they are probably best avoided, especially when relationships are valued and considered worth cultivating.

2. **Think about the appropriate amount of self-disclosure** Researchers have suggested that "relational satisfaction" is likely to be greater at moderate levels of disclosure (Gilbert, 1976). It's not necessarily the case that ever-increasing self-disclosure leads to ever more intimate and stronger relationships. This idea is only true when both people in a relationship have healthy self-concepts, when both are prepared to take risks, and when each displays unconditional positive regard toward the other. When these things are lacking there is a "curvilinear relationship" between self-disclosure and relational satisfaction. Thus, there can be too much, as well as too little, self-disclosure between people. As a general rule of thumb, self-disclose in moderation.

Table 7.1   Listening and Responding to Other People's Self-Disclosures

1. **Pay close attention** There's a difference between hearing and listening. It's possible to be miles away in thought while someone is speaking. Concentrate on what is said. Be present in mind as well as body. If necessary, offer to change locations to reduce external noise and interference. Don't just hear what is said, but really listen. Sometimes it's as important to hear what isn't said as what is.

2. **Suspend judgment** A critical attitude is not likely to encourage others' self-disclosure. Try to suspend judgment when people self-disclose. If you tend to be judgmental, others will probably become defensive and less likely to share personal information. You can facilitate openness by acceptance. You don't have to like everything that is self-disclosed; on the other hand, though, you don't always have to blame, condemn and judge. Ask yourself if you would be more or less likely to self-disclose to those who pronounce judgment on you.

3. **Reflect back to the speaker what is said** By paraphrasing what others self-disclose you can show personal interest and your level of understanding. If an individual perceives you as empathic and truly interested, self-disclosures are more likely to occur.

4. **Remember other people's self-disclosures** If you easily forget self-disclosed information that is considered important and divulged at some risk on the part of the other, you may indirectly communicate the message that you don't care. Besides hurting the other person emotionally, it can cause distance and lessen the chance for further self-disclosures.

5. **Listen with honesty and integrity** Don't try to fool people that you're interested in them when all you really want is someone's "good dirt" to spread around to other people. This action surely constitutes some sort of personal violation. Know why you are choosing to listen. Don't abuse the confidence of others. Respect their right to privacy.

6. **Reassure and support** Help people feel that they have made the right choice by self-disclosing. Support them as individuals and reassure them that what has been told to you has been received in confidence and with sincere efforts to understand and appreciate. This reassurance can be communicated directly with words or indirectly through nonverbal cues (e.g., eye contact or touch).

7. **Reciprocate with appropriate self-disclosures of your own** Communication is a two-way street. When someone self-discloses, that person often takes a psychological risk. A certain amount of trust may be placed in you. By responding with your own appropriate self-disclosures, you can begin to build a relationship of mutual trust (see the guidelines for self-disclosure earlier in the chapter).

3. **Pick your spots** Don't self-disclose indiscriminately. Make sure the disclosure occurs at the right time, at the right place and with the right person. Try to avoid making intimate self-disclosures with strangers. Ask if the self-disclosure you are about to make naturally flows out of the situation or relationship. Bringing up your personal ambitions at a funeral is not likely to be appropriate.

4. **Pay attention to others' self-disclosures** After self-disclosing, allow your listener time to reciprocate with his own disclosures. If there is no reciprocation, you may be getting the message that your disclosures are not wanted or appreciated. Self-disclosure is a two-way street. Clues about what you should disclose can be gained by carefully paying attention to others.

5. **Be prepared to live with what you reveal about yourself** Disclose only things about yourself that you are prepared to have others know. Self-disclosures cannot be erased from the minds of others. Once you reveal facts about yourself, they are public knowledge. Don't reveal what you're going to regret revealing. While self-disclosure requires a certain amount of risk, it should not be based on unwise or imprudent judgments.

Self-Esteem

We learned earlier that self-concept is the cognitive part of self-perception. As individuals, we all have perceptions of ourselves that we can describe. Someone could say, "I'm short," "I'm tall," "I'm a Chinese-Canadian, or "I'm Protestant." In all of these purely descriptive statements, notice the neutrality. Being short or tall is not presented as either good or bad. Presenting oneself as a Protestant or a Chinese-Canadian is regarded neither as praiseworthy nor blameworthy. Descriptive labels do exactly what they are designed to do, that is, describe.

With **self-esteem**, however, an emotional or affective component is added to self-perception (Hamachek, 1992). Not only do we have different perceptions of ourselves, but we also make value judgments based on those perceptions. Seeing yourself as short is one thing; liking what you see is another. Perhaps you dislike your height. Maybe you wish you were taller. Maybe you think of yourself as a "shrimp." If so, you may experience some negative feelings every time you consider your physical stature. Take note here that greater height, in itself, is neither good nor bad. An oriental student in one of my classes once told me how tall people are shunned in his culture. Apparently, in some regions of Japan, they are regarded as untrustworthy. They stand out as unacceptably different. However, height in North American culture is something almost cherished. Some men wish they were tall, dark and handsome. Some women complain they are too short and believe that clothes always look better on taller, slimmer people (just ask the fashion industry). Of course, the value judgments made on self-perceptions are ultimately a matter of personal responsibility. Nobody can make you feel unhappy or insecure about yourself without your permission. This is not to say that cultural ideals and group norms have no impact on self-esteem; they do if you let them. Maintaining self-esteem in the face of societal standards and social values is not always easy. A few inspirational words from e.e. cummings might be in order here.

> To be nobody but yourself — in a world which is doing its best, night and day, to make you everybody else — means to fight the hardest battle which any human being can fight, and never stop fighting.

It's worth underscoring here the fact that self-esteem does not equal egoism (Reece and Brandt, 1990). Having self-esteem is not about self-glorification at the expense of others. It also does not involve any attempt to diminish

Be *the* Star *that* You Are

7.9

The objective of this exercise is to facilitate self-disclosure in a small group. To respond to each of the questions below, first copy the star (Figure 7.8) on a large piece of paper and then draw a picture in the appropriate corresponding part. Don't worry about your artistic talent. What is more important is what you choose to say about each illustration. Once your pictures are finished, join a small group (three to five people) to share information about yourself. Have others in the group respond to your self-disclosures. See what you learn from their reactions.

Questions

1. What is the most important value or belief in your life?
2. What is the best thing you've ever done or had happen to you?
3. What was the happiest moment in your life?
4. What activity do you like?
5. If you could be described in one word, what would it be?
6. What would you like others to know about you?

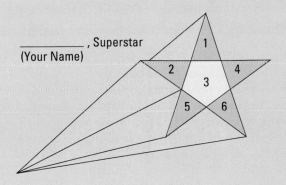

_____ , Superstar
(Your Name)

Figure 7.8
Be the Star that You Are

others or denigrate them for purposes of personal elevation. If you ever see people appearing arrogant and boastful, or if you witness them overestimating themselves in public, you're probably observing inadequate self-esteem in action. It's almost folk wisdom now to say that people who brag and put others down are trying to make themselves feel better. Be careful then to distinguish between healthy self-esteem (self-respect) and the insecure egotistical personality. Bragging for purposes of a "put down" certainly doesn't help others to feel better about themselves and, in the long run, it probably doesn't help you either.

A person's level of self-esteem is influenced by a number of factors. As suggested above, cultural ideals and social comparisons play a role. People trying to achieve a sense of self often look to others to see how they measure up.

We compare grades to see how smart we are. We compare salaries to see how successful we are. We compare clothes to see how fashionable we are. Social comparison allows us to place ourselves somewhere in the hierarchy of life. Many people feel a need to see themselves in relation to others and make self-evaluative judgments on that basis, saying things like, "Compared to that guy, I'm not so bad." In this case, social comparison helps the person feel better about herself.

Self-esteem is also influenced by personal aspirations (Hamachek, 1992). If we continually set unrealistic goals for ourselves and fail in their pursuit, for instance, we will probably develop low self-esteem and consider ourselves as losers. By contrast, if we set attainable goals and achieve them, we're likely to feel better about ourselves. Another factor influencing self-esteem is feedback from others. What people say about us and how they respond to us can obviously have an impact on self-concept and self-esteem. If others are constantly praising our good efforts and congratulating us on our accomplishments, we may begin to see ourselves as successful and feel good about that. Childhood upbringing also influences self-esteem. Researchers have observed that children who are brought up in a permissive environment tend to develop lower self-esteem than children who are raised in a firmer and more demanding home (Reece and Brandt, 1990). In the latter case, expectations are high, discipline is more consistent and greater parental involvement in the lives of children is evident. In short, our current level of self-esteem has probably been influenced, in part at least, by childhood experiences.

It's possible that self-esteem is also affected by gender and sex-role definitions (Monteiro, 1978). One report included in *The New York Times* tells of a study of female undergraduates at six prestigious colleges in the northeast region of the United States. Researchers found that women generally displayed lower self-esteem and lower aspirations then men, even though their grades were roughly equivalent. Given that all people in the study were about the same in terms of academic success, the possibility that gender expectations and cultural views negatively affect women is quite real.

Clearly, self-esteem is very important to human relations. See Table 7.2 for a summary of the effects of high and low self-esteem on interpersonal communication. This material is based on the work of Brooks and Emmert (1976).

Given the significant effects of self-esteem on interpersonal relations, it's important that we try to enhance it in ourselves if we wish to be more effective with people and happier about ourselves. Here are a few suggestions made by writers in the field of human relations to help you enhance your self-esteem (see DeVito, 1993; Napoli et al., 1992).

How to Enhance Self-Esteem

1. **Engage in positive self-talk** We all carry on inner dialogues, or to put it another way, we all talk to ourselves in our minds. The next time you do, experiment with some self-affirmations. Say good things about yourself. Remind yourself of past victories and successes. Think about your positive qualities, your strengths and your attributes. Tell yourself about

Table 7.2   Some Effects of Self-Esteem on Interpersonal Communication

Low Self-Esteem	High Self-Esteem
People with low self-esteem	People with high self-esteem
• Are overly sensitive to criticism; they must be handled with care	• Regard themselves as others' equals
• Overreact to praise; they make too much out of little comments of support and encouragement	• Feel confident about handling problems or situations as they arise; they welcome challenge
• Display hypercritical attitudes; they frequently complain, criticize and find fault	• Accept praise without embarrassment or self-indulgence
• Respond pessimistically to competitive situations	• Acknowledge and accept all aspects of the self (good as well as not good)
	• Seek improvement; they accept responsibility for themselves; they openly receive suggestions and criticisms

future possibilities; don't talk about your weaknesses and limitations.

2. **Surround yourself with supportive people**   I once heard a famous motivational speaker talk about his successful career. He claimed that part of his success was due to the fact that he chose to hang around only those people who were positive and supportive. Such people nourished his soul and energized his mind. He made the point that it is hard to feel good about yourself and to accomplish things if others around you are always finding fault with you or discouraging your efforts.

3. **Set realistic goals for yourself**   If you seek unattainable goals, you're setting yourself up for failure and all the disappointment and ill feelings that accompany it. Be sure to go after the achievable. One success will build upon the next until success will become a way of life and a part of your self-concept.

4. **Disregard counterproductive irrational beliefs**   If you believe, for example, that you must always please everyone all of the time, you're likely to drive yourself crazy. Don't get down on yourself. It's simply unreasonable to think you can always satisfy everybody. Experience demonstrates this idea. If you continue thinking and believing irrational thoughts (e.g., one broken date means nobody loves you), you will undermine your own self-esteem.

5. **Change your presentation of self**   Try to communicate more positively about yourself to others. If you value and appreciate yourself, you will influence others to value and appreciate you as well. People who present themselves as energetic, enthusiastic, interesting and fun-loving, for example, will probably elicit different responses from people who present themselves as listless, apathetic and bored. Whom would you prefer to be with?

STUDY GUIDE

Key Terms

perception (230)	closing (235)	self-serving bias (241)
empiricists (230)	interpreting (236)	proximity (241)
rationalist thinkers (230)	perceptual errors (237)	roles (242)
	stereotyping (237)	self (246)
interactionist theory of knowledge (231)	selectivity (238)	self-concept (246)
	self-fulfilling prophecy (238)	self-awareness (247)
construction (231)		open self (247)
categories (232)	Pygmalion effect (239)	blind self (248)
perceptual filtering (233)	halo effect (239)	unknown self (248)
	reverse halo effect (240)	hidden self (249)
selecting (234)		self-disclosure (250)
organizing (235)	attribution errors (240)	self-esteem (254)
enlarging (235)	actor-observer differences (240)	
simplifying (235)		

PROGRESS CHECK 7.1 ✔

Fill-in-the-Blank Questions

Instructions: Fill in each blank with the appropriate response from the list below.

interactionist	active
perceptual filters	halo effect
responsibility	attribution errors
self-concept	open self
perception	empiricists
static	self-esteem
self-disclosure	self-talk
personal responsibility	self-awareness
social comparison	stereotyping
selective	interpretation

1. _____ is an important key to mastering human relations.

2. According to _____, the mind is like a blank slate; it simply records events in the external world.

3. According to the _____ perspective, the mind organizes sensory data received as external stimuli.

4. The process of perception is _____.

5. People perceive things differently because they have different _____.

6. The process of perceptual construction involves selection, organization and _____.

7. The way I choose to see the world is my _____.

8. Whenever people wrongly lump others together and attribute to them common characteristics that they don't possess, they are guilty of _____.

9. When we meet somebody, we don't perceive everything about that person; we are _____ in our perception.

10. Forming a general impression of someone based on a single characteristic gives rise to the _____.

11. An effort to locate the source of behaviours as internal or external can sometimes lead to _____.

12. _____ refers to the overall way you see and understand yourself.

13. Self-concepts are not _____.

14. Self-disclosure hinges on _____.

15. The _____ is that part of yourself known by you and shared with others.

16. _____ is the act of revealing information about yourself to others.

17. The positive or negative evaluations we make about our self-concepts contribute to our _____.

18. The value judgments you make about yourself are a matter of _____.

19. Self-esteem can be affected by _____.

20. People can raise their self-esteem through the use of affirmations or positive _____.

True/False Questions

Instructions: Circle the appropriate letter next to each statement.

T F 1. Psychological perception is irrelevant to social relations.

T F 2. Rationalists believe that "what you see is what you get." Knowledge is based on experience.

T F 3. The figure made up of three dots has only one correct meaning.

T F 4. According to the interactionist viewpoint, perception is an active process.

T F 5. The filtering system of perception filters out erroneous messages to give us a truer picture of reality.

T F 6. The mind has a natural tendency to impose closure on incoming stimuli to make sense of the world.

T F 7. You can exercise considerable responsibility when it comes to how you choose to see life.

T F 8. The halo effect causes us to see "bad" people as "good" people.

T F 9. When we attribute behaviour to causal factors that are lasting or ongoing, we can say that the causes are stable.

T F 10. Students who fail an exam are likely to attribute their failure to external causes.

T F 11. Proximity, as a factor in perception, can be either physical or psychological.

T F 12. The notion of self-concept includes all of your self-referring values, beliefs, attitudes and feelings.

T F 13. There is only one self.

T F 14. The self-concept is static.

T F 15. Self-disclosure always improves relationships.

T F 16. The hidden self contains information about yourself that is buried in the unconscious.

T F 17. Introverts are likely to find self-disclosure more difficult than are extraverts.

T F 18. The Johari Window is a theoretical device used to explain the mechanisms of perception.

T F 19. People who rarely self-disclose have less effective immune systems compared to those who self-disclose more frequently.

T F 20. Egotism is another word for self-esteem.

Focus Questions

1. How does perception work? Is it always an accurate reflection of reality? Why?
2. Can certain knowledge be based on perception? Why?
3. What does it mean to suggest that personal and social reality are "constructed"?
4. What is meant by the concept of "perceptual filter?"
5. What sense can be made out of the assertion "How I see the world is my responsibility"?
6. Can perception be mistaken? If so, how?
7. What can be done to reduce perceptual errors?
8. What is meant by "self-concept"?
9. Why are people reluctant to tell others about themselves?
10. Can you outline some of the shoulds and shouldn'ts concerning self-disclosure?
11. What are some of the factors influencing self-esteem?
12. How does self-esteem influence interpersonal communication?
13. How can self-esteem be enhanced?

Summary

1. How is perception important to human relations?
   • they are intimately related
   • through perception we gain awareness, experience people, attribute causes, give meaning and form impressions of others

2. How is perception an (inter)active process?
   • perception involves construction (i.e., application of categories, assimilation to previous structures of understanding, accommodation)
   • perception is a filtering process
   • it involves selecting, organizing and interpreting

3. What are some common perceptual errors?
   • **stereotyping**: lumping individuals together and attributing to them common characteristics
   • **self-fulfilling prophecy**: seeing what one expects to see as a result of one's behaviour or expectations
   • **halo effect**: taking one characteristic (either positive or negative) and perceiving others as related, when in fact they're not
   • **attributional errors**: making mistakes when attributing causes or sources of behaviour
   • **proximity** (physical or psychological): misperceiving because of distance. Evaluations may be biased in favour of those who display similar attributes to our own.
   • **roles**: playing roles skews our perceptions

4. How can errors in perception be reduced?
   • avoid hasty conclusions
   • allow yourself more time
   • make yourself available
   • commit yourself to situations
   • create the proper climate
   • make adjustments when necessary

5. What is self-concept?
   • the overall way you see and understand yourself
   • all of your self-referring beliefs and attitudes, as well as your values, feelings, behavioural dispositions and preferences
   • it is multi-faceted (e.g., there is your work self, your ideal self and your serious self)

6. What is the importance of self-concept to human relations?
   • what you know about yourself, how you feel about yourself and what you reveal about yourself to others affects others' reactions to you

7. What are the four "panes" of the Johari Window?
   • **open self**: known by yourself and others
   • **hidden self**: known by yourself, not revealed to others
   • **blind self**: known by others, not recognized in yourself
   • **unknown self**: not known by yourself or others

8. How can self-awareness be increased?
   • adopt the perspective of others
   • create a list of your attitudes, behaviours and tendencies
   • pay close attention to how others react to you
   • increase openness to others to reduce the size of your blind self

9. What is self-disclosure?
   • the intentional act of revealing information about yourself to others
   • not about laying blame or emotional dumping

- sharing parts of yourself with others in a way that respects them

10. Why are people reluctant to self-disclose?
    - fear that self-disclosure may be used against the self-discloser
    - fear of rejection
    - fear of others' reactions
    - fear of hurting others
    - fear of projecting an unwanted image

11. Why is self-disclosure important to social relationships?
    - mutual self-disclosure paves the way for friendship and intimacy
    - it allows for caring, sharing and empathy
    - it offers others an opportunity to respond to us
    - it enhances personal well-being, improves effectiveness of immune system and supports good mental health

12. What are some guidelines for appropriate self-disclosure?
    - examine and evaluate your intentions
    - think about the appropriate amount of self-disclosure
    - pick your spots for self-disclosure
    - pay attention to others' self-disclosure
    - be prepared to live with what you reveal about yourself

13. What is self-esteem?
    - the value judgment we make on our self-concept
    - a self-referring feeling
    - not self-glorification, arrogance, boastfulness or egoism
    - healthy self-respect

14. What are some factors influencing self-esteem?
    - social comparison
    - personal aspirations
    - feedback from others
    - childhood upbringing
    - gender and sex-role definitions

15. What are some effects of self-esteem on interpersonal relations?
    Low self-esteem makes people
    - overly sensitive to criticism
    - overreact to praise
    - adopt hypercritical attitudes
    - respond pessimistically
    - avoid competitive challenges

    High self-esteem makes people
    - treat other people as equals
    - welcome challenges
    - accept praise without embarrassment
    - become more self-accepting
    - desire to improve themselves
    - accept personal responsibility

16. How can you enhance your self-esteem?
    - engage in positive self-talk

- surround yourself with supportive people
- set realistic goals for yourself
- discard irrational beliefs
- change your self-presentation

Related Readings

Branden, Nathaniel (1987). *The Psychology of Self-Esteem*. New York: Bantam.
——— (1987). *How to Raise Your Self-Esteem.* New York: Bantam.
Napoli, Vince, James L. Kilbride and Donald E. Tebbs (1992). *Adjustment and Growth in a Changing World*. 4th edition. St. Paul: West Publishing Co.
Piaget, Jean (1969). *The Mechanisms of Perception*. London: Routledge.
Satir, Virginia (1988). *The New Peoplemaking*. Mountainview, CA: Science & Behaviour Books Inc.

Weblinks

1. National Association for Self-Esteem
   www.self-esteem-nase.org/

   The association's aim is to fully integrate self-esteem into the fabric of American society so that every individual, no matter what his or her age or background, experiences personal worth and happiness.

2. Arizona Centre for Self-Help
   www.selfhelpcenter.com/

   This centre offers a web site describing products available to help people break habits of smoking, overeating, anxiety, depression and addictions.

3. Self-disclosure and openness
   www.cmhc.com/psyhelp/chap13i.htm

   Visit this web site for information about self-disclosure, emotional openness and effective communication.

...women speak and hear a language of connection and intimacy, while men speak and hear a language of status and independence.

–Deborah Tannen

GENDER, CULTURE AND NONVERBAL CUES

CHAPTER OVERVIEW

LEARNING OUTCOMES

After successfully completing this chapter, you will be able to

8.1 Appreciate how gender impacts on interpersonal communications

8.2 Account for male-female differences in moral thinking by reference to early identity formation

8.3 Give examples of gender differences in language usage

8.4 Discuss the importance of culture to interpersonal dynamics

8.5 Provide four different forms of intercultural communication

8.6 Give illustrations of miscommunication stemming from intercultural transactions

8.7 Improve intercultural communication

8.8 Define nonverbal behaviour

8.9 Better understand the functional relationship between verbal and nonverbal communication

8.10 Classify types of nonverbal behaviour

8.11 "Read" people better on the basis of their clothing and physical appearance

8.12 Illustrate how space and time send nonverbal messages

8.13 Explain how we communicate by touch

Coming and Going

i have noticed
that men
somewhere around forty
tend to come in from the field
with a sigh
and removing their coat in the hall
call into the kitchen
You were right
Grace
it ain't out there
just like you've always said
and she
with the children gone at last
breathless
puts her hat on her head
the hell it ain't!
coming and going
they pass
in the doorway

Ric Masten

Source: From *Ric Masten Speaking*, Papier-Mache Press. Copyright Sunflower Inc., 37931 Palo Colorado Rd., Carmel, CA 93923.

In this concluding chapter of Part II, Factors Influencing Interpersonal Relations, we'll be looking at gender, culture and nonverbal communication. At first glance, these topics may appear to be dissimilar. However, many examples and illustrations can be provided to reveal how they're actually quite closely connected. Gender relations, for instance, are often dictated by cultural norms and values. Who gets served first at dinner is a function of age and gender in Japan. Where men and women sit in an Israeli synagogue hinges on custom and religious tradition. Like gender relations, nonverbal signals can also depend on cultural factors. For example, when I was growing up in Brantford, Ontario, the "thumbs up" signal meant "Go to hell." (I remember delighting in its naughty use as a kid!) Years later, when I travelled to Europe, I was surprised to discover that it meant "Good luck." I guess Canadians import hand signals the way they do European fashions because the thumbs-up signal apparently now means "Good luck" in Paris, Ontario, just as it does in Paris, France. We'll continue to discuss nonverbal cues a little later on in the chapter, but for now, let's examine more closely the effects of gender on interpersonal communication.

GENDER COMMUNICATION: HE SAID, SHE SAID

8.1

How people communicate and get along with one another can be affected by **gender**, one's sex or sexual identity. Studies suggest that men and women use language differently, that their behaviour is often influenced by gender-role expectations, and that they tend to interpret the moral dimensions of life in different terms (Gilligan, 1982; Tannen, 1990). These differences are important to note. If we want to reduce gender-based misunderstandings, we should take into account the contrasting perceptual tendencies, communication styles and reasoning patterns of men and women. Let's begin, then, by examining how men and women tend to perceive interpersonal conflicts differently when matters of morality (right/wrong or good/bad) are concerned. To help your understanding, do Application Exercise 8.1.

Interpreting Your Responses

The dilemma on page 268 comes from the work of the late Lawrence Kohlberg (1976). Kohlberg was a Harvard psychologist who studied moral reasoning development for more than two decades. He used the "Joe dilemma" and others like it to gain information about the evolution of thinking when it comes to people's reasoning about moral matters. On the basis of his research, he concluded that **moral reasoning** progresses sequentially through six stages, falling under three basic levels of development.

At level one (pre-conventional morality), people respond to cultural labels of good/bad and right/wrong. They interpret these labels with respect to the physical or hedonistic consequences of action or in terms of the physical

Dad or Joe: Who Should Go?

Instructions: Read the moral dilemma below. After you have answered the questions privately, discuss your answers with others. You might wish to divide the class into smaller all-male and all-female groups. This division would help you to see if any gender-based differences arise. If the class is broken up into smaller gender-based groups, have each subgroup report to the class as a whole in order to compare answers.

1. Joe is a 14-year-old boy who wanted to go to camp very much. His father promised him he could go if he saved up the money himself. Joe worked hard at his paper route and saved up the $40 it cost to go to camp, with a little money left over. But just before camp was going to start, his father changed his mind. Some of his friends decided to go on a special fishing trip, and Joe's father was short the money it would cost. So he told Joe to give him the money he had saved from the paper route. Joe didn't want to give up going to camp, so he thought of refusing to give his father the money.

Should Joe refuse to give his father the money or should he give it to him? Why?

2. Further discussion about this dilemma can be generated by adding the following information:

Joe lied and said he only made $10 and went to camp with the $40 he made. Joe had an older brother named Bob. Before Joe went to camp he told Bob about the money and about lying to their father. Should Bob tell their father?

---

powers of those who make and enforce the rules. In other words, wrong is defined by what gets punished; right is defined by what gets praised, rewarded or allowed. At level two (conventional morality), people try to live up to the expectations of their family, group or nation. They act out of loyalty and for the maintenance of the existing social order. Good behaviour is that which pleases or helps others. Good is also defined by that which conforms to existing laws and rules of conduct. At level three (post-conventional morality), people define their own moral values and principles apart from any particular authority, group or cultural norm. Moral judgments are rational and objective. At level three, moral judgment is not biased by personal interest (level one) or group loyalty (level two). Instead, judgments possess a universal prescriptive quality. They apply to all people regardless of space-time considerations. Appreciating this information now, you may wish to review your personal responses to Application Exercise 8.1. In terms of Kohlberg's scheme, where does your reasoning fall?

Morality in a Different Voice: Carol Gilligan

If you did not score as highly as you might have liked on Kohlberg's scheme, you can take some comfort (especially if you're female) in the fact that Carol Gilligan, another noted Harvard researcher, has been critical of Kohlberg's work. She points out that females tend to score at lower levels of development than males in terms of Kohlberg's stage theory. Rather than accept these findings, Gilligan criticizes the moral assumptions underlying Kohlberg's theory. She draws attention to the fact that women have a tendency to speak to moral issues "in a different voice" from men, as she puts it. Perhaps you found this yourself when comparing male and female responses to the "Joe" dilemma in class. In any case, according to Gilligan, the different **moral voice** of women is what actually causes the lower scores. Since women make different psychological assumptions about morality, they display different reasoning patterns than do men. Unfortunately, male researchers such as Kohlberg have not been sensitive to these differences in the past. The result is that male norms have been used to judge moral reasoning adequacy.

With the new insights offered to us by feminists such as Gilligan, ignored differences between the sexes are being taken seriously in social scientific research. Theories and research methodologies, once considered sexually neutral in their scientific objectivity, are now being found to reflect consistent observational and evaluative biases. This certainly is true with Kohlberg, if Gilligan is correct.

Kohlberg's initial experimental studies were based on an all-male sample of subjects. This fact, once unnoticed or considered unimportant by the scientific community, is now astonishing in its gender bias. Making broad generalizations about people's moral reasoning development based on a small sample of males is clearly unacceptable. Furthermore, the dilemmas like "Joe" were also constructed by Kohlberg himself. He did not permit subjects to define the moral domain or to interpret moral conflict in their own terms. The dilemmas were all hypothetical, impersonal and abstract. These facts are important, for, as Gilligan points out, women tend to view moral situations more personally and concretely. Gilligan's critique of Kohlberg thus underscores the contaminating effects of the male bias and the abstract, unreal nature of the hypothetical situations.

The "different voice of morality" that Gilligan addresses is characterized more by theme than by gender (Gilligan, 1982: 2). As she says, "Its association with women is an empirical observation....But this association is not absolute....[T]he contrasts between male and female voices are presented here to highlight a distinction between two modes of thought and to focus on a problem of interpretation rather than to represent a generalization about either sex." In other words, male and female differences in moral reasoning can be observed though there's nothing necessary or innate about them. Nothing prevents women from displaying "typically male" reasoning patterns or men from displaying "typically female" reasoning patterns. Gilligan refers to Nancy Chodorow's (1974) work on identity formation to help account for apparent masculine and feminine differences in moral thinking.

8.2

According to Chodorow, **identity formation** in males and females is quite different. For females, identity formation occurs in a context of ongoing relationships. As she puts it, "[M]others tend to experience their daughters as more like, and continuous with, themselves (Chodorow, cited in Gilligan, 1982: 7). As daughters form their female identities, they perceive and experience themselves as being much like their mothers. The process of identity formation thus involves a significant element of attachment.

When it comes to boys, "mothers experience their sons as a male opposite" (Chodorow, cited in Gilligan, 1982: 8). Boys, in defining themselves as masculine, separate themselves from their mothers. They curtail "their primary love and sense of empathic tie." The net result is that male development entails more emphasis on the process of separation, individuation and a "more defensive firming of experienced ego boundaries" (Chodorow, 1974). If Chodorow is correct about male and female differences regarding the period of early identity formation, we can better understand how girls emerge from it with a greater capacity for empathy built into their primary definition of self. The early attachment and identification of girls with their same-sex mother provides them with a stronger basis for experiencing other people's needs or feelings as their own. Early identification with a same-sex parent means that girls tend to experience themselves "as less differentiated than boys, as more continuous with and related to the external object-world, and as differently oriented to their inner object-world as well" (Chodorow, cited in Gilligan, 1982: 9).

Male and female differences regarding early identity formation affect interpersonal relations and moral thinking. "Since masculinity is defined through separation while femininity is defined through attachment, male gender identity is threatened by intimacy while female gender identity is threatened by separation. Thus, males tend to have difficulty with relationships, while females tend to have problems with individuation (8). Male and female differences, with respect to identity formation, take us back to the inherent problems of Kohlberg's research on moral reasoning. Gilligan claims that by designing hypothetical dilemmas to emphasize justice considerations (legalistic rights, fairness and competing interests), Kohlberg has set up situations requiring detachment, rational objectivity, impartiality and the cold impersonal application of rules and principles. The legalistic, "rights" element in each of the dilemmas caters to the masculine psychology of separation. The better or more adequate moral solution to any dilemma is determined by justifications based on abstract principles of justice and fairness. Any reasoning that is subjective, personal, contextual, emotional or relationally based is deemed less adequate or less developed (because it's reflective of conventional, level-two thinking). Male life is thus taken as the norm. Abstract principles are preferred to real people and their personal interests.

In contrast to Kohlberg, who thought of morality as a development from hedonism to a rule-regulated morality, Gilligan sees feminine morality as a progression from selfishness to the recognition of social responsibility (Lefrancois, 1990). Using research on women's reasoning for having or not having an abortion, she has identified three stages in female moral development. In the initial stage, women are moved primarily by selfish concerns, e.g., "This is what I want, what I need, and what I should do, or what would be best for me." In the second stage, women increase their recognition of responsibility to others. The third and final stage of female moral reasoning displays a woman's wish to do the greatest good for both herself and others. Below, Lefrancois, from the University of Alberta, sums up the male and female differences as they emerge from the work of Gilligan and Kohlberg.

> *It seems that, in general, girls are more responsive to social relationships and to the social consequences of their behaviour, more concerned with empathy and compassion, perhaps more in touch with real life, and less concerned with the hypothetical....Boys are perhaps more concerned with law and order than with the personally meaningful dimensions of morality. (1990: 443)*

We learn from Gilligan and Kohlberg that people can construct social morality differently. A Kohlbergian level-two, stage-three response (based on a need to maintain relationships) is not necessarily less mature, less adequate or less developed than a response that appeals to abstract principles—at least not when viewed from a feminine perspective. As in so many areas of life, inter-gender communication may call for some compromise and mutual understanding. Perhaps we should all learn to appreciate the feminine **morality of care** and **relationship** as well as the masculine **morality of impersonal justice**. If we took these differences into consideration, perhaps men would appear less cold and uncaring, and women would appear less inconsistent and immature. Maybe we need to care more about reason, and reason with more care.

The unlike is joined together, and from differences results the most beautiful harmony...

Heraclitus

Masculine and feminine values, together and in balance, yield complementary benefits that enrich life. When either overwhelms the other, neither is life-giving. In our society — deprived of soul and therefore of a conscious understanding of the feminine — we've been looking at the feminine through the wrong lens, the lens of masculine understanding. However, just as masculine values were never intended to be evaluated through a feminine perspective, feminine values can't be understood from a masculine viewpoint.

Kathleen Hurley and Theodore Dobson

ANIMA AND ANIMUS

According to Carl Jung, the founder of analytical psychology, both men and women display psychic characteristics usually attributed to the opposite sex. Thus, psychologically speaking, men are not entirely masculine or exclusively male. Men possess feminine qualities, attributes and intuitions. These things make up the **anima**. Because of culture and tradition, however, men are encouraged to repress traits of the anima that could be described as weak, soft or feminine. Women, on the other hand, are not entirely feminine or exclusively female. They possess an **animus** as part of their psyche. We find in the animus all that is thought to be traditionally male.

While the anima produces moods in men, the animus produces opinions in women.

There are some dangers associated with the anima and animus. First, it's possible that the psyche may fall under the exclusive influence of either one of these psychological archetypes. A man dominated by the anima may lose his masculinity; if dominated by the animus, he may lose his tenderness and intuitive powers. A woman dominated by the animus may lose her femininity; if dominated by the anima, she may lose her objective rational capacities. A general point to be made here is that balance is required. The anima and the animus are different, but complementary as-

pects of the unified self. If the anima or animus is repressed, both men and women will fail to achieve psychological wholeness. They will remain incomplete or somehow imbalanced. A healthy and whole person is psychologically androgynous, someone who displays a balance of male and female characteristics. Refer to the graphic of the self for an illustration.

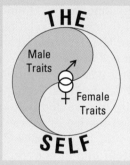

I used the preceding discussion to raise awareness of the fact that men and women tend to think differently about morality and interpersonal relations. In contrast to men, women speak in "a different voice," as Carol Gilligan puts it. In this part of the chapter, we'll continue to look at gender differences with respect to how men and women use language in everyday contexts. Knowing about language differences is important. First, it can help you to understand others better. Second, by being sensitive to your own language characteristics, you can better appreciate the impressions you make on others. Third, if you increase your understanding of others through a study of language differences, and others come to appreciate and understand you more, mutual empathy becomes a real possibility (Weaver, 1993).

In her best-selling book entitled *You Just Don't Understand: Women and Men in Conversation*, writer and researcher Deborah Tannen discusses a number of male and female differences in language usage. Her first observation is remarkably consistent with Gilligan's work. Tannen (1990: 42) says, "[W]omen speak and hear a language of connection and intimacy, while men speak and hear a language of status and independence...." Parallels can easily be drawn between a feminine morality of care and the language of connection, and between a masculine morality of rights and the language of independence (separation). A second observation made by Tannen is that male-female communication can be plagued by what she calls **asymmetries** (49–73). Because male and female speech lacks similarity of form, men and women often talk to each other at cross-purposes. For an example of an asymmetrical communication, read the dialogue below:

He: I'm really tired. I didn't sleep well last night.

She: I didn't sleep well either. I never do.

He: Why are you trying to belittle me?

She: I'm not! I'm just trying to show I understand. (51)

In the example above, the female had a particular intention behind her response. She was trying to establish a connection with the male; she was trying to show him that she understood his problem through her own experience. The male, on the other hand, took no comfort in the woman's response. He thought she was "trying to take something away from him by changing the uniqueness of his experience" (51). In this case, the man filtered the woman's attempt to establish connections through his concern with preserving personal autonomy and independence. Of course, problems of asymmetry can be reversed. Women can become annoyed or frustrated because men do not respond to their troubles by offering corresponding troubles—something they would appreciate.

A third gender difference in language, Tannen observes, involves speaking in private and public. She says, "More men feel comfortable doing '**public speaking**,' while more women feel comfortable doing '**private speaking**'" (77). Another way of capturing these differences is by using these terms: **report talk** and **rapport talk** (77). According to Tannen, rapport talk (done in private) is a language of conversation. It helps to establish connections and negotiate relationships. It emphasizes matching experiences. She explains, "From childhood, girls criticize peers who try to stand out or appear better than others" (77). Rapport talk tends to occur at home in private because that's where the closest connections are. By contrast, report talk usually takes place publicly. A man who barely speaks at home may appear confident and quite vocal to others as he uses report talk to exhibit knowledge and skill, preserve independence and maintain status in the hierarchical social order. "From childhood, men learn to use talking as a way to get and keep attention" (77). Thus, they become more comfortable in later life speaking in larger groups.

Gender differences can also be found in **gossip talk**. Both sexes gossip; only their subjects tend to differ. Men may gossip about business matters or sports, while women have a tendency to talk about feelings and what is currently happening in their lives. Such gossip talk forms the core of friendship (96–122). Here we see that gossip needn't necessarily be destructive; it can serve a useful function in establishing intimacy.

Male and female language usage differences are evident in the context of lecturing and listening as well. "[M]en are more comfortable than women in giving information and opinions and speaking in an authoritative way to a group, whereas women are more comfortable than men in supporting others" (Tannen, cited in Weaver, 1993: 242). Related to the business of who's talking and who's listening, Tannen points to research on gender and language that apparently reveals that men don't listen very well. By this point I mean that men tend to interrupt women more than women interrupt men (Tannen, 1990: 189). Interruptions should not be taken lightly, especially in close relationships. They can transmit metamessages to those whom we interrupt—messages like "I don't care enough to pay attention," "I don't listen" or "I'm not interested in what you're saying." Nobody likes to hear these metamessages because we all like to be heard and valued (189). When speaking to someone you care about, you might choose to be a little more careful about your interruptions.

Finally, when speaking in public situations, women are expected to be less boastful than men (223). Whereas males often use self-aggrandizing information to achieve status, females typically do not "wear their achievements on their sleeves," so to speak (Weaver, 1993: 244). Unfortunately, they do tend to be underestimated as a result. When addressing gender language differences, Richard Weaver (1993) cautions us about our generalizations and I think his caution is well recommended. After all, people are individuals and do not always fit the generalizations. What people do or say may vary from time to time, place to place and group to group. Furthermore, gender studies on language are at this point still inconclusive—gender tendencies seem to be present in some studies but not in others. Finally, group composition (the number of males and females) can also influence speech patterns. For example, language differences may be less evident in groups where gender mix is about equal. Be sure, then, not to make any gross generalizations or to predict people's behaviour solely on the basis of gender.

 ## CULTURE AND COMMUNICATION: INSIDE LOOKING OUT, OUTSIDE LOOKING IN

> It may be doubtful, at first, whether a person is an enemy or friend.
> Meat, if not properly digested, becomes poison;
> But poison, if used rightly, may turn medicinal.
>
> Saskya Pandita (1182–1251)

So far in this text we have studied individual differences and their impact on interpersonal communication. We have learned, for instance, how differing personality types, temperaments and conflict resolution styles can affect how we deal with others, both personally and professionally. At this point, we'll consider how sociocultural factors influence interpersonal dynamics.

If Canada were a purely homogeneous society, that is, if everyone dressed the same, spoke the same language, professed the same faith, originated from the same ethnic and racial background and shared the same sexual preferences and inclinations, all communication would likely be very easy. However, as former prime minister Joe Clark once stated, the nation of Canada is a "community of communities." We are, in fact, both a **pluralistic** society and a **multicultural** one as well. These terms refer to our social reality and our national identity. If we are to live democratically and communicate effectively with one another as friends, neighbours and citizens, we must learn to deal with cultural diversity. We must make an honest effort to listen to each other. We must accept differences, work with them and use them to enhance the quality of our collective life.

Not only has pluralism forced us to focus on the importance of culture in communications, but so too has economics. In a global economy, consisting of multinational corporations, foreign markets and international trade agreements, many people are forced to do their business in other countries and with other cultures. They must travel and remain constantly mobile. They must be able to understand, adapt to and accommodate people and circumstances in which they find themselves. **Economic interdependence** now requires us to communicate more effectively across different cultures. Furthermore, advances in technology and telecommunications have brought the world to our doorstep. We can witness events as they happen, live from around the world, by simply turning on the TV. Computers and information superhighways allow us to communicate across borders and gain access to information in amounts and at rates that would have dumbfounded earlier generations. We can attend teleconferences and communicate with people thousands of miles away. If we are not to misunderstand them, we must learn to appreciate cultural contexts out of which communications arise.

Politics also point to the importance of culture on communication. In a nation such as Canada, regional differences often cause tension and conflict. For example, there are Maritimers and Quebeckers, Aboriginals and Westerners, and these groups' needs and demands are often very different. In federal governmental affairs, it seems sometimes that every region wants to have a "voice," but is not willing to really listen to others. In light of this, one could argue that the survival of Canada depends on better communication among its various regions.

What Is Culture?

Since we're focusing here on the importance of culture to communication, it makes sense to define what we mean by culture. **Culture** refers to a group of people living a more or less defined and recognizable lifestyle. This group is collectively bonded by their shared values, ideals, beliefs, behaviours and accepted ways of communicating and doing things. All of the above are transmitted from one generation to the next (DeVito, 1992: 254–255). Culture is not genetically determined; it is not inborn or innate. Through our experiences with parents, teachers, peers, religious authorities and social institutions, we absorb the culture we have been raised in and become part of it ourselves, contributing to the **enculturation** of the next generation.

Related to enculturation is the notion of **acculturation**. In this process, an individual's "culture is modified through direct contact or exposure to another culture" (255). Immigrants to this country, for example, may acculturate by assimilating to our Canadian lifestyle and adopting many of our values as their own. Also, a member of one ethnic subcultural community may acculturate to another by incorporating some or any of its ways. I recently heard of a wedding, for example, between a Polish-Canadian woman and a Jamaican-Canadian man. At the wedding reception, cabbage rolls were served and reggae music was played. The combination probably represents, symbolically at least, some kind of cultural bridging or mutual acculturation between two subcultural groups. Members of both communities adopted preferences of the other and made them part of their own experience.

A language professor once suggested to me that you could tell when someone had successfully acculturated into any given society. He said that people are not acculturated until they understand the newly adopted culture's sense of humour. Personally speaking, I tend to agree. I remember how alienated I once felt in Quebec years ago as a student when I couldn't appreciate the jokes that were told at social gatherings, though I understood the vocabulary that was used. Cultural context (i.e., history and politics) added humour to otherwise neutral language, creating a humour that could not be grasped by at least one anglophone from Ontario.

8.5 ▶ There are four different forms of **intercultural communication** (DeVito, 1993: 256). The first form is international and could refer to communication between Germany and Japan or between the Ukraine and Italy, for example. The second form is interracial and could refer to the communication between blacks and Chinese people or between Native people and whites. The third type is inter-ethnic and could refer to communication between French-Canadians and Vietnamese-Canadians. The fourth type is religious and could be the sort of communication that takes place between Buddhists and Jews, Catholics and Protestants, or Hindus and Moslems. Occupational groups also form subcultures in a society. It's always interesting to hear doctors and lawyers communicate, for instance, especially in court! The technical "computerese" spoken by programmers is always an intriguing contrast to the "psycho-babble" spoken by behavioural scientists. Communication can also take place between a dominant culture and a particular subculture, such as the heterosexual and gay communities. Finally, it's possible to distinguish communication on the basis of gender groupings, such as between men and women, as we did in the preceding section. What needs to be stressed here is that communication can and often does go beyond simple transactions between two individuals. Not only does psychological type filter communication (see Chapter 2), but so too does the culture and cultural subgroup to which one belongs. See Figure 8.1 for a depiction of the communication process incorporating a cultural overlay.

Intercultural Communication

8.6 ▶

When people from different cultures or subcultural groups interact, miscommunication can sometimes arise. Language may not be understood, intentions may be misread or customs may be unconsciously violated. For

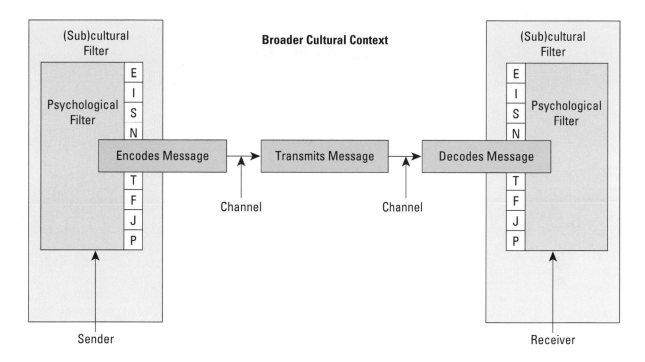

Sender

Receiver

Figure 8.1

The Communication Process with Cultural Overlay

example, a Canadian tourist in Japan might stop to take pictures of a Buddhist wedding in progress. For the Canadian, weddings are a time of great joy and celebration. Taking pictures comes naturally and spontaneously on such happy occasions. However, for Buddhists, weddings have a different purpose and picture taking is offensive to them. To do what seems innocent to the Canadian is wrong to the Japanese Buddhist. From this illustration, we can appreciate how cultural diversity can sometimes be a source of unfortunate misunderstanding. (Samovar, Porter and Jain, 1990: 395).

Communication can also suffer from **ethnocentrism**. Think of this as the social equivalent to psychological egocentrism. Egocentric people can only see the world from their own perspective. Like children, they can't see the broader picture. Their perceptions are slanted by subjectivity and personal bias. They are unable to detach themselves from their own wants, preferences, values and beliefs to see things as others see them. If we expand psychological egocentrism to include the collective psyche of a culture, nation or particular subgroup within it, we create a kind of ethnic egocentrism or ethnocentrism for short. Peoples, races, minorities, occupational groups, subcultures and religious denominations, for instance, may suffer from ethnocentrism. Around the globe you often hear people criticizing U.S. citizens, objecting to a viewpoint that they rightly or wrongly attribute to them, namely, "What's good for America is good for the world." This idea is obviously not so, and for any American to think this would be disrespectful of other cultures. The world is not the U.S. and the U.S. is not the world. By the way, not to be outdone by our U.S. cousins, we too have our own examples of ethnocentrism within Canada. Ontarians are sometimes perceived as ethnocentric from the vantage point of Maritimers, Quebeckers and Westerners. Some would argue that Ontarians are so self-centred that they

LOTUSLAND AND HOGTOWN IN COMMUNICATION

These two articles are humorous examples of intercultural communication that occurred between two regions of Canada during the 1994 Stanley Cup playoffs. Rosie DiManno of the *Toronto Star* sends her regards to *Vancouver Sun* columnist Denny Boyd, who shares his thoughts about his beloved coastal city and his perceptions of Toronto and Torontonians.

TAKE VANCOUVER AND SHOVE IT...

BY ROSIE DIMANNO

Vancouver — What a bimbo town.

If Vancouver were a dame, it would be a harlot starlet, pressing its cantilevered cleavage into your face and whispering huskily in your ear.

No talent, but a great set of...twin peaks.

It reclines here on the edge of terra firma, like a courtesan on a chaise longue, purring and preening and puckering its lips.

Put another way, Vancouver is spiritually, psychically and tempermentally blonde: a vapid airhead of a burg, substituting good looks for brains and giggles for conversation.

They really should have called their hockey team the Vancouver Vanities.

But the Canucks it is, and the Canucks it was, last night anyway. A 4–0 win over the Toronto Maple Leafs in a game that will not win any marks for artistic impression, or class, or sportsmanship.

And that was even before the flying fists, and the boxing gloves that were hurled to the ice, and the unidentified projectile that came crashing through the glass in the press box.

Things deteriorated so badly that both teams were ordered off the ice, with just over three minutes remaining, and were summoned back to finish off this rancid mess only after tempers had cooled.

That's some playoff style they've got going here, no? And style is so very crucial out here too. Style over substance, baby.

Oy, is this hamlet self-absorbed or what? Culturally bereft, politically inconsequential and geographically isolated from the commonweal of the Canadian experience, it has created a cult out of itself. There's a kind of Moonie attitude that permeates every aspect of life-as-they-know-it in Lotusland, an indolent haze-daze that renders its denizens glassy-eyed and intellectually fried.

Vancouverites are all the time bleating about Toronto. Their insecurity is staggering but understandable. What, after all, does Vancouver have going for it except a confluence of geological elements—the mountains and the sea—and the massive influx of Asian dollars?

Vancouverites have never met a fad they couldn't embrace, and right now the pet rocks of choice are the Canuckleheads.

Vancouverites are like mood rings: they change their colours, and their sensibilities, according to the whims of fortune. So one day they're touchy-feely aesthetes—tree-huggers, whale-petters, tofu-eaters—and the next they're trying to masquerade as hockey-frenzied Canuck devotees.

We're not buying it.

Vancouverites sneer and call us Hogtown even as they make piggy-grunts toward their ideological cousins in southern California. If Confederation is someday dismantled—and Premier Mike Harcourt's ill-advised comments this week, that Quebec would become British Columbia's enemy should the separatists prevail, can only hasten such an eventuality—Lotusland could petition La-la-land for official adoption. They are joined at the ego anyway.

Source: Reprinted with permission—The Toronto Star Syndicate.

WE HAVE IT ALL: COJONES, CALZONES AND HEAVEN, TOO

BY DENNY BOYD

Vancouver — Warm memo to all visiting members of the Toronto sporting media. Abusive remarks to follow, the moment you relax:

Gentlemen and ladies. I believe your flight arrived half an hour after ours descended into a characteristically sub-tropical morning Thursday.

Fish are jumping and the cotton is high. It's the type of weather we favour for hockey playoffs. Gives the players the opportunity for some beach time between games.

Your first obligation, if you have a shred of decency, will be to boot up your laptops and write retractions for all dingy remarks you have been making about the West, westerners and western lifestyle. You are here now, you see now, and you know now that you were wrong. Write it, say you're sorry, then kick back and put some sprouts in your avocado sandwiches while you await the third game of the playoffs.

One of you, I understand, made a down-putting remark on a presumed lack of cojones in the West. Let me assure you, my dear, not only do we have cojones in numbers and size but we also have calzones, frijoles, fajitas and pizzas to go.

We hope you have begun to appreciate the privilege you stepped into the moment you deplaned, blinking in the bright light. You have entered heaven without having to die, even a little bit. Surely you can see that, even through your winter-rimed eastern eyes.

In all modesty, we think our climate could whip your climate with July and August tied behind its back. Just look around.

Straight up, that's the best sky you can find anywhere. It's blue, the colour you only see on hockey sweaters. Now over there, those are our mountains. You may get your yah-yahs by looking at all those soaring bank towers in downtown Toronto, but when our souls need jarring, we look at the mountains.

And that wet blue patch, that's the eternity of the Pacific Ocean. It has the magical property of being able to chill us out and warm our souls at the same time.

I hope you know what I'm talking about. Some of these concepts may be alien to an easterner. I recall trying to explain to a friend from Ontario that when the Spanish explorer Bodega y Quadra saw the bluffs at Point Grey for the first time, he fainted on the poopdeck. My Ontario friend asked, "Had he skipped breakfast?"

We are genuinely sorry that you missed the annual explosion of the cherry blossoms last month. It was, as usual, enchanting. But the tulips have been up for weeks, the roses are budding and the watermelon and pineapples will be ripe in no time.

While you are here, for God's sake, try to relax. I saw so many people in Toronto who only blink twice a minute. It's from watching market results tick past on the TSE boards in an eastern economy that is so depressed it could cry. I also saw many signs of onychophagia, the compulsive urge to bite one's nails.

While walking our streets, you may be alarmed at the number of Vancouver people you see looking up. It's an old habit. You see we are either drinking sweet rain or thanking God for favours.

Walk around our city, but try not to break anything. Visit Stanley Park, watch the tide come in, check out the sunset, when the sun drops into the ocean with a boiling hiss.

In Toronto Wednesday, I went down to the lakeshore. I wouldn't want to drink it but it was very nice strolling along the boardwalk. I'm thinking of having the West Vancouver sea-walk redone in wood. The boardwalk pigeons were doing some kind of mating dance. The males with their cheeks and chests all puffed up, were strutting around and making hooting sounds, trying to impress the females. Sort of like Pat Burns and the referees.

Again, welcome to Vancouver. Have a nice day. You're overdue for one and we have enough to go round.

Source: Denny Boyd, *The Vancouver Sun.*

cannot appreciate the situation in the rest of Canada. (For example, "They think what's good for Ontario is good for the nation as a whole.") Now, depending on which part of Canada you come from, you may be cheering or sneering at this suggestion. In either case, it's important to note that to the extent anybody is guilty of ethnocentrism, it serves as an irritant to others and blocks effective communication. Since ethnocentric people are usually unaware of their ethnocentrism, it's important that we develop greater self-consciousness in this regard. Whenever we display a "tendency to interpret or to judge all other groups, their environments and their communications according to the categories and values of our culture" (Samovar et al., 1990: 296), we exhibit ethnocentrism.

Perception of difference is yet another potential obstacle to effective intercultural communication (Samovar et al., 1990: 396; also see DeVito, 1992: 258–260). When dealing with unfamiliar cultures, we sometimes tend to perceive differences as greater than they really are (Samovar et al., 1990: 297). We then allow these unrealistic differences to inhibit communication. We lack the trust to communicate and get along. Therefore, creating a **false perception of difference** is sometimes politically or militarily useful, even if ethically questionable. If soldiers are indoctrinated to believe that the enemy is inhuman, that "it" does not value life or that "it" is inferior to one's own group, attack becomes easier. A violent encounter is facilitated when the other group is depersonalized, dehumanized and made to look different—something like a monster.

While it is true that some differences are fabricated for instrumental purposes, occasionally we ignore real differences between ourselves and others. We may wrongly assume similarities exist and that differences don't. DeVito says, "When you assume similarities and ignore differences, you implicitly communicate to others that yours are the right ways and that their ways are not important to you" (1992: 259). Let me give you an example. As a professor, I have always been concerned by American speakers who cite U.S. statistics when addressing Canadian audiences. They often make generalizations about Canada by asking Canadians to divide U.S. statistics by 10, since in terms of population we are about one-tenth the size of the U.S. In fact, Canadian college and university students have read so many foreign textbooks that cite U.S. research statistics that they do this division almost automatically. I have received many papers that cite U.S. data from my students. The American misperception that Canadians are very similar has apparently led some Canadians, namely my students, to believe it themselves.

If we compare the number of murders committed by U.S. residents annually (20 000–25 000) with the hundreds committed in Canada, we can appreciate the fact that socioculturally we are not Americans, one-tenth the size. (In 1993, Statistics Canada cited a 1987 United Nations report indicating that 2.1 murders are committed in Canada per 100 000 people. In the U.S., the figure is nine per 100 000. Estimating the 1987 population of Canada at 25 million and the U.S. population at 250 million, this fact would mean that 22 500 people were murdered in the U.S. while 525 were murdered in Canada. However, 10 percent of the U.S. rate is 2250. Clearly, American culture is much more violent than Canadian culture. Therefore, differences should not be ignored or dismissed when describing people or when dealing with them interculturally.

Of course, describing the United States as a more violent culture than ours does not mean that every American is violent. When it comes to perceiving those in other cultures, we should be careful not to **stereotype**—to make generalizations about people and ignore individual differences. Not all Americans carry guns, nor do they all kill innocent people in the streets. Within any culture there is a great deal of diversity. On this note, it would be dangerous to say that all Canadians favour a constitutional monarchy, especially if you said this to a political militant in Quebec. Furthermore, to suggest that all Canadians are bilingual simply because Canada is a bilingual society is wrong.

On the subject of language, you should note that we cannot discount intercultural differences in the meanings attributed to words. Meanings do not exist in words, but in the people using them. For instance, the word "religion" may mean different things to different individuals. To singer Edie Brickell it is a "smile on a dog"; to the German communist Karl Marx it's "the opiate of the masses"; and for believing Catholics it's an "institution" created by God. Words are often laden with values and underlying connotations. As I mentioned earlier, nonverbal language also involves intercultural differences that can cause miscommunication. In this country a "V" sign made with the index and middle fingers stands for victory, or for the number two. To some South Americans, it is an obscene gesture (DeVito, 1992). To use inappropriate nonverbal language in a particular cultural context could get you into serious trouble.

Failure to appreciate and take into account all the differences observed above adds to another general problem with intercultural communication, namely, lack of empathy (Samovar et al., 1990: 397). **Empathy** involves an element of role taking. People who empathize with others are able to understand others' feelings and place themselves in others' shoes. Whenever you say things like "I know how you feel" or "I've been there; I know what you mean," you express empathy. Of course, empathizing is difficult for an ethnocentric person, who cannot shift from his own cultural perspective and really appreciate what things look like from another cultural vantage point. If we stereotype others, empathizing is also difficult, if not impossible. If we fail to see people as they truly are and ascribe to them inappropriate cultural stereotypes, given individual diversity within cultures, we will fail to understand them, their thoughts and their feelings. In interacting with others, we project onto them many of our own fears, insecurities and misguided notions.

How to Improve Intercultural Communication

8.7

Given the virtual inevitability and necessity of intercultural dialogue and interaction, a mastery of human relations demands that we take positive steps to break down barriers to effective communication. Listed below are some helpful recommendations (Samovar et al., 1990: 399–404).

1. Know Thyself

In many ways self-knowledge is a prerequisite for effective communication, both intercultural and interpersonal. If we are unaware of our ignorance or prejudicial tendencies, for example, we will not notice when our social perceptions are based on incomplete information or unjustifiable stereotypes. If we are blind to our negative attitudes toward homosexuals, for instance, we may not be aware of how our **precommunication attitudes** colour transactions between us and them (assuming the "us" is heterosexual). An accepting precommunication attitude among homosexuals may help to establish positive tones in communication that could be difficult to achieve between heterosexuals and homosexuals, if the former were unconsciously fearful of the latter. A climate of fear and distrust usually acts as an impediment to effective social interaction. It is well advised, then, that you learn as much as you can about yourself so that latent fears, buried hostilities and unconscious insecurities and tensions can be reduced.

Knowing yourself also involves being aware of the image you present to others. For example, how are Canadians perceived abroad? How are Sikhs perceived in Manitoba? How are French Canadians looked upon in Alberta or British Columbia? Or how are lawyers perceived by the medical establishment? If we wish to improve our intercultural or intergroup communication and understand the reactions of others toward us, we must have some idea of how other people see us (Samovat et al., 1990: 400).

If we know that others are likely to be hostile toward us or to project certain images upon us, we can take steps to diffuse any anger and dispel any undesirable stereotypes and preconceptions. For instance, we could try to empathize with the other groups in order to understand the basis of their anger or negativity. In other words, we could try to put ourselves in their shoes to see ourselves as they do. Using humour is another possibility. Personally speaking, I find self-deprecating humour to be an effective means of relieving tension. If we can laugh about our differences and intercultural misperceptions, we can begin to create an atmosphere for more productive communication. I think many black, Jewish and physically-challenged comedians have understood this principle for a long time. By listening to blind comedians joke about their blindness, for instance, we learn to appreciate their experience of life and, as a result, develop a better understanding of people who are blind. An increased understanding of others can often facilitate better communication.

2. Use a Common Language

It's obviously difficult to communicate with people if you don't speak their language. North Americans travelling in Europe can attest to this fact. People can try to make themselves understood with the help of dictionaries and hand gestures, but interactions could clearly run much more smoothly if people spoke the same language. When travelling abroad, then, a crash course in the language of the country you plan to visit or work in could be quite beneficial.

You will also see bilingual signs in the newly emerging Greektown in Toronto.

Within any country, linguistic barriers can also exist. Take any major metropolitan centre, for example. City neighbourhoods are sometimes identified by their ethnic and linguistic characteristics. In Toronto, people often refer to Chinatown and Little Italy. In those areas, a good portion of the population speaks either Chinese or Italian. Street signs are bilingual (English and Chinese, or English and Italian) and governmental agencies and stores offer services in the foreign languages represented there. In fact, some immigrants to Canada settle in ethnic communities and lead productive lives without ever learning either one of our two national languages. My maternal Lithuanian-Canadian grandmother, for example (who at the time of writing is 98), speaks barely a word of English and no French. She has lived in Canada for more than 40 years. For her, telephone conversations are complicated by her lack of English. She gets along fine, on the other hand, within her Lithuanian community.

Language difficulties derive not only from different national origins, but also from people belonging to different professional and technical fields. Specialists in any given field often use jargon. **Jargon** is really a kind of sublanguage that can create barriers if it is used to impress or confuse others (DeVito, 1992: 261). Good illustrations of sub-language can be found in insurance policies and legal documents. Academics and physicians also tend to use their own technical languages to say the simplest things. An orthopaedic surgeon may refer to the crest of your hip bone as the "anterior-superior iliac spine"; a general practitioner may use "medicalese" when telling you that you suffer from a "bilateral periorbital haematoma." If you don't ask for clarification on this one, you may not know you have a black eye. Using the jargon of "computerese," let me suggest that we should try to make our communications with others more "user friendly," especially when interacting with people outside our areas of technical expertise. Opt for the simplest and clearest way to say things. We should shift from our own point of view and try to understand what our jargon sounds like to others. We shouldn't assume that others always understand our specialized terminology. People are sometimes too embarrassed to admit their ignorance.

As an academic who sometimes uses jargon (this book is full of it—literally, I hope not figuratively), I wish to draw your attention to the fact that technical sub-languages do have their legitimate place. Terms and concepts are sometimes invented to describe and label (in exact terms) experiences, phenomena and events in the world. People who use technical language may be trying to develop a certain precision in their speech, to establish clarity and label new discoveries for those within their disciplines. Jargon that is confusing to you as a layperson may be perfectly understandable to an expert. The use of jargon, in itself, is not good or bad. It depends on the people involved and the situational context. If you're currently having difficulty understanding classroom lectures, your instructor may not be trying to show off by using big words. Maybe jargon is needed to capture a certain idea accurately. Perhaps the instructor is unaware of the impact her speech is having on the class. The instructor may be trying to communicate in a classroom situation in the same way that she communicates with colleagues at professional conferences. Therein may lie the problem.

3. Take Time Before Pronouncing Judgment

Finally, when dealing with people from different cultures and cultural subgroups, it's probably a good idea to delay or suspend judgment. We shouldn't jump to conclusions about others and presume to know what they are like. I once had a theatre arts student take my philosophy class as a required general education course. Having barely introduced myself in the first class, the student abruptly interrupted me and said he wanted nothing to do with me or my course. He informed me that his older sister had once dated a philosopher and that the "guy was a pompous jerk." Barely able to pronounce my name, never having spoken to me before and not allowing me a chance to introduce him to the study of philosophy, he dismissed me in one verbal assault. I guess in his mind all philosophers are pompous jerks. Now this may or may not be true, but I never got the opportunity to prove his point. The suggestion I'd like to make is that before we evaluate any culture or subgroup (e.g., philosophers), we should take the time to familiarize ourselves with those who belong to it. We should try to get to know their values and ideals. Otherwise, we are likely to arrive at false conclusions. (My own experience indicates that only 37.3 percent of philosophers are pompous jerks, not 100 percent as the student concluded!) In any case, preconceived notions, precommunication attitudes and prejudgments about this group obviously had a negative influence on this student's perceptions of me in my class. The student jumped to what I like to believe is an incorrect conclusion.

ART OF COMMUNICATION IS AS VARIED AS THE WORLD'S CULTURE

BY ARTHUR BLACK

According to Marshall McLuhan, "Language is a form of organized stutter." McLuhan was right. Every syllable of spoken word we know, from Hamlet's soliloquy on the battlements to Jean Chrétien's sound bites on Prime Time News—nothing but organized stutter.

How did that come to be? Nobody knows precisely when Grok the Caveman grew tired of waving his hairy arms around and decided to use grunts, growls, and snorts to express himself, but anthropologists know that the human throat was capable of speech anywhere from 20 000 to 35 000 years ago, so it's a safe bet that we nattered at each other for several thousand years before somebody got a bright idea and said, "I say chaps, how be we call all these noises we're making 'English'?"

And not just English. There are some 9 000 languages and dialects spoken around the world. The most popular is Mandarin Chinese. English is second, then Hindi, Russian, and Spanish.

Ottawa Valley Speak is not in the top 100.

Not all languages are spoken either. The deaf and the mute have sign language. Boy Scouts and aircraft carrier signalmen use semaphore. Various Indian tribes used to communicate by smoke signal. There is Morse Code, Braille, NHL referee hand signals.

And there is the drum.

Most of us in North America don't consider the drum to be a prime source of communication among human beings. For us, the drum is a loud, rather tiresome quasi-musical instrument employed to drown out other musicians. It owes its current popularity to Mister Ringo Starr, a large-nosed Liverpudlian, who regularly assaulted a drum kit on behalf of the Beatles.

But we in North America don't know diddley-squat about drums.

They do in West Africa. The Akan people—who are found throughout the West African countries—have been using drums to talk with each other for centuries.

Very effectively, too. A good West African drummer can pound out a message that will carry for nearly 40 miles. That message will, in turn, be picked up by other drummers in all directions who will each transmit it to their "listening audience."

In hours a message can sweep across thousands of miles without the benefit of telephone poles, highways, or communications satellite.

And how does a drum message "read"? Not cut and dried like Morse Code. More like a soliloquy from Hamlet. West African drumspeak is highly poetic and beautiful. A plane crash translates as "a canoe that flies like a bird has fallen out of the sky."

And when the much-revered President of the Ivory Coast died last year, the tribal drums throbbed out a dirge that translated as—"The great elephant has lost its teeth. The leopard has lost its spots. The baobab (tree) has crashed down."

A little more majestic than "KENNEDY SHOT!" wouldn't you say?

Reminds me of my most memorable encounter with a non-spoken language. Actually, it was a second-hand encounter. I heard the story from two wandering Canucks I met on a Spanish freighter waddling along the west coast of Africa. The two Canadians had been living on the island of Gomera—a tiny, volcanic atoll among the Canary Islands. They told a story of climbing one of the many rugged mountains on the island.

What they couldn't understand was how every villager they met seemed to be expecting them. Odd, considering they were climbing a goat path and there were no roads or telephones on their route. When they reached a village on the top of the mountain, they were astounded to find that the townsfolk had killed and cooked a goat in their honor. Yes, the head man told them, they'd been expecting "two foreigners." "Bienvenido."

But how? How could they know?

The two Canucks were masters of suspense. They waited until I paid for a round of drinks in the ship's saloon before they explained.

It was whistling. The people on the island of Gomera speak a language of whistles called silbo. The piercing whistles carry so well across valleys (or up mountains) that a "speaker" can be heard up to five miles away.

I wonder what Marshall McLuhan would say about that.

Source: Reprinted by permission of Arthur Black.

NONVERBAL COMMUNICATION: YOU DON'T SAY!

Well-timed silence hath more eloquence than speech.

Martin Tupper

There are things in the heart too deep, if not for tears, most certainly for words.

Ralph Connor

Rainy day people never talk, they just listen 'till they've heard it all.

Gordon Lightfoot

The cruellest lies are often told in silence.

Virginibus Puerisque

Have you ever had the uncomfortable experience of receiving a mixed message? Perhaps people told you one thing yesterday, but another thing today. Contradictory messages of this sort often result in emotional upset and confusion. The ambiguity or inconsistency causes a psychological fog, so to speak, making interpersonal navigation unsure and potentially dangerous. Sometimes the mixed messages we receive are more subtle and complex. One message may be verbal, the other nonverbal. There may be a gap between *what* people say and *how* they say it, or between what they say and what their body language communicates. For example, if you've ever witnessed people grit their teeth, clench their fists or stare without blinking, and then say, "I'm not mad," you can appreciate what I mean. People's nonverbal messages often belie what they say. It is possible, of course, to have consistency between verbal and nonverbal behaviour. What is expressed nonverbally can match what's actually said. For example, an angry person may act angrily and speak in angry terms (e.g., $*#@!).

In what follows, we'll explore the nature of nonverbal communication and its various expressions. What you'll learn in this section should help you to become a keener observer of people. Your increased powers of observation should help you to read people better, to be more sensitive to them and to hear what is *not* said, but communicated indirectly through nonverbal cues. Being sensitive to your own nonverbal communication will also help you to manage your behaviour more effectively. You'll become better able to govern the impressions you make on others. This ability could help you to get through certain "doors of life." In a very informal study done by TV celebrity hostess Oprah Winfrey, efforts were made to find out what it takes to get into some of the finest nightclubs and hotspots in America. She discovered that attitude (the way you carry yourself) was a determining factor. It wasn't always what people said that got them through the door, but how people handled themselves. Demeanour and deportment often meant direct entry. (A cash bribe didn't hurt either!)

 8.8

The Nature of Nonverbal Communication

As stated, messages between people can be sent at verbal and nonverbal levels. Verbal communication deals with words, which can be spoken or written. They can be sent in face-to-face conversation, over the telephone, by fax or through the mail. Thus, while some verbal communication can be *vocal* (i.e., oral), it can also be nonvocal, say, electronic (Stewart and D'Angelo, 1980).

Nonverbal communication can be defined as "communication without words" (Adler and Rodman, 1994: 157). Like verbal communication, it can also have vocal dimensions. Accompanying what anyone says is the tone of voice, volume, pitch, rate and articulation, which is referred to as paralanguage, something we'll look at in a moment. Nonverbal communication is multichanneled (Adler and Rodman, 1994). Nonverbal messages are sent through a number of sub-channels. For example, information may be sent by means of gestures, physical movements, facial expressions, eye movements, uses of space and time, personal appearance and touch. In contrast to paralanguage, these expressions of nonverbal communication are nonvocal. Nonverbal messages can also be sent intentionally or unintentionally. People are not always aware of the nonverbal messages they send. In any case, nonverbal communication cannot simply be turned off. Nonverbal messages occur spontaneously with or without the person realizing it (Weiten, Lloyd and Lashley, 1991). Do Application Exercise 8.2 now to prove this point.

The exercise below illustrates how nonverbal communication is multi-channeled and how it provides a constant source of information about yourself and others. If you didn't really want to do this exercise or thought you didn't participate fully, chances are pretty good that your nonverbal cues told your partner this. What did your face say? What did you tell your partner by your posture and eye movements? In the debriefing portion of this exercise you may have learned that nonverbal communication is ambiguous. You may have misread your partner. Inferences made about other people based on their nonverbal cues are sometimes wrong. People may remain silent because they're shy, angry, insecure, reluctant, introverted, or, as in this case, because they're instructed to be that way. Silence, like other nonverbal communication, can be hard to read. Be careful, then, not to jump to conclusions. It's precarious to make assumptions about people based solely on nonverbal factors. What is said, who says it, and the context in which it's said, should be considered as well.

Nonverbal communication has a social function (Adler and Rodman, 1994). By means of dress, posture and facial expression, for instance, we

Don't Talk to Me!

APPLICATION EXERCISE 8.2

This exercise can be done very easily in small or large groups. Select the person sitting next to you as your partner. If numbers are uneven, the instructor may participate as well. On cue, spend one minute looking at your partner without saying a word. Do not communicate verbally. Then record on a piece of paper all of the impressions, feelings and thoughts that were transmitted to you by your partner. In other words, what was communicated nonverbally? Share your observations first with your partner. Then listen for your partner's reactions. Did you and your partner read each other accurately? Willing participants can share what they learned with the rest of the class.

may try to present ourselves as friendly and outgoing. We may try to manage our identities and the images of ourselves that we project. In addition, we may use nonverbal communication to define the kind of relationship we wish to establish. If we want to remain distant and uninvolved, we can avoid all physical contact. By contrast, if we want to welcome someone, a warm handshake, hug or smile will do the trick. Finally, we may use nonverbal communication to express our feelings and attitudes; sometimes we do this unconsciously. Without knowing it, we can express our disinterest or enthusiasm by what our body "says." Through eye contact we may show interest in another person; by eye contact avoidance, we may communicate apathy, discomfort, upset or preoccupation.

Culture also affects nonverbal communication, an idea that was hinted at earlier. As we learned, certain hand gestures can mean different things in different cultures. As well, various cultures may have characteristically different forms of nonverbal communication. In one study, researchers observed Fiorello LaGuardia, the mayor of New York City from 1933 to 1945, who spoke fluent English, Italian and Yiddish. They watched films of his campaign speeches with the sound turned off. Without actually hearing LaGuardia's addresses, the observers were able to identify the language he was speaking by his nonverbal behaviour (Birdwhistell, 1970, cited in Adler and Rodman, 1994). Do you know any immigrants or first-generation Canadians? Do they import into English some of their nonverbal behaviours from other linguistic and cultural contexts? Is their nonverbal communication with you different from how it is with those from their culture of origin? What, if anything, have you observed? What impact have these differences had on your interpersonal communications?

On the issue of culture and nonverbal communication, I would like to stress one last point. While differences do exist, some nonverbal behaviours are seemingly universal; they mean the same thing everywhere. For example, in every culture, laughter and a smiling face are universal signs of positive emotion. A sour expression conveys displeasure, no matter where you go (Adler and Rodman, 1994: 165). Charles Darwin hypothesized that nonverbal expressions such as these functioned as survival mechanisms, allowing early humans to communicate feelings or states of emotion before the development of language.

The Relationship Between Verbal and Nonverbal Communication

Implicit in what has been covered so far is the idea that verbal and nonverbal communication are related. At a bare minimum they can be consistent or inconsistent with each other. Here I'd like to discuss, in a bit more detail, the function of nonverbal communication as it pertains to its verbal counterpart. Nonverbal communication can do a number of things. It can accent, complement, contradict, regulate, repeat or substitute for the spoken word (DeVito, 1993). Let's see how. To **accent** a verbal message, we could bang a fist on a table to underscore our objection. We could also throw a nerf ball at the television while complaining about the officiating of the game being televised. Another thing we do nonverbally is **complement** what we say. For instance, we could laugh while telling a joke or shake our head when expressing disbelief. As you already know, verbal messages can **contradict** what we do nonverbally. We might display a devilish grin when saying "Trust me!" As a student you might insist to your instructor that you are interested in the course, yet always look out the window during class. Nonverbal communication can also **regulate**. Leaning forward in your chair and raising your hand may indicate that you are anxious to answer a question. Your body language may be saying, "I wish to speak now." Leaning back in your seat and orienting to the speaker may communicate, "It's your turn; I'm ready to listen." Nonverbal communication can **repeat** what you say. If you were a server in a restaurant, you might ask, "Was that one cheeseburger or two?," first raising your index finger and then your middle finger (or your thumb and index finger, if you prefer!) Finally, nonverbal communication can interact with verbal communication through **substitution**. Instead of saying "yes" or "no," for instance, we could indicate our choice by nodding our head or shaking it. We needn't actually say anything. Our answer can be transmitted nonverbally. So you see, verbal and nonverbal communication can be interconnected.

Classifying Nonverbal Communication

We can better understand nonverbal communication by classifying it in terms of the following eight categories: paralanguage, environment, artifactual communication, physical appearance, posture and body movement (kinesics), space communication (proxemics), time communication (chronemics) and touch communication (haptics).

Paralanguage

How we say something can be as important as what we say. Volume, rate, pitch, articulation and emphasis are all important. They add communication value to our verbal messages. The sentences below illustrate the point that the same statement can communicate different ideas, depending on where the emphasis falls. As you read the variations of the same statement, emphasize the italicized words.

1. *Cynthia* took the human relations course for personal growth.
2. Cynthia took the *human relations* course for personal growth.
3. Cynthia took the human relations course for *personal growth*.
4. Cynthia *took* the human relations course for personal growth.
5. Cynthia took *the* human relations course for personal growth.

How is each statement different? What different things are communicated by emphasizing different parts of the same sentence?

Paralanguage, or the manner in which you say something, involves not only emphasis, but also volume. Soft and loud talk may communicate very different things. Asking someone, in a whisper, to shut the door communicates something very different compared with screaming the same request at the top of your lungs. In the latter case, the speaker conveys upset or anger, and in the former case only a simple request.

The speed (or rate) at which you speak also falls under paralanguage. It is important because of the impressions it creates. Studies have indicated that people who speak more quickly are stereotyped as more competent than slower speakers (see Mulac and Rudd, 1977, cited in Adler and Rodman, 1994: 456). Of course, if you speak too quickly, others will be less able to understand you and follow what you're saying. This reminds me of the time I was teaching at Sir Wilfred Grenfell College in Corner Brook, Newfoundland. As most Canadians already know, Newfoundlanders have a unique accent. Being a mainlander, I sometimes found conversations difficult to follow as rapid speech, combined with a regional dialect, made things virtually incomprehensible. Appreciating the kind of difficulty mainlanders experience, a fish processing company that advertised its products on TV once had a Newfoundland fisherman promote its food products while subtitles ran across the bottom of the screen to help those outside Newfoundland understand what he was saying.

It wasn't only rate of speech that caused difficulty for me in Newfoundland, but also the accent and articulation. Within Canada, indeed within many nations, regional and ethnic dialects are found that convey nonverbal messages, and not always favourable ones. The "Georgia Cracker" accent or "Southern drawl" is often regarded as less favourable or less desirable in the United States as compared with a midwest accent. In fact, many Canadian newscasters are deliberately hired by U.S. stations in part because of their neutral-sounding accents. Peter Jennings, Morley Safer, Hillary Bowker, J.D. Roberts and Mary Garafalo (the latter two both formerly with CityTV in Toronto) now work for U.S. networks.

Articulation involves our pronunciation. When we articulate, we may leave off parts of words (deletion), we may replace a part of a word (substitute), we may add parts to words (addition) or we may slur our words (Adler and Rodman, 1994). A common deletion involves words that end in "ing." Hoping, thinking and praying become hopin', thinkin' and prayin'. In my own case, I often use deletion as a way of making my speech more friendly and informal. In more formal, professional settings, I usually make an effort to articulate clearly all my "ing" endings for fear of appearing uneducated or a little "rough around the edges."

Substitution is another aspect of articulation that occurs when parts of words are replaced by incorrect sounds. The "th" ending of a word may become a "t." Found at the beginning of a word, "th" may become a "d" sound. A classic book out east, *Death on the Ice*, is pronounced by some Newfoundlanders as *Det own dee Ice*. Addition is another aspect of articulation that involves adding extra parts to words that don't belong; for example, you would say "normalicy" instead of normalcy or "sufferage" instead of suffrage (the right to vote in political elections). In northern Ontario, people sometimes say "youse" instead of "you." Addition also makes use of "tag questions"

(459). Canadians are notorious for saying "eh" at the end of their sentences. Sometimes we add words like "right" or "you know" (for example, "I saw this guy, right" or "He was a big dude, you know") to the end of sentences. The danger with additions is that they can become irritating to listeners, eh? (The American translation is "huh.") Slurring is yet another aspect of articulation. When we slur, words run together or overlap. The word "of" is often transformed by slurring. "This kind of thing" becomes "This kinda thing." "Sort of" becomes "sorta." "Want to" changes to "wanna." Slurring can become problematic if it makes you look unintelligent or interferes with comprehension.

Pitch is the last dimension of paralanguage we'll look at here. Pitch points to the highness or lowness of your voice and tends to be related to rate and volume. When people speed up their speech or increase their volume, pitch tends to rise. Since pitch is also associated with muscle tension in the throat (specifically in the vocal folds), nervous speakers may sometimes squeak while talking. It's important to take pitch into account when communicating. A continuously high, squeaking pitch may irritate others, while a low drone may put them to sleep. It's best to modulate your pitch, as well as your rate and volume, according to the demands of the situation and the messages to be relayed. Be aware of what you're saying, how you're saying it, to whom you're speaking and what impression you are giving off by virtue of your nonverbal speech characteristics.

Environment

People don't communicate in a vacuum. Their communications obviously take place in a particular physical location or **environment**. Sometimes the location can have a significant impact on the quality and nature of the interaction itself. If you've ever said in conversation, "Here is not the place to be discussing this," you've recognized at an intuitive level what constitutes a proper or improper environment for certain kinds of interpersonal communications. You probably appreciate how environment can affect our moods, actions and choice of words. For example, some things that you say on the street, you would never say in church. Also, you may find that you are more relaxed, more friendly, in a better mood or more polite in certain locations. You may communicate differently on a beach in Nassau compared with your office at work or in the college library. In fact, company executives who recognize this often hold professional retreats off-location to boost morale and to create an environment conducive to better human relations.

Things falling under physical environment include "furniture, architectural style, interior decorating, lighting conditions, colours, temperature, additional noises or music, and the like, in which the interaction occurs" (Knapp and Hall, 1992: 13). Obviously, inanimate objects cannot talk, yet don't we often say things like, "This furniture makes a statement" and "The decor in this room tells me a lot about you; you're obviously an artsy/practical/tasteful person." We can also make statements about ourselves nonverbally by how we arrange our environments—by the materials, fabrics and shapes we include in it or by the surfaces of objects found there. Suppose, for example, that you were invited to someone's apartment for coffee. What impression

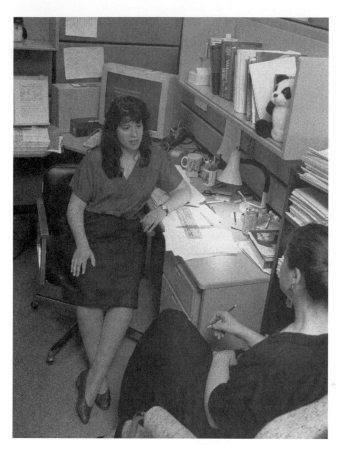

What does this work environment communicate to you?

would be made on you if you drank from fine, imported china cups worth $200 each? What would you think if you were given a used paper cup from which to drink? What would the two different cups say to you? On the subject of materials, don't many people attribute higher status to genuine leather compared with vinyl or rubber imitation? We seem to place certain value judgments on materials in this culture and describe people who know how to select and choose properly among them as discriminating consumers, or people with taste. We tend to be impressed by those who can distinguish between quality and cheap substitutes. Real wood communicates something different from inexpensive veneer. Of course, what it communicates is open to interpretation. Remember nonverbal communication is fraught with ambiguity.

Artifactual Communication

The decoration of space involving the physical environment is sometimes discussed under **artifactual communication** (DeVito, 1993). I've included it under the category of the communication environment. Under artifactual communication we'll focus on colour, clothing and bodily adornment.

Colour

Colours can have different meanings. They convey different messages, often depending on culture. For instance, green can mean environmentally friendly or envious. Yellow transmits the idea of divinity at the Vatican in Rome, while the same colour describes a coward in North America. Furthermore, the same colours can mean different things within any one culture. On the subject of yellow, I recall one evening calling out, "Go, Yellow!" in support of my fellow Bruins hockey players during one of my men's league hockey games (our sweaters were yellow). Another player on the bench asked if I could use the word "gold" instead of "yellow." He didn't like the negative connotations of yellow. As a matter of fact, I recall team morale being somewhat down because the league did not issue us the authentic black NHL Bruins uniforms, but a weak yellow version instead. (Black is seen as tough and intimidating.)

The importance of colour should not be discounted, especially when it comes to clothes. Whether or not we accept a person may depend on the colours he wears. I re-

> Beware of all enterprises that require new clothes.
>
> Henry David Thoreau

call when Frank Miller became leader of the Conservative Party in Ontario. He had a habit of wearing red-and-green plaid sports jackets that became targets of humour and political satire. Miller was disparagingly described by some as looking like a farmer or a used car salesman. Of course, there is nothing wrong with farmers or salespeople, but in government many people want leaders to look like leaders and this means wearing certain colours and not others. Miller quietly changed much of his wardrobe, probably on the advice of image consultants. The importance of colour to occupation has been noted by Bernice Kanner, a colour expert. In the context of the U.S. legal profession she writes, "If you have to pick the wardrobe for your defence lawyer heading into court and choose anything but blue, you deserve to lose the case"(DeVito, 1993: 111). Apparently black is so powerful a colour that it can work against the lawyer's interests with the jury. Brown isn't authoritative enough, while green could give rise to negative reactions (111). It might be interesting for you to consider what colours you most often wear and what colours you'd never be caught dead in. What colours, if any, send unappealing messages to you? Look around the room the next time you're in class; what colours are most often worn by others? What do these colours tell you?

Clothing

Clothing can also send messages to others. It can reveal how modest or immodest you are, how liberal or conservative you are, to which cultural or subcultural groups you belong, or what your income bracket is likely to be. People make inferences about you all the time. They do this in part by the way you dress. In one study, college students perceived an instructor who was informally dressed as enthusiastic, friendly, fair and flexible. When the same instructor dressed formally, college students perceived the person to be knowledgeable, prepared and organized (111). Correctly or incorrectly we say that "clothes make the person." While I think you'd agree this phrase is a bit of an overstatement, it's hard to deny that our perceptions of people are influenced by clothes. I once heard an upper middle-class woman express scepticism about a social worker who was assigned to help her. She said to me something along these lines: "How can someone wearing sandals and blue jeans possibly be of any use to me?" Obviously, this woman's interactions with the social worker were undermined by her perceptions. From her perspective, the social worker lacked credibility due to the way he was dressed. In another place and with other people, he may have appeared "cool," but the woman was not interested in "cool" and consequently was not interested in talking to him.

Bodily Adornment

In addition to clothing, jewelry constitutes part of bodily adornment. Wearing an inexpensive Timex watch may communicate to others that you are frugal and practical; wearing a Rolex or Gucci timepiece may say that you are wealthy and established. In fact, some people like to look wealthy and established even if they're not, which is the reason why a blackmarket exists for "label" merchandise. It's possible to buy a fake Gucci watch (one made by

Source: MISS PEACH, Courtesy of Mel Lazarus and Creators Syndicate. © 1990, Mel Lazarus.

another manufacturer but displaying the Gucci label) for a fraction of what the genuine one costs. (I know this because I have been approached to buy one!) People buy the label and wear the watch to communicate nonverbally that they're successful. Many of us hear and accept that message. Other artifacts of personal adornment that send out messages include such things as hairpieces, false eyelashes, lipstick and attaché cases (Knapp and Hall, 1992: 14). The attaché case may say, "I'm in business," while an obvious wig might communicate, "I don't like my real hair."

APPLICATION EXERCISE 8.3

8.11

Clothes Talk

Following are descriptions of people dressed and adorned in different ways. If you saw these people, what would you think to yourself? What would their appearance say to you? Share your answers with classmates.

1. A young woman is dressed in a very short, tight, blue-jean skirt. She is wearing black nylons and black high-heeled shoes. Her black top is lacy and see-through, revealing a black bra underneath. She is wearing heavy makeup: bright red lipstick, dark eye shadow, false eyelashes and a painted mole on one cheek. What is this young woman saying to you nonverbally?

_____

_____

2. A young man is wearing black Doc Martens, black socks, black jeans, a black T-shirt and black leather jacket. His one ear is pierced with some kind of silver earring symbolizing death. His hair is completely shaven except for a

goatee and he has adorned his arms with numerous satanic tattoos. What is this young man saying to you nonverbally?

_____

_____

3. A male student enters the class. He is wearing Birkenstock sandals, faded blue jeans and a tie-dyed shirt. His long hair is pulled back in a pony tail and he carries with him an army bag filled with philosophy books. The only facial hair is a little tuft just under his lower lip. What is this male student expressing to you nonverbally?

_____

_____

4. A female student sits near you in the cafeteria. She places down next to her a Christian Dior bag. Her hair is dyed blond and she has blue-tinted contact lenses. She's wearing a gold necklace, a Piaget watch and a one-carat diamond ring. This student is also wearing a dark blue suit with dark nylons and pumps. Her blouse is white and its frilly collar flops out onto her jacket. She pulls out a gold lighter and French cigarettes while apparently looking for something in her soft leather wallet. What is this female student saying to you?

_____

_____

Physical Appearance

Closely tied to clothing, colour and adornment is **physical appearance**. Some things about our appearance we can change or mask through clothes, for example, but other things we can't. We communicate messages about ourselves simply by our body type, attractiveness, height, weight and skin colour. Hair can be dyed another shade but its texture and thickness cannot really be changed all that much. Even hair transplants can create an unnatural look. In many ways our genetic heritage fixes our physical appearance. We may be destined to be tall or short, thick or thin, pretty, handsome or modest in our attractiveness to others (as culturally defined). Some research suggests that people may be genetically predisposed to be heavier, rather than lighter. Some people apparently have more fat cells than others. Let's look now at how physical appearance affects nonverbal communication.

Physical appearance has a lot to do with body type. People's body types can fall under one of three basic categories: endomorph (fat), ectomorph (thin) and mesomorph (athletic). See Figure 8.2 for a visual depiction of each type.

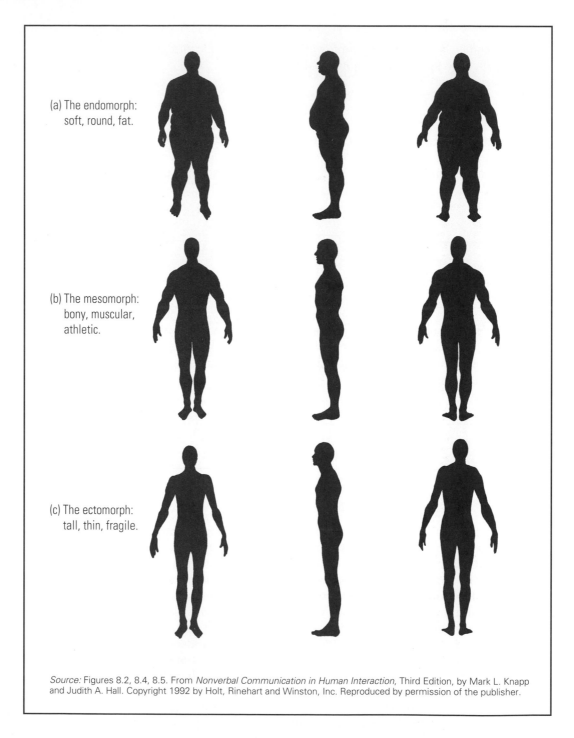

(a) The endomorph: soft, round, fat.

(b) The mesomorph: bony, muscular, athletic.

(c) The ectomorph: tall, thin, fragile.

Source: Figures 8.2, 8.4, 8.5. From *Nonverbal Communication in Human Interaction*, Third Edition, by Mark L. Knapp and Judith A. Hall. Copyright 1992 by Holt, Rinehart and Winston, Inc. Reproduced by permission of the publisher.

Figure 8.2
Body Types

In studies, people who were shown silhouette drawings of each of the body types were asked to rate them on a variety of scales. Below are Knapp and Hall's (1992: 110) findings on what each of the body types communicated to people and how each was perceived.

Endomorph	Mesomorph	Ectomorph
fatter	stronger	thinner
older	more masculine	younger
shorter	better looking	more ambitious
more old-fashioned	more adventurous	taller
less strong physically	younger	more suspicious
less good-looking	taller	more tense
more talkative	more mature	more nervous
more warmhearted	more self-reliant	less masculine
sympathetic		more stubborn
more good-natured		inclined to be difficult
agreeable		more pessimistic
more dependent on others		quieter
more trusting of others		

Certainly another important dimension of physical appearance is **attractiveness**. Physically attractive people are often perceived as possessing many desirable traits. Attractiveness seems to say, "Look, I'm more interesting, poised, sociable, independent, exciting and sexually warmer than unattractive people" (Brigham, 1980: 365). People also tend to believe that attractive individuals are more intelligent and more pleasant. Studies indicate, for instance, that essays allegedly written by attractive women receive higher grades and better evaluations than those written by unattractive women (Landy and Sigall, 1974, cited in Weiten et al., 1991: 144). Apparently, good looks communicate competence.

Height is another feature of physical appearance that influences what's communicated in interpersonal relations. Some women feel embarrassed about dating shorter men, while men often feel the same way about dating taller women. Everyday experience illustrates, then, that height can affect partner selection and interpersonal attraction. (Don't be surprised, however, if you find short men preferring tall women or tall women preferring short men.) For some people, height is associated with leadership. Trait theorists have tried to link particular physical characteristics like height to the ability to lead. While correlations remain suspect, you may wish to compare the average height of CEOs and successful business executives with low-level employees and middle managers. Is it true that successful professionals tend to be taller? What does height say about a person? Why does the taller candidate in U.S. presidential elections usually win? Why do some women fantasize about men who are tall, dark and handsome, not short, dark and handsome, or short, fair and plain? Height, like other nonverbal factors in communication, is ambiguous and culturally bound. What does it mean to you?

> Let me have men about me that are fat;
> Sleek-headed men and such as sleep o'nights;
> Yon Cassius has a lean and hungry look;
> He thinks too much; such men are dangerous.
>
> William Shakespeare,
> Julius Caesar, Act 1, Scene 2

Skin colour is yet another physical characteristic that communicates nonverbally. Simply being "lily white" in some neighbourhoods may say to others that you're spoiled, privileged or "white trash." To a racist individual, or to one guilty of stereotyping, someone's skin colour may say, "You can't trust me." Skin colour may not be vocal, but, paradoxically, it can sometimes speak very loudly, for better or for worse.

In casual conversation, we see how "weight" speaks to people. One's weight may nonverbally communicate the message, "I like and take care of myself" or "I have no self-respect and abuse my body." Caution is advised, however. I remember my mother not being impressed by some of the thin girls I dated in high school. My Eastern European mama would describe them as "skinny chickens." Their light weight told her that they were obviously underfed and lacked the stamina necessary to bear children and do hard work. I believe my dates thought their thin bodies were communicating something else. We see here how nonverbal communication is ambiguous. A single factor such as thinness can communicate different messages to different individuals.

Posture and Body Movement

Since we are on the topic of the body, we can smoothly move into a discussion of how **bodily movement (kinesics)** has a language all its own. How we hold our bodies and the ways in which we move them can communicate many different things.

Posture

A forward-leaning posture is generally associated with higher interest and involvement. When we "sit up and pay attention," we move closer physically and psychologically. We tell the other person that "we're with them." This posture has also been associated with liking and, interestingly, to lower status in situations where those interacting do not know each other very well (Knapp and Hall, 1992). Research indicates as well that posture is a key communicator of emotional states. A person with a drooping posture communicates sadness. One with a rigid, tense posture communicates anger (Knapp and Hall, 1992). During a conversation, one person may "mirror" the posture of another. When this happens, one communicates rapport or attempts to build it.

How would you feel if one evening you were on a date and after leaning forward toward your partner, he or she did likewise? How would you see this move? What other "right moves" could you make to communicate your friendly intentions? (We won't get into this any further here!)

Physical Gestures

In addition to posture, body language is communicated by the use of physical gestures. When the film critics Siskel and Ebert signify "two thumbs up" for a movie, they are expressing approval for the film. When someone gives the "Trudeau salute" (showing the raised middle finger), anger and defiance are typically communicated. (This gesture was made a part of our national heritage during a train trip taken across western Canada by then prime minister Pierre Elliot Trudeau.) Preening behaviour like applying makeup, re-arranging one's clothes or combing one's hair may indicate interest in another party or be some kind of unconscious come-on (Adler and Rodman, 1994). It can also mean disinterest and preoccupation.

By means of gestures, we can illustrate what me mean. Using our hands, we can show how big the fish was that we caught. Through gestures we can communicate our emotions. We can also meet physical needs by, say, scratching our head when it's itchy. Finally, gestures can help us to regulate communication. By raising our arm and displaying the palm, we can tell others to stop—the movement that traffic cops make at intersections. By means of a sweeping arm movement, they tell us to go through.

Face and Eye Movements
Face and eye movements have as much communication value as, if not more than, posture and other physical gestures. The eyes, for example, send many kinds of messages. You can elicit feedback or convey to others that the channel of communication is open. You can provide signals about the nature of a relationship or psychologically reduce the distance between yourself and another. A combination of rolling your eyes and giving a knowing glance from one person to another, across a room, can say, "I'm with you. Can you believe what we're witnessing here?" or "I'm on your side." Even when eye contact is avoided, messages continue to be sent. Eye avoidance can express disinterest. It can also express nervousness or guilt. Sometimes we avoid eye contact to enable others to maintain their privacy. When we're in close quarters, such as in an elevator, we often avoid eye contact to maintain our own privacy as well.

As with many aspects of nonverbal communication, gender and culture affect how we use our eyes to communicate. In North American culture, direct eye contact usually communicates honesty and forthrightness. In Japanese culture, it indicates lack of respect. In times of grief, women tend to make more eye contact than men and usually maintain it for longer periods. This appears to be so whether they are speaking or listening to others (DeVito, 1993).

An interesting hypothesis about eye movements has been raised by neurolinguistic programmers (NLPs) Joseph O'Connor and John Seymour (1990). They claim that people move their eyes in different directions depending on how they are thinking. To illustrate their point, they ask people to think of the first thing they see as they walk through the front door of their homes. They say that in thinking about the answer, right-handed people usually look up and left. When asked how it would feel to have velvet next to their skin, people typically look down and to the right. According to O'Connor and Seymour (1990), visual cues let us know how people access information. See Figure 8.3 for a visual representation of NLPs' claims about eye movements and information access.

The face is also an important vehicle of nonverbal communication. By means of facial expressions, we communicate universal emotions such as surprise, disgust, happiness, sadness, fear and anger. However, facial expressions can be difficult to read sometimes, if for no other reason than that they can change so quickly. People also try to mask their true feelings by

Figure 8.3

The Eyes Say It All

Fixed unfocused eyes: visualizing real or imagined event.

Eyes right and up: envisioning event never seen before.

Eyes left and up: recalling a previously experienced event.

Eyes right: constructing sounds.

Eyes left: remembering sounds.

Eyes right and down: processing bodily sensations.

Eyes left and down: carrying on internal dialogue.

putting on a "false face" or a "good front." When facial expressions become somewhat exaggerated, it usually indicates that efforts are being made to deceive. If you want to read faces better, examine them carefully when those observed are not likely to be thinking about the way they look at a particular moment in time. Look for quick flashes of emotional expression that differ from the ones the person observed is seeking to convey. You might also pay close attention to contradictions found on the face itself. The message sent by the eyes may not be consistent with the one sent by the mouth and eyebrows (Adler and Rodman, 1994: 175).

Space Talk: Close Encounters and Space Invaders

8.12

Next we'll discuss **space communication (proxemics)**. We can communicate much by our use of space. Each one of us lives in a kind of invisible space bubble that either expands or contracts, depending upon particular conditions and circumstances. Knapp and Hall (1992: 160–167) have identified a number of primary factors that affect space and space communication. I've provided an example for each factor.

1. Sex   In natural settings, females predominantly choose to interact with other people (of either sex) more closely than males do.

2. Age   Young children interact more closely than adults. Interaction distance appears to expand incrementally from about the age of six to early adolescence. By that time adult norms seem to be operative.

3. Culture and Ethnic Background   Diverse cultures' norms produce different distances for communication. Cultures may be loosely described as "contact" or "noncontact" in nature. People in contact cultures (southern Europeans, Latin Americans) tend to face one another when communicating, interact in closer proximity, touch more often and make more eye contact. People in noncontact cultures, by contrast, make less eye contact and touch less often.

4. Topic or Subject Matter   Topic can influence conversational distance. Student subjects, for example, were given negative, positive and neutral comments upon entering a room. Studies showed that "[s]tudents given the negative comment sat furthest from the experimenter while those who were praised sat closest." After being insulted, people generally assume a greater distance than usual from the person with whom they're communicating.

5. Setting for Interaction   In formal or unfamiliar settings, people maintain a greater distance from unknown others and a closer distance to known others.

6. Physical Characteristics   Obese people are accorded greater interaction distances. People interacting with stigmatized individuals choose greater initial speaking distances than with non-stigmatized "normal" people. This distance diminishes as the length of interaction increases.

7. Attitudinal and Emotional Orientation   People choose to maintain greater distance when communicating with people perceived as unfriendly. Variations in our emotional conditions can also influence how close or how distant we wish to be with others. States of depression, fatigue, excitement or joy all have their spatial expressions. It's interesting to note that individuals who choose to maintain closer distances are frequently perceived as warmer, more empathetic and more understanding.

8. Characteristics of the Interpersonal Relationship   Strangers begin conversations farther away from each other than do acquaintances. Findings suggest that "closer relationships are likely to be associated with closer interaction distance" (Hall, 1966: 110).

9. Personality Characteristics   In conversation introverts display a tendency to stand farther away than extraverts. They seem to prefer greater interpersonal distances.

Spatial Distances

We have just learned a little bit about "space talk." We can now see better how the distances we maintain from others in interaction depend on a variety of factors and circumstances. The specific distances we maintain have been given names by anthropologist Edward T. Hall (1966). They are intimate distance, personal distance, social distance and public distance. Below are brief descriptions of each. Each distance has what Hall refers to as a "close phase" and a "far phase." The former moves toward greater closeness, the latter toward lesser closeness.

Intimate Distance (skin contact to 1/2 m.)   The close phase of intimate distance includes the space we use for such things as lovemaking, wrestling, comforting and protecting. At the far phase, touch can be achieved by hand extension. This is not usually a distance considered proper for stranger-to-stranger interaction.

Personal Distance (1/2 to 1 1/3 m.)   One can still hold or grasp the other person at this distance. Perceptual acuity is still very strong. At the far phase of this distance, we can keep someone at arm's length, if we wish. It is also at this distance that we discuss subjects of personal interest and involvement.

Social Distance (1 1/3 to 2 1/3 m.)   At this distance visual acuity begins to diminish. It is here that we typically conduct business and interact at social gatherings. When maintaining social distance it is important to maintain eye contact and to speak up in order to be heard. A feature of social distance is that it liberates us from nonstop interactions with those surrounding us, and does so without making us seem rude.

Public Distance (4 to 8 1/3 m. or more)   This is the distance your college or university instructor probably uses in the classroom. If one moves away more than 8 1/3 m., interpersonal communication becomes difficult. Public distance allows people to take evasive or defensive action if threatened. From this distance, nonverbal communication must be exaggerated or amplified (e.g., facial expressions, gestures and posture) if it is to be perceived. We tend to reserve this distance for public figures and for formal occasions.

Territoriality

Not only do people seek to maintain spatial distance from one another, but they also try to grab space itself. The possessive reaction to occupy space and objects within it is referred to as **territoriality**. By means of territoriality we communicate ownership and status (DeVito, 1992). We do this in a variety of ways. Whether territoriality is an innate predisposition or something learned is a continuing topic of debate in the world of psychology between behaviourists and ethologists.

If you own a pet, you've probably already witnessed territoriality in action. Dogs will defend their turf against the mail deliverer or the person who brings your daily newspaper. They will bark, snarl and sometimes bite. While humans don't usually do such things (though I know some who do), they have their own way of protecting their territories and threatening potential intruders. For example, my son Michael once wanted me to buy a doormat for the entrance to our house. It had a gun printed on it with the words, "We don't call 911." We can also protect and defend our territories by posting "No Trespassing" or "Beware of Dog" signs. My personal favourite sign indicating territorial possession was found on a Harley Davidson motorcycle owned by a gang member. It read, "Life after death? Touch this bike and find out." (The language was actually a bit more colourful, but some editorial licence was necessary to protect the innocent!)

There are three different types of territories: primary, secondary and public (DeVito, 1992). Primary territories are ones you would call your own. They belong exclusively to you. Things included in your primary territory could be your Sega system, stereo or desk. Secondary territories don't actually belong to you; nonetheless, you have used or occupied them so much that they become associated with you. The first seat in the first row of the class is not technically yours. You don't own it, you don't have legal rights to it. Yet people may recognize it as "yours" because you always sit there. I once went to an English pub in a small town south of London. Without knowing it, I took the seat of a regular customer. Upon arriving at "his" seat, he communicated nonverbally—his expressions of annoyance and irritation communicated his disapproval—that I was sitting in the wrong place. Public territories are open to all. The West Edmonton Mall does not belong exclusively to you or me, nor does the movie theatre down the street or the lawn at the provincial legislature. We all have access.

People indicate possession of territory by use of markers. You might leave your books on a chair, for example, or spread them across a desk in the library to indicate occupancy as well as a desire to be alone. We can mark possessions in many other ways as well. Maybe you label your gym bag and sporting equipment with your name, or place a fence between your property and your neighbour's yard. Still another way to mark your territory is by personalizing the space you occupy, such as your college residence. You may recall a scene from the movie *Wolf*, where Jack Nicholson, in wolf-like fashion, marked his territory in the men's bathroom by urinating on the walls and floor. This form of territorial marking is OK for wolves, but is considered ill-advised for normal humans!

Status and Space

The size of the territory we mark off is quite often a reflection of status. Success is often symbolized by the size of office, desk or property we own. In any organization, higher status individuals are not likely to possess the smaller desk, office or residence. Furthermore, with respect to status, territorial invasions are "socially and professionally permissible" only when higher status individuals encroach on the space of lower status individuals. The opposite is not true. While the boss may take and use the secretary's pen without asking, the secretary is well advised not to do likewise. Tolerated invasions of space are status-dependent. Notice I use the description "tolerated." It's probably rude, at any time, to borrow without asking or to encroach without permission. The fact that people do it to demonstrate status or dominance does not make it right, justifiable or polite. Applying the Golden Rule is probably a good idea here: "Do unto others as you would have others do unto you."

Time Talk

In Canadian society, time is highly valued. In fact, we often say, "Time is money." Given the importance attributed to it, how we use **time communication (chronemics)** can express nonverbal messages, both intentional and unintentional. Our personal use of time is often influenced by the psychological orientation we take toward it. Some of us see time in exact terms. Nine o'clock means nine o'clock. Others see time as diffused or approximate. Nine o'clock could mean anything between 8:45 and 9:15. When two people adopt different time orientations, frustration can arise. If one person has a diffused orientation toward time and promises to meet you at 9:00, that person may in her mind be only 15 minutes late when she arrives at 9:30. Let's say you are highly punctual and make it a point to arrive 10 to 15 minutes early for all your appointments. In this case, you could end up waiting 45 minutes for someone who believes they are almost on time. If the latecomer doesn't understand your upset, it's probably because time is not perceived the same way. Thus, when arranging meetings and appointments, it's probably a good idea to clarify what you mean by a specified time. Personally speaking, I have a relative who is chronically late for everything. The strategy adopted by many members in the family is to say, "If you're not here by *whatever* o'clock, we'll get started without you," or "We'll meet you there" or "We'll see you when you arrive."

Time and Culture

Sometimes culture can affect our use of time and the messages sent by it. A number of years ago I taught a Native Canadian at Brock University in St. Catharines. According to his experience, many traditionally minded Six Nation Indians on the reserve, near Brantford, relate differently than most of us do with respect to time. He explained to me how a number of his Native friends could not understand why their employers were so upset whenever they arrived late for work. If they were being paid for eight hours of work, they were quite willing to work hard for eight hours. The "white man's" preoccupation with starting on time at 7:00 a.m. or 9 a.m. every day was puzzling for my student's friends. Why people always had to eat lunch at 12 p.m. or relax for 15 minutes at 3:15 p.m. every day was a bit of a mystery. The natural flow of life seemed to be disrupted by the need to do things according to a schedule. Of course, for many whites in mainstream culture, punctuality, efficiency and productivity are largely defined in terms of time. People working by different time lines are therefore sometimes described as irresponsible, inefficient and unproductive. Perhaps some crosscultural miscommunication could be alleviated by a more creative use of time, or one that respects the values of all. We see this happening in fact with "flex-time" work schedules and flexible vacation periods. Time off is also being granted more and more to people of different faiths and cultures so that they can celebrate their traditions. Not allowing time off can communicate things like disrespect or contempt for differences. If this is what an employer is communicating nonverbally, we shouldn't be surprised if a loyal and motivated workforce fails to emerge.

Status and Time

Time can be used to communicate status. Executives and highly placed people often make it a point to arrive fashionably late. An early arrival could communicate eagerness and anticipation. Some think it's undignified to be a "keener." If you're concerned about communicating your own personal importance to others, you may think others should eagerly anticipate your arrival. To wait for others is to place yourself in a diminished position.

We often witness time being used as a status symbol in professional relationships. For example, instructors can arrive late to class and expect no protest. If students arrive late, however, speeches, threats and grade deductions may follow. Also, so-called "important" people may see you by appointment only, while it is permissible for you to drop by without notice on equal-status peers and colleagues. Furthermore, although it's allowable for prospective bosses to keep you waiting outside their offices, it would not be well-advised for you to show up late for an interview and keep them waiting. That delay would send the wrong message.

Finally, status seems to exempt "important" people from having to endure the waiting that most of us face in life. An acquaintance recently told me of a woman who called her husband's restaurant for a reservation. The wait for a table was going to be at least 90 minutes. When the woman identified herself as Dolly Parton, a table was made available immediately. Time talks. In this case, it says you're too special and important to be kept waiting. This may not be fair in any objective sense, but seems to be the way it is in the real world.

Touch Communication

The importance of **touch communication (haptics)** to healthy human development was briefly alluded to in Chapter 4. Recall the observation that infants desperate for strokes (human touch) often fail to thrive when physical contact is not forthcoming from caretakers. Institutionalized infants during the late 19th and early 20th centuries who were deprived of physical strokes often suffered from marasmus (a Greek

> ...*paradise is attained by touch.*
>
> Helen Keller

Touch can communicate emotion and help to solidify relationships.

word meaning "wasting away"). Some even died. In Ashley Montague's *Touching: The Human Significance of the Skin*, findings indicate that at Bellevue Hospital in New York, "mortality rates for infants under one year fell from 30 to 35 percent to less than 10 percent," following the institution of "mothering" on the pediatric wards. Touching, caressing and holding seemed to keep these babies alive. Incredible as it may seem, touch appears to be necessary for survival.

Touch is also important to human communication. By means of touch, such as shaking someone's hand, we can show appreciation. We can console our friends or give support by lending a shoulder to lean on. A gentle caress could indicate our interest or sexual attraction. A physical nudge or soft push could be a form of playful aggression. A slap on the back may be someone's way of giving encouragement. By means of touch we can also communicate things like inclusion, affection, compliance, attention, greeting and departure (Weaver, 1993: 310). Studies and observations of touch point to some positive effects. For instance, librarians who touched patrons when returning library cards were evaluated more favourably. Waitresses who touched diners received bigger tips; psychologists who touched students discovered greater compliance, while therapists who touched their clients accelerated the process of healing. This last finding underscores again the "therapeutic" benefits of touch. On this note, when tactile people ("touchers") were compared with "nontouchers," it was found that the latter "report more anxiety and tension in their lives, less satisfaction with their bodies, more suspicion of others, and are more socially withdrawn and more likely to be rigid or authoritarian in their beliefs" (Knapp and Hall, 1992: 234).

Of course, not all touch is beneficial, as survivors of child molestation and sexual abuse will attest. They may be suspicious of touch for very good reasons. Thus, it is a good idea to ask permission before touching someone whom you suspect might respond negatively to your physical contact.

As you might have guessed, touch, as a form of nonverbal communication, is also affected by culture and gender. In one study, Sidney Jourard counted the frequency of contact between couples in cafés in various cities throughout the world. He reported the following: in San Juan, Puerto Rico, couples physically made contact 180 times every hour; in Paris, France, the frequency was reduced to 110; in Gainesville, Florida, people touched two times; in London, England, they didn't touch at all. (This research is cited in

Knapp and Hall, 1992: 251.) In another study, Japanese and U.S. students were observed for their touching patterns (Barnlund, 1975, cited in Knapp and Hall, 1992: 251). Americans apparently touch about twice as much as the Japanese. They are also more accessible to touch. See Figure 8.4.

When it comes to touching, we also find gender differences. For example, females tend to engage in more same-sex touching than do males. They also tend to respond more favourably to touching than do men (at least in North America). Men and women are similar insofar as both respond favourably to touch when the one who originates it has higher status (Weiten, Lloyd and Lashley, 1991).

Interested in knowing what body parts people think are most often touched, Jourard administered a questionnaire to students, who revealed which (of 24) body parts they had seen or touched on others or that others

Figure 8.4

Physical Contact Patterns in Japan and the United States

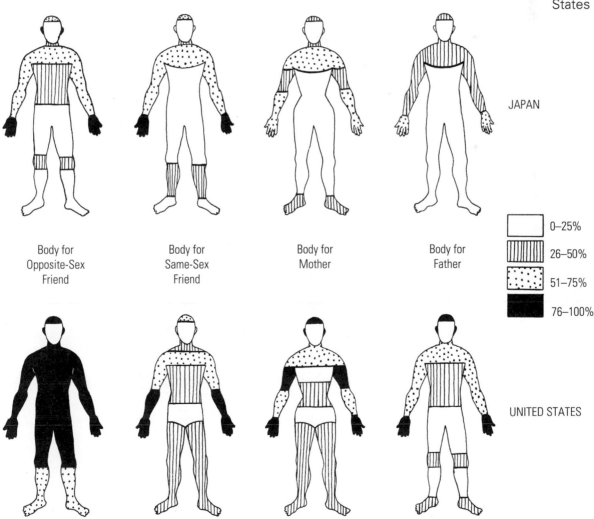

Body for Opposite-Sex Friend

Body for Same-Sex Friend

Body for Mother

Body for Father

JAPAN

UNITED STATES

0–25%

26–50%

51–75%

76–100%

had seen or touched on them within a one-year period. The "others" were designated as father, mother, same-sex friend and opposite-sex friend. Findings indicated that females are significantly more accessible to touch by all people compared to males. Most touching occurred between friends and with others. Many fathers were recalled as touching little more than the hands of subjects. Jourard's finding are visually displayed in Figure 8.5.

Figure 8.5

Areas of the Body Involved in Bodily Contact

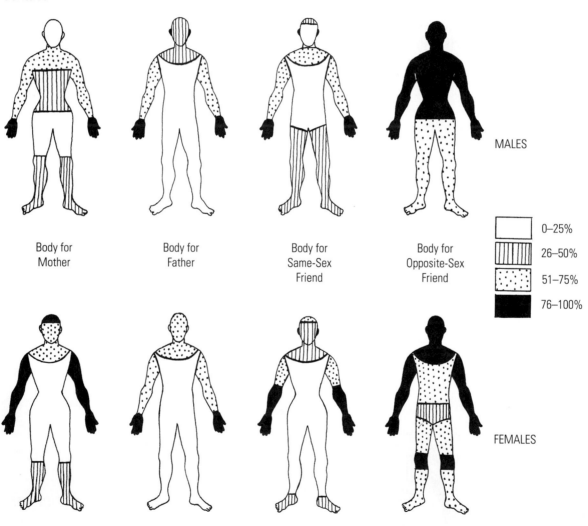

Body for Mother

Body for Father

Body for Same-Sex Friend

Body for Opposite-Sex Friend

MALES

0–25%

26–50%

51–75%

76–100%

FEMALES

How Tactile Are You?

Instructions: This instrument comprises 18 statements concerning how you feel about touching other people and being touched. Please indicate the degree to which each statement applies to you by considering whether you

1 = strongly agree
2 = agree
3 = are undecided
4 = disagree
5 = strongly disagree

_____ 1. A hug from a same-sex friend is a true sign of friendship.
_____ 2. Opposite-sex friends enjoy it when I touch them.
_____ 3. I often put my arm around friends of the same sex.
_____ 4. When I see two friends of the same sex hugging, it revolts me.
_____ 5. I like it when members of the opposite sex touch me.
_____ 6. People shouldn't be so uptight about touching people of the same sex.
_____ 7. I think it is vulgar when members of the opposite sex touch me.
_____ 8. When a member of the opposite sex touches me, I find it unpleasant.
_____ 9. I wish I were free to show emotions by touching members of the same sex.
_____ 10. I'd enjoy giving a massage to an opposite-sex friend.
_____ 11. I enjoy kissing a person of the same sex.
_____ 12. I like to touch friends that are the same sex as I am.
_____ 13. Touching a friend of the same sex does not make me uncomfortable.
_____ 14. I find it enjoyable when my date and I embrace.
_____ 15. I enjoy getting a back rub from a member of the opposite sex.
_____ 16. I dislike kissing relatives of the same sex.
_____ 17. Intimate touching with members of the opposite sex is pleasurable.
_____ 18. I find it difficult to be touched by a member of my own sex.

Scoring

To score your self-diagnostic, follow these procedures:
1. Reverse your scores for items 4, 7, 8, 16 and 18. Use these reversed scores in all future calculations.
2. To obtain your same-sex touch avoidance score (the extent to which you avoid touching members of your sex), total the scores for items 1, 3, 4, 6, 9, 11, 12, 13, 16 and 18
3. To obtain your opposite-sex touch avoidance score (the extent to which you avoid touching members of the opposite sex), total the scores for items 2, 5, 7, 8, 10, 14, 15 and 17.
4. To obtain your total avoidance score, add the subtotals from steps 2 and 3. The higher the score, the higher the touch avoidance—that is, the greater

your tendency to avoid touch. In studies by Andersen and Leibowitz (1978), who constructed this test, average opposite-sex touch avoidance scores for males was 12.9 and for females was 14.85. Average same-sex touch avoidance scores were 26.43 for males and 21.70 for females.

Touch Tips

Since touch, like other forms of nonverbal communication, is ambiguous and because so much hinges on the people and circumstances involved, it's virtually impossible to set down concrete guidelines for appropriate touching. At best, a number of general considerations can be put forward. These should help you decide when or when not to touch. Any given instance of touching could be appropriate or inappropriate depending on

a. the nature of the relationship between the person touching and the one being touched
b. the circumstances in which the touching occurs
c. the response of the one touched
d. the amount of pressure used
e. the length of the touch
f. the part of the body that is touched
g. what part of the body does the touching (Adler and Rodman, 1994: 178–179)

Source: From *The Development and Nature of Construct Touch Avoidance* by Peter Anderson and Liebowitz as in *Environmental Psychology and Nonverbal Behaviour 3*: 89–196, 1978. Reprinted by permission of Human Sciences Press, Inc. and the authors.

STUDY GUIDE

Key Terms

gender (267)	anima (272)	multicultural (275)
moral reasoning (267)	animus (272)	economic
moral voice (269)	asymmetries (273)	interdependence
identity formation (270)	public speaking (273)	(275)
	private speaking (273)	politics (275)
morality of care (271)	report talk (273)	culture (275)
relationship (271)	rapport talk (273)	enculturation (275)
morality of impersonal justice (271)	gossip talk (273)	acculturation (275)
	pluralistic (275)	

intercultural communication (276)	accent (288)	bodily movement (kinesics) (298)
ethnocentrism (277)	complement (289)	space communication (proxemics) (301)
perception of difference (280)	contradict (289)	intimate distance (302)
false perception of difference (280)	regulate (289)	personal distance (302)
stereotype (281)	repeat (289)	
empathy (281)	substitution (289)	social distance (302)
precommunication attitudes (282)	paralanguage (290)	public distance (302)
jargon (283)	articulation (290)	territoriality (303)
nonverbal communication (287)	pitch (291)	time communication (chronemics) (304)
	environment (291)	
	artifactual communication (292)	
	physical appearance (295)	touch communication (haptics) (305)
	attractiveness (297)	

Fill-in-the-Blank Questions

PROGRESS CHECK 8.1

Instructions: Fill in each blank with the appropriate response from the list below.

Deborah Tannen	women
men	articulation
care and relationship	artifactual
ethnocentrism	kinesics
jargon	neurolinguistic programmers
paralanguage	
Lawrence Kohlberg	ambiguous
body type	nonverbal communication
acculturation	empathy
Carol Gilligan	cultural context
public distance	Charles Darwin
justice and fairness	

1. According to _____, moral development occurs sequentially in six stages.
2. _____ claims that cognitive-developmental reasoning has an inherent gender bias.
3. According to _____, women speak a language of connection and intimacy, while men speak and hear a language of status and independence.
4. _____ have a tendency to interrupt _____ more often in conversation.
5. In matters of interpersonal conflict, men speak more the language of _____, while women are more interested in matters of _____.
6. Through the process of _____, a person from one culture is modified through direct or indirect exposure to another.

7. The process of interpersonal communication takes place in a broader _____.

8. When people are only able to see things from their own cultural perspective, not objectively, they exhibit _____.

9. _____ involves an element of role taking, placing ourselves in the shoes of the other.

10. _____ is a type of sub-language that can cause problems with interpersonal communication.

11. _____ can be vocal or nonvocal.

12. Under the umbrella of _____ is included tone of voice, pitch and rate.

13. Nonverbal cues are not always easily read because they are often _____.

14. According to _____, nonverbal expressions served as early survival mechanisms, prior to the development of language.

15. When we leave off parts of words, add parts that shouldn't be there or slur words, we are guilty of bad _____.

16. What we "say" by colour, clothing and bodily adornment is an aspect of _____ communication.

17. Endomorphy, mesomorphy and ectomorphy are all examples of _____.

18. The study of body movement is called _____.

19. According to _____, eyes move according to how people think and process information.

20. The space kept between you and your instructor during class is called _____.

True/False Questions

Instructions: Circle the appropriate letter next to each statement.

T F 1. The need to seize and occupy space is called territoriality.

T F 2. Space is often used as a symbol of status.

T F 3. Because of concerns over child abuse and sexual violence, it's always a good idea to refrain from touching other people.

T F 4. According to Sidney Jourard's crosscultural observations, French couples touch each other in cafés more often than do couples of any other nationality.

T F 5. The "V" sign made with the right hand is a universal sign for victory.

T F 6. Male-female differences in moral reasoning are innate, i.e., genetically determined, according to Carol Gilligan.

T F 7. According to Carl Jung, both men and women possess innate tendencies stereotypically attributed to the opposite sex.

T F 8. According to Deborah Tannen, asymmetries in male-female communication often lead to miscommunication.

T F 9. Ethnocentric people have superior powers of observation.

T F 10. Knowing yourself better can improve social communication.

T F 11. The expression "user friendly" is an example of jargon.

T F 12. Sometimes we receive mixed messages because what people communicate verbally is inconsistent with their nonverbal messages.

T F 13. Nonverbal communication is never vocal.

T F 14. Nonverbal communication can be used to accent, complement, regulate, contradict, repeat or substitute for the spoken word.

T F 15. Use of time can indicate status.

T F 16. Attractive people are usually looked upon with greater suspicion than are unattractive people.

T F 17. Being thin always sends a positive message.

T F 18. Preening behaviour could be interpreted as a conscious or unconscious come-on.

T F 19. It's possible to refrain from nonverbal communication.

T F 20. People who arrive chronically late are irresponsible.

Focus Questions

1. How do women speak in "a different voice" from men?
2. What accounts for male and female differences when communicating about interpersonal (moral) conflict?
3. How do men and women speak a different language, according to Deborah Tannen?
4. Why must culture be taken into account in the context of interpersonal communication?
5. What are some examples of intercultural miscommunication?
6. How can your intercultural communication be improved?
7. What are the different types of nonverbal communication?
8. Can you illustrate how statements can be made nonverbally? How so?
9. Given your usual physical appearance, posture and paralanguage, as well as your use of space and time, what nonverbal messages do you send to others? What specifically could you do to change these messages?

Summary

1. Why is a consideration of gender important to human relations development?
   - men and women use language differently
   - they behave according to different gender-role expectations
   - they tend to perceive and interpret interpersonal conflict differently
2. How can interpersonal (moral) conflict be interpreted?
   - reward and punishment (stage 1)
   - payback and instrumentality (stage 2)

- being nice (stage 3)
- unbreakable rules (stage 4)
- negotiable duties and responsibilities (stage 5)
- universal considerations of justice (stage 6)

3. How do Carol Gilligan's views of morality differ from those of Lawrence Kohlberg? Morality is

Gilligan	Kohlberg
subjective	objective
personal	impersonal
concrete	abstract/hypothetical
relational/contextual	rational/universal
care-based	justice-based
focused on social responsibility	focused on individual rights

4. How do men and women tend to use language differently, according to Deborah Tannen?
   - women speak a language of "connection and intimacy"; men talk in terms of "status and independence"
   - male and female communication is often asymmetrical; women like people to express matching experiences as a way of showing empathy, men tend to see this as a form of discounting experience
   - men tend to be more comfortable doing public speaking (report talk) while women usually prefer private speaking (rapport talk)
   - topics of gossip differ for males and females
   - men like to give information and opinions; women are more comfortable in supporting
   - men interrupt more than women
   - men are more self-aggrandizing; women are less boastful

5. What form does intercultural communication take?
   - international (e.g., between Germany and Japan)
   - interracial (e.g., between blacks and Chinese people)
   - interethnic (e.g., between French-Canadians and Finnish-Canadians)
   - interreligious (e.g., between Catholics and Protestants)
   - interoccupational (e,g., between doctors and lawyers)
   - intergender (i.e., between males and females)

6. What are some problems related to intercultural communication?
   - language
   - misread intentions
   - violations of values and customs
   - misunderstandings
   - ethnocentrism
   - perceiving differences as greater than they are
   - ignoring important differences
   - different meanings attributed to the same word
   - differing nonverbal cues
   - stereotyping and lack of empathy

7. How can intercultural communication be improved?
   - know yourself better (your prejudices, precommunication attitudes and projected image)
   - use a common language (minimize jargon and agree to meanings of terms)
   - suspend judgment (take your time before making evaluations)

8. What is the nature of nonverbal communication?
   - it is language without words
   - it may or may not be vocal (tone, pitch)
   - it is multichanneled
   - it is ambiguous
   - it has a social function (e.g., it can express fear or define a relationship)

9. What is the relationship between verbal and nonverbal communication?
   - nonverbal communication can accent, complement, regulate, contradict, repeat and substitute for the spoken word

10. What are the possible classifications for nonverbal communication?
    - paralanguage
    - environment
    - artifactual communication
    - physical appearance
    - posture and body movements
    - space communication (proxemics)
    - time communication (chronemics)
    - touch communication (haptics)

11. What are the different spatial distances?
    - intimate distance (skin contact to 1/2 m.)
    - personal distance (1/2 to 1 1/3 m.)
    - social distance (1 1/3 to 2 1/3 m.)
    - public distance (4 to 8 1/3 m. or more)

12. What is territoriality? What kinds are there?
    - territoriality is the possessive reaction to occupy space and objects within it
    - a way of communicating status and ownership
    - the three types are primary, secondary and public

Related Readings

Ardrey, Robert (1966). *The Territorial Imperative*. New York: Atheneum.

Chodorow, Nancy (1974). "Family Structure and Feminine Personality." Pp. 43–44 and 166–167 in M.Z. Rosaldo and L. Lamphere (eds.), *Women, Culture and Society*. Stanford: Stanford University Press.

Duska, Ronald and Mariellen Whelan (1975). *Moral Development: A Guide to Piaget and Kohlberg*. New York: Paulist Press.

Kohlberg, Lawrence (1976). "Moral Stages and Moralization: The Cognitive-

Developmental Approach." In T. Lickona (ed.), *Moral Development and Behaviour*. New York: Holt, Rinehart and Winston.

Montagu, Ashley (1971). *Touching: The Human Significance of the Skin*. San Francisco: Harper & Row.

 ## Weblinks

1. S.U.N.Y. Buffalo
   www.wings.buffalo.edu/academic/department/communication/com486/Service/index.html

   See what genders are thinking about each other in today's world, compared to 20 years ago.

2. Raising a Son, Raising a Daughter
   www.parentsplace.com/

   This parenting resource on the web offers advice regarding gender, relationship and parenting communication.

3. Qweb Sweden: A Women's Empowerment Base
   www.Qweb.kvinnoforum.se/

   Qweb Sweden is a global communication network for exchange of knowledge, experience and ideas on women's health and gender issues.

4. Test your nonverbal communication skills
   www.westwords.com/Guffey/nonvrb.html

   Visit this site to find out how tuned in you are to nonverbal communication.

CHAPTER 9

Strong lives are motivated by dynamic purposes.

–Kenneth Hildebrand

MOTIVATION MATTERS: WHY YOU DO THE THINGS YOU DO

CHAPTER OVERVIEW

LEARNING OUTCOMES

*After successfully completing this chapter, you will
be able to*

9.1 Explain the general nature of motivation

9.2 Determine your locus of control

9.3 Outline a psychoanalytic explanation of motivation

9.4 Describe Abraham Maslow's humanistic theory of motivation

9.5 Profile self-actualized individuals

9.6 Give a behaviourist account of motivation

9.7 Identify your personal motivations using a thematic apperception test

9.8 Explain how social behaviour can be learned

9.9 Give a choice-theory account of motivation

9.10 Gain greater control of your personal behaviour

MOTIVATIONAL MYSTERIES

When Jamal was a young boy, everybody considered him to be an intelligent, above-average student. He worked hard and tried his best at everything he did. Jamal was a likable guy, the kind of person who brought out the best in others. At his grade eight graduation, virtually everyone picked Jamal as the one who would excel in high school and be most likely to succeed later in life. Once Jamal entered high school, however, things suddenly began to change. His grades became inconsistent, his attendance became unpredictable and his boundless curiosity and enthusiasm for learning all but disappeared. He started to avoid people and engaged in self-destructive behaviours. He got into some minor trouble with the law and started taking drugs. He developed an apathetic attitude toward his personal responsibilities and life in general. Jamal somehow managed to graduate from high school and miraculously was admitted to the local college. Nobody expects very much from him now. If he squeaks through, everybody will be happy. Jamal doesn't have a clue what he'll do after college.

Althea is Jamal's younger sister. She has always been an average student, never excelling in anything she does. A bit self-conscious and overweight, she used to present herself as a shy person with not much to say about anything. The fact that Jamal was intelligent and well-liked in grade school served only to reinforce Althea's own feelings of inferiority. When Althea entered high school, things changed for her as well, only this time for the better. Althea's grades took a leap upwards and she worked hard to earn straight As. Althea shed some weight and began putting a lot of emphasis on improving her physical appearance. She decided to exercise regularly, buy fashionable clothing and use makeup to help her look more attractive. Althea, too, graduated from high school. She entered the local transfer college and plans to earn a liberal arts degree before eventually going on to law school. Althea is energized and "hungry" to acquire the material benefits of professional success.

Stories such as the two above are far from uncommon. Maybe you identified a little bit yourself with one of these fictional characters. Maybe there's a Jamal or Althea in your family or in your circle of friends. The point is that the Jamals and Altheas of the world leave us all wondering, "Why do people do what they do?" Why, for example, are some individuals motivated to achieve and others not? In this chapter, we'll look at different theoretical explanations that have been given for motivation and how it relates to human behaviour. This discussion should help you to understand why you (and others) do the things you do. With this understanding you will be able to take more effective control of your life. You will also learn how to become a positive motivational force in other people's lives. The information provided here, along with the application exercises and self-diagnostic, should help you to build a self-managed lifestyle, one that may not provide you with absolutely everything you *want*, but that will help you get much of what you really *need*.

THE NATURE OF MOTIVATION

Highly successful motivational speakers on television sometimes make it sound in their seminars as if **motivation**, the impetus to act, is a relatively easy concept to understand. These purveyors of personal success claim that "proven" behavioural techniques can be easily applied to anyone's life to maximize personal goal achievement. While their own success is witness to the fact that energy and enthusiasm are inspiring and motivational for many, I am not sure that life is so simple that their prescriptions for personal happiness should be so casually dispensed to a hungry public craving purpose and direction. Before going out to buy the next new and improved motivational book or tape on the market, you may wish to become an "informed consumer" of sorts. Acquaint yourself with some of the serious issues and psychologically important theories related to motivation discussed here.

Don't tell me what to do or I won't do it!

Adel Escent

Perhaps what we need is a kick in our complacency to prepare us for what lies ahead.

Captain Jean-Luc Picard, Star Trek: The Next Generation

Life can be pulled by goals just as surely as it can be pushed by drives.

Viktor Frankl

When the going gets tough, the tough go shopping!

Rumoured to be engraved on the tomb of the Unknown Consumer

Everybody's Motivated

In social conversation we sometimes hear it said that "so-and-so is motivated," but lament the fact that "so-and-so's brother or sister" is not. We also hear about motivated and unmotivated students or ambitious and unambitious employees. All this talk makes it sound like motivation is some kind of desirable character trait that not everyone possesses, and that anyone who lacks it is psychologically flawed. It also raises the idea that people can be categorized by one of two personality types: motivated or unmotivated. This categorization would be highly simplistic, as an individual might be motivated today, but not tomorrow. Maybe that person is motivated at work, but not at school. Perhaps some tasks are approached with a desire to do well, while others are approached lackadaisically. In fact, maybe the same task is approached by the same individual on two different days in qualitatively different ways—on one day with interest and enthusiasm and on the next with apathy and careless ease. In short, motivational levels can vary within and between individuals. They can vary as well among situations, tasks and the times at which things are done. In view of this variance, it could be argued that we're all motivated, we're just not motivated to do the same things in the same ways, at the same times and with the same people. It's probably true to say that when we describe others as unmotivated, what we are really saying is that those others are not doing what we want them to do in the way we want them to do it, at the time we want it done.

Reasons for Behaving

Motivation obviously has a lot to do with behaviour. When searching for the motivation for a behaviour, we try to discover the reason behind it. In general terms, we want to know why people do the things they do. Finding the reason for behaviour is no easy task. I suppose you could simply ask people why they do the things they do. You might on occasion even get an honest reply! However, suppose the person responding to you is hiding his real intentions. Answers to your question will not be very helpful. Maybe the individual lacks sufficient self-insight and does not really understand the reasons behind the behaviour she exhibits. Do *you* always know why you do things you do? Lack of self-awareness, then, as well as dishonesty, can make it difficult to determine people's motivations. Furthermore, we might, as observers, unwittingly project onto others our own motivations as we respond defensively toward them (see Chapter 3). In this case, the motivations we witness and attribute to them would actually be our own staring us in the face.

Conscious and Unconscious Motivations

Motivations can be either conscious or unconscious. **Conscious motivations** lead us to do things willfully and with self-awareness. With consciously motivated actions, we know what we're doing and we can provide rationales and explanations for them. **Unconscious motivations**, by contrast, give rise to actions performed without self-awareness and self-understanding. Lacking insight into ourselves, we may exhibit behaviour that we later regret. We may say to ourselves, "I don't know why I did that" or "How could I have said that?" Our own motivations can often be mysteries to us as much as they are to others. Repressed fears, buried anxieties or latent hostilities, for example, may manifest themselves in personal behaviour without warning and thereby catch us by surprise. Psychiatrists such as Sigmund Freud and Carl Jung would argue that much of our behaviour is indeed unconsciously motivated. On an optimistic note, they believe that clinical procedures can be used to bring a greater segment of human behaviour under the rational, conscious control of the ego. If we do not gain access to the unconscious, much of what appears to be freely chosen behaviour will in fact be determined by forces over which we have little control.

Internal versus External Locus of Control

Speaking of control, the question arises as to whether motivation is an "inside" or "outside" job. When you do something wrong, for example, did "the devil make you do it?" When you aggressively attack someone either verbally or physically, is it because that person "made" you angry? Is that person, not you, responsible for what happened? Is some behaviour simply beyond your control, caused by outside influences? As we'll consider in more depth shortly, some researchers believe that much of human behaviour is environmentally determined. Forces outside people cause them to be the way they are and condition them to act as they do. I suppose this is why defence lawyers often plead for reduced sentences on behalf of their guilty clients. They argue that external circumstances influenced the clients to do wrong. They were in many respects victims of circumstance. The "boys in the 'hood" made them bad. Society made them bad. The system made them bad. An alcoholic parent made them bad. Everything made them bad except themselves. To hold this position would be to assume that they experienced an **external locus of control** for behaviour. By contrast, if people accept responsibility for their actions, they assume an **internal locus of control**.

People who display a high internal locus of control see themselves as self-governed. They do not feel coerced and are not "victims of the system." What they do is a matter of personal choice. They really want to do what they're doing. They feel in charge of their destinies. The rewards derived from internally motivated activities often come from the activities themselves. We can observe that internally motivated people frequently do things for an action's intrinsic value. For example, when you behave virtuously, not to impress or to gain praise, but simply for the sake of duty, you implicitly recognize the inherent worth of virtuous acts. Virtue, for you, becomes its own reward. Others may act virtuously by giving to charity, but they may do so because fellow workers at the office have shamed them into it or because they want the tax deduction. The same action can be motivated by very different reasons. Reasons for behaviour can be external and coercive, or internal and voluntary.

It's not my aim here to convince you that some motivations are good or others are bad. Nor is it my intent to defend or discredit any one position on the nature of human motivation. In what follows, we'll examine several established motivational theories that seek to explain why we do the things we do. After completing our theoretical survey, a behavioural strategy for more effective and self-directed living will be introduced for your consideration and use.

SELF-DIAGNOSTIC

9.1

9.2

Internal Control Index

Please read each statement. Where there is a blank, indicate what your usual attitude, feeling or behaviour would be.

A = Rarely (less than 10 percent of the time)
B = Occasionally (about 30 percent of the time)
C = Sometimes (about half the time)
D = Frequently (about 70 percent of the time)
E = Usually (more than 90 percent of the time)

1. When faced with a problem I _____ try to forget it.
2. I _____ need frequent encouragement from others to keep working at a difficult task.
3. I _____ like jobs where I can make decisions and be responsible for my own work.
4. I _____ change my opinion when someone I admire disagrees with me.
5. If I want something I _____ work hard to get it.
6. I _____ prefer to learn the facts about something from someone else rather than to have to dig them up myself.
7. I will _____ accept jobs that require me to supervise others.
8. I _____ have a hard time saying "no" when someone trys to sell me something I don't want.
9. I _____ like to have a say in any decisions made by any group I'm in.
10. I _____ consider the different sides of an issue before making any decisions.
11. What other people think _____ has a great influence on my behaviour.
12. Whenever something good happens to me I _____ feel it is because I've earned it.
13. I _____ enjoy being in a position of leadership.
14. I _____ need someone else to praise my work before I am satisfied with what I've done.
15. I am _____ sure enough of my opinions to try and influence others.
16. When something is going to affect me I _____ learn as much about it as I can.
17. I _____ decide to do things on the spur of the moment.
18. For me, knowing I've done something well is _____ more important than being praised by someone else.
19. I _____ let other peoples' demands keep me from doing things I want to do.
20. I _____ stick to my opinions when someone disagrees with me.
21. I _____ do what I feel like doing, not what other people think I ought to do.
22. I _____ get discouraged when doing something that takes a long time to achieve results.

23. When part of a group, I _____ prefer to let other people make all the decisions.
24. When I have a problem I _____ follow the advice of friends or relatives.
25. I _____ enjoy trying to do difficult tasks more than I enjoy trying to do easy tasks.
26. I _____ prefer situations where I can depend on someone else's ability rather than just my own.
27. Having someone important tell me I did a good job is _____ more important to me than feeling I've done a good job.
28. When I'm involved in something I _____ try to find out all I can about what is going on, even when someone else is in charge.

Internal Control Index (ICI)

Author: Patricia Dutteiler

Purpose: To measure locus of control

Description: The ICI is a 28-item instrument designed to measure where a person looks for, or expects to obtain, reinforcement. An individual with an external locus of control believes that reinforcement is based on luck or chance, while an individual with an internal locus of control believes that reinforcement is based on his own behaviour. Locus of control is viewed as a personality trait that influences human behaviour across a wide range of situations related to learning and achievement. There are two factors contained in the ICI, one called self-confidence, and a second called autonomous behaviour (behaviour independent of social pressure).

Norms: The ICI was developed and tested with several samples of junior college, university undergraduate, and continuing education students. The total N involved 1365 respondents of both sexes. Means are available that are broken down by age, group, sex, race, and educational and socioeconomic level, and range from 99.3 and 120.8.

Scoring: Each item is scored on a 5-point scale from A ("rarely") to E ("usually"). Half the items are worded so that high internally oriented respondents are expected to answer half at the "usually" end of the scale and the other half at the "rarely" end. The "rarely" response is scored as 5 points on items 1, 2, 4, 6, 8, 11, 14, 17, 19, 22, 23, 24, 26 and 27; for the remainder of the items, the response "usually" is scored as 5 points. This produces a possible range of scores from 28 to 140, with higher scores reflecting higher internal locus of control.

Reliability: The ICI has very good internal consistency with alphas of .84 and .85. No test-retest correlations were reported.

Validity: The ICI has fair concurrent validity with a low but significant correlation with Mirels' Factor I of the Rotter I-E Scale.

Primary reference: Duttweiler, P.C. (1984). The Internal Control Index: A newly developed measure of locus of control, *Educational and Psychological Measurement* 44, 209–221. Instrument reproduced with permission of Patricia Duttweiler and *Educational and Psychological Measurement*.

Availability: Journal article.

Source: From *Educational and Psychology Measurement* by Corcoran and Fisher. Copyright 1987. Reprinted by permission of Sage Publications, Inc.

THEORIES OF MOTIVATION: WHAT MAKES ME TICK?

A Psychoanalytic Explanation

If you have been going through this book in sequence, you have already encountered Freud's **psychoanalytic theory** in Chapter 3. There you learned about the different psychic structures and the various mechanisms of defence. Here, we'll look at what fuels the functioning of human personality. By examining what makes people tick, you'll better understand what makes *you* tick.

Instincts — The Forces that Drive the Personality

When Freud developed his concept of personality, he was influenced by prevailing views within the biological and physical sciences. He adopted a then-accepted **energy model** to explain the workings of the human mind. According to Freud, human beings can be conceptualized as complex energy systems that require energy to do psychological work such as thinking, perceiving, remembering and dreaming (Carver and Scheier, 1988). The energy that is used to perform psychologically is generated and released through natural biological processes. Energy is continually used and released.

In this model of motivation, instincts are responsible for generating the psychic energy necessary to keep the human body functioning. Given this, behaviour has a biological basis. Instinctual drives are activated by bodily needs that motivate people to seek gratification. Biological need states cause psychological desires or wishes to emerge. If the body is suffering from a liquid deficiency, for instance, a bodily need gives rise to thirst, an urge to rectify an imbalanced condition. Once our thirst is satisfied, the need temporarily goes away and we are no longer motivated to drink or to seek out fluids.

> What I lack is not happiness, but peace of mind.
>
> Mortimer Adler, philosopher

Nirvana and Pleasure Principles

Implicit in what has just been stated is the notion of **homeostasis**. If Freud is correct, human behaviour aims to achieve a state of equilibrium. The psychic structure of personality functions according to the **nirvana principle**, meaning that it seeks to reduce excitation and tension. The mental apparatus tries to maintain a relatively stable state of stimulation-free existence (Monte, 1987). This principle was first called the constancy principle, a term borrowed from psychophysicist Gustav Fechner. Freud initially saw the nirvana principle of behaviour as inextricably linked to pleasure. For him, when people rid themselves of disturbing tensions and an excess of stimulation, they experience pleasure. Freud (1924) later distinguished between the nirvana principle and what he called the **pleasure principle**. He recognized, in the second principle, that some states of pleasure require an increase in excitation, rather than a reduction in stimulation. People who actively seek out tensions for the purpose of physical excitement live by this principle. On this note, Freud went on to regard the nirvana principle and the pleasure principle as separate but complementary forces in psychic life (Monte, 1987: 102).

Kinds of Instincts: Eros and Thanatos

To help us understand instinctual life, Freud distinguished between two basic types of instinct: *eros* and *thanatos*. Falling under **eros** are the life instincts and sexual instincts. They aim toward survival, self-preservation, procreation and pleasure. Collectively they belong to what people commonly refer to as the **libido**. Notice that the libido is not purely sexual. Hunger and pain avoidance can be considered life instincts, though they are not associated with erotic urges. In general terms, then, the libido is that which seeks physical and pleasurable feelings associated with the life instincts, both erotic and non-erotic (Monte, 1987). Instincts that do not fall under *eros* are placed under the heading of **thanatos**, which includes our death instincts. As Freud once said, "The aim of all life is death" (cited in Monte, 1987: 102). At first glance, such a proposal may seem a little ridiculous, but let's consider it seriously for a moment.

If we go back to the nirvana principle, we find that instincts are aroused so that we'll act in ways to reestablish homeostasis—a "state of peaceful freedom from need" (Monte, 1987: 102). For instance, when tension mounts from hunger, we eat and the tension is removed. Continually we seek under the pressure of instinct to achieve an earlier state of "organismic quietude" before the external world or internal needs made their disquieting demands upon us. Complete quietude—absolute freedom from need and tension and total independence from the world—comes only with death. Intuitively we understand this concept. We sometimes see expressions of peaceful bliss on the faces of deceased individuals. They look so still, so calm. We feel strangely uplifted and reassured, believing that they are now *resting* in peace, knowing perhaps that they did not *live* in peace. In a sense, death represents a final state of repose in which all struggles, tensions, torments and deprivations disappear.

A derivative of the death instinct is **aggression**. Tension can be reduced by a verbal, physical or symbolic attack. The objects of attack are usually others, though the self can be attacked as well. Aggressive urges that were once targeted at others could be redirected toward the self, resulting in acts of self-mutilation or even suicide. Expressions of humanity's aggressivity are present everywhere. People take dangerous drugs and laugh about their effects. Malicious people love to gossip and uncover "good dirt" that they can use against others. Individuals at work sabotage the efforts of colleagues. On the street, people physically assault their enemies. Contact sports are another obvious manifestation of the instinct of aggression. When I point to sports, I do not wish to pick on athletes. The next time you see a boxing match on television, watch the "bloodthirsty" spectators (some of whom would probably feel cheated if the fight ended in the first round with no blood or knockout punch). Or the next time you're at the "fights" and a hockey game breaks out, watch the fans yell, scream and pound on the glass in the vicinity of the action. Many fans of the game do not object to violence; they want it. That's what they pay for and that's what they like to see. Just ask the NHL expert Don Cherry! I guess in some ways he is unwittingly championing the cause of Freudian psychoanalysis. Don Cherry a Freudian? Think about that!

Figure 9.1

The Tension-Reducing Effects of Aggressive Acts

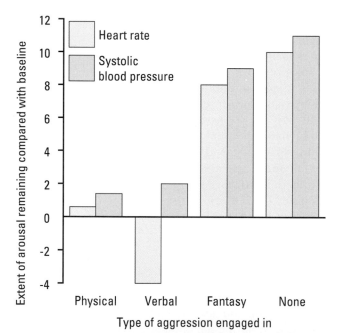

The figure portrays increases (positive values) and decreases (negative values) in heart rate and systolic blood pressure after various kinds of aggression, in comparison with levels before provocation. Both physical and verbal aggression were effective in returning subjects to (or below) their initial levels, whereas fantasy aggression was not (data from Hokanson & Burgess, 1962b).

Source: From Carver and Scheier, *Perspectives on Personality.* Copyright 1988 by Allyn and Bacon. Reprinted by permission.

The notion that aggressive instincts are motivating may seem to contradict the nirvana or homeostasis principles of psychoanalysis. Common sense would seem to suggest that when people display aggression, they become more aroused and physically excited. Research shows just the opposite, however. Aggressive acts serve as a **catharsis** or emotional release. In one study, subjects were harassed by an experimenter while they were working on a task. What resulted was a significant increase in heart rate and systolic blood pressure (indicators of tension). Afterwards, subjects were placed in four groups. One group was allowed to attack its tormentor physically by administering an electric shock; a second group was allowed verbal attack through experimenter rating; a third group was allowed to aggress in fantasy; a fourth group was given no chance to aggress in any fashion. The results displayed in Figure 9.1 indicate that there is an emotional catharsis when people have an opportunity to retaliate.

Control Your Instincts Before Your Instincts Control You

Recognizing that aggressive acts are emotionally cathartic should not suggest that we all become violent psychopathic killers, lashing out against people and objects in the world. Also, taking into account our instinctual sexual urges does not mean that we should sexually abuse others.

While life and death instincts constitute our ultimate source of motivational energy, they must be sublimated (see Chapter 3) into socially acceptable forms of expression. Police work, national defence, athletics and other competitive activities are good examples of ways to use aggression constructively. Artistic creation through photography, painting, movie making, writing or poetry would be good ways of sublimating sexuality, especially when expression of sexual urges would be inappropriate and morally prohibited. Instincts emanating from the id can also be better handled by raising levels of self-consciousness. The less that is denied or repressed in the unconscious, the greater rational control we have over our actions. Last, by reducing our defensiveness, we can learn to live with our biological nature and deal with it more effectively. Denying the reality of human biology is risky business; losing control of it is even worse. Think here of the roles that aggression and sexuality have played for famous people, such as Frank Gifford and O.J. Simpson, and what these roles have done to their careers and livelihoods. Maybe Freud was correct when he suggested that refusing to acknowledge the motivational force of biological instincts is just another expression of psychological defensiveness. Why is so much energy spent denying the importance of sexuality in human life?

Maslow's Humanistic Theory of Motivation

9.4

Abraham Maslow is another important figure in the historical development of motivational theory. In his books *The Farther Reaches of Human Nature*, *Motivation and Personality* and *Toward a Psychology of Being*, he presents a picture of human motivation that differs greatly from Freud's view.

Freud envisioned life as a constant struggle or conflict between the instinctive biological needs of the id and the moral demands imposed by the superego and society at large. He used clinical studies of neurotic and dysfunctional patients as the basis for his generalizations about human behaviour and motivation. By contrast, Maslow did not see psychological beings as people constantly at war with themselves and others. He viewed human nature as essentially good, not potentially evil and destructive. While Freud painted a dark picture of humanity focusing on its frailties, shortcom-

Abraham Maslow believed that all human beings are motivated to actualize themselves and to realize their potentialities.

ings and pathologies, Maslow emphasized human strength and virtue. He concentrated on the bright side of human reality. To study neurotics (as Freud did), in order to find out what normal people are like would be, for Maslow, like studying high school dropouts to develop a psychological profile of successful college or university graduates. In any case, to correct what he saw as inappropriate psychoanalytic conclusions drawn from a "sick" population, Maslow began to study healthy and well- adjusted individuals (e.g., extraordinary people he knew, as well as outstanding historical figures). He believed that the study of psychologically healthy people could provide a more adequate science of psychology and a better understanding of human motivation.

The Hierarchy of Human Needs

> Why aren't you ever satisfied?
>
> Universal complaint

I've heard it said that people are never satisfied. Usually when this assertion is made, the person making it is expressing displeasure, bewilderment or some kind of disapproval. It's as if wanting something more or wanting something different is inherently wrong. Maybe you've been criticized yourself for being restless and itchy, always searching for something you don't have. If so, you might take some comfort in Maslow's characterization of human beings as "wanting animals" who rarely reach a state of complete satisfaction (Hjelle and Ziegler, 1981). If you're never satisfied, maybe you're not a spoiled brat or a selfish malcontent, but simply a typical human being. For Maslow, psychological states of equilibrium or nirvana are short-lived. As soon as one need is satisfied, another demands satisfaction. To be human is to continually desire something. According to Maslow, our natural desires can be arranged in a **hierarchy of human needs**, a structure of ascending requirements. We have universal physiological needs, safety and security needs, social needs for love and belonging, esteem needs, cognitive needs, aesthetic needs and self-actualization needs. (Whether Maslow's hierarchical concept of motivation should be depicted with five or seven levels is open to discussion. In *Motivation and Personality*, he pays closest attention to physiological needs, safety and security needs, belonging and love needs, esteem needs and self-actualization needs. Cognitive and aesthetic needs are recognized as important, but are dealt with almost as an afterthought. Whether they belong to the higher levels of "basic needs" dealing with self-actualization or to the level of "metaneeds" beyond self-actualization is unclear to me. The cognitive needs for knowledge and understanding bear some resemblance to metaneeds for truth and meaning. Aesthetic needs seem to overlap with metaneeds for beauty and simplicity. For our purposes, I will put them at the higher level of the basic needs hierarchy). See these needs represented in Figure 9.2. We'll discuss each in a moment.

These innate needs motivate us to grow and develop. They serve to help us **actualize** ourselves; in other words, to help us become all that we are capable of becoming. Maslow does not see people as born inherently flawed or defective. They need not be redeemed, nor is there any instinctual devil that needs to be exorcised. For Maslow, the potential for healthy psychological growth and development is present at birth. Whether or not people fulfill themselves or actualize their potential will depend on the individuals themselves and on existing societal forces that will either serve to promote or inhibit self-actualization (Schultz, 1977). Different environments can stifle growth or encourage it.

As stated, the needs that have been listed as human motivators are hierarchical in nature. There is a **prepotency** to them. This means that lower-level needs must be satisfied before higher-level needs become salient or important in people's lives. At any given time, then, one level of needs dominates any individual's life. Which level it is depends on what other needs have already been satisfied. The further one's needs are satisfied up the hierarchy, the more self-realized the individual is. Let us now look at Maslow's hierarchy more closely.

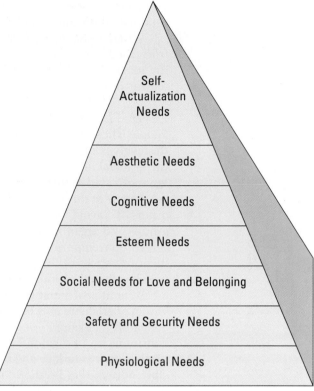

Figure 9.2
Maslow's Hierarchy of Human Needs

Level One: Physiological Needs

People at this level are most concerned with meeting their survival or **physiological needs**. They are preoccupied with obtaining such things as food and water. People struggling to survive may walk long distances for a bite to eat or for a life-saving sip of water necessary for continued existence. Physiological needs also include our need for air to breathe, and for sleep and sex. Without air we would obviously die. With continuous sleep deprivation, our mental and physical health would deteriorate. Without sex, the species would become extinct. (This statement has been true up until now; however, with new reproductive technologies such as in vitro fertilization, artificial insemination and newly developing cloning techniques, sex may become a redundant human need).

Level Two: Safety and Security Needs

In some cultures and societies where people are starving and the struggle to survive is an ongoing daily battle, higher order needs are not usually on their minds. If you're dying of thirst, realizing long-term ambitions does not occupy your attention. By contrast, in other cultures and societies where the basic needs of survival have been looked after, the physiological needs begin to play a less important role in daily life. **Safety and security needs** become prominent and exert themselves to ensure that there is stability, order, structure and certainty in one's environment. Children, for example, prefer routine and predictability. Uncertainty and unpredictability are difficult for everyone to cope with, but especially so for them. Take children out of their established routines and they show signs of distress.

When we finally get our safety and security needs met, we free ourselves from much fear and anxiety. Before meeting these needs, it is hard to see the magnificent horizons of our future; we are too busy defending and protecting our physical and psychological borders.

Level Three: Social Needs for Love and Belonging

People whose survival is ensured and security is guaranteed usually still find themselves dissatisfied. When the first two levels of needs are met, level three **social needs for belonging and love** begin to emerge. Individuals who are motivated at this level crave intimacy and caring relationships with others. People at this level need to feel a sense of belonging and togetherness with others. To avoid feeling lonely or socially ostracized, people will join clubs, groups and organizations.

In contemporary Canadian society, many of us experience difficulty meeting our level three needs. You may be a college or university student who has left all of your friends and family at home. Perhaps now you live in a basement apartment or residence where you know almost nobody. In time you may graduate as a business student, nurse, technician, social worker or educator, for example, and be forced to travel across the country, or even the continent, to find gainful employment. In this case, again, those who currently satisfy your love and belonging needs may be left behind, and quite possibly nobody will be there in your new location to make you feel that you belong or that you count. Even people who are not on the move due to their education or career find their level three needs frustrated. It's frequently the case that occupants of high-rise apartment buildings barely know their neighbours. Hundreds, if not thousands, of strangers can live close by and rarely make meaningful human contact. Being surrounded by people does not guarantee closeness and intimacy—a basic human need.

Level Four: Esteem Needs

Even if you are able to establish intimacy and a network of friends, life still remains incomplete. A husband might say to his wife, "I have a loving family, a good job, a roof over my head, financial security and food in my belly, but that's still not enough. I need something more!" At level four, esteem is the "something more." People need to feel good about themselves; in meeting their **esteem needs**, they receive respect from others. In Maslow's theory, esteem from others is primary (Schultz, 1977). This is understandable, for it can be very difficult to think well of ourselves if others don't. For example, if everybody else thinks you're a "schmuck," maybe you're not worthy of esteem. Some of the ways we try to gain the acceptance of others is by developing good reputations, achieving status or fame, gaining prestige or becoming a social success. We may also try to impress others by the car we drive, the clothes we wear, the neighbourhood we live in or by the knowledge and skills we display (Schultz, 1977).

Internal self-esteem is a universal need to feel worthy and adequate within ourselves. When this need is met, we feel confident and psychologically secure. We know ourselves well, we live by no grand self-delusions or inflated conceptions of self. We're able to assess our abilities and weaknesses in objective terms. When the need for self-esteem is frustrated, we experience a lack. We may feel inferior, discouraged or helpless. People with low self-esteem typically have poor self-concepts.

Level Five: Cognitive Needs

Once people have their esteem needs met, then higher level **cognitive needs** arise. These needs reflect our "impulse to satisfy curiosity, to know, to explain and to understand" (Maslow, 1987: 23). People who have level five needs frustrated may exhibit symptoms of boredom, loss of zest and steady deterioration of the intellectual life and its tastes. According to Maslow, the need to know is present in infancy and adulthood. As he puts it, "Children do not have to be taught to be curious. But they may be taught, as by institutionalization, not to be curious" (25).

Maslow also places understanding under the heading of cognitive needs. He points out that the need to know impels us, on the one hand, to minute details, while on the other hand, it moves us more and more toward developing a world philosophy, or theological perspective. This need can be labelled a search for meaning—"a desire to understand, to systematize, to organize, to analyze, to look for relations and meanings, to construct a system of values" (25).

Within the level of cognitive needs itself, a mini-hierarchy exists. The desire to know is prepotent over the desire to understand. Some discussions of Maslow's motivational theory leave out the cognitive needs as well as the aesthetic needs (see Ryckman, 1989: 346). This is unfortunate for, as Maslow himself says, "The desire to know and to understand...are as much personality needs as the basic needs we have already discussed" (1987: 25).

Level Six: Aesthetic Needs

Maslow addresses the issue of **aesthetic needs** somewhat tentatively. He believes that clinical observation indicates that, at least in some individuals, there is a truly basic aesthetic need. He maintains that people can get "sick" from ugliness and that cures can be found in beautiful surroundings. If you have any doubt about this idea you might try to imagine yourself being raised in a poverty-stricken ghetto, surrounded by dirt and squalor, graffiti-covered abandoned warehouses and severely deteriorating apartment complexes. Before I ever considered Maslow's notion of aesthetic needs, I remember thinking to myself that I would go crazy living in an ultramodern house decorated in the Bauhaus architectural style. For me, this type of architecture and corresponding furniture design are barren and cold. They create an ambience that is not nourishing to me psychologically. In any case, falling under the aesthetic category are needs for symmetry and closure, as well as needs for completion, system and structure (Maslow, 1987).

Level Seven: Self-Actualization Needs

Let's suppose that an individual—call her Kristine—has gained a lot of knowledge and has surrounded herself with beauty. Let's also say that she has developed positive self-esteem. She's respected and liked by others. Furthermore, Kristine belongs to many groups, has a solid network of friends, shares a loving intimate relationship with another person and is secure in her job, and certainly does not lack for the bare necessities of life. Yet Kristine is still dissatisfied. She wants something more. Since Kristine's needs at levels one through six are met, we would have to conclude that level seven **self-actualization needs** are probably becoming dominant in her life. At level seven, Kristine feels a need to actualize all of her potentialities; in other words, to become all of what she can be. Not to realize all her inborn potential would leave Kristine feeling frustrated. On this note, Maslow has written that "a new discontent and restlessness will soon develop unless the individual (Kristine) is doing what he or she, individually, is fitted for. Musicians must make music, artists must paint, poets must write if they are to be ultimately at peace with themselves. What humans can be, they must be. They must be true to their own nature. This need we may call self-actualization" (22).

As a college teacher I've met many Kristines. They are often returning students who are established and financially secure. They have family and friends. They are confident and able. They return to college to "grow" as people. They tell me that life before college was in some ways stifling them and interfering with their natural development as human beings. By coming to college they hope to realize themselves and their dreams.

A Psychological Portrait of Self-Actualized Individuals

Self-actualized people

1. Perceive clearly and efficiently. They have an unusual ability to detect dishonesty and to see concealed or confused realities.
2. Accept themselves, others and nature without guilt or complaint.
3. Behave spontaneously, with simplicity and naturalness.
4. Focus strongly on problems external to themselves, not on their own egos. They are frequently on a "mission" or have some life task to complete.
5. Enjoy privacy and solitude more than does the average person.
6. Are autonomous and resist enculteration. They are not dependent upon the physical and social environment.
7. Display a fresh appreciation for life. They experience life with awe, pleasure and wonder.
8. Have mystical and peak experiences.
9. Possess a deep feeling for humanity. They truly wish to help the human race.
10. Are honestly respectful and humble before others.
11. Have deep relationships with a limited number of people.
12. Are ethically strong, possessing definite moral standards.
13. Distinguish clearly between means and ends, focusing mostly on ends.
14. Display an unusual sense of humour, one that is philosophical and not hostile in nature.

Source: Summary is based on material from Maslow (1987: 128–142 and 1968: 26).

Life After Self-Actualization: Metamotivation and the Metaphysical Blues

Maslow's work with self-actualized individuals eventually led him to theorize that extremely healthy people were motivated by different things compared with average, normal and unhealthy people. He called his motivational theory for self-actualizing people **metamotivation**. He also calls it **being motivation**, or B-motivation, for short. To enable you to understand what's meant by this concept, it's helpful to draw attention to a distinction that Maslow makes between growth or B-motivation and deficit or **deficiency motivation** (D-motivation).

> What's left when having it all still isn't enough?
>
> Simplee A. Question

D-motivation serves the purpose of rectifying deficiencies in the person. Deficits in the body (lack of food, for example) produce pain and discomfort, as do psychological deficits. In response to biological and psychological deficiencies, hungry people are motivated to eat and insecure people are motivated to achieve, please or impress. Generally speaking, people with average to below average mental health are motivated by D-motives. Their behaviour aims primarily to gratify lower level requirements.

By contrast, self-actualizers are motivated by higher level needs. The term "needs" is used with caution here. Perhaps a better term would be "values." Self-actualizers do not live their lives preoccupied with reducing tensions or rectifying deficits. Rather, they aim to enrich and enlarge their experience of life (Schultz, 1977). Life for them is a kind of celebration; there's joy and ecstasy in simply being alive. As Schultz (1977: 66) puts it, "Self-actualizers are beyond striving, desiring, or wishing for something they need to correct a deficit; all their deficits have been corrected. They are no longer *becoming*, in the sense of satisfying the lower needs. Now they are in a state of *being*, of spontaneously, naturally, joyously expressing their full humanness. In that sense then, they are unmotivated." I may have witnessed an unmotivated self-actualized student in the hallway at school recently. She was wearing a T-shirt that read, "If I don't own it; I don't want it." I can only guess that all of her lower level material needs were met. If her life reflected what her T-shirt said, apparently she lacked for nothing, or at least she wished for nothing.

When people go after objects for purposes of need gratification, the objects become means to further ends. They possess an instrumental value for deficit reduction. Were there no deficit, the objects wouldn't be sought. By contrast, metamotivation addresses itself to things that have being value (B-value). Such things have intrinsic worth. They are ends in themselves. Metamotivation should be seen as involving states of being rather than intermediate steps to ultimate goals.

In some respects, B-values do act like needs, only on a higher plane. They can be referred to as metaneeds. Blocking of metaneeds does not produce typical neurosis or psychopathology, but rather, a kind of **existential frustration** or **metapathology**. Schultz (1977) describes metapathology as "a rather formless malaise; we feel alone, helpless, meaningless, depressed, and despairing, but we cannot point to something and say, 'There! That person, or that object, is the cause of my feeling this way.'" Personally, I call this kind of existential *angst* the "metaphysical blues." To help you recognize the various metapathologies resulting from frustrated metaneeds, see Table 9.1.

Table 9.1   Metaneeds or B-Values and Specific Metapathologies

Metaneeds or B-Values	Specific Metapathologies
1. Truth	Disbelief; mistrust; cynicism; skepticism; suspicion.
2. Goodness	Utter selfishness. Hatred; repulsion; disgust. Reliance only upon self and for self. Nihilism. Cynicism.
3. Beauty	Vulgarity. Specific unhappiness, restlessness, loss of taste, tension, fatigue. Philistinism. Bleakness.
4. Unity; Wholeness	Disintegration; "the world is falling apart." Arbitrariness.
4a. Dichotomy-Transcendence	Black-white thinking, either/or thinking. Seeing everything as a duel or a war, or a conflict. Low synergy. Simplistic view of life.
5. Aliveness; Process	Deadness. Robotizing. Feeling oneself to be totally determined. Loss of emotion. Boredom(?); loss of zest in life. Experiential emptiness.
6. Uniqueness	Loss of feeling of self and of individuality. Feeling oneself to be interchangeable, anonymous, not really needed.
7. Perfection	Discouragement(?); hopelessness; nothing to work for.
7a. Necessity	Chaos; unpredictability. Loss of safety. Vigilance.
8. Completion; Finality	Feelings of incompleteness with perseveration. Hopelessness. Cessation of striving and coping. No use trying.
9. Justice	Insecurity; anger; cynicism; mistrust; lawlessness; jungle worldview; total selfishness.
9a. Order	Insecurity. Wariness. Loss of safety, of predictability. Necessity for vigilance, alertness, tension, being on guard.
10. Simplicity	Overcomplexity; confusion; bewilderment, conflict, loss of orientation.
11. Richness; Totality	Depression; uneasiness; loss of interest in world. Comprehensiveness.
12. Effortlessness	Fatigue, strain, striving, clumsiness, awkwardness, gracelessness, stiffness.
13. Playfulness	Grimness; depression; paranoid humourlessness; loss of zest in life. Cheerlessness. Loss of ability to enjoy.
14. Self-sufficiency	Dependence upon(?) the perceiver(?). It becomes his responsibility.
15. Meaningfulness	Meaninglessness. Despair. Senselessness of life.

Source: Table 9.1 and Maslow quotations from *The Farther Reaches of Human Nature* by Abraham H. Maslow. Copyright 1971 by Bertha G. Maslow. Used by permission of Viking Penguin, a division of Penguin Books USA Inc.

A Behaviourist Account of Motivation

9.6

The two motivational theories we've looked at so far are based largely on the concept of needs. For Freud, needs were conceptualized as primarily biological in nature. Satisfying them required reducing tension within the organism. Maslow also saw motivation in terms of needs. As you've learned, he believed that there exists a hierarchy of human needs leading to self-actualization. As was the case for Freud, Maslow understood the gratification of (lower-level) needs as a way of making up for deficiencies and reducing tensions. Of course, Maslow went beyond Freud to talk about meta-needs, where the issue is not deficiency reduction, but states of being. Nonetheless, both theorists were concerned with needs as a way of explaining why we do the things we do.

A second feature common to Freud and Maslow is that they saw the origin of needs as internal, innate or biologically preprogrammed. For Freud, life and death instincts provided the energy necessary for all behaviour. One could not opt out, so to speak, of their influence. As for Maslow's hierarchy, people are born and destined to self-actualization. It is in people's nature to move in this direction.

Where Freud and Maslow probably differed most was on the issue of freedom and personal responsibility. Freud allowed unconscious forces to play a much greater determining role in life than did Maslow. The latter would surely accept the fact that people don't always understand themselves or control their behaviour, but he probably would argue that people's behaviour is under much more conscious and rational influence than Freud would allow. For example, I don't think Maslow would accept the often-cited Freudian proposition that "biology is destiny." Maslow regarded human beings as much more self-willed and self-determining than did Freud. Nevertheless, both theorists argued that internal forces (conscious or unconscious) play a prominent role in motivational explanations.

As we now move into a behaviourist account of motivation, we'll find no importance placed on unconscious factors. Behaviourists either don't believe an unconscious exists, that the notion is illogical, or that nothing scientifically valid can be said about it. Matters of free will and self-determination will also be put to the test. Strict, orthodox behaviourists don't believe in a free will that cannot be observed, tested or measured. In their efforts to make psychological explanations of motivation more scientifically respectable, they stress environmental and experiential factors that determine human action. Rather than focus on internal needs, states or psychodynamics as a way of explaining motivation, behaviourists emphasize external variables and learning principles. Let us now turn to a radically different conception of what makes us tick.

What We Do Is What We've Learned

According to **behavioural theory**, most behaviours exhibited by human beings are learned. Of course, actions such as breathing and blinking come naturally without learning. So too do digestive processes. We breathe, blink and digest food without prior training. On the other hand, apart from autonomic responses, most of our actions having psychological or social signifi-

APPLICATION EXERCISE 9.1

9.7 ▶

Picture, Picture in the Book

Instructions: Below you see a picture. Take a few seconds to look at it and then answer the questions that follow. Don't just describe what you see. Use your creative imagination to produce a detailed story.

1. What do you think is happening in this picture?
2. What events could possibly have preceded this situation? Did something happen in the past? If so, what?
3. What do you believe the woman in the picture is thinking? Does she want something? Does she need something? How does she feel?
4. Is something about to occur? What, exactly?

Volunteers may offer to read their stories to other members of the class.

Debriefing: The exercise you just completed is similar to a Thematic Apperception Test (TAT) originally developed by R. Murray. This test requires individuals to describe ambiguous pictures. If members of your class shared their stories with you, you can readily appreciate how ambiguous the photo is and, as a result, how many different interpretations can be given for it. In fact, there are no "correct" descriptions or interpretations. The idea is that people will project their own needs onto the content of the stories that they have created. The TAT is thus like a motivational inkblot test. By using it, you can begin to learn something about your own motivations. Maybe there is something in your story that reveals your underlying needs?

According to David McClelland (1962), people's needs are learned from the culture or society in which they're raised. Three of them emphasized by McClelland are the need for achievement, the need for affiliation and the need for power. The need for achievement captures the drive everyone has to excel, to rise above, to succeed or to achieve in view of some preselected standards of accomplishment or perfection. The need for affiliation is all about the desire to create and maintain interpersonal relationships that are friendly, caring and close. Finally, the need for power encompasses any individual's desire to make others behave in ways they would not have behaved without personal influence or control.

If you have high achievement motivation, your story may sound something like this one produced by a business executive.

> *The woman is an engineer at a computer. The picture is of her family. She has a problem and is concentrating on it. It is merely an everyday occurrence—a problem which requires thought. How can she get that bridge to take the stress of possible high winds? She wants to arrive at a good solution of the problem by herself. She will discuss the problem with a few other engineers and make a decision which will be a correct one—she has the earmarks of competence.*

If you have a high need for affiliation, your story may run along the lines of the one below.

> *The engineer is at work on Saturday when it is quiet and she has taken time to do a little daydreaming. She is the mother of the child in the picture— the wife of the man shown. She has a happy home life and is dreaming about some pleasant outing they have had. She is also looking forward to a repeat of the incident which is now giving her pleasure to think about. She plans on the following day, Sunday, to use the afternoon to take her family for a short trip.*

Finally, if you're highly motivated by power, your projected interpretation may read something like this scenario.

> *We have an engineer or architect here. She is trying to establish the best way to present her plan at the design committee meeting coming up soon. She has to persuade committee members that her plan is the best. She believes that the force of her ideas will defeat any sceptics. She doesn't anticipate any difficulty putting to rest criticisms that might come up. She thinks that if she wins the day with her plan, then nobody will stand in her way as she moves up the corporate ladder.*

Source: From "Business Drive and National Achievement" by David McClelland, *Harvard Business Review*, July/August 1962, pp. 99112.

cance are a product of learning and experience. We are not born with our attitudes. We are not biologically preprogrammed to speak French or English. How we perceive situations, act towards others, react emotionally or respond to pain will be largely a product of socialization. For example, my wife, who works in a hospital, informs me that some Italian-Canadian women love to scream at the top of their lungs during childbirth. Italian folk wisdom has "taught" them, apparently, that it's good luck. The louder the screaming, the healthier the baby. By contrast, oriental women tend to remain very quiet during labour. Their tradition has taught them to remain stoic while enduring pain. From these illustrations, we could say that behavioural responses to pain are not based on some kind of innate need or unconscious urge buried in the id, but on social conditioning. There are reasons for the screaming and the stoicism, and the reasons point to external cultural factors.

What Is Learning?

In simple terms, learning may be defined as "any relatively permanent change in behaviour that can be attributed to experience but not to fatigue, malnutrition, injury, and so forth" (Coon, 1991: 257). Several theories have been developed to explain this process: classical conditioning, operant conditioning and social learning theory. Let's look at each one briefly.

Classical Conditioning

9.8

Classical conditioning is based on a stimulus-response (S-R) model. It became formalized with the work of Russian physiologist **Ivan Pavlov**. In his studies on digestive processes in laboratory dogs, he noticed that they salivated not only in response to the presentation of food, as is natural, but also to other external stimuli that immediately preceded the food's presentation. He hypothesized that dogs were drawing some connection between preceding external stimuli and the food, and that others could be conditioned to do likewise. To test his hypothesis, he began pairing the sound of a bell with the presentation of meat powder to dogs. Hungry dogs naturally respond to food by salivating. They do not respond in this way to the sound of a bell. To dogs, a bell sound is a **neutral stimulus (NS)**. The meat powder, since it automatically produces an **unconditioned response (UCR)** in dogs, is called the **unconditioned stimulus (UCS)**. After repeatedly pairing the bell sound with the presentation of food, Pavlov went on to simply ring the bell without presenting the food. Interestingly, the experimental dogs began salivating at the sound of the bell. A formerly neutral stimulus (i.e., the bell) elicited a **conditioned response (CR)** (salivation), one which the dogs would never have given prior to the conditioning procedures. The dogs had learned to respond

Ivan Pavlov, a Russian physiologist, explained learning in terms of classical conditioning.

differently to the bell, now a **conditioned stimulus (CS)**. Their behaviour was changed as a product of experience.

Years ago I unintentionally classically conditioned a group of my students without them knowing it. At the beginning of the semester, nobody really cared much when I picked up the overhead projector (usually on the floor) and placed it on the table in front of me for use. The projector was like a neutral stimulus, eliciting no response from the students. Since I frequently made use of overheads and because students were required to take copious notes when I did, they learned to associate the overhead projector with a lot of work. Over time, I observed that notebooks were immediately opened and pens were drawn and placed ready in hand to write whenever I reached for the projector. Although earlier I had to ask the students to take out their notepads, whenever I readied the projector, they now did this automatically like Pavlovian dogs. The classical conditioning process is represented below in Figure 9.3.

Before Conditioning

During Conditioning

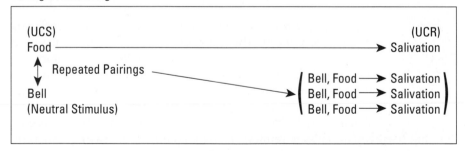

After Conditioning

Figure 9.3

The Process of Classical Conditioning

From Pavlov's research, we should recognize that many of our emotional and behavioural reactions to people, situations and events, though seemingly automatic or spontaneous, are actually learned over time. Just as I was not aware of the fact that I was conditioning my students, I doubt that any of the students thought of themselves as being conditioned. The point is that we are not always aware of our learnings. We don't always know what associations we're making. We're not always self-conscious about our reactions to stimulus events in the world. Just because we're not, however, doesn't mean learning isn't taking place. Learning can occur in uncontrolled life experiences, as well as in formal training situations.

Operant Conditioning

Another behavioural model that has been developed to explain why we do what we do is **operant conditioning**. This model has emerged primarily out of the work of **B.F. Skinner** and **Edward Thorndike**. Operant conditioning, as we know it today, is based on the **law of effect**, a notion originally conceptualized by Thorndike (1898, 1905) and adopted by Skinner. Essentially, the law of effect states that when a response is followed by a more satisfying state of affairs, the probability or likelihood of that behavioural response occurring in the future is increased. Conversely, if a behaviour or response is followed by a worse state or unsatisfactory state of affairs, the probability or likelihood of that behaviour occurring in the future is decreased. The law of effect helps to explain why some behaviours, and not others, begin to develop in our lives as habitual responses in certain kinds of situations (Carver and Scheier, 1988). In more direct language, let's say we are more likely to continue doing things that have a psychological payoff.

B. F. Skinner developed the operant conditioning theory.

Reinforcement and Punishment   The term "reinforcer" can be used to describe anything that creates a pleasant or satisfying state of affairs. Putting a coat on in cold weather is reinforcing. Having people laugh at your jokes is reinforcing. Being listened to and taken seriously is also reinforcing. Many things can be reinforcing, although the same things are not always reinforcing to different people. Time off to do nothing may be reinforcing to you, but boring to me. Where reinforcers are concerned, the saying "different strokes for different folks" really does apply.

Reinforcement can be positive or negative. As you'll see, both types should be distinguished from punishment. With **positive reinforcement**, an action is met with praise, reward or some kind of satisfying state of affairs. For example, if you give a good answer in class, your instructor might reward you by making a favourable comment about your insight and intelligence. If you're pleased with the consequences of answering, you'll be more likely to answer the next time a question is posed. Things are a bit different with **negative reinforcement**, which occurs when unpleasantness or an unsatisfying state of affairs is removed. It's negatively reinforcing to have a headache disappear after taking medication. The next time your head hurts, you're more likely to take the medication that helped you in the past; that's because it was proven to be negatively reinforcing. It is worth noting here that alcoholism and drug addiction likely begin as a function of negative reinforcement. If you're in physical or mental pain, a drink or an injection may turn agony into ecstasy. Obviously, other healthier ways should be found to remove pain.

Punishment can also have an impact on behaviour. Generally speaking, punishment creates unpleasantness or a worse state of affairs than before an action was taken. It can be described as aversive, noxious, painful or undesirable. When punishment follows as a consequence of someone's behaviour, the frequency of that behaviour is typically reduced. Actions followed by painful consequences are less likely to occur. People who favour retribution for wrongdoing usually assume this to be true. They may think that if you spare the rod, you'll spoil the child. In the minds of some people, physical punishment is an appropriate and effective means of controlling behaviour. When I was in grade school, the strap was still administered frequently to alter the behaviour of misbehaving students.

Punishment and reinforcement strategies cannot always guarantee behavioural change. In my grade six class, where it was good to be bad, the strap backfired. The status of getting the strap, and the satisfaction derived from bragging about it later, far outweighed any physical pain. Teachers could never understand why kids continued to endure beating after beating. What they didn't know is that they were unwittingly reinforcing behaviour they were hoping to extinguish. What they considered punishment was actually reinforcing to some "bad students" who were proud of being bad.

If reinforcers follow actions too long after they have been performed, they will be less effective. Reinforcers should closely follow the behaviours that they're designed to promote. As a young child or adolescent at school, for example, your study habits may not have been altered very much by parental promises of distant reward. Being asked to study tonight in order to get a reward six months from now isn't very reinforcing for many students. Getting a reward immediately after studying would work much better, provided the reward was truly satisfying.

Timing is important for punishment as well. For a parent to say to a misbehaving child, "Wait until your father/mother gets home!" may not do much to extinguish undesirable behaviour. Young children, who live in the eternal "now" and whose concentration and memory spans are often very limited, may make no connection between what they did wrong in the morning and the painful consequences that follow many hours later. Drawing no connection, young children can become bewildered if not resentful toward the punishing agent. In their minds, they may be asking, "What did I do wrong?" or "What's this punishment for? That happened a long time ago."

Motivational Implications: So What Should I Do Now?   According to operant conditioning theory, human behaviour is largely under the influence of external conditions. Systematically and often unsystematically, in controlled and in uncontrolled situations, our behaviour has been environmentally shaped by reinforcement factors according to the law of effect. The behaviours we exhibit most frequently are those that have, over time, been rewarded and praised most often. Behavioural habits become what some call our "personalities." Behaviours we don't exhibit may have been repeatedly punished in our earlier conditioning histories and consequently extinguished. Other behaviours we no longer display may seldom, if ever, have been reinforced. For this reason, their frequency is minimal.

By changing reinforcers to ones that are truly satisfying, by altering reinforcement schedules and by careful use of punishment, we can significantly and systematically engineer changes in behaviour, especially our own. If rewards are rarely administered from outside, we can begin to reward our own behaviour. We can decide what behaviour to encourage, what rewards and punishments we will self-administer, and how often they will be forthcoming. In other words, we can now proceed to develop a self-directed personalized behaviour modification plan. For example, if you love to eat, but hate to exercise, reward yourself with a light snack after each heavy workout. The frequency of your exercising may increase. Or, if you dislike work, but like the money it yields to buy things you want, you could reward your hard effort by getting yourself a gift at the end of each week. After all, you deserve it! Work could even become somewhat more satisfying if it allows you to be rewarded and pampered on an ongoing basis. In short, create a formal reward system for yourself, one that is likely to maintain the behavioural patterns you desire.

Albert Bandura's Social Learning Theory

Albert Bandura's **social learning theory** can be generally classified as belonging to the behaviourist school of thought. Having said this, I should immediately point out that it diverges in many important respects from traditional behaviouristic accounts of human functioning provided by classical and operant conditioning. These traditional accounts do, nevertheless, provide an excellent theoretical backdrop against which to view Bandura's work. It is in response to behaviourists such as Skinner and Pavlov that social learning theory has developed.

We saw with Pavlov that once associations are formed between neutral stimuli (e.g., a bell) and unconditioned stimuli (e.g., food), neutral stimuli can then elicit automatically what was once elicited only by unconditioned stimuli. The operative word here is "automatically." For Pavlov, classically conditioned behaviour can be understood in stimulus-response or S-R terms. No internal intervening variables need be discussed to explain behaviour (e.g., salivation, as in the case of the dogs). A given stimulus emits a certain response.

Skinner, too, seems to downplay internal factors in his behavioural explanations. He insists that learning only happens when responses are emitted in reaction to environmental stimuli and their consequences (i.e., punishments and reinforcements) are experienced. Remember the law of effect: positive and negative consequences of action will determine their frequency. For Skinner, learning is a relatively permanent change in behaviour, resulting from experience, and experience means reinforcement for behaviours emitted.

SHOWCASE PROFILE

Presenting Alberta's Native Son — Albert Bandura (1925–   )

Albert Bandura was born on December 4, 1925, in the small Alberta town of Mundare, population 600. The son of Polish-Canadian wheat farmers, he attended a tiny high school where he essentially educated himself. After graduating, he enrolled at the University of British Columbia in Vancouver, B.C. Upon receiving his bachelor's degree in 1949, he went to the University of Iowa where he eventually earned his doctorate in 1952. A clinical internship took him to the Wichita Kansas Guidance Centre in the U.S. Once finished there, he accepted a position in the psychology department of Stanford University where he has worked ever since. Typical of so many great Canadians, Bandura's fame was to be found in the U.S.

Bandura developed a social-learning theory approach to the study of personality and human behaviour. He has written numerous books and articles in the field and has been recognized often for his monumental contribution to the field of psychology. For example, in 1972 he received the Distinguished Scientist Award from the American Psychological Association (APA). The next year he was elected president of that prestigious organization, a position that has been held by such outstanding individuals as B.F. Skinner and Abraham Maslow. In the history of psychology, Albert Bandura has certainly earned a place among the intellectual giants. He ranks as one of the leading figures in the development of social learning theory. He will always be seen as a pioneering visionary of behaviour modification and a premier figure in studies of aggression. Not bad for a small town Alberta boy, eh? (Hjelle and Ziegler, 1981)

Source: From *Personality Theories: Basic Assumptions, Research and Applications* by L. Hjelle and D. Ziegler, 1991, McGraw-Hill, NY.

In contrast to Pavlov and Skinner, Bandura argues that much learning occurs through **observation**. Simply put, observational learning occurs whenever a new behaviour is acquired by means of observing the behaviour of another person. A person doesn't necessarily have to do something and experience the consequences before we can say learning has taken place. People can learn vicariously through others. They can imitate what they see others do. In addition to learning by trial and error, then, one can learn through observation and instruction (Smith and Vetter, 1991). This important fact allows for the notion that **internal variables** are at work in the learning process. If people are going to imitate someone, they must have some kind of mental or cognitive representation in their mind of that person's behaviour. Furthermore, if learning can take place without the necessity of actual trial-and-error practice, followed by external reinforcement, human behaviour is not the sole product of environmental conditioning. More must be happening. According to Bandura, personal, behavioural and situational factors continually interact to determine what people think and do.

Still another difference between the work of Bandura and that of Skinner and Pavlov is that the former has a distinctively social focus. Whereas Pavlov focused on physiological responses and Skinner concentrated on relatively simple behaviours, Bandura chose in his research to look at more complex, socially significant behaviours such as aggression, conformity, sex role differentiation and deviance (Smith and Vetter, 1991).

By pointing out that Bandura has studied aggression and that he takes into account internal variables between stimulus and response, I do not mean to suggest that he accepts Freudian notions such as instinct or the unconscious. According to Bandura, internal motivational drive states cannot properly account for variations in the strength and frequency of particular behaviours across people and across situations. They also lack scientific predictive powers. Now, understanding a little bit better Bandura's point of departure from classical and operant conditioning, as well as from Freudian psychoanalysis, let us look at where his theory takes us.

The Process of Observational Learning   **Observational learning** comprises four subprocesses that deal with attention, retention, motor reproduction and motivation. In order to learn by observation, a person must pay **attention** to certain key features of a model's behaviour. If, for example, you're trying to learn archery by observing expert archers, focusing on their clothing will probably not do you much good. Concentrating on their hands and posture probably will. The observer must select what's important and ignore what's irrelevant to the target behaviour to be learned. Second, for observational learning to take place, long-term memory of it must be produced. If you pay attention to the right things, but can't remember what you paid attention to, learning is not going to occur. You must **retain** what you have attended to. Third, observational learning requires that you translate symbolically coded memories into corresponding action. Knowing in your mind how to do something is different from actually doing it. **Motor reproduction** or rehearsal may be necessary. Finally, motivational processes are at work in observational learning. It doesn't matter how well you've paid attention to modelled behaviour, how much you've remembered or how able you are to behave like the model—if there is insufficient motivation to do so. Without some kind of **motivation** or incentive, you will not perform the modelled behaviour that you're capable of displaying (Hjelle and Ziegler, 1981). You will give no evidence that learning has occurred.

> Monkey see, monkey do.
>
> *Higher primate saying*

People can imitate behaviour in a variety of ways, two of which are direct or indirect imitation. Individuals using **direct imitation** behave in the same ways as people they observe. For example, in unfamiliar circumstances a stranger might choose to behave exactly as those around him who know the ropes, so to speak. If the person being observed responds to a waiter in French by saying "*merci*," so too could an insecure observer. With **indirect imitation**, people copy a class of behaviours, not a single act. They may observe someone being friendly to a coworker and then go on to exhibit friendly behaviour to everyone they meet.

Direct and indirect counter-imitation are also examples of observational learning (Liebert and Spiegler, 1990). Whenever you do exactly the opposite of what the observed person does, you engage in **direct counter-imitation**. I'm sure that to the chagrin of parents, many adolescents swear to themselves never to behave toward their children as their parents behaved towards them. They firmly resolve to do the opposite. Sometimes this resolution is a good thing. For instance, if your father gets abusive when drunk, you might learn never to drink. Even in this case, however, negative observed behaviour contributes to learning. (I guess that even if we seriously dislike what our parents say and do, they still teach us a lot!) With **indirect counter-imitation** an observer is less likely to engage in acts that belong to the same class as those performed by the model observed. For instance, a mother might cry in response to a conflict with her child. The observer child could "learn" never to get emotionally upset in confrontational circumstances, no matter where or with whom.

Whether or not a model will be imitated depends a lot on the consequences of the model's behaviour. These **vicarious consequences** can be positive, negative or neutral. Positive consequences can be called **vicarious rewards**. In this case, the model is reinforced for the behaviour. Witnessing vicarious positive reinforcement leads observers to infer that if they behave the way the model does, they too will be rewarded with something desirable. **Vicarious punishment,** by contrast, is a negative consequence resulting from a model's observed behaviour. Again, the punishment is administered to the model, not the observer. In this case as well, observers infer from what they have witnessed that like behaviour on their part will lead to like consequences. Finally, **neutral vicarious consequences** result when neither positive nor negative consequences follow a model's particular actions. Generally, no response is a neutral response. However, sometimes no response can be interpreted as a positive one, such as when no response means that you have permission to do something—a good thing (Bandura, Ross and Ross, 1963).

In 1963, Bandura and his colleagues tested the hypothesis that learning can take place merely through observation, without any subject response being emitted for reinforcement. The study involved nursery school kids who observed a model enter a room and attack a doll. Later, the children were placed in the room with the doll and other toys. Researchers discovered that the children performed more of the model's specific aggressive responses against the doll as compared with a control group of kids who had witnessed the same model behaving in a nonaggressive fashion toward the doll. The conclusion drawn was that children in the experimental group learned aggressive responses by observing the model. No prior aggressive responses on their part needed to be emitted or reinforced. With respect to (vicarious) reinforcement as well, research findings point to some interesting conclusions. Bandura (1965) has found that children who observe models punished for aggressive behaviour are less likely to exhibit the same aggressive responses themselves. On the other hand, children who saw the model rewarded for aggression exhibited more aggressive behaviour (Bandura, 1965). The research results suggest that consequences to modelled behaviour can effect the likelihood that observers will imitate the model or perform the response observed.

LIFE AFTER TV: *A Natural Experiment*

Canadian kids and adults spend a good part of their leisure time watching TV. What effect does this have on behaviour? A relatively recent study offers a fascinating look at life with the tube. A team of researchers found a town in northwestern Canada that did not receive TV broadcasts. Discovering that the town was about to get TV, a research team seized a rare opportunity. Tannis Williams (1986) and her colleagues carefully tested residents of the town just before TV arrived and again two years later. This natural experiment revealed that after TV came to town, the following changes occurred.

1. There was a significant increase in both verbal and physical aggression. It occurred for both boys and girls and applied equally to children who were high or low in aggression before they began watching TV (Joy et al., 1986).

2. Reading and development among children declined (Corteen and Williams, 1986).

3. Children's scores on creativity dropped (Harrison and Williams, 1986).

4. Children's perceptions of sex roles became more stereotyped (Kimball, 1986).

Concerning aggression, the results come as no surprise. Researchers have consistently found that television has a strong impact on aggression. In view of such findings, it is understandable that Canada, Norway and Switzerland have restricted the amount of permissible violence on television (Levinger, 1986).

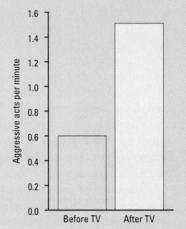

This graph shows the average number of aggressive acts per minute before and after television broadcasts were introduced into a Canadian town. The increase in aggression after television watching began was significant. Two other towns that already had television were used for comparison. Neither showed significant increases in aggression during the same time period. (Data compiled from Joy et al., 1986.)

Figure 9.4

9.9 *Choice Theory of Motivation*

The last model of motivation we'll consider in this chapter is William Glasser's **choice theory**. Glasser is a world famous psychiatrist and founding president of the Institute for Reality Therapy, now known as the William Glasser Institute. His motivational model of human behaviour provides us not only with therapeutic applications, but with educational, correctional and organizational ones. So whether you're training for a career in business, social work, allied health, education, or law and security, for example, you should find this treatment of choice theory helpful. (Note: in 1998, Dr. Glasser renamed his motivational model. It was formerly called control theory.)

William Glasser is the founder of reality therapy and president of the William Glasser Institute.

Our Basic Needs

William Glasser (1984: 5) says, "Built into our genetic instructions, into the very core of our being, is a group of basic needs that we must satisfy continually." This group of **basic needs** includes

1. The need to survive and reproduce.
2. The need to belong, love, share and cooperate.
3. The need for power.
4. The need for freedom.
5. The need for fun.

The Need to Survive and Reproduce

The **need to survive and reproduce** finds its biological roots in the most ancient part of our brain, which is located at the top of the spinal cord. Brain structures there keep our bodily machinery functioning and healthy. Vital operations such as breathing, digesting, perspiring and regulating blood pressure are controlled by this "old brain." Much of its activity occurs automatically, without us being aware of it. For instance, our immune systems go to work whenever foreign bacteria invade our bodies, and our heart rate goes up when we exercise to supply our greater requirements for oxygen.

In terms of human biological evolution, a cerebral cortex or "new brain" has developed to help out the old one to get needs met. Suppose, for instance, that you haven't eaten for a long time. Your old brain will detect this lack of nutrient as a threat to your survival. Since the old brain is not the seat of consciousness, nor the initiator of any intentional behaviour, it sends what Glasser calls a "help me" signal to the new brain. In this case, the signal is recognized as hunger. Once recognized, our conscious new brain directs us to search for food. We are motivated to seek out in the environment that which will satisfy our basic survival need of hunger. The process works the same with thirst, air, sex and physical comfort.

The Need to Belong

While it's easily recognized that the need to survive is basic and genetically programmed, Glasser argues that it's not prepotent in Abraham Maslow's sense. Survival needs can be and sometimes are overridden by other social needs, such as the **need to belong**. Glasser points out that most people who attempt suicide describe devastating loneliness as the reason. He concludes that "the need for friends, family, and love—best described as the need to belong—occupies as large a place in [your] my mind as the need to survive" (1984: 9). Just as people are motivated or "genetically instructed" to eat and drink, so too are they directed to belong, love, share and cooperate.

The Need for Power

For Glasser, everyday experience demonstrates clearly that people have a **need for power**. Wealthy individuals can sometimes spend a lot of money trying to get into positions of political influence. Managers and leaders may try to exert their power by getting subordinates and followers to do what they otherwise wouldn't do. We constantly compare ourselves with others to see who's stronger, better, more attractive, richer or who lives in the more exclusive neighbourhood. As Glasser points out, while nonhuman animals struggle for power in terms of territorial behaviour, it is only humans who compete for power simply for the sake of power itself. History is a testimony to this; so too are contemporary "empire builders," whether they're found in government, business, politics, the battlefield or on the street.

The Need for Freedom

As with power, the **need for freedom** is apparent in everyday life. People will often say that they don't want to be tied down and don't want to be told what to do. Wars and revolutions are sometimes fought in the name of freedom and political liberty. People from ethnic and racial minorities frequently talk about the struggle that is really a name for their quest for freedom from oppressors. No matter where you go, it seems, somebody is searching for freedom. Life is virtually an endless struggle of removing obstacles, taking detours or coping with adversity so that we can eventually do what we want to do, when we want to do it.

The Need for Fun

By including the **need for fun** under the heading of basic needs, Glasser seems to take us away from some of the more traditional motivational theories. (Do you think the death instinct was fun for Freud?) Glasser notes that most of us do not feel as driven by this need as by the need for power, freedom or belonging, but he nonetheless believes that it is as much a basic need as any other (Glasser, 1984). He states, "I believe that fun is a basic genetic instruction for all higher animals because it is the way they learn" (14). If you

Satisfying the need for fun can keep you feeling young.

doubt this statement's truth, talk to any primary school teacher. I'll bet you that person often uses games and fun as a way of promoting learning. To support his claims, Glasser points to research done with female apes and monkeys. If they are isolated and deprived of normal social play in early development, they fail to learn even the simplest of social interactions, such as mothering their offspring. Since humans are primates, research with monkeys and apes is highly suggestive. Glasser claims that forgetting how to play and have fun in life is a sign of mental deterioration, especially in older people (14).

Pictures in Our Minds

As mentioned by Glasser, all of our basic needs are produced by genetics and biology. They are universal throughout the human species. What is not universal is how people *satisfy* their basic needs. At birth, infants do not know how to meet their needs. They feel uncomfortable, and instinctively cry and show other symptoms of distress. In time a

> ... life without a picture to satisfy the need to belong is really life without hope.
>
> William Glasser

child may begin to associate a particular face with food, physical comfort or security. A **picture** may be taken of the caretaker as an agent of need satisfaction. Once the child is mobile, he may seek out the caretaker whenever physical security or physical nourishment needs must be satisfied. If this occurs, we have evidence that a need-satisfying picture of the caretaker has been stored in what Glasser metaphorically refers to as the "picture album" in the child's head.

Everyone has a picture album in her head. In that album we store images of what we want and things that have satisfied one or more basic needs in the past. These pictures are not exclusively visual. Our sensory apparatus makes for quite an extraordinary device that can record not only visual pictures, but also auditory, gustatory, olfactory and tactile pictures. Pictures are important for Glasser because they serve as the specific motivations for all we attempt to do with our lives (Glasser, 1984). Throughout our lifetime, we probably develop hundreds, if not thousands, of pictures that satisfy an individual need. The picture album of wants we put together begins to make up a selective part of our memories—the **ideal world** or **quality world** that we want right now. Glasser says that the power of pictures as a motivator for action is complete. Every day we make endless efforts to satisfy our wants. We may sometimes do what, in the estimation of others, are crazy and wild things in order to get what we want. We may even behave in ways that endanger our lives. The point is that pictures in our heads don't necessarily have to be rational or sane. They don't have to make sense. Someone may satisfy his need for power by trying to become recognized as the greatest mass murderer of this century; another may seek power by winning a college basketball championship. Different pictures and different wants take us in different directions to our commonly sought, ultimate destination of basic need satisfaction.

The pictures in our minds do not necessarily remain there forever. As we live our lives, we continually add and occasionally subtract pictures that are no longer need satisfying. Sometimes this removal is necessary, especially in therapeutic situations. People sometimes develop unrealistic pictures of what they want and what would be need satisfying. Getting what's currently wanted may be very difficult, if not impossible. If a spouse has died, for example, relying on that person to continue satisfying one's needs would make little sense. Memories are satisfying, but you can't build a satisfying life on memories. Another picture of a loving, caring person may have to be found and placed in the internal world if future belonging needs are going to be met. As people commonly say after a period of bereavement, "It's time to get on with my life." To live in the past (preoccupied with the picture of how life was) is counterproductive to living in the present.

Humans as Behavioural Control Systems: Taking Action

If what we're getting from life is roughly equivalent to what we want, we experience relatively little frustration, limited displeasure and we are more or less in effective control of our lives. However, to the extent that our inner perceptions of reality are radically different from what we want, as defined by pictures in our internal quality world, we experience pain and frustration. The greater the frustration, the greater the impetus or motivation to act. Our **behavioural system** is activated so that we can get what we want.

According to Glasser, when people are understood as behavioural control systems, we can better appreciate why they do the things they do. He imagines the human structure as very similar to a thermostat. When a thermostat is set at 22 degrees and the air temperature is the same, the furnace sits idle. However, once the thermostat senses that the air temperature has dropped, instructions are sent to the furnace to turn on. Likewise, when people aren't getting what they want, they fly into action. Furthermore, just as thermostats turn off once the proper temperature is reached, so too do people stop behaving once they get what they want. For example, if you like sweet lemonade but the glass you just bought tastes sour, you can add a teaspoon of sugar. You taste the lemonade again. If it is sweeter but still too sour for your taste, you can add another teaspoon. You keep doing this until the lemonade is just the way you want it. At this point, you stop adding sugar. The behavioural system shuts down when your wants are satisfied.

As adults, we have during our lifetime placed many actions into our behavioural systems. Think of your behavioural system as the repertoire of actions you've accumulated over the years, actions that have proven to be need satisfying. We can call upon any action in our behavioural system at any time to satisfy our wants. Adding sugar is but one example of an action to rely on whenever you want to decrease sourness. (Someone else could add an artificial sweetener.) Unfortunately, we don't always have actions ready in our behavioural systems to deal with all our frustrated wants and emotional pains. If you're just breaking up with your first boyfriend or girlfriend, you've never encountered this situation before. You may not know how to behave. You need to care and be cared for, so what do you do? When previous behaviours don't work to satisfy our wants (e.g., calling to apologize, but having the apology rejected), newly organized behaviours have to be created to deal with the frustration and pain. The reorganized behaviours can seem silly or stupid to others; however, for the person engaged in them, they represent a best attempt at the time to get basic needs met.

Behaviour Is Total

When it comes to behaviour, people often make what Glasser would consider illegitimate distinctions. For instance, people often separate how they think from how they feel, or how they feel from how they act, or how they act from how they function physically. For Glasser, thinking, feeling, doing and functioning physiologically are all interdependent parts of what he calls **total behaviour**. In any given situation, a particular aspect of behaviour (e.g., feelings) is dominant, but it's not divorced from all other components of total behaviour. For instance, if you are sad, what is the reason for your sadness? What are you thinking that is making you sad? Even if you are unable to articulate in precise terms the thinking behind the sadness, it doesn't mean that there's no thinking at all. Be sure, too, that the body is responding physiologically to sadness. It's a fact that sad and depressed people tend to get sick more often than happy people because their immune systems are affected by emotional states. Are you tired right now as you read? What if I informed you that you had just won $3.7 million? Chances are pretty good, I'll bet, that you'd suddenly wake up and feel energized. Thinking about your winnings would brighten you up fairly quickly. We see then how thinking and feeling can affect the body. Conversely, body functioning can affect your thinking. How? Bodily fatigue and hunger affect your thinking and emotions. If you're like many, you probably get irritable, impatient or pessimistic when tired or hungry. Doesn't the world look a lot better after a nutritious meal and a good night's sleep?

To put total behaviour in choice theory context, Glasser points out that our internal pictures of our wants steer our behaviour in a certain direction. He uses the metaphor of a car to explain this idea. He says that basic needs are like the engine of an automobile because they provide the energy or motivational force for the vehicle. The wants act as the steering wheel that determines the direction the automobile will take. Thinking, feeling, acting and physiological responses serve as the wheels of transportation to get us to our destination and get us what we want. See Figure 9.5 for an illustration of the choice-theory auto.

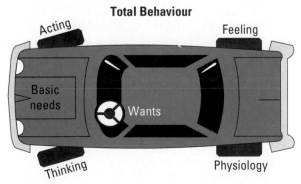

Total Behaviour

Acting
Feeling
Basic needs
Wants
Thinking
Physiology

Source: Choice theory material reprinted by permission of William Glasser.

Figure 9.5
Choice-Theory Auto

Behaviour as a Feedback Loop

Once we behave in some fashion to get what we want, we then examine, either consciously or unconsciously, the consequences of our actions. We perceive the effects of our actions and then evaluate them. Some of our perceptions will turn out to be positive, some will be negative, while others will be neutral. How perceptions are evaluated depends on what's in our quality world. If we're getting what we want, the evaluation is positive. If our actions do not get us what we want, the evaluation is negative. If our actions have little or no impact on our wants, the evaluation is neutral. The point to underscore here is that internal values and wants determine whether our perceptions are appraised as good or bad. We keep behaving until we get what we want.

Glasser believes that human motivation has an internal locus of control. Pictures represent wants and wants are what propel us into action. Nothing in the real world makes us sad, glad or happy or forces us to do certain things. We are not like Pavlovian dogs automatically responding to stimuli. An insult (stimulus) may or may not affect us; it all depends on the value we place on it. If we value the opinion of the one who insulted us, we may be hurt (response). If we don't, the insult leaves us unaffected (another possible response). Similarly, a red light is not a stimulus event that automatically causes us to stop in response. In any emergency, we may choose to ignore the light to get to our destination more quickly, if this is what we want. People respond to wants, not to external stimuli.

In this context, it's worth recalling our earlier discussion of reinforcement under behaviourism. According to Glasser's choice theory, punishment can't make school children stop misbehaving. If they want to be bad, punishment will actually give them exactly what they desire (status and confirmation of their badness). Even bandits can't force you to do anything. Glasser tells the story of someone who refused to surrender a wallet when held up at gunpoint. Defiantly, the victim said, "No, you can't have my wallet; you'll have to shoot me first." The bandit fled. Don't think, from this example, that all actions are easy or without risk. But just because someone is trying to coerce us doesn't mean we don't have choices. Our choices may be limited and difficult. The consequences of these choices may be mixed or unpleasant. In any event, we are ultimately in control. We choose what we want and we value what we choose. Our values filter our perceptions, and our internal pictures impel us into action. While what happens to us is sometimes beyond our control, how we choose to respond is our responsibility. Acceptance of this responsibility gives us freedom and power to determine our personal destinies.

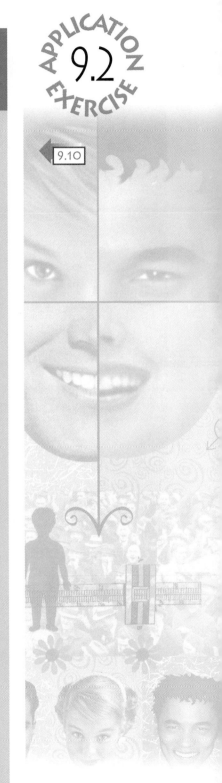

APPLICATION EXERCISE 9.2

9.10

The TBWA—Total Behaviour and Wants Analysis

This tool can be used to promote individual effectiveness through basic need satisfaction. It is a self-exploratory exercise based on William Glasser's choice theory of behaviour and human motivation. The TBWA will help you identify a current want and become aware of the actions you're taking to get what you want. It will also enable you to evaluate the effectiveness of your current actions and plan for future success in terms of getting what you desire. Follow the directions as described.

Step 1: Identify a Want

Consider an important want you currently have. It could be a thing, an ideal or a positive situation. If this step is difficult, think of what you dislike or don't want. If you got rid of what you don't want, what would you have? What you would have is in fact what you want. Once you've clearly established a want in your mind, write it below.

I want _____.

Step 2: Describe Your (Total) Behaviour in Relation to Your Stated Want

In relation to my stated want above, what am I likely to be

Thinking:_____

_____

Feeling:_____

_____

Doing:_____

_____

Experiencing Physically:_____

_____

Step 3: Evaluate Your Total Behaviour

Given what I'm thinking, am I more or less likely to get what I want? Explain.

_____

_____

Given what I'm feeling, am I more or less likely to get what I want? Explain.

_____

_____

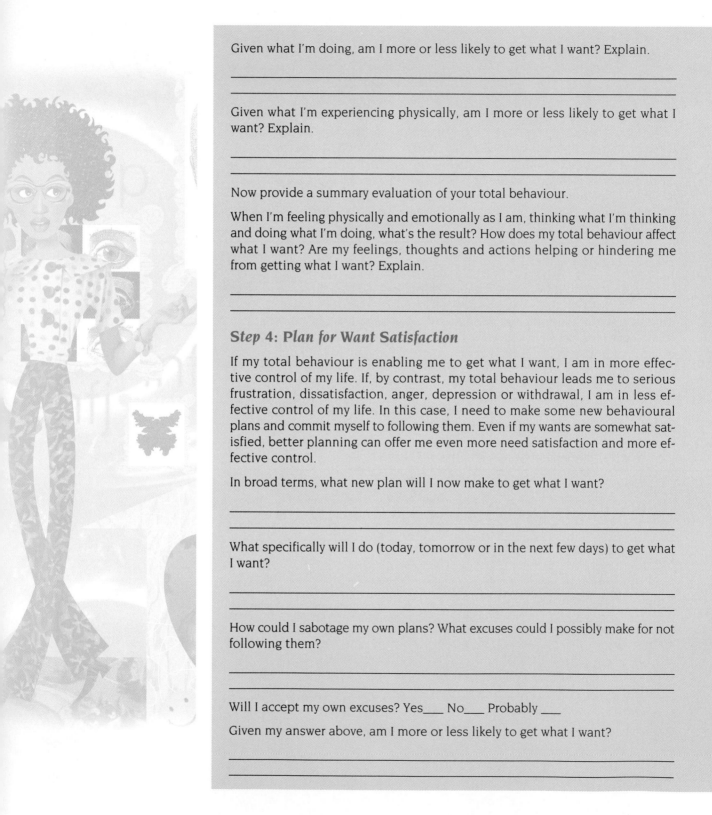

Given what I'm doing, am I more or less likely to get what I want? Explain.

_____

_____

Given what I'm experiencing physically, am I more or less likely to get what I want? Explain.

_____

_____

Now provide a summary evaluation of your total behaviour.

When I'm feeling physically and emotionally as I am, thinking what I'm thinking and doing what I'm doing, what's the result? How does my total behaviour affect what I want? Are my feelings, thoughts and actions helping or hindering me from getting what I want? Explain.

_____

_____

Step 4: Plan for Want Satisfaction

If my total behaviour is enabling me to get what I want, I am in more effective control of my life. If, by contrast, my total behaviour leads me to serious frustration, dissatisfaction, anger, depression or withdrawal, I am in less effective control of my life. In this case, I need to make some new behavioural plans and commit myself to following them. Even if my wants are somewhat satisfied, better planning can offer me even more need satisfaction and more effective control.

In broad terms, what new plan will I now make to get what I want?

_____

_____

What specifically will I do (today, tomorrow or in the next few days) to get what I want?

_____

_____

How could I sabotage my own plans? What excuses could I possibly make for not following them?

_____

_____

Will I accept my own excuses? Yes___ No___ Probably ___

Given my answer above, am I more or less likely to get what I want?

_____

_____

Am I fully committed, then, to getting what I want?

_____

_____

If I accept my excuses, if I am not fully committed to getting my wants satisfied, or if my total behaviour hinders me from meeting my basic needs, who is truly responsible for the resulting frustration? Who must change? Who must take alternative courses of action?

_____

_____

Debriefing: The TBWA process can be simplified using the acronym WDEP, which stands for

W — Wants: What do I want?

D — Doing: What am I doing?

E — Evaluation: Is what I'm doing helping or hindering me?

P — Planning: How must I plan for success?

The TBWA assumes that

- All human behaviours are internally motivated. We are not victims of the environment, socioeconomic circumstances or early childhood histories.

- A human is designed as a control system that operates in the world to satisfy wants or pictures of what is wanted at a given time.

- Human beings are responsible for their thoughts, feelings and actions. Behaviour is holistic and can be self-controlled. Actions, thoughts, feelings and physiological reactions are all part of the same total behaviour.

- At any given time, we are either in more or in less effective control of our lives.

- While wants vary from person to person and from time to time, basic needs remain the same.

- Personal and professional success in life requires that we gain more effective control.

STUDY GUIDE

Key Terms

motivation (321)
conscious and unconscious motivations (322)
external locus of control (323)
internal locus of control (323)
psychoanalytic theory (326)
energy model (326)
homeostasis (327)
nirvana principle (327)
pleasure principle (327)
eros (327)
libido (327)
thanatos (327)
aggression (327)
catharsis (328)
Abraham Maslow (329)
hierarchy of human needs (330)
actualize (330)
prepotency (331)
physiological needs (331)
safety and security needs (331)
social needs for belonging and love (332)
esteem needs (332)
cognitive needs (333)
aesthetic needs (333)
self-actualization needs (334)
metamotivation (335)

being motivation (335)
deficiency motivation (335)
existential frustration (335)
metapathology (335)
behavioural theory (337)
classical conditioning (340)
Ivan Pavlov (340)
neutral stimulus (NS) (340)
unconditioned response (UCR) (340)
unconditioned stimulus (UCS) (340)
conditioned response (CR) (340)
conditioned stimulus (CS) (341)
operant conditioning (342)
B.F. Skinner (342)
Edward Thorndike (342)
law of effect (342)
reinforcement (342)
positive reinforcement (342)
negative reinforcement (342)
punishment (343)
social learning theory (344)
observation (345)

internal variables (345)
observational learning (346)
attention (346)
retain (346)
motor reproduction (346)
motivation (346)
direct imitation (346)
indirect imitation (346)
direct counter-imitation (347)
indirect counter-imitation (347)
vicarious consequences (347)
vicarious rewards (347)
vicarious punishment (347)
neutral vicarious consequences (347)
choice theory (348)
basic needs (349)
need to survive and reproduce (349)
need to belong (349)
need for power (349)
need for freedom (350)
need for fun (350)
picture (351)
ideal world (351)
quality world (351)
behavioural system (352)
total behaviour (353)

Fill-in-the-Blank Questions

Instructions: Fill in each blank with the appropriate response from the list below.

motivations	nirvana principle
healthy	prepotency
hierarchy of human needs	vicarious consequences
learning	basic needs
punishment	thermostat
thematic apperception test	law of effect
total behaviour	metamotivations
classical conditioning	locus of control
aesthetic needs	desirous
instinct	*thanatos*
social learning theory	negative reinforcement
pictures	

1. Human behaviour can have conscious and unconscious _____.

2. Debate as to whether behaviour is motivated internally or externally centres on the notion of _____.

3. The _____ is a Freudian concept used to explain how people are motivated to reduce disturbing tensions and excess stimulations in their lives.

4. A(n) _____ has its source in some bodily need or deficit.

5. _____ is another name for the death instinct.

6. Abraham Maslow's humanistic account of motivation is based on the study of _____ individuals.

7. To be human is to be continually _____ of something.

8. According to Maslow, human behaviour is motivated by a(n) _____.

9. In Maslow's scheme, needs possess a _____. Lower ones must be satisfied before higher ones.

10. The requirement people have for such things as beauty, symmetry and elegance points to our _____.

11. Self-actualized persons are not without needs. They are driven by _____ or B-values.

12. When we witness a relatively permanent change of behaviour as a product of experience, we can say that _____ has occurred.

13. Dogs can be taught to salivate in response to neutral stimuli such as bells or tones by processes of _____.

14. The _____ states that if an action is followed by pleasurable consequences or by a more satisfying state of affairs, the likelihood of that action occurring in the future is increased.

15. _____ involves administering unpleasant consequences after a particular behaviour has occurred.

16. _____ involves the removal of unpleasant, painful or noxious stimuli.

17. Albert Bandura is most noted for developing _____ as an explanation of human behaviour.

18. According to Bandura, people can learn by observing _____. Observers can infer that if they behave just like the model they're considering imitating, then they too will be subjected to similar rewards or punishments.

19. The _____ can be used to determine people's needs for achievement, power and affiliation.

20. According to William Glasser, all human behaviour is internally motivated by _____.

21. In choice-theory terms, people develop motivating _____ of what they want, which in turn satisfy what they basically need.

22. Glasser is opposed to stimulus-response accounts of behaviour. His choice theory holds that human behaviour is regulated more like a _____.

23. A choice-theory account of motivation does not completely separate thinking and feeling or doing and physiological reactions. They are all seen as related parts of _____.

True/False Questions

Instructions: Circle the appropriate letter next to each statement.

T F 1. There are two kinds of people, motivated and unmotivated.

T F 2. When it comes to motivation, we always know why we do the things we do.

T F 3. People with a high internal locus of control see themselves as self-governed.

T F 4. The Freudian nirvana principle states that the human organism functions to reduce tension and excitations.

T F 5. Aggressive acts can serve as a catharsis.

T F 6. Abraham Maslow is a behaviourist.

T F 7. According to Maslow, lower level needs are prepotent with respect to self-actualization needs.

T F 8. Maslow's theory explains why it is wrong never to be satisfied with what one has.

T F 9. B-values act in the same way as needs, only on a lower plane.

T F 10. Learning can be defined as any relatively permanent change in behaviour that results from experience.

T F 11. Classical conditioning techniques were developed by Albert Bandura.

T F 12. According to operant conditioning, if an action is followed by positive consequences, the likelihood of that action occurring in the future is increased.

T F 13. Negative reinforcement is a type of punishment.

T F 14. Bandura agrees with Skinner that people must experience things directly and with reinforcement if they are to learn them.

T F 15. For William Glasser, the need to survive is prepotent as compared with the need to belong.

T F 16. Choice theory was developed to help people take control over others.

T F 17. The instinct of *eros* deals exclusively with sexuality.

T F 18. Like Freud, Abraham Maslow based his studies on neurotic patients.

T F 19. Self-actualized people tend to have deep relationships with lots of people.

T F 20. In classical conditioning, a neutral stimulus cannot ever cause a response.

Focus Questions

1. Do unmotivated people exist? Explain.

2. Is it true that people always know what motivates them? Why?

3. Is all behaviour caused? Can people make you glad, mad or sad? Are you forced by determining factors to do what you do? Discuss.

4. Is biology relevant or irrelevant to human motivation? Explain.

5. What explanation could be given for why people are seemingly always dissatisfied?

6. What does it mean to be self-actualized? Do you know any self-actualized individuals? What are they like?

7. How does the behaviourist account of motivation differ fundamentally from psychoanalysis and humanism?

8. Do rewards and punishments always motivate others as intended? Why?

9. What is a thematic apperception test? What does it reveal about human motivation?

10. How can human behaviour be governed like a thermostat?

11. Does it make any sense to suggest that we're responsible for our feelings? How so?

Summary

1. What can be said generally about the nature of motivation?
   - everybody is motivated
   - it can be conscious or unconscious
   - the locus of motivational control may be internal or external

2. What does Sigmund Freud say about human motivation?
   - personality is driven by instinctual energy
   - instincts belong either to *eros* (life) or *thanatos* (death)
   - behaviour is based on nirvana and pleasure principles
   - instincts must be sublimated for acceptable social expression
   - aggression and sexuality are two powerful motivations in everyone's life

3. How does Abraham Maslow conceptualize motivation?
   - people are driven by needs
   - needs are found on a hierarchy
   - lower level needs must be satisfied before higher level needs become potent motivating forces
   - humans can be classified as "wanting animals"
   - once lower level D-needs are satisfied (e.g., survival and esteem), higher level B-motivations kick into operation (e.g., the need for truth, beauty and goodness)
   - failure to live by B-motivations can lead to metapathologies

4. What does behaviourism tell us about motivation?
   - most behaviour is learned through experience
   - classical conditioning, operant conditioning and observational learning can account for why we do the things we do
   - there is no need to refer to instincts, unconscious factors or higher level goals to explain human behaviour
   - the environment shapes us and our so-called personalities
   - our behaviour is a product of conditioning

5. How does William Glasser conceptualize motivation?
   - everyone is motivated
   - motivation ultimately stems from basic need satisfaction
   - needs give rise to wants represented by motivating mental pictures
   - when wants are frustrated, people are motivated to act
   - behaviour is not a mechanical response to stimuli; it works in the same way as a control system or thermostat
   - behaviour is energized when wants go unsatisfied
   - we are ultimately in control of our behaviour, the motivating pictures we place in our mental picture albums, and we are responsible for how we choose to respond to people, situations and events in our lives
   - people are either in more or in less effective control of their lives

Related Readings

Freud, S. (1973). New Introductory Lectures on Psychoanalysis. London: Penguin Books.

Glasser, William (1981). *Stations of the Mind: New Directions for Reality Therapy*. New York: Harper & Row.

Maslow, Abraham (1968). *Toward a Psychology of Being*. Location: Van Nostrand Reinhold Co.

Rathus, Spencer and Jeffrey Nevid (1992). *Adjustment and Growth: The Challenge of Life*, 5th edition. Fort Worth, TX: Holt, Rinehart and Winston.

Skinner, B.F. (1979). *Beyond Freedom and Dignity*. Toronto: Bantam Books.

——— (1953). *Science and Human Behaviour*. New York: MacMillan.

Weblinks

1. New developments in William Glasser's work
   www.indigo.ie/~irti/newideas.htm

   Keep on top of recent developments in William Glasser's choice theory model of human motivation.

2. Gender differences and self-actualization
   www.mwsc.edu/~psych/research/psy302/spring96/melissavelasquez.html

   You can find research here on the relationship between gender needs and self-actualization.

3. Youth Motivation Institute
   www.a-motive.com/

   The corporate education and family resource for motivational programs and materials offers a Champions for Life Success System for Youth.

4. Motivational tapes and videos
   www.achievement.com/motivati.htm

   See this site for a list of audio and video tapes produced by well-known authors and speakers on the subject of motivation, achievement and success.

CHAPTER 10

Are you...
Stressed out and sleepless in Saskatchewan?
Nervous in Nova Scotia, New Brunswick or Newfoundland?
Terrified in the Territories?
Quivering in Quebec?
Yowling in the Yukon?
Anxious in Alberta?
Burned out in British Columbia?
Manic in Manitoba?
Peeved in Prince Edward Island?
Or, obsessed in Ontario?
Don't worry, be happy!...Stress is in the mind of the beholder.

–I.M. Nervus

STRESS AND LIFESTYLE MANAGEMENT: GOOD NEWS FOR JITTERBUGS AND ADRENALIN JUNKIES

CHAPTER OVERVIEW

LEARNING OUTCOMES

After successfully completing this chapter, you will be able to

10.1 Explain the nature of stress from three theoretical perspectives

10.2 Gauge your stress level using Holmes and Rahe's Social Readjustment Rating Scale

10.3 Determine if, and to what extent, stress is affecting your academic performance

10.4 Distinguish between stress and eustress

10.5 List and describe effective and ineffective strategies to cope with stress

10.6 See to what extent your thinking style is contributing to your personal stress levels

10.7 Practise cognitive strategies for coping with stress

10.8 Use meditation for purposes of stress reduction

> As long as man is capable of anxiety,
> he is capable of passing through it to
> a genuine human destiny.
>
> Northrop Frye

Imagine this scenario. You just woke up in response to your neighbour's barking dog. Looking at your clock, you realize your alarm did not go off. As you leap out of bed, you remember that you have a test to write in precisely one hour. College is a 65-minute drive away. Skipping breakfast and your daily shower, you feverishly start to dress, only to discover stains on both sleeves of your sweater. Hurrying to gather your books together, you jump into your car. In disbelief, you discover the battery is dead. You ask your mom if you can use her car. She says OK, but then you find that you're riding on empty. You stop at a service station and use your last two loonies to buy gas—so much for lunch! Once you get back on the road, you see that cars are lined up bumper to bumper and you learn that all possible detours are under construction. Eventually, you make it to class only to get blown away by your instructor, who lectures you on the virtues of punctuality. As you continue to get blasted, you notice that you are now left with 15 minutes to complete a 50-minute test. So, in view of all this, may I ask how you are feeling today?

Contrary to what some people may think, student life is not always simple and easy; the example above is a good illustration. Students really don't have it easy. Like everyone else, they experience stress stemming from the demands of everyday life. In what follows, we'll look at the nature of stress, its contributing factors, its consequences, and what you can do to handle it. Being able to deal with stress in constructive ways will help you to live a more productive and satisfying life.

THE NATURE OF STRESS

> To be totally without stress is to be
> dead.
>
> Hans Selye

Stress is an experience that many of us know intimately, yet it is difficult to explain. A review of the literature on stress indicates that definitions of it tend to come from three different perspectives. Some researchers explain stress from the viewpoint of the stressor itself. This viewpoint operates on the assumption that there are stimulus events in the world that cause stressful responses in people. By contrast, a second perspective focuses on stress in terms of responses. From this perspective, the stress is not in the stressor, but in the reactions of the individual experiencing it, whether they be emotional, psychological or behavioural. Finally, a third perspective conceptualizes stress in terms of an interaction between the stimulus event and the individual experiencing it. Between the stressor and the stressful reaction comes the perception and cognitive appraisal of the person. Whether or not a stressor is perceived and experienced as stressful depends on what the person thinks about it. Later we'll look at the importance of cognitive appraisals as we learn how thinking styles can affect how well we cope with stress. Until then, let's get back to the business of defining stress itself.

UNDERSTANDING STRESS IN TERMS OF STRESSORS

As mentioned, one perspective on stress research emphasizes the role of stressors. **Stressors** can be classified in different ways. For our purposes here, let's categorize them under four headings: life-event stressors, occupational stressors, psychological stressors and daily hassles.

Life-Event Stressors

10.2

Holmes and Rahe's research (1967) suggests that **life-event stressors**, or various life changes and events, can create stress within individuals. Their findings indicate that as the number of significant life changes increases (what they call LCUs or *life change units*), the risk of illness grows. They have found that people can suffer ill effects from stressors for as long as one year afterwards. To help us assess the stress potential of various events in our lives, Holmes and Rahe (1967) have constructed what they call the social readjustment rating scale (see Table 10.1 on p. 368).

You might wish to check off those items that pertain to you and add up your score using the values attached to each. If your score is somewhere between 150 to 199, you are probably experiencing a mild life crisis. A score between 200 and 299 reflects the likelihood of a moderate crisis, and any score over 300 points, a major crisis. (These norms take into account differences in age, sex and race.)

Occupational Stressors

If you're a typical college or university student, chances are pretty good that you have a part-time job. If you do, there's probably no great need to point out that work can be stressful and that you face **occupational stressors**. Consider the physical environment in which you work. Fluorescent lighting, excessive noise, uncomfortable temperatures and stale air are all factors that can act as stressors. Perhaps your boss is unreasonable. Maybe he overworks you, issues conflicting demands, doesn't specify clearly what should be done or somehow places you in a compromising position of role conflict. At work you might also experience difficulties with your fellow employees, or with those working under your authority. Bad interpersonal relations can be stressors indeed. Finally, as we enter the 21st century, rapid technological advances have also become stressors. We may be given little opportunity to do things for any period of time in any kind of stable, established ways. New developments and new technologies may almost always keep us vigilant and on our toes, ready for the next required adjustment. In this kind of environment people fear "falling behind" or getting out of date.

> God grant me the serenity to accept the things I cannot change, courage to change the things I can, and the wisdom to know the difference.
>
> Reinhold Niebuhr

Table 10.1 Social Readjustment Rating Scale

Rank	Life Event	Mean Value
1	Death of spouse	100
2	Divorce	73
3	Marital separation	65
4	Jail term	63
5	Death of close family member	63
6	Personal injury or illness	53
7	Marriage	50
8	Fired at work	47
9	Marital reconciliation	45
10	Retirement	45
11	Change in health of family member	44
12	Pregnancy	40
13	Sex difficulties	39
14	Gain of new family member	39
15	Business readjustment	39
16	Change in financial state	38
17	Death of close friend	37
18	Change to different line of work	36
19	Change in number of arguments with spouse	35
20	Mortgage over $10,000	31
21	Foreclosure of mortgage or loan	30
22	Change in responsibilities at work	29
23	Son or daughter leaving home	29
24	Trouble with in-laws	29
25	Outstanding personal achievement	28
26	Wife begins or stops work	26
27	Begin or end school	26
28	Change in living conditions	25
29	Revision of personal habits	24
30	Trouble with boss	23
31	Change in work hours or conditions	20
32	Change in residence	20
33	Change in schools	20
34	Change in recreation	19
35	Change in church activities	19
36	Change in social activities	18
37	Mortgage or loan less than $10,000	17
38	Change in sleeping habits	16
39	Change in number of family get-togethers	15
40	Change in eating habits	15
41	Vacation	13
42	Christmas	12
43	Minor violations of the law	11

Source: Reprinted with permission from *Journal of Psychosomatic Research*, Vol. 11, pp. 213-218, Holmes and Rahe, "The Social Readjustment Scale," 1967, Elsevier Science Ltd., Pergamon Imprint, Oxford, England.

Psychological Stressors

Type A and Type B Personalities

A number of years ago cardiologists Meyer Friedman and Ray Rosenman (1974) suggested that people who display certain behavioural patterns and who suffer from certain **psychological stressors** are more likely to suffer (stress-induced) heart attacks. They distinguished between **Type A personalities** and **Type B personalities**, claiming that those people with the former type were more likely than the latter to suffer from heart disease. To whatever extent you display tendencies to behave in ways listed below, to that same extent you are a Type A personality (see Friedman and Rosenman, 1974: 100–102).

You are a Type A personality if you

1. Explosively accentuate key words in ordinary speech.

2. Always walk, talk and eat rapidly.

3. Are impatient about the rate at which most things get done.

4. Frequently try to do two or more things at once.

5. Are preoccupied with your own thoughts and often try to swing conversations to topics that interest you.

6. Feel guilty when relaxing.

7. Fail to notice interesting and beautiful objects in your surroundings.

8. Are constantly seeking to get things, rather than to enjoy them as they are.

9. Try to do more and more in less and less time.

10. Feel challenged by other Type A personalities.

11. Exhibit characteristic gestures or nervous tics such as clenching your fists or banging your hand on a table.

12. Take pride in being able to do things better because you are faster.

13. Translate everything everyone does in terms of "numbers" (e.g., time, amount, distance).

Source: Reprinted by permission of Alfred A. Knopf.

Friedman and Rosenman (1974: 14) say that a Type A personality exhibits

> *a particular complex of personality traits, including excessive competitive drive, aggressiveness, impatience, and a harrying sense of time urgency. Individuals displaying this pattern seem to be engaged in a chronic, ceaseless, and often fruitless struggle with themselves, with others, with circumstances, with time, and sometimes with life itself. They also frequently exhibit a free-floating but well-rationalized form of hostility, and almost always a deep-seated insecurity.*

Source: Reprinted by permission of Alfred A. Knopf.

> *The harder you push yourself, the harder your self pushes back.*
>
> Anonymous

By contrast to the Type A personality, the Type B personality rarely suffers from a sense of time urgency with the impatience that accompanies it. Type B individuals carry with them no free-floating hostility. They have no need to display themselves or to discuss their achievements publicly. At playtime, Type B people actually play for fun, not necessarily to win and exhibit superiority at any cost. They are also able to relax without feeling guilty. In short, we see in the Type B personality a mirror opposite of the Type A. Type Bs are free of the habits and traits that harass the severely stressed Type A person (Friedman and Rosenman, 1974).

Some relatively recent studies have failed to show a link between Type A behaviour and heart disease. Critics of these studies claim that people involved in them were not accurately classified as Type A or Type B in the beginning, therefore negating any conclusions (Coon, 1991). Some evidence suggests that it's the anger and hostility components of Type As that correlate with heart attacks, not the other aspects of this personality profile (see Chesney and Rosenman, 1985; Friedman and Booth-Kewley, 1987; and Wright, 1988). In view of the fact that hundreds of other studies have supported the hypothesis about Type A being linked to heart disease, let's say that the jury is still out on this one. Nonetheless, if you are a Type A personality, you may wish to consider changing some of your behavioural patterns. As Dennis Coon (1991) points out, one large-scale study of heart attack victims found that the rate of repeat heart attacks could be significantly reduced by modifying Type A behaviours. Perhaps by changing Type A behaviours at the outset, the first "big one" could be avoided as well.

Pressure

Whether you exhibit a Type A or a Type B personality, you've probably felt **pressure** at some point in your life. Maybe your parents have pressured you to do well at school or to make concrete plans for your future. Perhaps you've been under pressure to juggle many different responsibilities at the same time. People may think of you as "superman" or "superwoman" as they form great expectations and heap loads of them upon you. It could be that you are "supposed to" produce, regardless of the difficulties and competing demands. In short, pressure is all about expectations and demands and how they make us behave in certain ways.

There are two subtypes of pressure (Weiten and Lloyd, 1994): the pressure to perform and the pressure to conform. In the first instance you may be expected to successfully complete tasks and execute responsibilities in a quick and efficient manner. For instance, you may have to meet quotas, deadlines and minimal standards of quality. As a student, you may be under pressure to earn at least a B average in your studies to be considered as a candidate for a post-graduate program. Police officers are sometimes pressured to meet their quotas of traffic tickets. Academics can be pressured to submit grant applications before specified deadlines.

Pressure can also relate to conformity. People are often pressured to conform to others' expectations. Fears, anxieties and insecurities about how we should dress, act, speak or think often arise when we are unclear about what others expect of us. We may wish to please, obey, or fit in, but remain uncertain as how to do so exactly. If we are clear about others' expectations, we may still have fears about not being able to live up to them. If the expectation for a male executive is to wear a jacket and tie to work, he may still worry about whether or not they coordinate properly, or whether they fit the corporate image required.

Regardless of whether people are under pressure to perform or conform, preliminary research suggests a strong relationship between pressure and psychological symptomatology (Weiten, 1988; Weiten and Dixon, 1984). In fact, pressure may be more strongly tied to stress-related disturbances than change as measured by Holmes and Rahe's social readjustment rating scale.

Frustration

Frustration can often be a stimulus event that leads to stress. Generally speaking, "frustration occurs in any situation in which the pursuit of some goal is thwarted" (Weiten and Lloyd, 1994). Whenever you are denied what you want, your goal is not attained and you become frustrated. If you can get what you want, but must wait longer than you would like before getting it, frustration results again.

Two common kinds of frustration involve failure and loss (Weiten and Lloyd, 1994). If you want to pass a test, but fail, you can experience stress over the failure and over the fact that your chances of graduating may be jeopardized. On the other hand, your girlfriend or boyfriend may break up with you and leave you at a loss, stressed out about what to do next.

Conflict

In Chapter 6, we looked at the nature of **conflict**. We learned that it can result when we must choose between two positives, the lesser of two evils, or when we must make any other choice that has both positive and negative elements attached. Conflicts can be internal or interpersonal. I may want something but my moral conscience may condemn my desire. The guilt or self-blame I lay on myself could be a source of stress. By contrast, the conflict I experience may not be within my psyche, but between us. You and I may want the same thing at the same time (e.g., a job) when only one of us can have it. Whenever we experience "me against you" or "us against them" situations, stress is likely to result. We may fear that we may not get our share of scarce resources, and that others will overpower us. Anxious about the eventual outcomes, we experience stress.

Daily Hassles

Studies in stress research seem to indicate that **daily hassles** and frustrations in life can be collectively as upsetting as major life traumas (Delongis et al., 1982; Lazarus, 1981). From an objective point of view, having to wait in bumper to bumper traffic is really a rather trivial inconvenience. However, don't tell that to angry daily commuters when someone cuts into traffic in front of them. Especially for impatient (Type A) people, having to wait is stressful. The wait could be in traffic, in the line at the grocery store or over the phone. When communicating with a Type A person over the phone, put that individual "on hold" at your own risk. Being forced to wait is one of life's daily hassles that drives some people crazy.

STRESS AS A RESPONSE: GENERAL ADAPTATION SYNDROME (GAS)

> It's all right to have butterflies in your stomach. Just get them to fly in formation.
>
> Dr. Rob Gilbert

Of all the definitions of stress, the one provided by Canadian stress researcher Hans Selye (1974, 1976) has been one of the most influential. A professor at McGill University and director of the Institute of Experimental Medicine and Surgery at the University of Montreal, he developed his theory of the **general adaptation syndrome (GAS)** as a way of explaining the body's reaction to stress. According to Selye (1974: 27), "Stress is the nonspecific response of the body to any demand made upon it." To say that stress involves a nonspecific response means that regardless of the stressor, the bodily reaction remains the same. Bodily responses to earthquakes, firings, poisonous snakes, bungee-jumping and term tests are all physiologically identical. Stress induced by fear or apprehension, regardless of its source, produces the same effects.

SHOWCASE PROFILE

Hans Selye

Dr. Hans Selye (1907–1982) was a pioneering visionary in the field of medicine and stress research. His work has helped us to understand how the body reacts negatively to stress. His research has also opened up the way for many new types of treatment programs for stress-related diseases. During his lifetime, Selye was a professor at McGill University and director of the Institute of Experimental Medicine and Surgery at the University of Montreal. He held doctoral degrees in philosophy and science, as well as in medicine. Selye received 16 honourary degrees in addition to many awards, medals and honourary citizenships. He was also made a Companion of the Order of Canada, this country's highest honour.

You can't look at a stress-induced bodily reaction and say, "Oh, this one comes from an earthquake" or "That one results from test anxiety." The body's response to stress is stereotypically the same. The general adaptation syndrome has three basic stages: the alarm reaction, the resistance phase and the exhaustion stage.

The Alarm Reaction

You will understand the stage of **alarm reaction** better (and the GAS more broadly) if you place it in a biological, evolutionary context. To begin with, the body is genetically programmed to maintain a homeostatic balance. We all carry within ourselves something like a "biological thermometer" that regulates such things as our body temperature, heart rate and respiration. When all is well, things operate more or less smoothly. However, when a stressor (e.g., a frightening stimulus) is presented, the homeostatic balance of the body is upset as it prepares to deal with the presented threat.

To understand how, let's go back to prehistoric times to meet Conan the cave-dweller. Let's suppose that our friend Conan was suddenly confronted by a sabre-toothed tiger. Faced with this predicament, Conan could choose to stay and fight the predator or take flight to save himself. To help him meet the demands presented by this frightening stressor, Conan's autonomic nervous system would kick in and prepare him for a "fight-or-flight" response. Conan's digestion would slow so that more blood could be directed to his muscles and brain. His respiration rate would increase to supply increased oxygen to the muscles. His heartbeat would accelerate and his blood pressure would soar, forcing blood to the parts of the body that needed it. Perspiration would increase to cool the body; muscles would tense in preparation for action; chemicals would be released into the blood to make it clot more rapidly in case of injury, while sugars and fats would be poured into the bloodstream to provide fuel for quick energy needs. In short, Conan's body would prepare to meet the demands of the life-threatening situation. Such bodily preparations would serve to enhance the chances of Conan's continued survival. If Conan stayed and slayed the beast, the threat would be over and his body would return to its normal homeostatic balance. If Conan chose to flee the situation, the same thing would happen. (See Table 10.1 for a list of physiological reactions that follow a stressor.)

Table 10.1   The Physiology of the Alarm Reaction

blood pressure increases	respiration rate increases
muscles tense	digestion is inhibited
heart rate increases	corticosteroids are secreted
blood coagulability increases	blood flow increases to skeletal musculature
adrenalin is secreted	perspiration increases

In contrast to our friend Conan, however, we in the latter part of the 20th century are not likely to be confronted by prehistoric predators, but rather by personal ghosts, environmental demons and organizational bogeymen (metaphorically speaking, of course). There may be some kind of beast (e.g., an imposing uncle) or dragon (a pushy aunt) that we have to contend with. Maybe we are afraid of some personal ghosts in our psychological closets, or we feel unsure about ourselves, afraid to take risks where others are involved. It could be that our boss at work is an ogre who is constantly on our case, so much so that we're worried that we might get fired. We could also be anxious about the state of the economy. With all the recent downsizing and restructuring, we may feel trapped and victimized about our future prospects. Add to this our apprehension about falling behind at school, keeping up with technological advances and getting our finances in order, and Conan's tiger begins to look a bit like a pussy cat, don't you think?

I don't wish to suggest that our early ancestors lived an easy life compared to us, but at least Conan's fears were temporary and short-lived. Once the tiger was killed or an escape was accomplished, life returned to normal. For us, some stressful situations (e.g., traffic jams) do come and go relatively quickly; others, though, can last for days, weeks, months or even years. We may find ourselves in stressful and threatening situations (e.g., a bad economy) from which we cannot easily escape or which we cannot do much about. The result is that our bodies, like Conan's, make ready for a "fight-or-flight" response—but for a very long time. What should normally be a brief, temporary state of physiological arousal to deal with an external threat becomes for us a longer-term scenario. Our bodies are often constantly on red alert to attack the threat or flee from it if necessary.

Threats to Conan were tangible and real, because when the tiger disappeared, so did the threats. This means that Conan's body was given the chance to rest and return to normal. For us, as highly evolved relatives of Conan, things become somewhat more complicated. The evolution of our cerebral cortex allows us to anticipate and predict dangers and threats, which certainly has biological advantages. It allows us to prepare for dangers before they present themselves. We can plan our escapes and ready ourselves for challenges and confrontations. On the downside, however, the evolved human brain also leads us to perceive threats and dangers that are nonexistent in reality, but present in our minds. In other words, it's possible to be afraid of nothing except what we imagine to be true or think likely to occur. The saying, "You have nothing to fear but fear itself" seems especially relevant here. At this juncture, you might wish to ask yourself how much time you have wasted thus far in your life worrying about things that have never happened. I trust you get my point! We can literally worry ourselves sick over nothing. The ultimate source of our stress may sometimes not be out there, but in our minds.

If the alarm reaction continues for any significant length of time, physical symptoms may result. For example, people could develop sleep disorders, hypertension, headaches, low-grade fevers, aching joints or loss of appetite. (More will be said about symptoms shortly.)

The Resistance Phase

When a stressor persists, the body adapts by moving into the **resistance phase** of the GAS. In this phase, the bodily signs characteristic of the alarm reaction virtually disappear (Selye, 1974). Resistance actually rises to above normal. Neural and glandular systems become hyperactive. We remain in a constant state of overstimulation and are continually mobilized for defence. Thus, in the resistance phase we have learned to cope with the stressors in our lives, and do so by functioning at higher than normal levels of physiological arousal.

The Exhaustion Stage

While it's a nice thought, human beings do not possess unlimited energy. Following long-term exposure to stressors to which the body has adjusted, the body eventually exhausts its energy supply. This happens because the glands of the body are not given an opportunity to rest and restore their normal levels of activity. The result is that they become overtaxed and no longer function well. In the **exhaustion stage**, physical signs and symptoms of stress originally evident in the alarm reaction reappear (Selye, 1974). The difference is that many of these symptoms are now irreversible. Damage to the body can be permanent. The ultimate consequence is death. If high blood pressure—one symptom of prolonged stress—is called the "silent killer" by doctors, perhaps stress—as one factor that gives rise to it (no pun intended)—should be named the "deadly coconspirator." Stress and high blood pressure are partners in crime and all of us are potential victims. (See Figure 10.1 for an illustration of the GAS.)

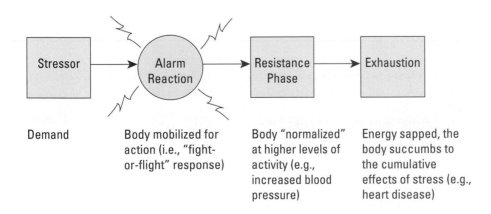

Demand — Body mobilized for action (i.e., "fight-or-flight" response) — Body "normalized" at higher levels of activity (e.g., increased blood pressure) — Energy sapped, the body succumbs to the cumulative effects of stress (e.g., heart disease)

Figure 10.1

Hans Selye's Model of the General Adaptation Syndrome

SELF-DIAGNOSTIC 10.1

10.3

Stress...Let Me Sum It Up!

Aim: This self-diagnostic will help you reflect on the amount of stress you have experienced recently in your personal life and as a college student. Findings suggest that the amount of stress reported by college students is directly related to their general health. Furthermore, stress seems to be related to academic performance (see Napoli, Kilbride and Tebbs, 1992). Students who experience many life changes and stressful events tend to get lower grades than do those who experience fewer changes and fewer stressors. This self-diagnostic will help you to compare your stress level with that of other students.

Instructions: Below are 47 events that can affect your stress level. Check those that apply to you. For each event that is checked, multiply its numerical value by the number of times it occurred to you within the last year. If, for example, you changed your living conditions (number 21) twice, then multiply 42×2 to get 84. After making your selections and doing the multiplication, add all your subtotals together to get a grand total. Scores below 347 place you in the low stress category. Scores above 1435 put you in the high stress category as compared with other college students. If you have been ill lately or if your grades have fallen, perhaps stress has something to do with it.

	Event	Numerical Value
1	Entered college	50
2	Married	77
3	Trouble with your boss	38
4	Held a job while attending school	43
5	Experienced the death of a spouse	87
6	Major change in sleeping habits	34
7	Experienced the death of a close family member	77
8	Major change in eating habits	30
9	Change in or choice of major field of study	41
10	Revision of personal habits	45
11	Experienced the death of a close friend	68
12	Found guilty of minor violations of the law	22
13	Had an outstanding personal achievement	40
14	Experienced pregnancy or fathered a pregnancy	68
15	Major change in health or behaviour of a family member	56
16	Had sexual difficulties	58
17	Had trouble with in-laws	42
18	Major change in number of family get-togethers	26
19	Major change in financial state	53
20	Gained a new family member	50
21	Change in residence or living conditions	42
22	Major conflict or change in values	50
23	Major change in church activities	36
24	Marital reconciliation with your mate	58

25	Fired from work	62
26	Were divorced	76
27	Changed to a different line of work	50
28	Major change in number of arguments with spouse	50
29	Major change in responsibilities at work	47
30	Had your spouse begin or cease work outside the home	41
31	Major change in working hours or conditions	42
32	Marital separation from mate	74
33	Major change in type and/or amount of recreation	37
34	Major change in use of drugs	52
35	Took on mortgage or loan of less than $10,000	52
36	Major personal injury or illness	65
37	Major change in use of alcohol	46
38	Major change in social activities	43
39	Major change in amount of participation in school activities	38
40	Major change in amount of independence and responsibility	49
41	Took a trip or a vacation	33
42	Were engaged to be married	54
43	Changed to a new school	50
44	Changed dating habits	41
45	Trouble with school administration	44
46	Broke or had broken a marital engagement or a steady relationship	60
47	Major change in self-concept or self-awareness	5

Source: Reprinted with permission from "*Journal of Psychosomatic Research*, Vol. 19, p. 97, Vince Napoli, James Kilbridie and Donald Tebbs, The Influence of Recent...," 1975, Elsevier Science Ltd. Pergamon Imprint, Oxford, England.

DISTRESS VERSUS EUSTRESS

The fact that Selye (1976) defines stress as a "nonspecific response of the body to any demand" means that stress is something that cannot be avoided. Life constantly makes demands on us. As a result, our biological homeostasis is continually being upset whether we are aware of it or not. As Selye said, to be totally without stress is to be dead. You shouldn't stress yourself, therefore, trying to lead an entirely stress-free life. To want to do this is to dream the impossible dream.

If stress is unavoidable, you may be inclined to think that we're all headed toward the exhaustion stage of Selye's general adaptation syndrome. This is not necessarily so. To begin with, stress is not all bad, as you might think. There are **high sensation seekers** who actively pursue experiences that many people would find very stressful (Weiten, Lloyd and Lashley, 1991). These "adrenalin junkies" prefer, and may even need, higher levels of stimulation

> Stress is like the tension on a violin string. You need enough tension so that you can make music, but not so much that it snaps.
>
> Anonymous

Adrenalin junkies find excitement relaxing.

to maintain their well-being. They may skydive, bungee-jump or drive race cars in order to relax. If they experience too little stimulation, they may fall prey to **hypostress**, a stress brought on by boredom (Lafferty, 1984). Of course, **low sensation seekers** prefer a peaceful, slower-paced life. Selye labels what I call adrenalin junkies as "race horses." The second group he calls "turtles." In short, a lifestyle that would be exhausting to one person may be healthy to another. This difference raises the next point.

Stress may in fact play a role in healthy human functioning. Let's use the analogy of a muscle. If you don't use it, the muscle will atrophy and lose its strength. Likewise, an unused mind will not fully develop. As for stress, some tension or resistance is necessary for healthy functioning. A certain amount of stress keeps us operating at peak performance levels (Lafferty, 1984). Being pushed or challenged can help us to "get up" for the game or to get "pumped up" for the presentation. Of course, how much stress any one person requires to do her personal best is an individual matter.

Recognizing that the same stressor (e.g., skydiving) may have different effects on individuals, Selye (1976) distinguishes between distress and eustress. Stressors that lead to **distress** elicit uncomfortable feelings and harmful physical consequences. Distress is bad. It is something that we dislike and seek to avoid. By contrast, stressors that lead to **eustress** produce positive feelings and no apparent ill-effects (the prefix "eu" means good in Greek). When we're experiencing eustress, we typically develop a motivating surge of energy that can improve the efficiency and quality of whatever we're doing (Lafferty, 1984). Important to note again is that one person's distress can be another's eustress. This brings us to the third perspective on stress, one which locates it not exclusively in the stressor, nor entirely in the bodily reactions of the stressed individual, but in the interaction between the stressor and the person involved.

STRESS AS AN INTERACTION

According to interactionist accounts of stress, how much stress is experienced and whether a specific stimulus event will give rise to eustress or dis-

> *Understand that you do not respond to anything directly, but to your interpretation of it. Your interpretation thus becomes the justification for the response.*
>
> A Course In Miracles

tress hinges on any particular individual's appraisal of it. In other words, responses to the same potential stressor will vary from person to person depending on how the stressor is interpreted and evaluated. According to Lazarus and Folkman (1984), upon initial exposure to a potential stressor or stimulus event, we first appraise it by determining its relevance to us. Is the event or stimulus relevant or irrelevant to us given our position and circumstances in life? Second, if the stimulus event is found to be relevant, we must determine whether or not it is threatening. On the basis of this determination, we decide whether or not the event is stressful. After this initial appraisal, we are likely to make a secondary appraisal. We assess our coping resources and options for dealing with the stressor presented. The fewer the resources and the greater the threat, the more intense the stress becomes. You can see here that **cognitive appraisal,** or what you might prefer to call a mental evaluation, plays an important role in an interactionist account of stress. In what follows, we'll examine a number of key variables that affect our cognitive appraisals of potentially stressful stimulus events: interests, values, personal wants, beliefs, familiarity, controllability, predictability and imminence.

Interests

Different **interests** lead people to appraise the same situation in different ways. Let's say, for instance, that you and I hear the same bad news about a fall in stock market prices. I may panic and become distressed about the situation, whereas you might be left essentially unaffected. Since you have no money invested, you have nothing to lose in the price fall. However, as I perceive (appraise) the situation, I stand to lose a lot of money. Consequently, I become worried, angry and upset at my stockbroker for not anticipating the crash. From this illustration, we can clearly see how interests can come between (potential) stressors and (alternative) responses. When I perceive my interests are jeopardized by poor stock market performance, I respond in a way that you probably would not. (I'm assuming of course that you're a poverty-stricken student, even if you do drive a better car than I do!)

Values

Values can also act as intervening variables between stressor and response. If I value your opinion and you say something nice about me, I'm likely to respond favourably to what you say. However, suppose you say something very negative and critical about my teaching performance or the content of this textbook; then, I am quite likely to experience some distress. If I didn't value your opinion, your critical comments would be irrelevant to me. They would leave me unaffected. But since I value your evaluations, negative ones cause me psychological and emotional discomfort. Note that it's not what is said that pains me, but the value placed on what is said. Of course, the value judgment resides in my mind. You might also wish to note that this entire situation could be reversed. What your instructor says about your academic work may or may not stress you, depending in large part on the importance you place on the instructor's evaluations. If you do not value the instructor's opinions or if you do not care about your grades, you will not be distressed by any negative commentary.

Personal Wants

Whether or not a stimulus event contributes to distress, eustress or no stress often depends on our **personal wants**. If you are a friendly but shy person, content with doing routine tasks at work, for example, being required to assume a prominent leadership role with new responsibilities could be quite distressful. By comparison, if you see yourself as an aggressive mover and shaker who desires a high level of material and professional success, being asked to assume the same leadership role would be quite eustressful. You may appraise the new responsibilities not as a threat, but as an opportunity to rise to the occasion, to demonstrate your talents, skills and abilities. When it comes to stress, the equation is this: the same situation plus different wants equals different reactions.

Beliefs

Your **beliefs** can also affect the kind and amount of stress you experience. If you believe in a punishing and vengeful God, for example, you will feel differently about an action that could be considered immoral (e.g., premarital sex) than would an atheist who does not believe that God exists. Whether or not an action, as a stimulus event, eventually results in guilt and fear (emotional symptoms of distress) or joy and elation (eustress) depends again not on the event itself, but on how the belief intervenes between the stimulus and the response. Shortly we'll look a little more closely at a number of irrational beliefs that contribute to people's distress. Getting rid of irrational beliefs is one way to reduce the amount of unwanted stress in our lives.

Familiarity

Research has shown that **familiarity** with potentially stressful events reduces the amount of threat people are likely to feel (Weiten, Lloyd and Lashley, 1991). When we are familiar with challenges and events as they present themselves, we can often make difficult obstacles easier to overcome. If you've been there and done it before, going there and doing it again may not be so threatening. Going to a new college with new people, new expectations and unfamiliar circumstances is probably a lot more stressful for most compared with going back to visit your old high school. Walking down recognizable hallways and experiencing familiar sights and sounds is typically less threatening than going into unknown territory. I remember the first time I travelled to Europe. Being a stranger there was occasionally a bit scary for me. Returning as I did years later for a second visit, the same places were not as intimidating. I felt more relaxed and stress-free.

Controllability

How much control you have over your affairs can also affect the amount and type of stress you experience. Generally speaking, the more **controllability** you have, the less stress you tend to feel. Ask people who say their lives are out of control how stressed they are. Chances are pretty good they'll admit to high levels of stress and anxiety. If you feel that you're in effective control of your life, you are probably experiencing greater levels of happiness and personal well-being. An exception to this statement is found with people who have control (responsibility), but who worry about external evaluations by others. If you know that you are responsible and in control, you cannot blame others for your failures and inadequacies. Having someone else to blame instead of ourselves can be less stressful, even if it is dishonest.

Predictability

Whether or not a potential stressor is experienced as (dis)stressful also can depend on **predictability**. Usually people like to have warning when something unpleasant is going to occur. When a devastating situation can be anticipated, it is generally easier to cope with. If a company is making plans to downsize, and informs employees that many workers will be let go, layoffs are less likely to be taken personally. Laid-off individuals may be spared feelings of inadequacy and poor self-esteem. In fact, positive steps could be taken to prepare for what is likely to come. A job search could begin and prospects could be explored. By the time the layoff actually comes, those who could predict it might be well on their way to establishing new careers and new directions in life. Compare this scenario with individuals who one day are called into the office unexpectedly and fired. Of course, some people would rather not know things in advance. I guess this just serves to support the interactionist thesis. Predictability's role in stress cannot be properly understood apart from the individual's attitude toward it.

Imminence

Imminence is the last key factor we'll discuss here that is important to the interactionist account of stress. Let's say that you do have prior knowledge or advance warning that a threatening event is going to occur. The closer the threat comes, the more stress results. It is a surprise to many when they discover that experiencing a stressful event is in fact far less stressful than anticipating it. Worrying about going to the dentist, for example, may prove to be worse than the actual discomfort involved in replacing a worn filling. We may be pleasantly surprised that the experience wasn't as bad as we anticipated. See Figure 10.2 on depicting stress as an interaction.

Figure 10.2

An Interactionist
Model of Stress

| Stressor | + | Cognitive Appraisal | → | Emotional Response (e.g., anger, excitement, fear) / Physiological Response (e.g., alarm reaction) / Behavioural Response (e.g., fight-or-flight) | → | Distress (damaging to health) / Results (either/or) / (no apparent ill effects) Eustress |

A demand,
potentially
threatening
stimulus or event

Thoughts about
stressor in view of
one's values,
interests and
familiarity, etc.

Responses to
stressor

Consequences of
responses

Source: Calvin and Hobbes by Bill Watterson. Reprinted by permission of Universal Press Syndicate.

 10.5

WAYS TO COPE WITH STRESS: EFFECTIVE AND INEFFECTIVE STRATEGIES

If researchers such as Hans Selye are correct when they say that stress is a necessary and unavoidable part of life, it's well-advised that we begin to develop coping strategies. If we can't live *without* stress, we might as well learn to live *with* it. We certainly don't want to be overwhelmed by distress or to suffer its long-term ill effects. In what follows, we'll look at some effective and ineffective strategies people use to deal with stress. A number of these strategies you may be using already. This section will give you an opportunity to reconsider your coping efforts in order to determine if you ought to be doing something else or something more. Maybe you'll discover that what you're doing is in fact not getting you what you want.

Coping Strategies with Limited Effectiveness

In their desperation to reduce and eliminate stress, people often engage in behaviours that work temporarily but make things worse later on. Temporary relief is no substitute for long-term solutions. What works for the moment can have negative consequences later on. Let's see how.

Withdrawal

Nobody should be a masochist. If a stressor is unnecessarily causing you mental pain or physical illness, it might be wise simply to remove yourself from the stressful situation. Maybe you're involved in a relationship or marriage within which there are irreconcilable differences. If loving feelings are quickly fading, or if they have vanished entirely, it might be wise to get out. To accept unnecessary pain and suffering is to cause yourself avoidable stress. Maybe you're in a job or studying a subject at college or university that doesn't fit your temperament and personality. Leaving may be the best thing for you. To say that quitting, leaving and getting out are occasionally advised is not to suggest that these forms of withdrawal and escape are, generally speaking, the best means of coping with stress. You can't always deal with stressful situations by "checking out." People who do are often described as immature and irresponsible. A mature and responsible approach to life requires that we deal with stress in direct and intelligent ways. The reason some people give up on life is that they believe there is nothing they can do to change the situation causing their stress. Researcher Martin Seligman (1974) calls this response to stress "learned helplessness." As people no longer try to effect positive change in their lives, they are more likely to become anxious and depressed. Extreme withdrawal can lead to psychosis, which is obviously no solution to the problem of stress. In fact, it is far worse than the problem itself. As a general strategy, then, withdrawal is not a good coping strategy.

Aggression

Some people cope with stress by getting mad. They may lash out and attack others, either physically or verbally. They intend to hurt people or inflict pain on innocent targets (e.g., kicking a pet). Social psychological researchers have hypothesized in the past that frustration (in combination with other factors) can often give rise to aggressive behaviours. If you are frustrated by being denied what you want, you may strike out at some innocent or defenceless person to make yourself feel better. Of course, if feeling better requires you to hurt others and aggress toward them, you can easily appreciate how people in your life might begin to disappear. From their vantage point, your stress does not justify your hurting them. Cursing, verbally abusing or physically assaulting someone may help you to feel better momentarily, but you must live with the stress of the subsequent guilt and shame, not to mention the ostracism and possible criminal charges that could ensue. Furthermore, others could choose to strike back at you in response to your aggression. They may no longer wish to play the role of victim in your episodes of stress-induced violence. Being the target of others' attacks can only increase your own stress in the long run. Aggression as a coping strategy is likely to give you only short-term gain for long-term pain.

Self-Deception

A third way to handle stress involves covering up any anxiety through self-deception. We can ignore stress, put it to the side, push it down, and escape from it by being dishonest with ourselves. This fact is most vividly illustrated by examples of Freudian psychological defence mechanisms (see Chapter 3). If our behaviour is perceived by us as somehow deficient or unacceptable, we can rationalize it rather than consciously accept the stress that it produces. If we feel anxious and worried after being chewed out by our instructors at school, we can go home and unload our stress and pent-up hostility on our family (displacement). We can always refuse to accept the feelings associated with stress and behave exactly opposite to the way we feel (reaction formation). We can also choose to escape stressful situations in our imaginations by fantasizing our way out of them. When things get unpleasant for us, we can always intellectualize our predicament and provide logical-sounding explanations instead of coming to terms with the pain or hurt resulting from stress. On top of all this, we may choose to manage our stress by denying that unpleasant emotions exist. By refusing to acknowledge the emotions, at some level we may think that stress and related anxiety will just disappear.

As psychoanalysis has demonstrated, anxiety covered up by psychological self-deception does not just disappear. Defensiveness consumes energy. Over time, our resources dwindle until unpleasant feelings and urges manifest themselves in thoughts, feelings and actions. After years of repression and denial, stressful feelings are not much under the rational control of the ego. Irrational urges may take control of our lives in the form of neurotic obsessions, compulsions and, at worst, in symptoms related to psychosis. To deny, repress, displace and otherwise lie to ourselves about the stressful anxiety in our lives is to set ourselves up for later psychological difficulties. Extensive use of psychological defensiveness is no solution to the stress problem; it's only a cover-up.

Effective Coping Strategies

Cognitive Approaches to Stress Management

Instead of withdrawing from life, aggressing against others or playing a game of self-deception, there are other more constructive ways to cope with the stress in our lives. In view of what interactionists have to say about stress, we'll first take a look at several cognitive approaches to stress management. Our goal will be to learn how to make psychological appraisals of life's potential stressors in more reasonable and productive ways. To the extent that we are able to accomplish this goal, we will be able to promote more rational and responsible living. In addition, we'll also explore how stress can be better handled through behavioural modification strategies and lifestyle management. By altering not only what we think, but also what we do, we can effect positive change with respect to how we deal with the problem of stress. Effective stress management is important, for it can significantly affect the quality of our lives.

Albert Ellis's A-B-C Model of Emotional Response

Albert Ellis is an internationally recognized psychologist and the developer of rational-emotive therapy. According to him, people feel the way they do largely because of how they think. He says that "what we label our emotional reactions are mainly caused by our conscious and unconscious evaluations, interpretations and philosophies" (Ellis, 1973: 56). When we feel anxious, worried or stressed, it is frequently due to the irrational assumptions we make and the foolish beliefs to which we cling. If we could identify our irrational assumptions and beliefs and then abandon them, we would begin to live a more rational lifestyle, one with significantly less stress and less negative emotion. By clinging to irrationality, we become architects of our own stress. We create more stress for ourselves than necessary. To help us understand how this is so, Ellis designed an **A-B-C model of psychological functioning** that he incorporates into his system of rational-emotive therapy. By using this model, Ellis believes, we can positively change our emotional reactions to stress. We do this by altering our appraisals of potentially stressful events.

> *...for there is nothing either good or bad, but thinking makes it so.*
>
> William Shakespeare

The "A" in Ellis's model stands for the activating event. Given what we know already about stress, we might label it the "potential stressor." According to Ellis, an activating event is anything with the capacity to disturb or upset an individual. It could be a failing grade on a test, a missed bus or a confrontation with a gang member. Common sense might seem to dictate that such stressors would automatically cause some sort of stressful response. This would be consistent with an S-R (stimulus-response) understanding of human behaviour. Contrary to this common sense perspective, however, Ellis claims that between the activating event (the stimulus) and the response or emotional consequence (labelled "C") comes a cognitive appraisal. This appraisal is based on a "belief" about the stressor. The belief component of Ellis's model is not surprisingly labelled "B."

Now, depending on what exactly is believed (B) about

Albert Ellis believes that stress and unpleasant emotion result from irrational thinking.

> *If you are pained by any external thing, it is not the thing that disturbs you, but your judgment about it. And, it is in your power to wipe out this judgment now.*
>
> Marcus Aurelius

the activating event (A), the consequences (C) will vary. In other words, the same activating event can lead to different emotional consequences depending on how it is interpreted and appraised. See Figures 10.3 and 10.4 for an illustration of common sense S-R thinking and how it differs from Ellis's A-B-C model.

In Ellis's (1962) book *Reason and Emotion in Psychotherapy*, a number of **irrational beliefs** are listed—these are ones that contribute to unnecessary emotional upset. For each irrational belief, Ellis provides us with a more rational alternative, one that will probably lead to less stress and ill-feeling. For Ellis, the belief that "It's catastrophic when things don't turn out the way

Figure 10.3

Common Sense S-R Thinking About Stress

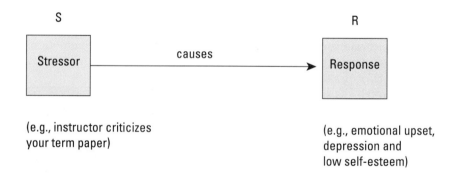

Figure 10.4

A-B-C Model of Emotional Responses to Stress

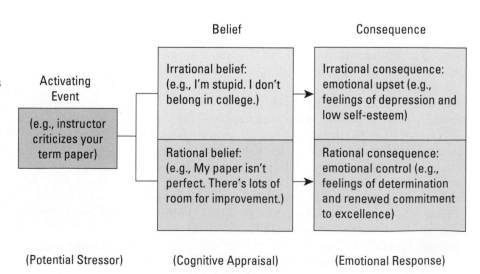

I'd like them to" is irrational and likely to lead to emotional pain and disappointment. The alternative belief: "Frustrating situations are challenges that can be useful for personal change" is more productive. Such a belief is more likely to be emotionally calming and stress reducing. It is also irrational to believe that you must be loved and approved of by everyone. The better alternative is to accept the notion that you can't please all of the people, all of the time. By believing that you should develop self-respect by being good, say, or by doing what should be done, and by accepting the idea that feelings of self-worth should not entirely hinge on the fickle opinions of others, is to liberate yourself from a lot of psychological misery.

Human Synergistics

In the early 1980s, a program of stress management called SCOPE was developed by Lorraine Colletti and Ronald Phillips. SCOPE stands for System for Creating Organizational and Personal Effectiveness. A key component of this stress program is the stress processing report (SPR). In consultation with Hans Selye, J.C. Lafferty and his staff developed the SPR to help people identify their particular **thinking styles** so that they could assess the extent to which their own thinking was contributing to the stress in their lives. Lafferty hypothesized that if a potential stressor could give rise either to distress or eustress, as Selye discovered, a critical factor determining the outcome was "thinking." One's thoughts about any given stressor could cause it to be emotionally energizing or upsetting. This hypothesis was supported by empirical research done with a group of managers and executives (Lafferty, 1984). Apparently, not all such people who experience stress succumb to the physical symptoms usually associated with it. According to Lafferty's findings, there are healthy and unhealthy ways to think about the stressors in anyone's life. Certain thinking patterns are more likely to cause distress than others. By changing your thinking patterns, then, you can more effectively manage the stress in your life.

> Men are disturbed not by things, but by the view which they take of them.
>
> Epictetus, Stoic philosopher

The Role of Thinking in Distress   When an event is perceived, the mind internalizes it and then sends signals to the body. The body, in turn, attempts to interpret the signals. When people think negatively about stimulus events and potential stressors, they often engage in a form of "self-talk," which is self-defeating. They may say things like, "I must be perfect in everything I do," "I must always finish first and beat all the competition," "I'm no good if I can't do that," or "If we break up, there's no reason to keep on living." Such self-talk contains cata-

Dr. Lorraine Colletti-Lafferty and the late Dr. J. Clayton Lafferty are psychological practitioners whose work on stress has been influenced by the insights of Hans Selye.

strophic thinking, unreasonable assumptions and unrealistic conclusions. Regardless of how self-defeating and irrational such self-talk may be, the hypothalamus of the brain nonetheless receives and processes information about stressors as provided by the cerebral cortex. The hypothalamus sends threatening messages to the pituitary and adrenal glands that combine to create the physiological alarm reaction of the body (Selye's idea). Even if the threat is not real, the body responds as if it were. The body responds to "thinking" about the stressor, not to the stressor itself. Optimistically speaking, this means that if we begin to engage in more positive self-talk and if we change our self-defeating thinking patterns, we can reduce our levels of distress, regardless of the stressors in our lives. While we may not be able to change the world, we can always change our thinking about it. Controlling our thoughts can significantly help us to control our stress levels. Researchers at Human Synergistics appear to confirm the insight offered earlier that "stress lies in the mind of the beholder" or, as some would say, "It's all in your head." The notion that stress is an "inside job" can be graphically illustrated. See Figure 10.5.

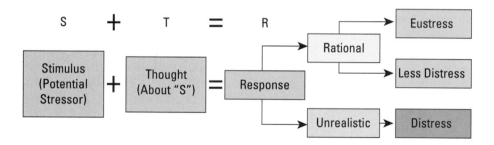

Figure 10.5

Human Synergistics Stress Equation

Think About Thinking: The Purpose of the Stress Processing Report (SPR)
To help us better understand how thinking can affect stress and stress-related symptomatology, Lafferty et al. (1988) developed the SPR. The basic mission of the SPR is to measure, with reliability and validity, the key ingredients in human thought processes. Human Synergistics has aimed this diagnostic instrument and its associated support program (SCOPE) at helping participants to change their thinking and behaviour so that they are less prone to the negative effects of change and stress.

Lafferty et al. (1988) have grouped 19 different thinking patterns into four major clusters: self, others, process and goals. Of major importance to our mental health is how we think about ourselves. Self-perceptions and our personal belief system affect how we deal with the stressors in our lives. In terms of others, our social perceptions can affect our relationships and how we feel about them. The process or way we go about our lives, and how we accomplish what we have chosen to, do all influence our stress levels, as will our goal directedness. If we have goals, know what we want and have a plan to get there, stress levels will lower (Lafferty et al., 1988). Below are the domains of thought that belong to each cluster.

Self Cluster	Others Cluster
self-image	inclusion
past view	interpersonal (thoughts)
control	intimacy
approval	trust
growth	
effectiveness	
Process Cluster	**Goals Cluster**
receptiveness	satisfaction
synergy	directedness
cooperation	expectations
time orientation	future view
time utilization	

How Is My Current Thinking Contributing to My Personal Stress?

SELF-DIAGNOSTIC

10.2

10.6

One way for you to determine whether your current thinking is insulating you from stress or contributing to it would be to complete the entire Stress Processing Report (available from Human Synergistics in Plymouth, MI). While this is not possible given space limitations imposed by the text, Dr. Colletti-Lafferty has extracted from the SPR two domains of thinking and kindly produced, especially for us here, a mini self-diagnostic. It is based on the SPR and can help us to begin assessing the extent to which our thinking in two selected domains contributes to personal stress. The two domains are "directedness" and "expectations" in the goals cluster. Directedness refers to the sense of where we're going and the sense of certainty we have about getting there. Expectations refers to the anticipation and assurance of achieving reasonably challenging objectives. These two domains, like the others, proceed on a continuum from the negative to the positive. Thinking in the negative direction will produce stress, while thinking in the positive will limit, and may even insulate us from stress.

Instructions: Draw a circle around the number that best describes the extent to which you agree with each statement.

0   Don't agree at all
1   Slightly agree
2   Somewhat agree

3   Agree
4   Strongly agree

0	1	2	3	4	I know what I want to do with my life.
0	1	2	3	4	Setting goals is difficult for me because things are always changing.
0	1	2	3	4	I feel little sense of direction or purpose in my life.
0	1	2	3	4	I think about how things could be and work toward that image.
0	1	2	3	4	I take concrete steps to move toward the future I have planned.
0	1	2	3	4	I have few personal goals that are important to me.
0	1	2	3	4	Where I am going with my life seems vague and uncertain.
0	1	2	3	4	I feel I'm not very good at the things I do.
0	1	2	3	4	I worry about failing before I even start.
0	1	2	3	4	At home or at work I'm successful at the tasks I take on.
0	1	2	3	4	I am confident even when I take on difficult tasks.
0	1	2	3	4	The possibility of failing prevents me from trying new things.
0	1	2	3	4	I have trouble doing things as well as I would like.
0	1	2	3	4	I can succeed at almost anything I try.
0	1	2	3	4	When I make an effort to do something, I can perform at the level I expect.

Total Score: _____

A score between 20 and 32 indicates that you have a clear-cut sense of where you are going and a sense of continuity about getting there. In other words, you display goal-directed behaviour. A score of 0 to 20 indicates less direction in life with more vagueness and undetermined goals. The lower the score, the more probable the chance of experiencing greater stress around this issue.

Prescription for Change: To develop a sense of direction, you must first change your self-defeating thought patterns and set some goals for yourself. Begin with a modest personal goal. List the steps necessary to reach it. Visualize the results and take action to achieve them. Enjoy the satisfaction of achievement and you'll be motivated to tackle more goals. If you think about yourself in a more positive fashion and become more self-accepting, you will probably experience less distress and fewer unpleasant emotions compared to people who reject themselves and others. Remember, how you think about life is a choice, and the choice is *yours*.

Source: Reprinted with permission of Human Synergistics.

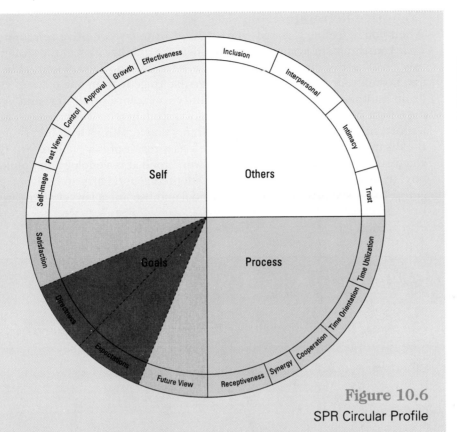

Figure 10.6
SPR Circular Profile

Just in case you're discouraged about your current thinking patterns, here's the story of a man who

> *Failed in business in 1831*
> *Was defeated for the Legislature in 1832*
> *Failed again in business in 1834*
> *Lost his sweetheart in 1835*
> *Had a nervous breakdown in 1836*
> *Was defeated in election in 1838*
> *Was defeated for Congress in 1843*
> *Was defeated again for Congress in 1846*
> *Was defeated a third time for Congress in 1848*
> *Was defeated for the Senate in 1855*
> *Was defeated for vice-president in 1856*
> *Was defeated for the Senate in 1858*
> *Was elected President of the United States in 1860*

That man was Abraham Lincoln. And you think you've got problems! What do you imagine Honest Abe was thinking?

Cognitive Reframing

When you're feeling stressed, you might want to try **cognitive reframing** to view your situation again. In other words, take another look at the situation. Any "bad" set of circumstances can be reframed to reveal potential bene-fits. Losing your job may seem like a terrible tragedy from one point of view. From another, it becomes an opportunity to explore other new and excit-ing career possibilities. Recently, I taught a student who was unsuccessful in a sports injury management program. In my conversations with her, I sensed the disappointment and anxiety she felt as a result of her "failure." In time she discovered, however, that she was very good at psychology and philoso-phy; in fact, she excelled in her newly adopted general arts and science pro-gram. Today she plans to attend law school and become a lawyer after earning

APPLICATION EXERCISE

10.1

10.7

Practice in Cognitive Coping

Part I: Read the brief description of the situation presented below and then an-swer (in private) the questions that follow.

Situation: You walk into an upstairs bedroom at a house party to find your boyfriend or girlfriend hugging someone else.

Questions

1. How will you respond?
2. What will you say?
3. How will you feel?
4. What will your physical state be?
5. What thoughts would or did you have just before responding?
6. What assumptions did you make upon seeing the two of them together?

Part II: Form small groups. Explore and identify the different assumptions peo-ple made about the situation.

Questions

1. What different assumptions could be made about this situation?
2. Are all the possible assumptions about the situation negative? Explain.
3. What other assumptions could one make about the situation that your group has not identified?
4. What new thoughts follow from these assumptions?
5. Would these new and different thoughts give rise to different emotions? If so, how?
6. What thoughts about this situation could reduce stress?
7. Select those thoughts about this situation that would reduce emotional upset. Pick thoughts that are reasonable, mature and responsible.

her degree. Had this student recognized at the time that her failure opened a door to an exciting future, she probably wouldn't have been so anxious and disappointed. Reframing our little setbacks within the general scheme of life or travelling into the future in our minds to look back on the problems we face today can help us to cope. The emotional upset of stress can be reduced by looking at life from a broader perspective or at least from a different one.

Physical and Behavioural Approaches to Stress Management

Practise Meditation

Sometimes it's difficult, if not impossible, to think your way out of stress. In fact, thinking may be part of your problem. Maybe you are obsessive in your thoughts. Perhaps your mind always races and it's difficult for you to relax or fall asleep. Engaging in more thinking will probably not help you very much; it may even make things worse.

> ...to gain insight into the depths of our reality...requires a very calm and quiet mind. It is impossible to see into the depths of a pool of water when it is turbulent.
>
> S.N. Goenka

An entirely different, "nonthinking" approach to stress management is **meditation**. The kind of meditation I'm referring to here does not deal with any kind of intellectual contemplation or rational reflection about the universe. When we meditate to reduce stress, we're not analysing concepts or seeking truth. We're not examining beliefs or studying cognitive thought processes. (I'm getting stressed just thinking about it!) Rather, we practise meditation for stress reduction to gain "mastery over attention" (Pelletier, 1992: 193). Meditation focuses on concentration. People who meditate learn to fix their attention firmly upon a given task for progressively longer and longer periods of time. By concentrating attention, we develop the ability to overcome the mind's usual habit of jumping from one thought to another. When the incessant activity of the mind is stilled, the meditator experiences that aspect of being that is prior to and distinct from her thoughts and from attention itself (Pelletier, 1992: 193). At most profound levels, this state of **deep relaxation** has been described as transcendental awareness, cosmic consciousness or "satori." Some believe that the deep inner peace achieved by meditation can open the doorway to higher levels of self-knowledge not possible through rational thought or cognitive thought processes. Whether you believe this or not is unimportant for our purposes here. The fact is that scientific research supports the notion that meditation can help reduce arousal levels associated with stress. I'll say more about this in a moment; for now, let's look at a couple of ways we can learn to fix our attention for purposes of stress reduction.

Types of Meditation   While meditation is a relatively recent phenomenon in North America and the western world, many eastern religions have practised it for centuries. They have found different ways to focus attention. In one form of Zen meditation, people focus on common external objects such as landscapes, mountain tops or ocean horizons. By contrast, Tibetan Buddhists practise their power of concentration by using a **mandala**, a geometric figure that has spiritual or philosophical importance (see Figure 10.7). Buddhists may

Figure 10.7
A Mandala

also use a **mantra** or a silently repeated sound such as "ohm" (Greenberg, 1990). Adapting this last strategy into secular, nonreligious practice, many North Americans simply close their eyes and silently repeat words such as "in, out" while breathing. The chosen words or sounds are not really important. Their purpose is to focus awareness.

If you choose to focus on a mantra or mandala when meditating, internal and external stimuli may sometimes divert your attention. When this happens, no resistance should be offered. Simply allow distractions to flow through you. Become aware of them and then let them go. In time and with practice, distracting thoughts should become less frequent. Deep concentration will also serve to filter out external noise.

Now that you have some idea of what a meditation is, we will conduct one in Application Exercise 10.2. In this meditation, we'll learn to focus our attention by becoming aware of our breathing and different parts of the body. We won't be using external objects or mantras, but the calming effects should still be the same.

APPLICATION EXERCISE 10.2

10.8

Achieving Calm Through Focused Attention

Aim: This meditation exercise has two purposes. It will help you to practise **focused attention** and it will enable you to experience firsthand the calming effects of meditation.

Instructions: Have the instructor or a student volunteer slowly read the text below. If available, play relaxing background music, such as Pachelbel's "Canon in D" or something from the *Solitudes* series of tapes produced by Canadian Dan Gibson.

Please take a moment to find a comfortable position in your chair...pause...you might like to sit with a straightened back. Unfold your arms and uncross your legs. Now, what I'd like you to do is take a deep breath...hold it...exhale...hold...inhale...hold for a moment...exhale...hold...inhale...hold...exhale. I invite you now to close your eyes. As you take note of the darkness, begin to focus on your breathing...Feel the air as it passes through your nostrils...Is there a difference in temperature between the air inhaled and the air exhaled? Focus on this for a moment...

Now direct your attention to your face and head...Are there any areas that are tense? Are your eyes pulsating? Are your lips twitching? Is there a stiffness at the back of your skull where your head attaches to your neck? Focus on these tension areas...Now, every time you exhale, I want you to imagine you're blowing out those tensions...

Focus now on your neck...How does it feel? Do you need to swallow? Is there a lump in your throat? Imagine any tensions you have draining downward. Feel how heavy your neck is...Let's visualize now how all these squeezed down tensions are moving down your arms and out your fingertips...Feel your arms relax. Now focus on your stomach. Do you hear any noises...feel any sensations? Can you picture your diaphragm moving up and down as you breathe? Concentrate now on your seat. Are your buttocks comfortable? Do you need to move or readjust yourself? Do so, if necessary...How do your legs feel? Is there pressure on your knees?...

How about your calves?...Focus on your toes. See if you can feel each one in isolation from the others...Every time you breath and exhale see the little remaining tension trickle down, out your toes...

Enjoy for a moment the calm that has come through focused concentration...Feel the tranquillity and inner peace...Rest assured that you can achieve this state of calm any time you wish. All you need to do is to sit still and focus...When you are ready, open your eyes refreshed and energized, present to the moment, yourself and others. Notice how things appear different to a calm mind.

Exercise and Physical Activity

You will recall from our discussion of Hans Selye's general adaptation syndrome that when stressful demands are placed upon us, the body responds with the alarm reaction. It prepares for fight or flight. Our levels of physiological arousal increase to adapt to the stressors in our lives. Recall how heart rate and perspiration increase along with blood pressure. A number of physiological changes prepare us to deal with whatever threat is at hand.

In response to threats and related stress, some of us strike out at others. We may attack physically or verbally. As we've learned, aggressing against others is not a very effective physical way of coping. A better alternative for letting off steam before we explode (in anger) is to engage in **physical exercise**. We can use our physiological arousal productively in sports and in other exercise activities. By means of such things we can beneficially use our bodies in some active way without hurting others (Greenberg, 1990).

If you're a serious jogger or know of someone who is, you've probably heard of the "jogger's high." Those who jog often experience a feeling of well-being while exercising. Personally speaking, as a jogger for more than 20 years, I experience the "high" immediately upon starting the cool-down phase of my jog (i.e., when I walk home the last half kilometre or so). I recognize this feeling, I know what it is and I purposely jog to experience it and feel euphoric. To suggest that a feeling of euphoria can accompany strenuous physical exercise is not an exaggeration. While jogging, the brain releases endorphins into the bodily system. Endorphins are a little like morphine. They serve to dull pain and to produce feelings of well-being (Greenberg, 1990). If you wish to get naturally high, then you should exercise. Feeling euphoric is certainly better than feeling stressed and anxious. Of course, due care should be taken as well. Illness or bad health may place restrictions on what types of exercise are best for you. Consult your physician before embarking on any kind of rigorous exercise program.

Clinical Biofeedback Techniques

Another way of reducing physiological levels of arousal associated with stress is through **clinical biofeedback procedures**. Biofeedback is based on the premise that many autonomic or involuntary nervous-system functions can be brought under conscious control. By using mechanical devices to monitor such things as brain wave patterns, heart rate, muscle tension and body temperature, people can learn to make physiological changes in their bodily systems (Pelletier, 1992). In other words, by becoming aware of internal bodily processes that we don't usually notice, we can bring them under voluntary control (Davis, Eschelman and McKay, 1988). Biofeedback helps us discover which parts of our nervous system are more or less relaxed. It can help us to gain awareness of what total relaxation feels like and can assist us in achieving that state. By means of biofeedback procedures, we can learn to lower such things as muscle tension and blood pressure whenever we need to respond to a stressful situation. The assumption is that changes in our physiological state will be accompanied by positive changes in our mental and emotional states, whether conscious or unconscious.

EMG (**electromyogram**) training is one biofeedback technique. The EMG is a machine that monitors skeletal muscle tension. Connected to the EMG are sensors or electrodes that are placed on the forehead, jaw and hunches of the shoulders of the person using the machine. Muscles at these locations typically tighten or become tense when responding to stressful situations. By learning to reduce tension at these sites, greater relaxation can be induced. Another biofeedback technique involves EEG training or using the **electroencephalogram**. The EEG can help you to create brain wave patterns associated with states of calm. It has been used to treat insomnia and epilepsy. A third biofeedback technique makes use of the GSR or **galvanic skin response**. In this case, a skin graph or dermograph monitors minute changes in the concentration of salt and water in the body's sweat gland ducts (Davis et al., 1988). An imperceptible electrical current is passed through the skin. When sweat glands become more active, the GSR machine registers the skin's increased ability to conduct electricity. Remember that according to Selye's notion of the alarm reaction, we perspire more when nervous, in order to cool the body. Increased perspiration will show up in changes to the GSR. The lower the measurable voltage of electrical skin conductibility, the less sweat gland activity. By controlling our GSR, we can thereby control physiological reactions associated with stress. If you are interested in learning more about biofeedback techniques, I suggest you look at *The Relaxation and Stress Reduction Workbook* by Davis et al., *Mind as Healer, Mind as Slayer* by Pelletier, and *Comprehensive Stress Management* by Greenberg.

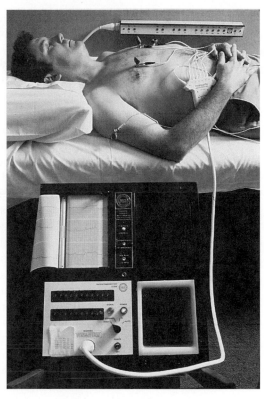

Clinical biofeedback procedures can help people learn to make physiological changes in their bodily systems.

Autogenic Training

Autogenic training (AT) is another effective means for dealing with the problem of stress. It was developed by the German psychiatrist Johannes H. Schultz in 1932 to help people adapt to an overstressed environment (Pelletier, 1992). Through autogenic training, people can learn to regulate their autonomic nervous systems and normalize physical, mental and emotional processes that become imbalanced due to stress (Davis, Eschelman and McKay, 1988). The goal of AT, then, is much like that of meditation. If practised correctly, AT achieves "a state of mind and body which have many of the same characteristics as the low arousal state achieved through meditation" (Pelletier, 1992: 231). Whereas meditation uses the mind to relax the body, AT uses physical sensations to first relax the body before using visual imagery to expand the relaxed state of the mind. In both meditation and AT, the results are similar. They both reduce blood pressure, respiration rates, muscle tension and serum cholesterol levels. Brain wave activity (i.e., alpha waves) associated with states of relaxation increase in both instances as well.

Reality Therapy's WDEP Method of Lifestyle Management and Stress Control

In learning how to handle stress, we've looked at some effective and ineffective coping strategies. Before we conclude this discussion, I would like to suggest that negative emotions related to stress can be reduced by taking greater and more effective control of our lives. People who perceive themselves as powerless or out of control tend to be more stressed than do those who have a self-directed and self-managed lifestyle. In order to take more effective control of your life, I strongly suggest you reflect on the work of William Glasser, as discussed in Chapter 9. Recall that Glasser developed reality therapy. By using a choice-theory systems approach to explaining human behaviour and motivation, he shows us how to get what we want from life in more rational, responsible and effective ways. To manage the stress in our lives better, we could use the **WDEP method** based on reality therapy principles. First, we must identify our *wants*. We must become clear about our goals, desires and aspirations. Second, we must examine our actions or total behaviour, as Glasser would say. What are we *doing* to get what we want from life? Third, we must *evaluate* our actions. Is what we are currently doing helping us or hindering us from getting what we want? Finally, if what we're doing is not working, and thereby creating stress for us, we must *plan* for success. We must come up with alternative courses of action and we must act on the best alternatives. By using reality therapy's WDEP strategy, we can use what is, in effect, a problem-solving strategy to deal with the stress in our lives. Using choice-theory psychology, we can learn to control stress before it controls us!

STUDY GUIDE

Key Terms

stress (366)
stressors (367)
life-event stressors (367)
occupational stressors (367)
psychological stressors (369)
Type A personalities (369)

Type B personalities (369)
pressure (370)
frustration (371)
conflict (371)
daily hassles (371)
General Adaptation Syndrome (GAS) (372)
alarm reaction (373)

resistance phase (375)
exhaustion stage (375)
high sensation seekers (377)
hypo-stress (378)
low sensation seekers (378)
distress (378)

eustress (378)	A-B-C model of psy- chological function- ing (385)	focused attention (395)
cognitive appraisal (379)		physical exercise (396)
interests (379)	irrational beliefs (386)	clinical biofeedback procedures (396)
values (379)	thinking styles (387)	electromyogram (397)
personal wants (380)	cognitive reframing (392)	electroencephalogram (397)
beliefs (380)		
familiarity (380)	meditation (393)	galvanic skin response (397)
controllability (381)	deep relaxation (393)	
predictability (381)	mandala (393)	autogenic training (397)
imminence (381)	mantra (394)	WDEP method (398)

Fill-in-the-Blank Questions

PROGRESS CHECK 10.1 ✓

Instructions: Fill in each blank with the appropriate response from the list below.

Type A personality	interactionist
general adaptation syndrome	defence mechanisms
eustress	mandala
ineffective coping strategies	fight-or-flight
irrational beliefs	stressors
thinking styles	reframe
clinical biofeedback	alarm reaction
endorphin	conform
meditation	cognitive appraisal
occupational stressors	control

1. According to one account, stress is caused by _____.

2. In the context of work, bad lighting, stale air and uncomfortable temperatures are all examples of _____.

3. Stressed individuals who are impatient, competitive and aggressive probably have a _____.

4. Stressed people are sometimes under pressure to perform and _____.

5. Hans Selye has explained the stress response in terms of the _____.

6. In the context of Selye's work, increased blood pressure, increased heart rate and increased adrenalin secretions, when combined, help to create the _____ (or fight-or-flight response).

7. Not all stress is bad. Good stress is called _____.

8. According to the _____ account of stress, values, beliefs, wants and interests all intervene between stressors and reactions to particular stimulus events.

9. Self-deception, withdrawal and aggression are all examples of _____.

10. Self-deception is accomplished by the use of _____.

11. According to Albert Ellis, much of our stress is self-induced because of catastrophic thinking and _____.

12. The "B" element in Ellis's A-B-C model of emotional responses to stress involves a form of _____.

13. According to Clayton Lafferty at Human Synergistics, there are healthy and unhealthy _____ that can either insulate people from stress or contribute to it.

14. When you look at the same stressful situation from a different angle or from a different perspective, you are trying to _____ the situation.

15. One nonthinking approach to stress management is called _____.

16. A _____ is a geometric figure used to induce states of relaxation.

17. Physical exercise can give us a sense of well-being, in part due to the release of _____ into the bodily system.

18. According to advocates of _____, autonomic nervous system functions can be brought under conscious control.

19. Standard exercises of autogenic training can be used to reverse the physiological _____ response.

20. According to William Glasser, people can reduce the stress in their lives by taking more effective _____.

True/False Questions

Instructions: Circle the appropriate letter next to each statement.

T F 1. Student life is stress-free.

T F 2. According to Selye, the human organism needs some stress to remain alive.

T F 3. Marriage, divorce, retirement and change are all examples of life-event stressors.

T F 4. Type B personality types are at a higher risk than Type A personality types of having heart attacks.

T F 5. Daily hassles are a normal part of living. They give rise to no stress.

T F 6. During the resistance phase of the GAS, bodily symptoms present in the alarm reaction disappear.

T F 7. Eustress can be energizing.

T F 8. The same things cause stress for all people.

T F 9. According to the interactionist account of stress, cognitive appraisal comes between potential stressor and emotional response.

T F 10. Usually the more familiar we are with a stressful situation, the less stress we experience.

T F 11. Being able to predict a stressful event always creates greater stress.

T F 12. The closer the threat, the greater the stress.

T F 13. Withdrawing from a stressful situation is usually the best thing to do.

T F 14. In response to stress, some people get mad and aggress toward others.

T F 15. We can discard a lot of stress in our lives by ridding ourselves of irrational beliefs.

T F 16. According to the interactionist account, stress is caused by a single stimulus.

T F 17. There are healthy and unhealthy ways to think about time.

T F 18. Stressful situations can be "cognitively reframed" to create less stress.

T F 19. Meditation works exactly like autogenic training.

T F 20. Stress can be reduced by taking more effective control of our lives.

Focus Questions

1. Do students have a relatively stress-free life compared with other adults? Explain.
2. What is meant by saying that stress is a response?
3. How can stress be understood as an interaction?
4. Is stress simply caused by stressors? Please explain.
5. How is personality related to stress?
6. What is the physiology of stress as described by researchers such as Hans Selye?
7. Is all stress bad? Why or why not?
8. What are some ineffective ways to cope with stress?
9. What are some effective coping strategies?
10. How does Albert Ellis help us to manage stress?
11. How is thinking style related to stress?
12. What is cognitive reframing?
13. How is autogenic training similar to and different from meditation?
14. What can be learned about stress management from William Glasser?

Summary

1. How can stress be defined?
   - as a stressor
   - as a response
   - as an interaction
2. What are the major categories of stressors?
   - life-event stressors
   - occupational stressors
   - psychological stressors
   - daily hassles

3. Which personality type is most likely to suffer from heart disease? What is this personality type like?
   - Type A
   - accentuates key words, talks and walks rapidly, is impatient, preoccupied, hostile, aggressive, has nervous ticks, translates performance into numbers and is competitive

4. Apart from personality type, what are some other psychological factors contributing to stress?
   - pressure
   - frustration
   - conflict

5. What makes up the general adaptation syndrome?
   - alarm reaction (fight-or-flight response)
   - resistance phase
   - exhaustion stage

6. What occurs in the alarm reaction?
   - blood pressure increases
   - muscle tension increases
   - heart rate increases
   - blood coagulability increases
   - adrenalin secretions increase
   - digestion slows
   - corticosteroids are secreted
   - perspiration increases
   - blood flow to skeletal musculature increases

7. How are distress and eustress different?
   - distress is bad and takes a physical toll
   - eustress is good, energizing and doesn't harm the body

8. How does cognitive appraisal affect stress?
   - cognitive variables (e.g., values and beliefs) determine whether a stimulus will be experienced as stressful

9. What are some intervening variables affecting cognitive appraisals?
   - interests
   - familiarity
   - values
   - controllability
   - personal wants
   - predictability
   - beliefs
   - imminence

10. What are some ineffective ways to cope with stress?
   - withdrawal
   - aggression
   - self-deception

11. What are some effective coping strategies?
   - monitor and discard irrational beliefs (Ellis)

- develop a stress-insulating thinking style (Human Synergistics)
- cognitively reframe stress-causing situations
- practise meditation
- engage in exercise and physical activity
- use clinical biofeedback techniques
- use autogenic training
- take control of your life using WDEP strategy

Related Readings

Ader, R. (1993). Conditioned Responses. In B. Moyers (ed.), *Healing and the Mind*. New York: Doubleday.

Berenbaum, H. and Connelly, J. (1993). The Effect of Stress on Hedonic Capacity. *Journal of Abnormal Psychology*: 102, 474–481.

Charlesworth, Edward A. and Ronald G. Nathan (1984). *Stress Management*. New York: Athenaeum.

Culligan, M. and K. Sedlacek (1976). *How to Kill Stress Before It Kills You*. New York: Grosset & Dunlap Publishers.

Weblinks

1. Awareness and relaxation training
   www.healthlocator.com/stress.html

   Mindfulness-Based Stress Reduction is a program of stress reduction developed at The Stress Reduction and Relaxation Clinic, University of Massachusetts Medical Centre. This program can be used in medical settings, schools, corporations and in the public sector.

2. Centre for Anxiety and Stress Treatment
   www.stressrelease.com/

   The centre offers online resources for anxiety and stress reduction, as well as anxiety-management workshops, counselling and consulting services.

3. Institute for Stress Management
   www.hyperstress.com/mainpage.htm

   This institute offers products and services designed to help you gain greater control in your life.

4. The Mindspa Place
   204.131.249.82/mindspa/

   Learn how neurofeedback can be used to deal with pain control, peak performance enhancement, addictions prevention, depression and attention deficit disorder.

CHAPTER 11

Eventually everyone begins to recognize, however dimly, that there must be a better way.

–A Course in Miracles

THE ROAD TO SELF-TRANSCENDENCE

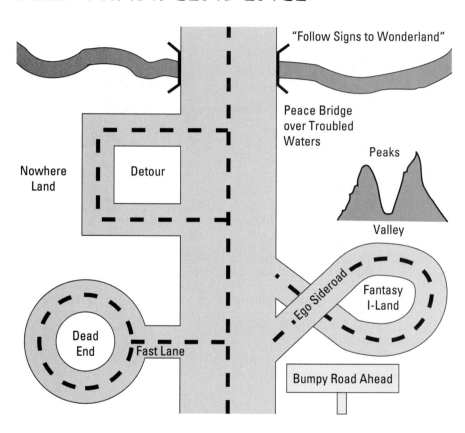

CHAPTER OVERVIEW

LEARNING OUTCOMES

After successfully completing this chapter, you will be able to

11.1 Outline enneagram theory and describe its relationship to traditional and contemporary psychology

11.2 Form an hypothesis of your enneagram personality type

11.3 Find personal direction in view of your enneagram type

11.4 Identify healthy and unhealthy expressions of your enneagram personality type

11.5 Use the insights of Viktor Frankl's logotherapy to deal more effectively with the spiritual concerns of life

11.6 Locate the sources of meaninglessness in contemporary life

11.7 Work toward greater meaning in your life

11.8 Promote self-development using archetypal psychology's concept of "the heroic journey"

11.9 Determine which psychological archetypes are dominant in your life at this time, thereby establishing the stage you are at in life's journey

THE SELF AND SELF-TRANSCENDENCE

The longest journey begins with the first step.

Chinese proverb

In this final chapter, we'll pursue three very lofty goals. The first is **personal liberation**. This liberation has nothing to do with political struggle or socioeconomic injustice. Rather, the liberation we'll be addressing involves freeing ourselves from the limiting aspects of our personalities—what spiritual writers often refer to as the **ego** or **false self**. This self inevitably develops through interactions with our families, friends, cultures and societal institutions. In our efforts to adapt to our social worlds we all move away from our true selves. We learn to play mind games. We put on social masks. We detach ourselves from our innermost feelings. We unwittingly fall prey to those things that will hurt us most. We become obsessive in our thoughts and compulsive in our actions as we defend ourselves against the world. We do all this to protect our precious ego selves. It is from the limiting and harmful aspects of our personalities, therefore, that we wish to become liberated.

Perhaps on the surface, at least, you're currently quite happy. Maybe you like being extraverted or introverted in attitude, Promethean in temperament, or visionary in leadership style. Moreover, you may take pride in your psychological preferences and personality traits. In your everyday experience of life you may not feel particularly limited or constrained. You may feel that you're very much in control of your own destiny. Yet studies in existential, transpersonal, archetypal and spiritual psychology would suggest you are constrained, even if unknowingly. According to these psychologies, there is often more going on in the self (personality) than meets the eye. For example, without knowing it you may be falling prey to a lot of self-deception (e.g., maybe you're trying to convince yourself you're happy when you're not). Lying to yourself can lead to **false consciousness** or what existentialists call **bad faith**. When suffering from this state you begin to believe your own lies about yourself. For instance, you may not be upset for the reasons you think. You may not truly be motivated by what you believe. You may be doing and saying all the right things, but for a lot of dishonest reasons you won't admit to. In addition, you may overly identify with one or two aspects of your personality and thereby neglect other important dimensions of your humanity. If so, this would leave you unwhole and unfulfilled. Or, in protecting of the self, you may uncontrollably behave in ways that are injurious to your health or detrimental to your long-term well-being. In short, all this bad faith, defensiveness and underdevelopment produces a false self with which we identify. We call this the "ego self" or "I."

As you can well appreciate, failure to see our own psychological enslavement may be the worst kind of bondage. Not knowing that you're bound is far worse than being bound and knowing it. It's like not *knowing* that you don't know. To continue the analogy, if you *know* what you don't know, at least you can take steps to obtain information and thereby rectify the situation. So too with personal freedom. Once you know how you've been imprisoned by your personality, you can then take positive steps to free yourself and realize your full potential. Creating an awareness of the limits imposed by our personalities will therefore be one of our goals. Now is the time for all of us to face the enemy, for indeed, we are the enemy.

To help us face the enemy we'll turn to the spiritual psychology of the enneagram. The **enneagram** (pronounced any-a-gram) is an ancient and powerful symbol of the human personality that can facilitate the process of **self-transformation**. This symbol can help us to identify the traps set for us by our egos. It can show us how to avoid these traps. It can offer hope and direction for future liberation from our limiting personalities. The enneagram can also bring to our awareness the spiritual dimensions of life, an awareness that has unfortunately been deadened in many people. If you've ever wondered about who you are, about the universe, human nature or the purpose of life, you have indeed faced spiritual questions.

> You have no enemy except yourself and you are the enemy indeed to him because you do not know him as yourself.
>
> A Course in Miracles

Our second goal in this chapter is to find greater meaning in our lives. To this end, we'll focus on the work of existential psychiatrist Viktor Frankl. He claims that the greatest meaning in life is found in **self-transcendence**. By getting beyond our egos and by overcoming ourselves, we can commit to things, forget our self-preoccupations and ultimately experience happiness in life. Frankl offers us a diagnosis of society's "metaphysical malaise of meaninglessness" and provides a prescription to remedy this widespread existential ailment. If you personally feel apathetic and bored with life, or if you're depressed and fatalistic, Frankl's insights will prove helpful to you.

Our third goal in this chapter is to find dignity, purpose and hope in our lives. To do so, we will look at the **archetypal/transpersonal psychology** of Carol Pearson. She uses the metaphor of the "hero's journey" to map our developmental stages and transitional periods of life. She interprets human development in terms of a spiral process. We all begin life by establishing ego boundaries, then develop what she calls soul, before we reach the final destination of the real or **authentic self**—that which allows us to experience wholeness and integrity as people. It's a bit misleading to say "final destination," for achievement of the authentic self then allows us to go back and redefine our ego boundaries and enrich our souls in new ways not possible before the development of self. In time, continuing soul and ego developments make possible new experiences and expressions of the authentic self. The journey to wholeness is a spiralling process that only ends in death. In other words, "It ain't over 'til it's over!" People are not like pastries baked in an oven; there never comes a moment in time when we're baked to perfection. The human journey is itself the destination. To think you've ever finally "made it" in life or that for once and for all you've "got your act totally together" is probably a self-deception. Your life is like an incomplete masterpiece, beautiful for what it is, but incomplete nonetheless.

THE ENNEAGRAM: A PATH TO PERSONAL LIBERATION

The enneagram is a system of **transformational/spiritual psychology** that uses a geometric symbol to represent nine basic personality types and their interrelationships. The term is derived from the Greek words *ennea*, meaning nine, and *gram*, meaning graph or drawing. The symbol begins with a circle. Around the circle are placed nine equidistant points, each having a number. The numbers refer to different personality types, so somebody could be a one, an eight, or a five, for example. Note that no number is better or worse than any other; the numbers are value-neutral. On the enneagram, the number nine is top and centre. Number one is found to the right of it, while the rest of the numbers follow clockwise in sequence. Within the circle itself, you will find an equilateral triangle and another six-pointed shape. See the enneagram symbol below in Figure 11.1.

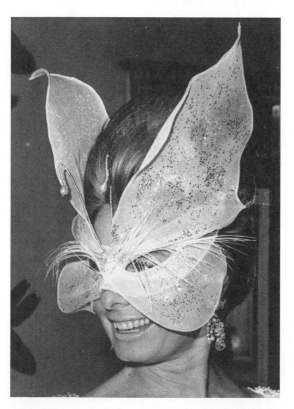

Is the mask you wear keeping you from facing the enemy?

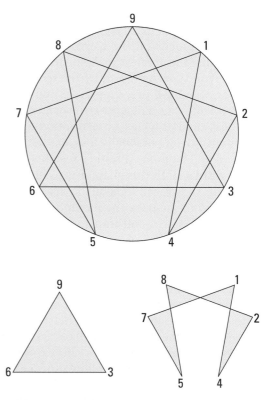

Figure 11.1

The Enneagram

Source: Figures 11.1, 11.2, 11.3, 11.4. Don Richard Riso, best-selling author of *Personality Types, Understanding the Enneagram, The Riso-Hudson Enneagram Type Indicators* and *Enneagram Transformations*.

> One's own self is well hidden from one's own self: of all mines of treasure, one's own is the last to be unearthed.
>
> Friedrich Nietzsche

> ...forget not that no concept of yourself will stand against the truth of what you are.
>
> A Course in Miracles

> Clad in this "self," the creation of irresponsible and ignorant persons, meaningless honours and catalogued acts—strapped into the straight jacket of the immediate.
> To step out of all this, and stand naked on the precipice invulnerable, free: in the Light, with the Light, of the Light.
> Whole, real in the Whole.
> Out of myself as a stumbling block, into myself as fulfilment.
>
> Dag Hammarskjold

Relationship to Traditional and Contemporary Psychology

The enneagram has ancient origins. It dates back at least to the Islamic Sufi Brotherhoods in the 14th and 15th centuries. Some believe the enneagram originates with the Greek thinker Pythagoras, who believed the universe could be explained in numerical terms. In any case, the enneagram's psychological insights have been passed down orally for hundreds of years. Building upon what they've learned about the enneagram from spiritual teachers who have come into contact with it, current developers of it, such as Don Richard Riso (1990), have incorporated the work of Karen Horney, Sigmund Freud and Carl Jung in efforts to explain the psychodynamics of the various enneagram personality types. In this vein, Riso has pointed out that his descriptions of the enneagram types correlate not only with Jungian types (described in Chapter 1) but also with personality disorders as described in the *Diagnostic and Statistical Manual of Mental Disorders*, essentially the bible of the psychiatric profession. For example, number eight (in its unhealthy expressions) corresponds to the antisocial personality disorder, while a dysfunctional number one displays symptoms characteristic of the compulsive personality disorder. Renee Baron and Elizabeth Wagele (1994) have also tried to correlate Jungian personality types with enneagram types. See Figure 11.2 for an illustration. Your enneagram type may thus help to verify your Myers-Briggs's Jungian type and vice versa. For purposes of type verification, do Self-Diagnostic 11.1, What's My Enneagram Type?.

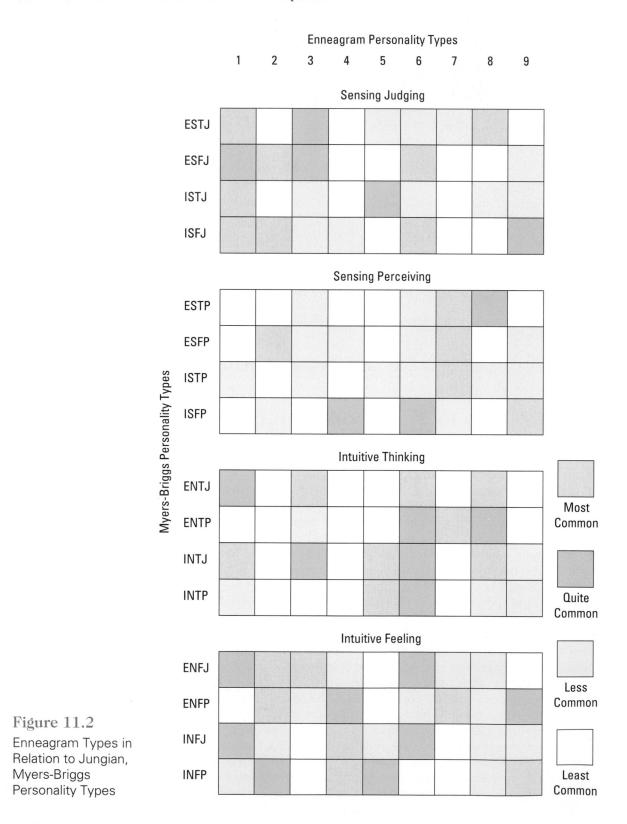

Figure 11.2

Enneagram Types in
Relation to Jungian,
Myers-Briggs
Personality Types

SELF-DIAGNOSTIC 11.1

What's My Enneagram Type?

Aim: This self-diagnostic will enable you to form an initial hypothesis of your enneagram personality type. Results obtained will be useful in finding whole new liberating directions for personal self-transcendence. They should enable you later on to remove self-created obstacles to your higher development as a spiritual being.

Instructions: Listed below are 45 statements. Next to each one, indicate how well it reflects what you're like as a person. The person we're addressing here is not your "social self," "family self," or "school self," but the "self inside" that you know to be the most authentic expression of who you are.

1 = Not like me at all

2 = Not very much like me

3 = A little bit like me

4 = Frequently like me

5 = Almost always like me

_____ 1. It's important for me to be morally correct. I want to do the right things for the right reasons.

_____ 2. How others see me is important.

_____ 3. I focus more on goals than on relationships.

_____ 4. I want to understand myself. I want others to understand me as well.

_____ 5. I am very observant, seeing things most people overlook.

_____ 6. I am a traditionalist, strongly identifying with groups, institutions and friends.

_____ 7. I am unpredictable, spontaneous and fun-loving.

_____ 8. I am direct, able to motivate and take charge when necessary.

_____ 9. Keeping the peace is very important to me.

_____ 10. I try to achieve perfection in my work. Others should do the same.

_____ 11. I wouldn't want to live with people who don't care about or appreciate me.

_____ 12. It's important that I make something of myself.

_____ 13. Beauty and taste are important to me. My physical surroundings strongly influence my moods.

_____ 14. I have a deep desire to gain knowledge and to understand the world around me.

_____ 15. I am severely hurt when betrayed by others.

_____ 16. In my opinion, people need to lighten up.

_____ 17. I enjoy opposition and confrontation.

_____ 18. I avoid disagreement and confrontation whenever I can.

_____ 19. I tend to be formal and idealistic.

_____ 20. It's important that I make people feel comfortable and welcome.

_____ 21. I try to make good first impressions on people.

_____ 22. I'm easily bothered or hurt by intrusions.

_____ 23. I hold on tightly to what I have acquired.

_____ 24. I need people to give me clear-cut guidelines so I know where I stand.

_____ 25. I like and enjoy people and they usually like and enjoy me.

_____ 26. I hate being used or manipulated by others.

_____ 27. I'm usually perceived as friendly and easygoing, though on occasion I can be extremely stubborn.

_____ 28. I get upset when people break the rules.

_____ 29. People sometimes see me as an interference, when I'm only trying to help.

_____ 30. I can adapt to whatever group of people I'm with.

_____ 31. I am often envious of what others have.

_____ 32. Being alone is not a problem for me. I love my privacy.

_____ 33. I'm more sensitive to danger and threat than most other people.

_____ 34. I really hate being bored, having no plans and having nothing to do.

_____ 35. I need to be in control and to exhibit my strengths.

_____ 36. I prefer to be optimistic rather than pessimistic.

_____ 37. I do what I say I'll do almost all of the time.

_____ 38. I easily show my feelings.

_____ 39. I'm competitive.

_____ 40. I often appear melancholy, sad or emotionally intense.

_____ 41. I have a tendency to intellectualize my problems.

_____ 42. I'm a practical, "meat and potatoes" kind of person.

_____ 43. I enjoy physical activity.

_____ 44. I emphasize practical results over abstract ideals.

_____ 45. I often need help or encouragement to get started on things. Once I get started, I'm usually OK. Getting started is the problem.

Scoring: The numbers of the preceding statements have been arranged into columns. Next to each statement number, place the numerical value you gave to it reflecting your level of agreement.

1: The Perfect Idealist	2: The Nurturing Helper	3: The Motivating Star
1. _____	2. _____	3. _____
10. _____	11. _____	12. _____
19. _____	20. _____	21. _____
28. _____	29. _____	30. _____
37. _____	38. _____	39. _____
Totals _____	_____	_____

4: The Sensitive Artist	5: The Observant Thinker	6: The Wary Loyalist
4. _____	5. _____	6. _____
13. _____	14. _____	15. _____
22. _____	23. _____	24. _____
31. _____	32. _____	33. _____
40. _____	41. _____	42. _____
Totals _____	_____	_____

7: The Enthusiastic Generalist	8: The Assertive Leader	9: The Easygoing Peacemaker
7. _____	8. _____	9. _____
16. _____	17. _____	18. _____
25. _____	26. _____	27. _____
34. _____	35. _____	36. _____
43. _____	44. _____	45. _____
Totals _____	_____	_____

My highest total is _____ under the _____ column.

To discover what your enneagram type is like, read the descriptions below.

1. The Perfect Idealist   Rational, hardworking, ethical, serious, emotionally rigid or unexpressive; can be wise and discerning; often impatient, angry and humourless

2. The Nurturing Helper   Caring and nurturing; friendly, self-sacrificing and altruistic; can also be possessive, proud and manipulative, creating dependency relationships

3. The Motivating Star   Adaptable and chameleon-like; motivated by success; ambitious and image conscious; can be overly competitive, emotionally shallow, driven, opportunistic and arrogant

4. The Sensitive Artist   Typically shy and introverted; quiet and gentle, inspired and creative; sees self as special, introspective; can be moody, melancholic, inhibited and self-pitying

5. The Observant Thinker   Intellectual, insightful and curious; independent and innovative; great capacity for knowledge and system building; can be emotionally distant, isolated, eccentric and awkward with people

6. The Wary Loyalist   Dependable and trustworthy; committed, reliable, security oriented, dependent on others, endearing; can also be defensive and suspicious, creating "in" and "out" groups; may hide fear by acting tough

7. The Enthusiastic Generalist   Usually energetic and enthusiastic with a real *joie de vivre*; playful and spontaneous, likable and optimistic; can be infantile, excessive and self-centred or insensitive to others

8. The Assertive Leader   Aggressive, powerful, forthright and decisive; strong, assertive and resourceful; can become belligerent and confrontational; overly controlling

9. The Easygoing Peacemaker   Stable, accommodating and trusting; blends into surroundings; at one with the world; avoids conflict, minimizes upset; can also be stubborn, inattentive, impenetrable and neglectful

How Did You Get Your Type?

To understand how you developed your type, it's helpful first to arrange the nine personality types into three triads. Riso (1996) calls them the instinctive triad, the feeling triad and the thinking triad. See Figure 11.3.

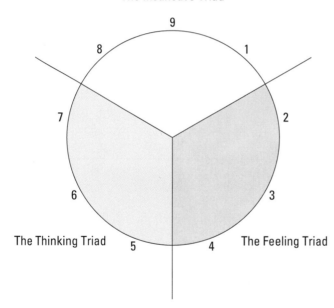

Figure 11.3
The Psychological Triads

In each of the triads, one type overexpresses the characteristic faculty of the triad, another underexpresses it and the third is most out of touch with it. See Figure 11.4.

We all have instinctive abilities, as well as the ability to think and to feel. However, beginning in childhood, we emphasize one faculty over the other two. The triad in which your personality type is found represents the overall way you consciously and unconsciously adapted to your family and the world (Riso, 1987). It's not that the other two triads disappear, but as Riso puts it, "all three faculties operate in an ever-changing balance to produce our personality" (1987: 26). The faculty that emerges and becomes dominant in our lives is a product of biology and early childhood experience. Concerning the latter influence, enneagram developers such as Riso (1996) give special importance to **childhood orientations** toward the parents when it comes to the development of type. You may, for example, have bonded and felt closely connected to the nurturing figure (usually the mother) or the protective figure (usually, though not necessarily, the father) in your life. Perhaps you positively connected with both. By contrast, maybe you felt disconnected from either one or both, or perhaps you felt ambivalent toward either one or both. Whatever the case, these initial childhood orientations to the nurturing and protective figures in your life helped to form your adult personality. By the way, the identifications that are, or are not, formed in childhood have little to do with the quality of parental caretaking. You could strongly

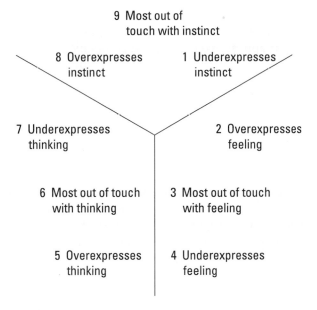

Figure 11.4
What Each Type
Does

identify with an abusive parent or disconnect with a loving one in whom you simply do not see yourself.

The Wings

According to enneagram theory, nobody is a "pure" personality type. Riso (1990) maintains that anyone's personality is a unique blend of his basic type and one or two of the types adjacent to it on the circumference of the enneagram. For example, the five can be coloured by its four or six wing, or both in differing degrees.

When the wings of personality are taken into account, we can understand how two people with the same basic personality type can exhibit subtle differences or different shades of the same character. For instance, a five with a strong four wing "looks" different from a five with a strong six wing. The traits of the four and five conflict with one another. Fives tend to withdraw and distance themselves from experience, whereas fours internalize everything to intensify their feelings (Riso, 1989). Combining elements of the two produces one of the richest subtypes. Possibilities for outstanding artistic achievement (number four trait) are combined with intellectual achievement (number five trait). Riso (1987) identifies Glenn Gould, the late great Canadian classical pianist as a five with a four wing. By contrast, a five with a six wing constitutes a personality type that is one of the most difficult to communicate with or to maintain a relationship with. The person's fiveness creates problems of trust, while the six wing reinforces anxiety, thereby making risk-taking in relationships difficult (Riso, 1987). Examples of fives with a strong six wing include Sigmund Freud and B.F. Skinner, two psychological theorists we've already studied. Not to fear, then, if you're a five with a six wing. It appears you're in good company.

Levels of Development

Every enneagram personality type has within it levels of development. You can express your personality in healthy, average and unhealthy ways (Riso, 1990). For instance, a healthy eight acts differently from an unhealthy eight or an average eight. At the highest level of development, the eight is heroic and magnanimous. At the lower levels, an eight can become confrontational, domineering and intimidating. At worst, the eight can become a sociopath (Keyes, 1991) or an antisocial personality (Riso, 1982).

What is so powerful about the enneagram is that it offers an explanation of the psychodynamics of the descent into dysfunction. On the upside, it also offers directions for climbing out of the abyss, overcoming the unhealthy debilitating expressions of our personalities and ultimately achieving personal liberation from ourselves.

Paths of Integration and Disintegration

According to enneagram theory, people change but their personalities remain the same for life. A seven cannot suddenly become a four, for instance. However, your personality is not fixed. As we just learned, people can move from unhealthy to healthy expressions of their personalities. As well, very healthy people can move beyond their basic personalities in the direction of integration, or choose the **path of integration**. Under stress or great anxiety, people can also choose the **path of disintegration** by moving in the direction of disintegration. In other words, people can grow or deteriorate and, in the process, they can begin to display behaviours characteristic of other personality types. Given this, in order to fully understand the workings of your personality, you need to know your basic type, your wing(s), your personal direction of integration (i.e., how you grow and develop by going beyond your basic type), and your direction of disintegration. See Figure 11.5 for an illustration of the paths of integration and disintegration.

From Figure 11.5 we see that as individuals become more healthy or unhealthy, they can move in different directions from their basic types. Riso (1987: 38–39) provides an example of how type six can integrate or disintegrate by either moving ahead to nine or deteriorating to three.

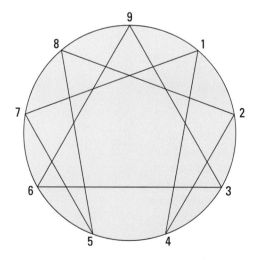

Paths of Integration
1–7–5–8–2–4–1
9–3–6–9

Paths of Disintegration
1–4–2–8–5–7–1
9–6–3–9

Figure 11.5
Paths of Integration and Disintegration

A brief example will illustrate what these movements mean. At personality type six, one line is drawn to nine, and another to three. This means that if a six were to become healthy and begin to actualize his potentials, he would move to nine, the direction of Integration specified by the Enneagram, activating what personality nine symbolizes for the six. When the Enneagram predicts that a healthy six will move to nine, we find that this is precisely the kind of psychological development we see in individuals who are sixes. Many of the six's problems have to do with insecurity and anxiety, and when the six moves to nine he or she becomes relaxed, accepting, and peaceful. This six at nine is more self-possessed and less anxious than ever before.

Conversely, the line to three indicates the six's direction of Disintegration. If a six were to become not merely neurotic, but even more unhealthy, he or she would do so by "going to three." The six's anxiety has made him extremely suspicious of others, and his feelings of inferiority and insecurity are rampant. A move to three marks a neurotic six's need to bolster his self-esteem by an extreme narcissistic overcompensation. The six at three will maliciously strike out at people to prove how tough he can be, and to triumph over anyone he thinks has threatened him. In short, the six at three becomes dangerously aggressive and psychopathic.

(Source: Riso (1987, 1990) quotations from *Personality Types, Understanding the Enneagram, The Riso-Hudson Enneagram Type Indicators* and *Enneagram Transformations*.)

The Problem with Your Personality

If you're typical of many college and university students, you've probably already wrestled for some time now with personal problems of self-concept and self-esteem. Finding out who you are, what you want and where you're going in life are no easy tasks. Add to this insecurities you might have about appearance, body type and how others see you, and you can well appreciate

...there is nothing on which people are so fixated as their self-image. We are literally prepared to go through hell just so we don't have to give it up. Ernest Becker rightly calls it 'character armour'. It determines most of what we do or don't do, say or don't say, what we occupy ourselves with and what we don't. We're all affected by it. The question is: Do I have the freedom to be anything else than this role and this image?

Richard Rohr

how developing a positive self-concept and healthy self-esteem are important life issues.

I hope this book has helped you to know yourself better. In addition to getting you to start thinking about your enneagram type, you have also been given a chance to reflect on your Jungian type, temperament type, as well as your communication, leadership and conflict resolution styles. I hope you know yourself and your preferences a little bit better now and that you feel more comfortable about yourself. I should be quick to add, however, that from an enneagram perspective, we've barely begun our work. Richard Rohr (1993: 4) says that

> [t]he discovery of regular patterns in human behaviour has meaning only when at the same time the possibility of change and liberation from the pressure of determinacy comes into view. This possibility, I believe, is opened up by the Enneagram.

Following up on Rohr, it could be said that knowing your type is not necessarily good in itself. We should not resign ourselves to our personalities, nor should we become completely satisfied and complacent about them. For example, it would be wrong to excuse ourselves for our behaviour by saying, "This is just the way I am." Resignation and complacency make for rigidity and defensiveness. To develop fully as human beings we must use our personalities as vehicles for self-liberation. We must not be confined by them. We shouldn't allow our personalities to control us.

Sadly, many of us fall under the spell of our personalities. We use them to defend ourselves from fully realizing how fearful we are. We adopt ingenious strategies for inflating the ego as a defence against insecurity and loneliness (Riso, 1987). In the process, we create self-fulfilling prophecies in our lives. We bring about the very things we fear most, and we lose what we most desire. Riso (1987: 346) continues:

> Looking at each of the personality types as a whole teaches us what we can expect if we inflate our ego at the expense of other values. By coercing others to love them, twos end by being hated. By aggrandizing themselves, threes end by being rejected. By exclusively following their feelings, fours end by wasting their lives. By imposing their ideas on reality, fives end by being out of touch with reality. By being too dependent on others, sixes end by being abandoned. By living for pleasure, sevens end by being frustrated and unsatisfied. By dominating others to get what they want, eights end by destroying everything. By accommodating themselves to others too much, nines end as undeveloped, fragmented shells. By attempting to be perfect with humanity, ones end by perverting their humanity. The way out of these inexorable conclusions is to become convinced that only by transcending the ego can we hope to find happiness. As wisdom has always recognized, it is only by dying to ourselves that we find life.

Another benefit of the enneagram stems from the way in which it exposes each personality type's self-deceptions, dead-end pursuits and destructive self-defeating tendencies. Identifying your enneagram type should therefore not be experienced as fun. The enneagram is not a game. The enneagram can reveal much about you that is not very pleasant. I remember not liking everything I learned about myself at a Riso enneagram training in Pennsylvania during the spring of 1994. The enneagram helped me to understand how the personal pride I took in my gifts, talents and accomplishments created traps for my own undoing. To the extent that my new psychological vision caused me discomfort, the training worked. Talking about the feelings that should result when one honestly comes to terms with his or her enneagram number type, Richard Rohr (1993: 13) says that

> [w]hoever is not humiliated has not yet found his or her "number". The more humiliating it is, the more one is looking the matter right in the eye. Anyone who says, "It's wonderful that I'm a Three" is either not a Three or hasn't really understood what I'm saying about type Three...The Enneagram uncovers the games we find ourselves tangled in. It will initially be experienced as embarrassing and perhaps shameful. For a time there will even be a loss of energy and motivation until we relearn how to operate from truth.

If you refer back to the descriptions of the enneagram types provided in Self-Diagnostic 11.1, you will see that each type has much to be disturbed and embarrassed about. For example, at lower levels of development, ones can be impersonal, rigid and impatient; twos can be manipulative and controlling; threes may be calculating, arrogant and opportunistic; fours are sometimes self-pitying and impractical; fives can be awkward and eccentric; sixes often scapegoat and rebel; sevens can be infantile and insensitive; eights are sometimes hard-hearted and openly belligerent; while nines can be stubborn, inattentive and neglectful.

Not wishing to leave you here completely humiliated and embarrassed (though if I were a dysfunctional eight, this option might be tempting!), let me suggest to you that by leaving behind a false self, filled with its deceptions, illusions, obsessions, misguided wants and compulsions, a kind of spiritual rebirth becomes possible. Repeating the ancient wisdom to which Riso draws our attention, "It is only by dying to ourselves that we find life" (Riso, 1987: 346). Nothing less than existential rebirth is required. To lay bare the psychological games we have played for so long and to see how our natural gifts have unconsciously been used as weapons of psychological self-defence against our basic fears is in itself liberating. Life can become more serene, for when we confront the lies of our life, when we expose our absurdity and when we finally see how ridiculous we can sometimes be, then we are in a position to call upon others to do the same (Rohr, 1993). Finally, we grow to love our true selves (not artificially created self-images) and to love others for who they really are. Ultimately, by shedding the character armour of our personalities, we free ourselves to the experience of love and joy in our lives.

ENNEAGRAM TRAVEL TIPS FOR LIFE 11.3

For Ones

1. Relax! The world will survive without you. Not everything will end in disaster if you're not there to be involved.
2. Stop telling yourself and others what should be done. It's not healthy. Instead of saying, "I should...," try saying, "I want to...." Rather than insisting, "That's wrong," say instead, "I don't like it when...." Make your statements of objective judgment more like statements of personal preference.
3. Inject some humour into your life. Don't always be so serious.
4. Get in touch with your feelings. They may not be perfect or rational, but they're nevertheless yours. Ignoring them doesn't mean that they will not exert unconscious influence. Come to terms with your anger in particular.
5. Take a class in stress reduction or engage in some sports and leisure activities. Stop working or doing whatever it is you do so compulsively.

For Twos

1. Do some pleasurable and self-satisfying things without others. Do something for yourself for a change.
2. Stop expecting a return for your generosity or kindness toward others. Don't guilt people into appreciating you; they likely won't appreciate either you or what you've done for them. At best, they'll feel guilty. At worst, they'll resent the guilt you've instilled.
3. If you become the target of unfair treatment, speak up immediately and rationally express your concerns.
4. Don't be possessive with your friends and loved ones. Share them with others.
5. Don't kid yourself about the benefits you derive personally by being nice or helpful to someone else. There's a payoff in being a self-sacrificial martyr. What's the payoff for you?

For Threes

1. Remember that no self-image can ever replace the truth of who you really are. Tell that to your image consultant!
2. Try not to manipulate people on your climb to the top. At the top of the ladder there's only one way to go, namely down. On your descent you might run into some of the people you passed on your way up to personal glory.
3. Give back to the community some of what the community has given to you. Do not feel entitled to get what you want at the expense of others (Riso, 1990).
4. Quit trying to be impressive. People may see you as a braggart—little could be more detrimental to your personal pursuit of success.
5. Don't let your competitive instincts cause bad feelings and contempt for others. Respect your opponents.

For Fours

1. Focus on the present. Avoid self-pity. If your needs were not met in the past, treat yourself with love and compassion now.
2. Get active and don't wait until you're in the mood. The right feelings may never come. Dedicate yourself to some type of meaningful work. Live by this dictum: "When the going gets depressed, the depressed get going."
3. Try not to take people's comments and behaviours so personally. "You would worry less about what others thought of you if you knew how little they did." Your propensity toward defensiveness is irritating to others; it doesn't help you either.
4. Give yourself time to be creative. Ideally, find work that uses your creative talents.
5. Don't overwhelm people with your emotions. For an emotional outlet, write letters to yourself that you don't mail (Baron and Wagele, 1994).

For Fives

1. Remember Gurdjieff's insight: "Books are like maps, but there is also the necessity of travelling." Do more and think less.
2. Get in touch with your body. Take up sports, physical activities and creative pursuits.
3. If you want to understand, concentrate on observing without judgment. Analyse less what you see.

4. Reject your natural tendency to withdraw. Support and nurture others. Try to approach and cooperate.
5. Remember that someone having less knowledge than you doesn't make that person less worthy. Don't use your knowledge as a way of building yourself up as you put others down. You probably like doing this, but this habit hasn't made you any friends lately or helped you to win any popularity contests.

For Sixes

1. Don't mask your insecurity with a tough façade. Accept and come to terms with your anxiety. Use it to energize yourself into productive action.
2. Surround yourself with people who are accepting, trustworthy and encouraging (Baron and Wagele, 1994).
3. Try to develop more trust in your life. Risk rejection as you try to develop close and meaningful relationships.
4. Don't allow yourself to get into patterns of negative thinking.
5. Don't "suck up" to authorities or worship them. Smart authorities will recognize your behaviour for what it is. Be your own self-respecting person. Remember, authorities can be wrong; they certainly conflict with one another.

For Sevens

1. Don't string yourself out doing too many things at the same time.
2. Don't let your "joie de vivre" or your pleasurable pursuits get in the way of duties and responsibilities.
3. Start to control your impulses. I know the Nike commercial says, "Just do it," but if you just do it without thinking, you may end up regretting what you've just done.
4. Try not to make happiness your ultimate life goal. It is a by-product of giving yourself to something worthwhile (Riso, 1990).
5. Be grateful and appreciative for what you have. Try to heed this Chinese proverb: "Before you wish for any one thing, first examine how happy are those who already have it." Here's another sobering Chinese zinger for you: "Want anything long enough and you don't."

For Eights

1. Remember that not everything in life is a contest. Allow others to take control sometimes. See what it's like to be a follower. Imagine what it would be like to be your follower.
2. Don't use your power to hurt or intimidate people. People will not accept your control if they hate you.
3. Keep in mind that you have a tendency to become restless

and impatient with others' incompetence or inability. Showing this side of yourself may scare people away or interfere with their performance.
4. Don't confuse honesty with rude bluntness. Try expressing criticism softly and tactfully. As for appreciation, express it loudly and frequently.
5. Monitor your tendency to pick fights with others. Ask yourself what you're trying to prove when you say or do provocative things.

For Nines

1. Take action when things aren't right. Don't just sit there wishing and hoping for better times.
2. Show initiative rather than always waiting for others to make the first move. Have others join you in your actions for a change.
3. Accept your negative feelings and impulses. If you don't express them, they will surface unexpectedly and interfere with the peace and harmony you want in your relationships.
4. Set goals and deadlines for yourself. Stick to them.
5. Don't allow yourself to be distracted from problems. Deal with them head-on. Remember, conflict is an opportunity for positive change.

Enneagram Types Before the Party

Enneagram Types After the Party

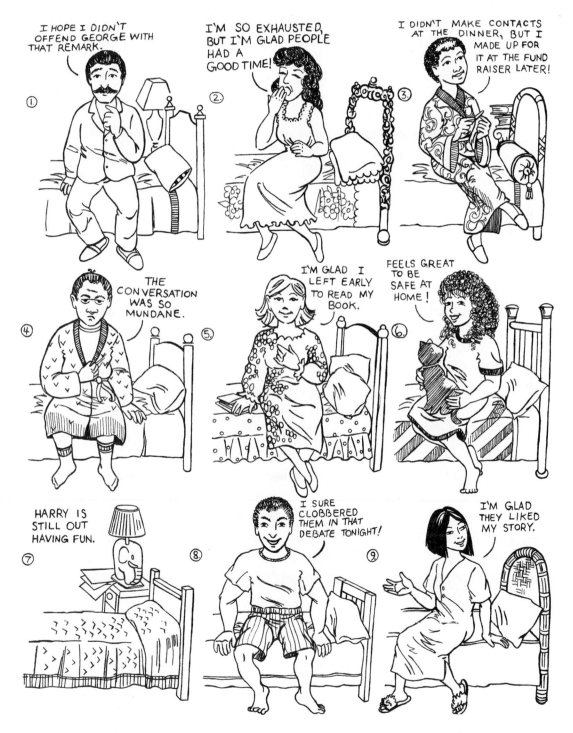

11.4

Self-Expressions

Part I: Under each of the categories that follow list one or two adjectives that describe healthy and unhealthy expressions of your particular enneagram personality type (for help, see Self-Diagnostic 11.1). For each descriptive adjective provide an illustration of it using your personal experience. According to your number, how in the past have you behaved in a healthy or unhealthy way?

My type: ____

Healthy

Descriptors: _____

Personal Illustrations:

_____

_____

The Medicine Wheel: **A Symbol of Native Spirituality**

The First Nations people of Canada have developed their own spiritual traditions independently from European, Middle Eastern, African and Asian influences. In Saskatchewan, for example, the Moose Mountain Medicine Wheel, a 2000-year-old physical structure, is believed to have spiritual and astrological significance.

As a teaching tool, the concept of the medicine wheel has been used for centuries by Native Indians across North America to help them gain self-awareness and spiritual enlightenment. However, little is recorded about it. As with the enneagram, knowledge and information about the medicine

wheel has been transmitted orally from one generation to the next. The best way for you to learn more is by speaking to a tribe elder at the nearest Indian reservation. Because of its oral tradition, details and descriptions of the medicine wheel differ between regions and tribes. In her discussions of the medicine wheel, Mary E. Loomis (1991) shares with us Native teachings as revealed to her by Harley Swiftdeer, a Cherokee medicine man.

Loomis tells us that the medicine wheel is first of all a circle. On the circle are placed the so-called Powers of the Four Directions: North, South, East and West. Native spiritualists believe everything that exists

can be organized according to these powers. For example, if you look at the medicine wheel included here, you will note that each direction has a colour associated with it (i.e., white, black, yellow and red). These colours represent the four races of humanity. The rainbow centre represents people of mixed race.

Each direction on the wheel provides specific life lessons for us to learn. The sun and fire of the East Power illuminate possibilities and spark the imagination. The Power of the West, using earth and blackness, teaches us the value of introspection and connection with the earth. The South Power, with plants that nourish us, teaches us to be trusting and innocent,

Unhealthy

Descriptors: _____

Personal Illustrations:

_____

_____

Part II: If you wish, you can share your insights and personal information with others in the class. This may be done in pairs or in small groups. Participation is optional. Share only that which you feel comfortable sharing.

while the Power of the North, using animal symbols, teaches us about perfection, wisdom and logic. At the centre of the wheel is found sexual energy. This catalytic energy is a creative force that combines masculine and feminine potentials in harmonious balance. In short, using the medicine wheel, we can learn to balance and harmonize the emotional, physical, mental, spiritual and sexual components of the human personality. The medicine wheel can facilitate the development of psychological wholeness and health. (For more information on the medicine wheel, read *Dancing the Wheel of Psychological Types* by Loomis.)

Air
Animals
White
Receives energy
Mental aspect
Wisdom and logic

Earth
Black
Holds energy
Physical aspect
Introspection and insight

N

W

Void
Rainbow
Catalyst energy
Sexual aspect

E

S

Fire
Sun
Yellow
Determines energy
Spiritual aspect
Illumination
and enlightenment

Water
Plants
Red
Gives energy
Emotional aspect
Trust and innocence

Figure 11.6

The Medicine Wheel: Powers of the Four Directions

Source: From Mary E. Loomis, *Dancing the Wheel of Psychological Types*, copyright 1991 by Mary E. Loomis, p. 5. Reprinted by permission of the publisher, Chiron Publications.

We should be prepared for some difficulty on the road to our spiritual rebirth. The enneagram would have us travel into unknown territory. We may have to express feelings, do things or relate in ways that are foreign to our current self-concepts. We may have to overcome past habits, confront old attitudes and identifications, and learn to leave the old ways behind (Riso, 1987). Only by transcending our ego selves can we find lasting happiness, peace and redemption (Rohr, 1993). In closing this discussion of the enneagram, let me leave you with some direction for each numbered type to follow on the continuous journey to personal freedom.

The two needs to overcome its tendency toward self-deception by moving toward the self-understanding of the healthy four. The three needs to overcome its malicious envy of others by moving toward the loyalty and commitment of the healthy six. The four needs to overcome its self-destructive subjectivity by moving toward the objectivity and self-discipline of the healthy one. The five needs to overcome its nihilism by moving toward the courage of the healthy eight. The six needs to overcome its suspicion of others by moving toward the receptivity of the healthy nine. The seven needs to overcome its impulsiveness by moving toward the involvement of the healthy five. The eight needs to overcome its egocentricity by moving toward the concern for others of the healthy two. The nine needs to overcome its complacency by moving toward the ambition of the healthy three. And the one needs to overcome its inflexibility by moving toward the productivity of the healthy seven (Riso, 1987: 348).

> Books are like maps but there is also the necessity of travelling.
>
> Gurdjieff
>
> Sometimes you have to go miles out of your way to go a short distance correctly.
>
> Edward Albee

LIFE...AND MAY I ASK, WHAT'S THE MEANING OF THIS?

In the book entitled *The Unheard Cry for Meaning*, Viktor Frankl tells us about 60 students at an American university who were interviewed after attempting suicide. Some 85 percent of them said the reason they tried to kill themselves was that for them "life seemed meaningless." This finding was particularly surprising in view of the fact that 93 percent of these students were actively engaged socially, performing well academically, and were on good terms with their families. Frankl believes that these stunning findings should serve as a wake-up call from our dreams. The North American dream for a long time has been material in nature. A majority of people believe that if we just improve the socioeconomic situation of people, everything will be fine and people will become happy. As Frankl puts it, however, "The truth is that as the struggle for survival has subsided, the question has emerged: survival for what? Ever more people have the means to live, but no meaning to live for" (Frankl, 1978:20-21).

In view of Frankl's experiences and findings with students, it would seem that not money, success nor a good social life can guarantee happiness. Even when people struggle for an entire lifetime to get what they want, the question still remains: "What do they want it for?" Unfortunately, many people do not seriously ask the "what for" question until middle age or later. When they do, they usually recognize at some level of consciousness that "having it all still isn't enough." They are surprised by the prospect that they have been travelling in the fast lane of life but that all along their destination has been a dead end. Then life takes on the quality of a "**spiritual emergency**." The mind and body may be functioning more or less adequately, but from neglect and malnourishment, the spirit finds itself in critical condition. Pills, profits and pleasures that often work to sustain physical and mental life prove to be ineffective when healing the spiritually diseased patient.

In hopes of saving you from a midlife crisis, or at least from a little bit of grief between now and then, I will turn your attention to the work of Viktor Frankl, world-famous psychiatrist and developer of **logotherapy**—a psychotherapeutic method of counselling that focuses on the spiritual problem of meaning.

> *Among all my patients in the second half of life, that is, over thirty-five, there has not been one whose problem in the last resort was not that of finding a religious outlook on life.*
>
> C.G. Jung

Dr. Frankl and the Soul

 11.5

So far in this text, there has been a lot of talk about basic needs. Recall, for example, how Freud argued that human beings are motivated by drives and instincts. Much of life, he maintained, is determined by the pleasure principle emanating from the id. Recall also how Abraham Maslow conceptualized his hierarchy of human needs. He talked about the basic needs of survival, safety and security, esteem and self-realization. William Glasser brought to the motivational table of life his own set of basic needs including fun and freedom, as well as power, survival, care, love and belonging. What Viktor Frankl claims is that deep within every person is an innate need to find meaning in life. He calls this the **will-to-meaning** (Frankl, 1973). A major problem in contemporary life, perhaps in your own, is that meaning escapes us. The search for meaning therefore becomes one of our most important life tasks.

The Three Dimensions of Life

Viktor Frankl (1973) brings to our attention the fact that life has three dimensions: the somatic or physical, the mental and the spiritual. He believes that modern psychology and psychiatry have overemphasized the importance of the mind and body to the virtual exclusion of spirituality. This is unfortunate according to Frankl (1973), since spirituality is what makes us

> But I myself feel that humanity has demonstrated ad nauseum in recent years that it has instincts, drives. Today it appears more important to remind man that he has a spirit, that he is a spiritual being.
>
> Viktor Frankl

distinctively human. Rats and weasels do not ask about the meaning of life, but humans do.

In today's fast-paced, results-oriented world, people who ask why things happen or ask questions of meaning are often regarded as disturbed, neurotic or maladjusted in some way. The point, it seems, is to get on with living and to quit worrying about life's significance. For many there is no purpose in asking about the value of life. In response, Frankl would say that "to be concerned about the meaning of life is not necessarily a sign of disease or of neurosis. It may be; but then again, spiritual agony may have little connection with a disease of the psyche. The proper diagnosis can be made only by someone who can see the spiritual side of man" (Frankl, 1973: x).

Existential Neurosis

In the context of classical psychoanalysis, blocking the expression of biologically based needs and drives gives rise to frustration that in turn can lead to clinical neurosis. Similarly, Frankl holds that when the will-to-meaning is blocked, **existential frustration** results. If such frustration is strong and persistent enough, a type of existential neurosis may arise. He says, "When existential frustration results in neurotic symptomatology, we are dealing with a new type of neurosis which we call '**noögenic neurosis**'" (Frankl, 1973: xii). Support for the existence of existential or noögenic neurosis is provided by empirical studies (see Frankl, 1973).

Meaninglessness in Modern Society

It's been said that young people growing up in the last decade of the 20th century are part of a lost generation, or X-generation, as it's been dubbed. Many of them suffer from what Frankl would label a **collective neurosis**. This neurosis is characterized by four symptoms. The first is planlessness. Some people just live day to day showing little or no energy or enthusiasm for life. For them, there are no five-year plans and no long-term goals. Many people live for today and today alone. A second symptom of collective neurosis involves developing a fatalistic attitude, essentially a feeling of helplessness. Fatalistic people feel powerless. They believe that their lives are controlled by forces beyond their control. These forces may be internal conditions or external circumstances. Having no plans and no control, people often display collective thinking as a third symptom of mass neurosis. Fearing their own individuality, and trying to escape individual responsibility, they immerse themselves in the crowd. They become like others. They simply do what others are doing. Finally, a life with a frustrated need for meaning may manifest itself as fanaticism. In contrast to those who surrender their personalities to the crowd, the fanatic ignores others who are different. The fanatic may

Nowhere Man

He's a real nowhere man
Sitting in his nowhere land
Making all his nowhere plans
for nobody.
Doesn't have a point of view
knows not where he's going to
Isn't he a bit like
you and me.
Nowhere man please listen
You don't know what you're missin'
Nowhere man,
the world is at your command.
He's as blind as he can be
Just sees what he wants to see
Nowhere man,
can you see me, at all.
Nowhere man, don't worry
Take your time. Don't hurry
Leave it all till somebody else
lends you a hand.

John Lennon and Paul McCartney

even hate and attack those who do not follow "the chosen path." Here, differences become the basis of hatred, a sick response to perceived meaninglessness. Thus, if Frankl is correct, it may be that neo-nazi racists, for example, are really just frightened people responding antisocially to the fear of emptiness in their lives. They may be trying to fill a painful vacuum with aggressions and racial hatred. Behind the tough exterior may be fearful and lost individuals.

Roots of Meaninglessness

Frankl believes that **meaninglessness** in life has fundamental root causes. The first, interestingly enough, has to do with evolutionary biology. In contrast to animals, humans are not so determined by genetics and hormones. Whereas animals unavoidably and necessarily respond to instinctual urges, humans have evolved in ways that allow them to rise above biology. We can choose not to eat when hungry, not to drink when thirsty, not to attack aggressively when provoked and not to engage in mating rituals when sexually aroused—try stopping an animal from making these choices! In short, instincts no longer tell us what we must do.

Second, Frankl points out that in society today, traditional values and institutions are declining in importance in people's lives. A good example is organized religion. It no longer has the influence it once had. For many, it has ceased to provide guidance and direction. In fact, it is often a target for cynical attack. Furthermore, the traditional nuclear family has been under seige in recent years. Once defined by bloodline, it now seems that any convenient arrangement of loving and caring people living together, regardless of gender combination, constitutes a family. Add to this dramatic changes in sexuality and ever-changing societal attitudes, and we can readily understand how some people have become confused by life. They no longer know what is right or wrong, good or bad. Simply, they no longer know what they should do.

So placed in a position where they no longer do what they must do by force of biology, and no longer knowing what they should do given the changing values and crumbling institutions of society, people no longer know what they *want* to do. They are lost and adrift on the turbulent sea of life. They see no way home and can find no shelter from the storm. In response to this frightening and dangerous situation, they fall ill to collective neurosis, made up of **conformity** and **fanaticism** (mindless obedience). They no longer accept personal responsibility for themselves or their lives. They become followers and foolish imitators in their desperate attempt to escape the anxiety of decision making in an uncertain world.

How to Find and Create Meaning in Your Life

A number of years ago on CBC's *Man Alive*, host Roy Bonisteel asked Viktor Frankl where meaning could be found. In response, Frankl said it can be found anywhere by anyone. Meaning can be found on the mountaintops and in the valleys of life. It can be found in the dingiest hut or in the fanciest mansion. Meaning is possible whether you're rich or poor, beautiful or ugly, male or female, hearty or sick, young or old, intelligent or unintelligent. Meaning is not the exclusive preserve of philosophers, geniuses or rich and accomplished people. In fact, Frankl points out that according to letters he's received, some of the deepest meaning is found by convicted prisoners in jail, those sentenced to be executed and living on death row. Given that meaning can be found even in jail, he laments the fact that so many young people today lack meaning in their lives, so much so that even when surrounded by the abundance of life in the latter part of the 20th century, they still find cause to kill themselves, to check out of life. Given this tragic situation, it's vitally important that we find meaning in our lives, but how can we begin the search?

> When the people lack a proper sense of awe, then some awful visitation will descend upon them.
>
> Lao Tzu

Self-Transcendence

As a logotherapist and existential psychiatrist, Frankl recognizes that meaning cannot be imposed on individuals. Nobody can lay life's meaning on someone else. There is not one single meaning that applies to everybody. Since all people are different, meaning is unique to each and every individual. Each person is challenged by life in different ways by the particular set of circumstances in which he finds himself. No two people find themselves in exactly the same situation. We've all been dealt a different hand in life. Only the requirement to respond is universal.

> ... man should not ask what he may expect from life, but should rather understand that life expects something from him.
>
> Viktor Frankl

According to Frankl, some people respond to life by seeking meaning in the pursuit of happiness. By feeding their appetites and satisfying their desires, and also by indulging in the pleasures of the body, some hope to find meaning. These people think of life in terms of "I want," "Me first" and "Gimme gimme." They believe the sayings, "Whoever dies with the most toys wins" and "You only live once, so you might as well go for the gusto and get everything you can."

In contrast to the pleasure-seeking self-indulgence of the above crowd, others try to find meaning in self-absorption. It could be argued that a whole segment of the book-publishing industry is devoted to narcissistic people who wish to analyse themselves, interpret themselves, intellectualize themselves—in short, to absorb themselves in themselves. For Frankl, this kind of self-absorption, along with the pursuits of the self-indulgent crowd, cannot ultimately lead to meaning and lasting life satisfaction. He likens self-absorbed people to the boomerang. He points out, contrary to popular belief, that the job of the boomerang is not to return to the hunter who throws it. If the boomerang returns, it means that the hunter failed to hit the prey he was aiming at. So too with humankind. When people focus on themselves too intently rather than on a target mission or life task external to themselves, they fail in their endeavour. Frankl prescribes **self-transcendence** as a requirement for meaningful and satisfying life. Frankl believes it's necessary to forget oneself, to quit caring so much about one's personal wants and needs if meaning is to be found. Obsessively focusing on the self will in the end be self-defeating. It's not that your basic needs and wants should be totally neglected, only that preoccupation with them will not help you find meaning.

Future Orientation

When the locus of meaning is placed outside the individual, life begins to take on a **future orientation**. One begins to perceive a gap between the way things are and the way things ought to be, or between the way one is and how one should be. This perceived gap between "is" and "ought" produces in the person a kind of healthy tension. People begin to feel motivated to act. They find reasons to get up in the morning, get active and start changing things. They want to make things better for the future. Looking for improvements, they constantly find new purposes to fulfill. Compare this to people who dwell in the past, either living in a pleasant fantasy that no longer exists, or bitterly resenting a personal history that cannot be undone. Neither option yields very much meaning, if any at all. Lamenting an unsatisfying present or complaining about current frustrated wants doesn't yield very much meaning either.

Meaning Is Found in Work, Love and Suffering

For Frankl, meaning in life is ultimately found in work, love and, if necessary, in suffering. Let's look at work first. **Work** provides all of us with an opportunity to find meaning in our lives. Through work we can express our personal creativity and realize values that are important to us. If you're an artist, your work enables you to fulfill your potentialities. If you're devoted to saving the planet, working for Greenpeace will help you champion a cause you consider important. Note that not all work is inherently creative or important in itself. Fortunately, it's not the work that yields meaning; rather, it's the way in which the work is performed. Show me somebody at work, at any job, who doesn't care or who just goes through the motions, and I'll show you a bored and dissatisfied person. On the other hand, show me a student, a janitor, an executive or parent who takes pride in her efforts and personal best, an individual who goes the extra mile without being asked, and I'll show you a person who's motivated and enthusiastic about life.

Work affords all of us the opportunity for self-transcendence. By investing ourselves in our work, we can get beyond our petty self-preoccupations. We can enrich our personal lives and the lives of others by giving ourselves to something greater than ourselves. Life can indeed take on the quality of a mission. We can commit and dedicate ourselves to worthwhile values and ideals. We can thereby give dignity to life and find purpose in our actions. Serving a cause greater than ourselves can provide a reason for living. Finding a cause or mission to which we want to commit ourselves is one of our ulti-

Meaning is not found in work itself, but in the way it is done.

mate life tasks. This doesn't necessarily entail jumping on some kind of so-cial bandwagon or becoming a pavement-pounding crusader. Your mission may be played out quietly and in private. It's all up to you. The expression of meaning is a personal choice.

Love is a second source of meaning. It too provides an opportunity for self-transcendence. In true love we forget ourselves. We experience someone else in his uniqueness. Rather than preoccupy ourselves with what *we* want or need, we focus on the other person. We give, share and care. We try to do for the other and take pleasure in doing so. In this context Frankl (1978) talks about the problem of sexual dysfunctions in intimate sexual relations. When people pursue sexual pleasure as an end in itself, when they try to impress their partner or when they seek self-satisfaction above all else, they often become sexually dysfunctional.

According to Frankl, it is precisely by not caring about yourself or your "performance" that you find the most satisfying sexual intimacy with an-other. For Frankl, happiness is a by-product of self-transcendence. When happiness (say through sex) is pursued directly, as a target objective, fail-ure and misery are sure to result. The **pursuit of happiness** is regarded as a contradiction in terms. Happiness can't be pursued, he says; instead it must ensue from giving oneself to another in a love, or, as I mentioned before, by offering oneself in service to a cause or mission greater than oneself. To worry about how happy you are today or how much pleasure you're currently enjoying is to make a wrong turn in life.

Love is but one example of an **experiential value**. Other such values in which we find meaning include goodness, beauty and truth. Glorious sunsets, cultural achievements, scientific discoveries, literary works, natural wonders, heroic acts, saintly examples of humanity and profound insights into human nature are all things that make life wondrous and worth living. They leave us awestruck, filled with joy, inspired about the future and eager to partake in the mystery of life. It is by losing ourselves in culture, nature, art and research that we find meaning.

Finally, meaning can be found in certain **attitudinal values**, especially those relating to how we respond to unavoidable suffering. Viktor Frankl says (1973: xiii) that "facing your fate without flinching is the highest achievement that has been granted to man." When **suffering** can be avoided, he thinks it should be. If you're sick and medication can make you well, you should take the medication. Unnecessary suffering does not yield any meaning. To accept avoidable suffering is masochistic. However, if you are faced with unavoidable suffering (e.g., incurable cancer or unemployment), meaning can be found in how you face your distress. The challenge presented by life here is to transform the tragedy into a personal triumph. To face suffering and difficulty with cheerful courage, in your particular style, is to make for greatness. It serves as an heroic example to others. Your response to suffering and life's difficulties can be inspiring. Frankl uses his own Nazi concentration camp experience of suffering to illustrate how such terrible

---

Try to apply seriously what I have told you, not that you might escape suffering—nobody can escape it—but that you may avoid the worst—blind suffering.

C.G. Jung

Macbeth: Canst thou not minister to a mind diseased,
　　　　　 Pluck from the memory a rooted sorrow,
　　　　　 Raze out the written troubles of the brain.
　　　　　 And with some sweet oblivious antidote
　　　　　 Cleanse the stuffed bosom of that perilous stuff
　　　　　 Which weights upon the heart?
Doctor: Therein the patient
　　　　　 Must minister to himself.
Macbeth: Throw physic to the dogs; I'll none of it.

William Shakespeare, Macbeth, Act 5, Scene 3

circumstances can bring out either the best or worst in people. Those who saw purpose in their suffering—to educate the world after the war—were more likely to survive. Those who saw no future and no purpose in their suffering were less likely to survive. Your **mission** in life, then, is to see the purpose in every tragedy, the gift in every problem and to respond in ways that ennoble yourself and others. You're on the existential stage of life and the whole world is waiting for your response.

THE HEROIC JOURNEY: LIVING BASED ON ARCHETYPAL PSYCHOLOGY

In this final section of the chapter we'll examine the **archetypal psychology** of Carol Pearson. She is the author of the well-known books *The Hero Within*: *Six Archetypes We Live By* and *Awakening the Heroes Within*: *Twelve Archetypes to Help Us Find Ourselves and Transform Our World*.

> Everyone who takes a journey is already a hero.
>
> Carol Pearson
>
> A disciple once complained, "You tell us stories, but you never reveal the meaning to us." Said the master, "How would you like it if someone offered you fruit and masticated it before giving it to you?"
>
> Anthony DeMello

What Is Archetypal Psychology? What Can It Do for Me?

Carol Pearson's archetypal theory is a cutting-edge developmental transpersonal psychology. It "take[s] a technique of literary criticism, combine[s] it with the central premises of Jungian psychology, and appl[ies] it to people" (Pearson, 1993). In addition to Jung, other influences on Pearson's psychological thinking include Joseph Campbell (author of *The Hero with a Thousand Faces)* and David Olfield, whose creative mythology methods enabled Pearson to work with archetypes and mythical material in experiential ways. Archetypal psychology outlines key stages of human development, each having its own lesson, task or gift. Pearson believes that the archetypal psychology's **heroic journey** concept is a universal metaphor (as evidenced in myth, art and literature) that can be used as a model for living in our complex modern world. It can help us realize current developmental challenges in our lives. It can open up new ways to personal growth. It can prepare us for more effective citizenship and for leadership roles in a democratic society. Archetypal psychology can also create a greater tolerance for diversity. It shows us that people differ not only racially, culturally and linguistically, but psychologically as well. At the higher reaches of human nature, archetypal psychology can be useful as a guide to spiritual development. It can transform us and help us transform the world. Archetypal psychology is best seen as an educational tool that helps people to discover themselves and their mission in life.

The Kingdom Is Sick

Archetypal psychology begins with the observation that there's sickness in the kingdom, so to speak. Frankl might describe this sickness as collective neurosis; other humanistic psychologists might refer to it as existential anxiety. I call it the **metaphysical blues**. According to Pearson's observations, some people in the kingdom (society) have grown ill because they are without "soul." Like Goethe's Faust, they have sold their souls to the devil for personal gain. While they have made it in the world by gaining fame and fortune, they nonetheless feel empty inside. They do all the right things and go through all the right motions, but in the end it's movement without meaning (Pearson, 1991). They just don't know what all their moving and shaking is for. To say that these people have sold out to the devil is not to suggest that they're necessarily destined for hell, as conceptualized by Christians, Jews and Muslims. Rather, it means that life remains for them unfulfilled. They remain unwhole. Some kind of lack is experienced, one that is disturbing to the very core of their being. This is hell enough. This is hell on earth.

Another disease in the human kingdom is **alienation**. People with this existential ailment feel connected to their souls, but cut off from the world (Pearson, 1991). They feel love, and experience life intensely, but they can't find meaningful work and satisfying relationships. They just can't "connect." They experience the external world as an imposition, placing constraints on their freedom. They consequently feel separate and apart.

Finally, you have those in the kingdom who are the worst off. These people are disconnected from their souls and disconnected from the world as well. The lives of such people are empty and unrewarding. Frankl would probably say they suffer from an **existential vacuum**. They don't know how to be true to themselves or how to make their way in the world (Pearson, 1991). They don't know who they are, how to relate, what they should do or what the meaning of life is.

The Hero's Journey as a Model for Living

If you currently suffer from one of the plagues devastating the kingdom, take heart. Self-knowledge, meaning and purpose are all possible and within your grasp. We can all find our way in life learning from heroes. Pearson explains:

> *Stories about heroes are deep and eternal. They link our own longing and pain and passion with those who have come before in such a way that we learn something about the essence of what it means to be human, and they also teach us how we are connected to the great cycles of the natural and spiritual worlds. The myths that can give our lives significance are deeply primal and archetypal and can strike terror into our hearts, but they can also free us from unauthentic lives and make us real. If we avoid what T.S. Eliot called this "primitive terror" at the heart of life, we*

miss our connection to life's intensity and mystery. Finding our own connection with such eternal patterns provides a sense of meaning and significance in even the most painful or alienated moments, and in this way restores nobility to life. (1991: 2)

Source: Pearson quotations from "Twelve Archetypes" and "Archetypes and Their Stories" from *Awakening the Heroes Within* by Carol S. Pearson. Copyright 1991 by Carol S. Pearson. Reprinted with permission of HarperCollins Publishers, Inc.

We can find our place in the world, then, through stories about mythical heroes. By means of them we can feel rooted in history and eternity. Our personal life stories are not unlike those of heroes who came before us. Our lives may not be as celebrated as the lives of mythic heroes, but they are in many ways essentially the same. Their quests are our quests. Their struggles are our struggles. The obstacles they overcome (e.g., dragons) are metaphors for the problems that we face. By seeing how our lives and the lives of others are heroic, we can begin to forge links between ourselves and all people of the world, regardless of time and place (Pearson, 1991). We can at last find our connection to humanity. We can begin to live in responsible community with one another. Through identification with heroes we can restore dignity and nobility to life. And when we do this, we heal ourselves and transform the world at the same time.

> It's not where you are. It's where you're headed that matters.
>
> Joseph R. Smallwood, former Premier of Newfoundland
>
> The destination is not the goal for all the learning is in the journey.
>
> Taoist saying

In classical mythology, how happy or how well a kingdom was often depended on the health of the king or queen. If the monarch was sick, injured or wounded, the kingdom degenerated into a wasteland. For the kingdom to be saved, it was typically necessary for a hero to undertake a quest. Some kind of challenge had to be met or some type of sacred object had to be found. Of course, many difficulties usually confronted the hero along the way. In the end, the hero had to return to the kingdom to heal the king or queen or take that monarch's place as ruler (Pearson, 1991).

Pearson sees parallels between the mythic hero's journey and life today. Stories of heroes reflect psychosocial realities. Our world is the ailing kingdom; our mission is the hero's quest. She continues:

Our world reflects many of the classic symptoms of the wasteland kingdom: famine, environmental damage to the natural world, economic uncertainty, rampant injustice, personal despair and alienation, and the threat of war and annihilation. Our "Kingdoms" reflect the state of our collective souls, not just those of our leaders. This is a time in human history when heroism is greatly needed. Like heroes of old, we aid in restoring life, health, and fecundity to the kingdom as a side benefit of taking our own journeys, finding our own destinies, and giving our unique gifts. It is as if the world were a giant puzzle and each of us who takes a journey returns with one piece. Collectively, as we contribute our part, the kingdom is transformed.

The transformation of the kingdom depends upon all of us. Understanding this helps us move beyond a competitive stance into a concern with empowering ourselves and others. If some people "lose" and do not make their potential contribution, we all lose. If we lack the courage to take our journeys, we create a void where our piece of the puzzle could have been, to the collective, as well as our personal, detriment. (2–3)

The point should be stressed here that your "heroic journey never ends. As soon as we return from one journey and enter a new phase of our lives, we are immediately propelled into a new sort of journey, the pattern is not linear or circular but spiral" (3). New journeys start at new levels, present new obstacles, new treasures and new transformative abilities.

The Call to the Quest

It furthers one to have somewhere to go.

          The I Ching

It is important for all of us to accept the **call to the quest** and to embark on our heroic journeys. We must take on the challenge, confront the dragons, find our treasures and finally return home from our quest to offer our gifts. We thereby transform the kingdom. To accept any **delusions of insignificance** is to engage in self-deception and ultimately to retreat from personal responsibility. To do so would be to give up our freedom. I guess if you think you're a "nobody" or a "psychological serf" you don't have to do anything in the kingdom of the world except feel lost and empty. If contemporary society's values have turned you into a self-disrespecting person or if you think of yourself as little more than a commodity to be sold in the job market to the highest bidder, more's the pity. Pearson contends that we must come to respect the human mind and soul as much more than tools of material acquisition. Those of us who have been duped into believing we are unimportant unfortunately "seek to fill our emptiness with food, or drink, or drugs, or obsessive and frantic activity. The much lamented pace of modern life is not inevitable—it is a cover for its emptiness. If we keep in motion, we create the illusion of meaning" (Pearson, 1991: 4).

This thought, that the only thing you are called to become is the individual that only you can be, places profound worth on each of us.

          Margaret Frings Keyes

You are more than you have become.

    From The Lion King, an animated movie

Some people will at first experience the call to the quest as an urge to improve themselves or their personalities. Society encourages us to measure up to standards of beauty and success. Life can become for many a kind of self-improvement project. By improving self-images, playing our roles better or by living up to perfectionistic standards imposed by others, some of us try to become what we're not. For Pearson, the point of life is not to become someone other than who you are, but to find your true self and discover what you were put on the face of the earth for. We are who we are. It's impossible for us to become someone else. We do not have to measure up to anything. We only have to be true to ourselves. We are not wrong. We are not misplaced. God did not make a mistake. We are all heroes. We are all here to embark on our life journeys. As I said before, we must face our dragons, find our personal treasures and heal the ailing kingdom. By our mere presence in the kingdom we are charged with the responsibility of transforming the world. (And you were bored, thinking you had nothing to do today!)

Psychological Archetypes: Inner Guides for the Journey

From her literary studies of the mythic hero's journey, Pearson has identified 12 **psychological archetypes** that influence our personal life travels. They include the Innocent, Orphan, Warrior, Caregiver, Seeker, Destroyer, Lover, Creator, Ruler, Magician, Sage and Fool. Each archetype "has a lesson to teach us, and each presides over a stage of the journey" (Pearson, 1991: 5). Archetypes are visible everywhere. They are outward manifestations of inner psychic realities. They are reflected in the recurring images of art, literature, myth and religion. We see them represented in all cultures and in all periods of history.

In Chapter 7, you learned how cognitive structures (i.e., mental concepts and ideas) can shape and organize incoming sensory stimuli in different ways. The mind provides the form or mould into which the contents of experience are poured. Well, archetypes work something like this. They are mental forms or patterns that condition what we perceive and how we experience the world. As different archetypes gain prominence in our psychological lives, we tend to focus on different things, establish different priorities, think in different ways and experience different emotions. As each archetype becomes operative in our psyche, it "brings with it a task, a lesson and ultimately a gift" (7). Collectively, the archetypes teach us how to live and realize the full human potential within ourselves.

According to Pearson, which archetypes become operative in anyone's psychic life at any given moment is determined by where the person is in terms of her heroic journey. At the **preparation stage**, the Orphan, Innocent, Caregiver and Warrior take prominence. At the **journey stage**, we find the Seeker, Destroyer, Lover and Creator. Finally, at the **return stage** of our personal journeys, the Ruler, Magician, Sage and Fool are most influential.

At this point, it might be fun and revealing for you to do Self-Diagnostic 11.2, a shortened adaptation of Pearson's Heroic Myth Index, as found in the appendix of *Awakening the Heroes Within*. This exercise will start you thinking about where you are in your life's journey and what things occupy your attention, given the dominant archetypes in your life. If you wish, you can verify your initial hypothesis by completing the Heroic Myth Index prepared by Pearson and her associates.

11.9

What Kind of Hero Are You, Anyway?

Instructions: Next to each statement below indicate your level of agreement or disagreement. Do these statements describe you or not? Do they reflect your feelings, thoughts and attitudes?

1 Strongly disagree
2 Disagree somewhat
3 Not quite sure
4 Agree somewhat
5 Strongly agree

Note: Be honest when completing this instrument, but try to avoid number 3 whenever possible. Choosing this number too frequently will not provide a very accurate archetypal profile.

1. _____ Thriving on chaos is something that makes sense to me.
2. _____ I often experience states of inner tranquillity.
3. _____ I'm good at leading people.
4. _____ I have faith in my intuitions or gut-level feelings about things.
5. _____ I hate playing roles; I prefer to be real and genuine with people.
6. _____ There are many things going on in my life right now; I feel disoriented.
7. _____ It's difficult for me to say "no" to people.
8. _____ Without self-discipline, there is little chance of personal success.
9. _____ Love makes the world go 'round.
10. _____ It's time for me to make a change and back away from certain significant others in my life.
11. _____ Life has not dealt me a fair hand.
12. _____ I tend to see the bright side of things.
13. _____ When situations get boring or lifeless, I try to get things going and generate activity.
14. _____ I try not to judge people, but accept them with all their imperfections.
15. _____ I like it when people look up to me for direction.
16. _____ Helping myself enables me to help others.
17. _____ I can sometimes accomplish a lot in ways that seemingly require little work or effort on my part.
18. _____ It's time for me to let go of attachments, things and activities that no longer fit me or my personality.
19. _____ I'm a giving person. I like to share before asking anything in return.
20. _____ I defend my beliefs and values, even when personal risks are involved.
21. _____ I'm aware of my sexiness and sensuality.
22. _____ I like to go my own way and find my own answers.
23. _____ I worry that people will leave me high and dry when they no longer need me.

24. _____ I think people are essentially good; if they hurt others they do so out of ignorance more than anything else.
25. _____ I'm a fun person, though sometimes perceived as irresponsible.
26. _____ I tend to see things from a distance, in objective terms.
27. _____ I know how to find the right person for the right job.
28. _____ I'm the kind of person who makes things happen and precipitates change.
29. _____ I have so many good ideas, I find it difficult to act on all of them.
30. _____ I sometimes think of myself as a loser, since I fail to live up to my self-expectations.
31. _____ I typically put others before myself.
32. _____ I'm not reluctant to stand up to objectionable people.
33. _____ I live to love, because love is life.
34. _____ I often feel restless, like I need to go somewhere or do something else.
35. _____ Most of the time I feel like I'm on my own with little help coming from anywhere.
36. _____ I think most people are trustworthy.

Scoring: Statements have been grouped together below according to the archetypes they reflect. Next to each statement number, place your answer. Add the columns. Provide combined totals where instructed.

Self Archetypes (Return Stage)

Fool	1 _____	Ruler	3 _____
	13 _____		15 _____
	25 _____		27 _____
	_____ Total		_____ Total
Sage	2 _____	Magician	4 _____
	14 _____		16 _____
	26 _____		28 _____
	_____ Total		_____ Total

Combined Totals for Self Archetypes _____

Soul Archetypes (Journey Stage)

Creator	5 _____	Destroyer	6 _____
	17 _____		18 _____
	29 _____		30 _____
	_____ Total		_____ Total
Lover	9 _____	Seeker	10 _____
	21 _____		22 _____
	33 _____		34 _____
	_____ Total		_____ Total

Combined Totals for Soul Archetypes _____

Ego Archetypes (Preparation Stage)

Innocent	12 _____		Warrior	8 _____	
	24 _____			20 _____	
	36 _____			32 _____	
	_____ Total			_____ Total	
Orphan	11 _____		Caregiver	7 _____	
	23 _____			19 _____	
	35 _____			31 _____	
	_____ Total			_____ Total	

Combined Total for Ego Archetypes _____

Scoring Summary

Highest score: _____   Dominant archetype: _____
Lowest score: _____   Least influential archetype: _____
Highest combined score: _____   (Ego, Self or Soul) _____
Lowest combined score: _____   (Ego, Self or Soul) _____

Currently, I am at the (preparation, journey, return) _____ stage of my heroic life quest. (To determine your answer, look at the combined totals for ego, self and soul archetypes.)

Interpretation

See Table 11.2 for the goals, fears, problems, life responses and gifts associated with each of the archetypes, including the one that is dominant for you. By looking at the same things associated with your lowest score, you can learn what is either not important to you right now or possibly repressed. Also, read the descriptions of the stages below to understand better where you are in your life, psychologically speaking. Pay closest attention to the stage that captures your highest combined score.

Ego Stage: If you are at the ego stage of development, your life right now is focused on establishing boundaries between yourself and the world. You're learning to adapt and to get your needs met. You are building the "container" for your future life.

Soul Stage: At this developmental stage you are trying to connect with the eternal. Life may be seen as a mystery to you. You are probably experiencing a sense of yearning. The will-to-meaning is likely consciously present at this time. You may be shedding a false identity and moving toward authenticity.

Self Stage: At this stage, you are moving into a whole new mode of being. Life is no longer a struggle. You appreciate its abundance. Your true inner self is coming out naturally and openly now. It's time to express yourself in the world and to give your gifts to the world.

Table 11.2 The 12 Archetypes

Archetype	Goal	Fear	Dragon/Problem	Response to Task	Gift/Virtue
Innocent	Remain in safety	Abandonment	Deny it or seek rescue	Fidelity, discernment	Trust, optimism
Orphan	Regain safety	Exploitation	Is victimized by it	Process and feel pain fully	Interdependence, realism
Warrior	Win	Weakness	Slay/confront it	Fight only for what really matters	Courage, discipline
Caregiver	Help others	Selfishness	Take care of it or those it harms	Give without maiming self or others	Compassion, generosity
Seeker	Search for better life	Conformity	Flee from it	Be true to deeper self	Autonomy, ambition
Lover	Bliss	Loss of love	Love it	Follow your bliss	Passion, commitment
Destroyer	Metamorphosis	Annihilation	Allow dragon to slay it	Let go	Humility
Creator	Identity	Inauthenticity	Claim it as part of the self	Self-creation, self-acceptance	Individuality, vocation
Ruler	Order	Chaos	Find its constructive uses	Take full responsibility for your life	Responsibility, control
Magician	Transformation	Evil sorcery	Transform it	Align self with cosmos	Personal power
Sage	Truth	Deception	Transcend it	Attain enlightenment	Wisdom, nonattachment
Fool	Enjoyment	"Nonaliveness"	Play tricks on it	Trust in the process	Joy, freedom

Source: Tables 11.2, 11.3. Pearson, Carol (1991). *Awakening the Heroes Within. Twelve Archetypes to Help Us Find Ourselves and Transform Our World.* New York: Harper San Francisco.

My Life Story Is a Heroic Myth

Part I

Instructions: Begin by drawing a timeline on a sheet of paper. One end of the line represents birth. The other end represents death. Place an "X" on your timeline at the appropriate spot, given your age. Now think of all the significant events and important people in your life. Mark these events and people on the timeline.

Part II

Once you've completed your timeline, write your autobiography using the information you've recorded. When you're done, translate your life story into mythic language. I've provided an example below.

Life Story

I was born into an average family. My mother was a school teacher and my father worked as a conductor on the railroad. As the youngest child, nobody paid much attention to me. My mom was working all day and my dad was away for days at a time....

Mythic Language Translation

Once upon a time, there was a very special child, born with a promise and a light within him that was so bright that it blinded all others and they did not dare to look at him. Even his mother, who knew of the way things worked, and his father, who officiated on caravans to distant realms, could not see him (Houston, 1987: 112).

Your life story:

_____

_____

Your life story translated into the mythic language:

_____

_____

Part III

Compare your life myth with those of the various archetypes (see Table 11.3). If your life contains many painful episodes, smashed illusions and the unveiling of a lot of phoniness, your formative myth may be a variation of the Destroyer's plot. If your life has been about proving yourself, getting your way or fighting against the world, maybe you have been living a variation of the Warrior's plot.

Table 11.3   Archetypes and Their Stories

Innocent	Paradise lost but faith retained; paradise regained.
Orphan	Paradise lost, resulting despair and alienation; gives up hope of paradise; and works with others to create better conditions in world as it is.
Warrior	Goes on journey; confronts and slays dragon; rescues victim.
Caregiver	Sacrifices and does what others ask; feels maimed or is manipulative of others; gains the capacity to choose to live as feels right and life-enriching.
Seeker	Feels alienated in community by perceived pressure to conform; goes off on journey alone; finds treasure of autonomy and vocation; finds real family and home.
Lover	Yearns to love; finds love; separated from love, and (in tragedy) dies or (in comedy) is reunited with loved one.
Destroyer	Experiences great loss and pain; loses illusions and inauthentic patterns; faces death and learns to make death an ally.
Creator	Discovers true self; explores ways of creating a life that facilitates the expression of that self.
Ruler	Is wounded and kingdom is a wasteland; takes responsibility for kingdom and own woundedness; kingdom is restored to fertility, harmony and peace.
Magician	Overcomes debilitating illness; through healing and transforming self learns to heal and transform others; experiences destructive effects of hubris or insecurity; learns to align will with that of universe.
Sage	Seeks truth through losing self; recognizes own subjectivity; affirms that subjectivity; experiences transcendent truth.
Fool	Lives for pleasure but without rootedness in self, community or cosmos; learns to commit and bond with people, nature, universe; is able to trust the process and live in harmony with universe; finds joy.

Part IV

Now that you have begun to identify the myth by which your life operates, answer the following questions to gain personal insight.

1. In my myth, what am I scripted to be? (e.g., Victim, Villain or Warrior)
2. Is my role in the script limiting in any way? If so, how?
3. What is the gift, lesson or treasure in this script?
4. What results personally if I choose to live by no other script?
5. What new challenges must I accept now to transform myself into an even greater hero? What other heroes are calling out to me for life responses?

According to Pearson, the heroic journey is not just some interesting and playful notion; it is a sacred task that should not be taken lightly, though it does not always have to be taken seriously. Just ask your resident psychic Fool! Advantages of identifying the heroic story of your life include the following:

1. You will be less likely to undercut or undervalue yourself.
2. You will be less likely to get confused by trivial and nonessential concerns.
3. You will be less likely to be manipulated by others.
4. You won't be talked into becoming less than you could be (Pearson, 1991).

If you are like many people, you have been travelling life until now without a map. Lacking a sense of history or destiny, you may not have felt grounded. Maybe you have not really understood where you have been, where you are now and where you're going in the future. By looking at life as a heroic journey, you can relate to the past and to the future. You can see where you are right now along the way, what dragons must be fought and what potential treasures can be discovered.

FAREWELL, YOUNG BRAVEHEART

As we say our final farewells, young Braveheart, I wish you luck on your heroic journey of life. I hope you have learned important lessons and discovered valuable gifts along the path to human relations mastery. I know you have confronted many dragons and obstacles along the way. I know too that you have been forced to travel at times in the shadows of darkness in pursuit of your destiny. But rest assured, young Braveheart, that your travels through the dark forest will soon take you to the sunny clearing on the other side. Perhaps you will be fortunate, as I have been, to encounter many a kind knight. They have all in their own way given me their gifts. They have helped me to discover my mission in life, Braveheart, namely to help you. They have given me much profound knowledge. May their gift to me now become my gift to you, as you depart again on the long and winding road of life.

STUDY GUIDE

Key Terms

personal liberation (406)
ego (406)
false self (406)
false consciousness (406)
bad faith (406)
enneagram (407)
self-transformation (407
self-transcendence (407)
archetypal/transpersonal psychology (407)
authentic self (407)
transformational/spiritual psychology (408)
childhood orientations (414)
path of integration (416)
path of disintegration (416)

spiritual emergency (427)
logotherapy (427)
will-to-meaning (427)
existential frustration (428)
noögenic neurosis (428)
collective neurosis (428)
meaninglessness (430)
conformity (430)
fanaticism (430)
self-transcendence (431)
future orientation (432)
work (432)
love (433)
pursuit of happiness (433)
experiential value (434)

attitudinal values (434)
suffering (434)
mission (435)
archetypal psychology (435)
heroic journey (435)
metaphysical blues (436)
alienation (436)
existential vacuum (436)
call to the quest (438)
delusions of insignificance (438)
psychological archetypes (439)
preparation stage (439)
journey stage (439)
return stage (439)

Fill-in-the-Blank Questions

Instructions: Fill in each blank with the appropriate response from the list below.

PROGRESS CHECK 11.1

triads
levels
self-image
archetypal
wing
gift
kingdom
spiritual

disintegration
mass neurosis
suffering
delusions of insignificance
inner guides
enneagram
meaning

1. The _____ is a Greek symbol used to describe nine different personality types.
2. Don Riso uses the concept of the _____ to talk about secondary personality characteristics.
3. The nine enneagram personality types can be categorized in terms of thinking, instinctive and feeling _____.
4. According to Riso, within each personality type there are healthy, average and unhealthy _____.
5. When an enneagram type two "goes" to eight, that type takes a path of _____.
6. According to Richard Rohr, the problem with people is that they get fixated on their _____.
7. According to Viktor Frankl, the most human of all needs is the need for _____.
8. For Frankl, the _____ dimension of life has been sorely neglected in contemporary society.
9. Meaninglessness is evidenced by the _____ of society.
10. Frankl believes meaning can be found in love, work and potentially through _____.
11. _____ psychology uses the hero's journey as a metaphor of life.
12. The reason people do not experience themselves as heroes, according to Carol Pearson, is because they suffer from _____.
13. Psychological archetypes can act as _____ on our personal journeys.
14. Each psychological archetype has a _____ to offer us.
15. Your task in life is to transform the _____.

True/False Questions

Instructions: Circle the appropriate letter next to each statement.

T F 1. Some enneagram types are better than others.

T F 2. Don Richard Riso is the sole inventor of the enneagram.

T F 3. Unhealthy enneagram types bear some resemblance to dysfunctional types as described by the *Diagnostic and Statistical Manual of Mental Disorders*.

T F 4. People's basic personalities change as they get older.

T F 5. Enneagram type sixes are most out of touch with thinking.

T F 6. People can express their personalities in healthy or unhealthy ways.

T F 7. It's fun and exciting to discover your true enneagram personality type.

T F 8. Viktor Frankl's system of counselling, called logotherapy, deals seriously with problems of meaning.

T F 9. People who search for meaning suffer from clinical neurosis.

T F 10. People suffering from an existential vacuum have no purpose in life. They are without direction.

T F 11. Suffering can yield no meaning, according to Frankl.

T F 12. Archetypal psychology is a transpersonal theory of human development.

T F 13. According to archetypal psychology, we are all called to be heroes in life.

T F 14. Heroic myths can ground us psychologically in history and in destiny.

T F 15. Certain psychological archetypes are to be repressed and avoided at all cost.

Focus Questions

1. How can you become your own worst enemy in life?

2. How can family relationships and early childhood orientations affect how you express yourself in the world?

3. Do people with the same personality characteristics necessarily act in the same ways? Why?

4. In what sense is it possible for people to get beyond their personalities?

5. How can self-knowledge be liberating?

6. According to Viktor Frankl, what dimensions of life do we tend to ignore in contemporary society? What is the result?

7. How can people live more satisfying lives? What must they find? Where must they find it?

8. What metaphor does Carol Pearson introduce as a model for living?

9. What illnesses plague the "social kingdom"?

10. How can we heal the kingdom? What must we do?

Summary

1. Why is it necessary for people to get beyond their personalities or ego selves?
   - for personal liberation
   - our personalities are limiting in some ways
   - to get in touch with our true selves
   - the ego personality leads to game playing, self-deception, compulsivity and obsessions
   - to realize their full potentials
   - self-preoccupation is self-defeating

2. How is the enneagram related to contemporary psychology?
   - recent developments are based on the insights of Karen Horney, Sigmund Freud and Carl Jung

  • the enneagram correlates to the *Diagnostic and Statistical Manual of Mental Disorders*

3. How do people get their enneagram type?
  • as a product of biology and early childhood experience
  • types of connection found with nurturing and protective figures have an influence on which triad one will find oneself in

4. What is a wing?
  • that aspect of your personality reflecting secondary traits and characteristics, which may have a large or small role

5. What are the levels of personality development?
  • healthy
  • unhealthy

6. What are the paths of personality integration?
  • 1 - 7 - 5 - 8 - 2 - 4 - 1
  • 9 - 3 - 6 - 9

7. What are the paths of personality disintegration?
  • 1 - 4 - 2 - 8 - 5 - 7 - 1
  • 9 - 6 - 3 - 9

8. What unfortunate consequence results if we inflate our ego and fall under the spell of our personality?
  • we bring about the very things we fear most and we lose what we most desire

9. What is the most basic of all human needs and drives, according to Frankl?
  • the will-to-meaning

10. People whose need for meaning is frustrated suffer from
  • mass neurosis, fatalism, helplessness and conformity
  • an existential vacuum/existential frustration
  • planlessness
  • directionlessness
  • noögenic neurosis

11. What are the three dimensions of life for Frankl?
  • the somatic or physical
  • the mental
  • the spiritual

12. What are the roots of meaninglessness?
  • evolutionary biology
  • waning values and declining traditional institutions
  • lack of clarity about personal wants

13. How does one find meaning?
  • through self-transcendence
    (e.g., getting beyond petty self-preoccupations, narcissism and self-indulgence)
  • adopt future orientation
  • see distinction between "is" and "ought"

14. Where is meaning to be found?
  - in love, work and suffering, if need be

15. What is archetypal psychology? What does it do?
  - a new, cutting-edge developmental, transpersonal psychology
  - it takes literary criticism, combines it with Jungian psychology, and applies it to people
  - it uses the "hero's journey" as a metaphor for life and applies this metaphor in the construction of a developmental model of human life

16. Why must we all take our heroic journeys?
  - to heal ourselves
  - to find our personal treasures
  - to heal the kingdom
  - to reach wholeness
  - to find our roots and our destinies
  - to find dignity and nobility in living
  - to get over our delusions of insignificance

17. What is a psychological archetype?
  - a pattern, form or cognitive structure that organizes our perceptions
  - an inner reality reflected in external recurring images (e.g., wise men, fools and warriors)

18. How do the psychological archetypes function?
  - they condition our perceptions
  - they offer gifts
  - they suggest directions
  - they make us focus on other aspects of life and experience

Related Readings

Frankl, Viktor (1967). *Psychotherapy and Existentialism: Selected Papers on Logotherapy*. New York: Simon and Schuster.

Hurley, Kathleen and Theodore Dobson (1991). *What's My Type?* New York: HarperSanFrancisco.

Keen, Sam and Ann Valley Fox (1989). *Your Mythic Journey: Finding Meaning in Your Life Through Writing and Story Telling*. Los Angeles: Jeremy Tarcher.

Naranjo, Claudio (1991). *Ennea-Type Structures: Self-Analysis for the Seeker*. Nevada City, CA: Gateways/IDHHB Inc.

Palmer, Helen (1995). *The Enneagram in Love and Work: Understanding Your Intimate and Business Relationships*. New York: Harper-SanFrancisco.

Pearson, Carol (1986). *The Hero Within: Six Archetypes We Live By*. San Francisco: Harper & Row. Revised edition, 1989.

Weblinks

1. *Enneagram Monthly* homepage
   www.ideodynamic.com/enneagram-monthly/index.htm

   The *Enneagram Monthly* is the largest and most complete enneagram journal today. The leading thinkers in the enneagram field are regularly featured, along with new talents.

2. Meaning-centred family therapy and resistance
   www.albany.net/~deavila/existft.html

   Refer to this site if you wish to learn more about how meaning fulfillment in life is the best protection against emotional instability and the best warrantor of psychological health.

3. The Association for Transpersonal Psychology
   www.igc.apc.org/atp

   You can actively explore the transpersonal perspective by participating in the Association for Transpersonal Psychology, the leading organization devoted to the field.

4. Learning and the enneagram
   www.enneagram-edge.com/

   Find out how enneagram insights apply to the teaching-learning process.

APPENDIX
Progress Check Answers

PROGRESS CHECK 1.1

Fill-in-the-Blank Questions

1. others
2. _ _ _ _, your type
3. outer
4. inner
5. bipolar
6. analytical
7. processes
8. realists
9. innovators
10. now
11. future
12. thinking
13. feeling
14. decision making
15. life-orientation
16. judging
17. perceptive
18. intuitive-feeling
19. patterns
20. Jung

True/False Questions

1. T
2. F
3. F
4. F
5. T
6. T
7. F
8. F
9. F
10. T
11. F
12. F
13. F
14. F
15. T or F

PROGRESS CHECK 2.1

Fill-in-the-Blank Questions

1. sender
2. receiver
3. encoded
4. channels
5. psychological type
6. communication style
7. experiences
8. speak
9. misunderstood
10. think
11. sequential
12. nitpicking
13. present
14. global
15. metaphors
16. facts
17. objective
18. cold
19. values
20. hearts
21. logic
22. surprises
23. closure
24. alternatives
25. indecisive

True/False Questions

1. T
2. F
3. T
4. F
5. T
6. F
7. F
8. F
9. F
10. T
11. F
12. T
13. F
14. F
15. T
16. T
17. T
18. F
19. F
20. F
21. F
22. T

PROGRESS CHECK 3.1

Fill-in-the-Blank Questions

1. reaction formation
2. repression
3. regression
4. displacement
5. projection
6. fantasy formation
7. denial
8. intellectualization/isolation
9. identification
10. rationalization
11. circular reasoning
12. straw man
13. *ad hominem*
14. two-wrongs
15. red herring

True/False Questions

1. F
2. F
3. T
4. T
5. F
6. T
7. F
8. F
9. T
10. F
11. T
12. T
13. T
14. F
15. F

PROGRESS CHECK 4.1

Fill-in-the-Blank Questions

1. transactional analysis
2. ego states
3. child
4. rational
5. adult
6. parent
7. transactions
8. crossed
9. ulterior
10. complementary
11. strokes
12. life position
13. marasmus
14. self-stroking
15. game-playing
16. victim
17. persecutor
18. crossed transactions
19. intimacy
20. unequal relationships

True/False Questions

1. F
2. F
3. T
4. T
5. F
6. F
7. T
8. T
9. F
10. T
11. F
12. T
13. T
14. T
15. T
16. F
17. T
18. T
19. F
20. T
21. T
22. T
23. F
24. F
25. F

PROGRESS CHECK 5.1

Fill-in-the-Blank Questions

1. leadership
2. temperament
3. appreciation
4. Epimethean
5. planning
6. trait theory
7. theory X
8. theory Y
9. three-factor theory
10. task-oriented
11. situational leadership theory
12. maturity
13. Dionysian
14. Promethean
15. Apollonian

True/False Questions

1. T
2. F
3. F
4. T

5. T
6. T
7. F
8. T
9. T
10. F
11. T
12. T
13. T
14. T
15. F

PROGRESS CHECK 6.1

Fill-in-the-Blank Questions

1. conflict
2. wrong
3. psychological
4. intragroup
5. approach-approach
6. dysfunctional
7. self-knowledge
8. conflict orientation
9. constructive
10. passive-defensive
11. aggressive-defensive
12. conflict management styles
13. competing shark
14. collaborating
15. win-win

True/False Questions

1. F
2. F
3. F
4. F
5. T

6. F
7. T
8. T
9. T
10. F
11. T
12. F
13. T
14. T
15. F

PROGRESS CHECK 7.1

Fill-in-the-Blank Questions

1. perception
2. empiricists
3. interactionist
4. active
5. perceptual filters
6. interpretation
7. responsibility
8. stereotyping
9. selective
10. halo effect
11. attribution errors
12. self-concept
13. static
14. self-awareness
15. open self
16. self-disclosure
17. self-esteem
18. personal responsibility
19. social comparison
20. self-talk

True/False Questions

1. F
2. F

3. F
4. T
5. F
6. T
7. T
8. F
9. T
10. T
11. T
12. T
13. F
14. F
15. F
16. F
17. T
18. F
19. T
20. F

PROGRESS CHECK 8.1

Fill-in-the-Blank Questions

1. Lawrence Kohlberg
2. Carol Gilligan
3. Deborah Tannen
4. men, women
5. justice and fairness, care and relationship
6. acculturation
7. cultural context
8. ethnocentrism
9. empathy
10. jargon
11. nonverbal communication
12. paralanguage
13. ambiguous
14. Charles Darwin
15. articulation

16. artifactual
17. body-type
18. kinesics
19. neurolinguistic programmers
20. public distance

True/False Questions

1. T
2. T
3. F
4. F
5. F
6. F
7. T
8. T
9. F
10. T
11. T
12. T
13. F
14. T
15. T
16. F
17. F
18. T
19. F
20. F

PROGRESS CHECK 9.1

Fill-in-the-Blank Questions

1. motivations
2. locus of control
3. nirvana principle
4. instinct
5. *thanatos*
6. healthy

7. desirous
8. hierarchy of human needs
9. prepotency
10. aesthetic needs
11. metamotivations
12. learning
13. classical conditioning
14. law of effect
15. punishment
16. negative reinforcement
17. social learning theory
18. vicarious consequences
19. thematic apperception test
20. basic needs
21. pictures
22. thermostat
23. total behaviour

True/False Questions

1. F
2. F
3. T
4. T
5. T
6. F
7. T
8. F
9. F
10. T
11. F
12. T
13. F
14. F
15. F
16. F
17. F
18. F
19. F
20. F

PROGRESS CHECK 10.1

Fill-in-the-Blank Questions

1. stressors
2. occupational stressors
3. type A personality
4. conform
5. general adaptation syndrome
6. alarm reaction
7. eustress
8. interactionist
9. ineffective coping strategies
10. defence mechanisms
11. irrational beliefs
12. cognitive appraisal
13. thinking styles
14. reframe
15. meditation
16. mandala
17. endorphins
18. clinical biofeedback
19. fight-or-flight
20. control

True/False Questions

1. F
2. T
3. T
4. F
5. F
6. T
7. T
8. F
9. T
10. T
11. F

12. T

13. F

14. T

15. T

16. F

17. T

18. T

19. F

20. T

PROGRESS CHECK 11.1

Fill-in-the-Blank Questions

1. enneagram
2. wing
3. triads
4. levels
5. disintegration
6. self-image
7. meaning
8. spiritual
9. mass neurosis
10. suffering
11. archetypal
12. delusions of insignificance
13. inner guides
14. gift
15. kingdom

True/False Questions

1. F
2. F
3. T
4. F
5. T
6. T
7. F
8. T
9. F
10. T
11. F
12. T
13. T
14. T
15. F

REFERENCES

Chapter 1

Briggs Myers, Isabel and Mary McCaulley (1985). *Manual. A Guide to the Development and Use of the Myers-Briggs Type Indicator*. Palo Alto, CA: Consulting Psychologists Press, Inc.

Keirsey, David and Marilyn Bates (1984). *Please Understand Me*. Del Mar, CA: Prometheus Nemesis Book Co.

Lawrence, Gordon (1996). *People Types and Tiger Stripes: A Practical Guide to Learning Styles*. Gainesville, FL: Center for the Applications of Psychological Type, Inc.

Chapter 2

Adler, Ronald B. and Neil Towne (1996). *Looking Out, Looking In*, 8th edition. Fort Worth, TX: Holt, Rinehart and Winston.

Hirsh, Sandra and Jean Kummerow (1989). *Lifetypes*. New York: Warner Books.

Keirsey, David and Marilyn Bates (1984). *Please Understand Me*. Del Mar, CA: Prometheus Nemesis Book Company.

_____ (1992). *Type Talk at Work*. New York: Delacorte Press.

Lawrence, Gordon (1996). *People Types and Tiger Stripes*. Gainesville, FL: Center for the Applications of Psychological Type, Inc.

Myers, Isabel Briggs and Mary H. McCaulley (1988). *Manual: A Guide to the Development and Use of the Myers-Briggs Type Indicator*. Palo Alto, CA: Consulting Psychologists Press.

Chapter 3

Atwater, Eastwood (1999). *Psychology of Adjustment*, 6th edition. Upper Saddle River, NJ; Prentice Hall.

Barocas, Harvey, Walter Reichman and Andrew Schwebel (1983). *Personal Adjustment and Growth*. New York: St. Martin's Press.

Barry, Vincent (1996). *Philosophy: A Text with Readings*, 6th edition. Belmont, CA: Wadsworth.

Engler, Barbara (1985). *Personality Traits: An Introduction*, 2nd edition. Boston: Houghton Mifflin Company.

Frager, Robert and James Fadiman (1984). *Personality and Growth*, 2nd edition. New York: Harper & Row Publishers.

Freud, Sigmund (1953) [1915]. "Repression." *The Complete Works of Sigmund Freud*, Standard Edition, Volume 14. London: Hogarth Press.

_____ (1973). *New Introductory Lectures on Psychoanalysis*. Middlesex, England: Pelican Books.

Hall, Calvin (1954). *A Primer of Freudian Psychology*. New York: New American Library.

Hjelle, Larry and Daniel Ziegler (1981). *Personality Theories: Basic Assumptions, Research and Applications*. New York: McGraw-Hill Book Company.

Masserman, J.H. (1961). *Principles of Dynamic Psychiatry*. Philadelphia: W.B. Saunders Company.

Stewart, David and Gene Blocker (1996). *Psychology Applied to Modern Life*, 5th edition. Pacific Grove, CA: Brooks/Cole Publishing Co.

Woodhouse, Mark B. (1993). *A Preface to Philosophy*, 5th edition. Belmont, CA: Wadsworth Publishing Co.

Chapter 4

Berne, Eric (1961). *Transactional Analysis in Psychotherapy*. New York: Ballantine Books.

_____ (1964). *Games People Play*. New York: Ballantine Books.

_____ (1976). *Beyond Games and Scripts*. New York. Grove Press, Inc.

Dusay, John and Katherine Dusay (1977). "Transactional Analysis." Pp. 374–427 in R.J. Corsini, *Current Psychotherapies*. Itasca, IL: F.E. Peacock.

Ernst, Ken (1972). *Games Students Play*. Berkeley: Celestial Arts.

Freed, Alvyn and Margaret Freed (1873). *T.A. for Kids*. Sacramento: Jalmar Press.

Gilliland, Burl, Richard James and James Bowman (1989). *Theories and Strategies in Counselling and Psychotherapy*, 2nd edition. Englewood Cliffs, NJ: Prentice Hall.

Goulding, M. and R. Goulding (1979). *Changing Lives Through Redecision Therapy*. New York: Brunner/Hazel.

Harris, Thomas (1969). *I'm OK—You're OK*. New York: Avon Books.

James, Muriel and Dorothy Jongeward (1971). *Born to Win*. New York: Signet.

_____ (1975). *The People Book: Transactional Analysis for Students*. Don Mills, ON: Addison-Wesley Publishing Co.

Levin Pamela (1988). *Becoming the Way We Are: An Introduction to Personal Development in Recovery and in Life*. Deerfield Beach, FL: Health Communications Inc.

_____ (1988). *Cycles of Power*. Deerfield Beach, FL: Health Communications Inc.

Lussier, Robert N. (1990). *Human Relations in Organizations: A Skill Building Approach*. Homewood, IL: Irwin.

Spitz, R. (1945). "Hospitalism: Genesis of Psychiatric Conditions in Early Childhood." *Psychoanalytic Study of the Child* 1: 53–74.

Steiner, Claude (1977). *The Original Warm Fuzzy Tale*. Sacramento: Jalmar Press.

Weiten, W., M. Lloyd and R. Lashley (1996). *Psychology Applied to Modern Life*, 5th edition. Pacific Grove, CA: Brooks/Cole Publishing Co.

Chapter 5

Barr, Lee and Norma Barr (1989). *The Leadership Equation*. Austin, TX: Eakin Press.

Benton, Douglas and Jack Halloran (1991). *Applied Human Relations*. Englewood Cliffs, NJ: Prentice Hall.

Callahan, Robert E. and Patrick C. Fleenor (1988). *Managing Human Relations: Concepts and Practices*. Toronto: Merrill Publishing.

Cleary, Thomas (ed./trans.) (1990). "Lesson from The Master of Huainan." In: *The Tao of Politics: Lessons of the Masters of Huainan*. Massachusetts, MA: Shambhala Publications Inc.

Hersey, Paul and Kenneth Blanchard (1982). *Management of Organizational Behavior: Utilizing Human Resources*, 4th edition. Englewood Cliffs, NJ: Prentice Hall.

Keirsey, David and Marilyn Bates (1984). *Please Understand Me*. Del Mar, CA: Prometheus Nemesis Book Co.

Kroeger, Otto and Karen Thuesen (1992). *Type Talk at Work*. New York: Delacorte Press.

Likert, Rensis (1961). *New Patterns of Management*. New York: McGraw-Hill.

Lussier, Robert N. (1990). *Human Relations in Organizations: A Skill-Building Approach*. Homewood, IL: Irwin.

McGregor, Douglas (1967). *The Human Side of Enterprise*. New York: McGraw-Hill.

Rahim, M.A. (1983). "A Measure of Styles of Handling Interpersonal Conflict." *Academy of Management Journal* (June): 368–76.

Robbins, Stephen P. (1993). *Organizational Behavior: Concepts, Controversies and Applications*, 6th edition. Englewood Cliffs, NJ: Prentice Hall.

Thomas, Kenneth W. (1977). "Toward Multi-Dimensional Values in Teaching: The Example of Conflict Behaviors." *Academy of Management Review*, 2:487.

Chapter 6

Johnson, David W. (1990). *Reaching Out: Interpersonal Effectiveness and Self-Realization*, 4th edition. Upper Saddle River: Prentice Hall.

Kreoger, Otto and Janet Thuesen (1992). *Type Talk at Work*. New York: Delacorte Press.

Lafferty, Clayton and Ron Phillips (1990). *LSI Conflict: Self-Development Guide*. Plymouth, MI: Human Synergistics.

Lussier, Robert N. (1990). *Human Relations in Organizations: A Skill-Building Approach. Homewood, IL: Irwin.*

Rahim, M.A. (1983). "A Measure of Styles of Handling Interpersonal Conflict." *Academy of Management Journal* (June): 368–76.

Robbins, Stephen P. (1993). *Organizational Behaviour: Concepts, Controversies and Applications*, 6th edition. Upper Saddle River, NJ: Prentice Hall.

Thomas, Kenneth W. (1977). "Toward Multi-Dimensional Values in Teaching: The Example of Conflict Behaviours." *Academy of Management Review*, 2:487.

Chapter 7

Atwater, Eastwood (1983). *Psychology of Adjustment*, 2nd edition. Englewood Cliffs, NJ: Prentice Hall.

Brooks, William D. and Phillip Emmert (1976). *Interpersonal Communication.* Dubuque, IA: William C. Brown Co.

Cozby, Paul (1973). "Self-Disclosure: A Literature Review." *Psychological Bulletin* 79: 73–91.

DeVito, Joseph (1992). *The Interpersonal Communication Book*, 6th edition. New York: HarperCollins.

——— (1993). *Essentials of Human Communication.* New York: HarperCollins.

Gilbert, Shirley J. (1976). "Empirical and Theoretical Extensions of Self-Disclosure." Pp. 197–216 in Gerald R. Miller (ed.), *Explorations in Interpersonal Communication.* Newbury Park, CA: Sage Publications Inc.

Good, Katherine C. and Lawrence R. Good (1973). "Attitude Similarity and Attraction to an Instructor." *Psychological Reports* 33 (August): 335–337.

Hamachek, Don E. (1982). *Encounters with Others: Interpersonal Relationships and You.* New York: Holt, Rinehart and Winston.

——— (1987). *Encounters with the Self*, 3rd edition. Holt, Rinehart and Winston.

——— (1992). *Encounters with the Self*, 4th edition. Fort Worth, TX: Harcourt, Brace and Jovanovich.

Johnson, David W. (1990). *Reaching Out: Interpersonal Effectiveness and Self-Actualization*, 4th edition. Englewood Cliffs, NJ: Prentice Hall.

Jones, E.E. and R.E. Nisbett (1971). *The Actor and the Observer: Divergent Perceptions of the Causes of Behaviour.* Morristown, NJ: General Learning Press.

Jourard, Sydney M. (1971). *Self-Disclosure: An Experimental Analysis of the Transparent Self.* Toronto: John Wiley & Sons Inc.

——— (1971). *The Transparent Self.* New York: D. Van Nostrand Co.

Luft, Joseph (1970). *Group Process: An Introduction to Group Dynamics*, 2nd edition. Palo Alto, CA: Mayfield Publishing Company.

Monteiro, L.A. (1978). "College Women and Self-Esteem." *The New York Times*. December 10, p. 85.

Pennebacker, James W. (1991). Opening Up: The Healing Power of Confiding in Others. New York: Morrow.

Reece, Barry L. and Rhonda Brandt (1990). *Human Relations: Principles and Practices*. Boston: Houghton Mifflin Co.

Rosenthal, Robert and L. Jacobson (1968). *Pygmalion in the Classroom*. New York: Holt, Rinehart and Winston.

Weaver, Richard (1993). *Understanding Interpersonal Communication*, 6th edition. New York: HarperCollins.

Weiten, Wayne, Margaret A. Lloyd and Robin L. Lashley (1991). *Psychology Applied to Modern Life: Adjustment in the 90s*, 3rd edition. Pacific Grove, CA: Brooks/Cole Publishing Co.

Chapter 8

Adler, Ronald B. and George Rodman (1994). *Understanding Human Communication*, 5th edition. Forth Worth, TX: Harcourt Brace College Publishers.

Andersen, Peter A. and Ken Leibowitz (1978). "The Development and Nature of the Construct Touch Avoidance." *Environmental Psychology and Nonverbal Behaviour* 3: 89–106.

Birdwhistle, R. (1970). Chapter 9 in *Kinesics and Context*. Philadelphia: University of Pennsylvania Press.

Brigham, J.C. (1980). "Limiting Conditions of the Physical Attractiveness Stereotype: Attribution about Divorce." *Journal of Research on Personality* 14: 365–375.

DeVito, Joseph A. (1992). *The Interpersonal Communication Book*, 6th edition. New York: HarperCollins.

—— (1993). *Essentials of Human Communication*. New York: HarperCollins.

Gilligan, Carol (1982). *In a Different Voice: Psychological Theory and Women's Development*. Cambridge: Harvard University Press.

Hall, Edward T. (1966). *The Hidden Dimension*. Garden City, NY: Doubleday and Co. Inc.

—— (1973). *The Silent Language*. Garden City, NY: Anchor Press/Doubleday.

Knapp, Mark L. and Judith A. Hall (1992). *Nonverbal Communication in Human Interaction*, 3rd edition. Fort Worth, TX: Holt, Rinehart and Winston.

Lefrancois, Guy R. (1990). *The Lifespan*, 3rd edition. Belmont, CA: Wadsworth Publishing Co.

Mulac, A. and M.J. Rudd (1977). "Effects of Selected American Regional Dialects upon Regional Audience Members." *Communication Monographs* 44: 184–195.

O'Connor, Joseph and John Seymour (1990). *Introducing Neuro-Linguistic*

Programming: The New Psychology of Personal Excellence. London: Mandala.

Samovar, Larry A., Richard E. Porter and Nemi C. Jain (1990). "Intercultural Communication Problems and Guidelines." Pp. 395–405 in John Stewart (ed.), *Bridges Not Walls.* New York: McGraw-Hill.

Stewart, John and Gary D'Angelo (1980). *Together: Communicating Interpersonally*, 2nd edition. Reading, MA: Addison-Wesley.

Tannen, Deborah (1990). *You Just Don't Understand: Women and Men in Conversation.* New York: Ballantine Books.

Weaver, Richard (1993). *Understanding Interpersonal Communication*, 6th edition. New York: HarperCollins.

Weiten, Wayne, Margaret A. Lloyd and Robin Lashley (1991). *Psychology Applied to Modern Life*, 3rd edition. Pacific Grove, CA: Brooks/Cole Publishing.

Wells, Fran and B. Siegel (1961). "Stereotype Somatypes." *Psychological Reports* 8: 1175–1178.

Chapter 9

Bandura, Albert (1965). "Influence of Model's Reinforcement Contingencies of the Acquisition of Imitative Responses." *Journal of Personality and Social Psychology* 1: 589–596.

Bandura, A., D. Ross and S.A. Ross (1963). "Imitation of Film-Mediated Aggressive Models." *Journal of Abnormal and Social Psychology* 66: 3–11.

Callahan, Robert E. and Patrick Fleenor (1988). *Managing Human Relations.* Columbus: Merrill Publishing Co.

Carver, C. and M. Scheier (1988). *Perspectives on Personality.* Boston: Allyn & Bacon.

Cherrington, David (1989). *Organizational Behaviour: The Management of Individual and Organizational Performance.* Boston: Allyn & Bacon.

Coon, Dennis (1991). *Essentials of Psychology: Exploration and Application*, 5th edition. St. Paul: West Publishing Co.

Fehr, L. (1983). *Introduction to Personality.* New York: MacMillan Publishing Co.

Freud, S. (1961). *Beyond the Pleasure Principle.* James Strachey (ed.). New York: W.W. Norton & Co.

——— (1961). *The Ego and the Id.* Joan Riviere (trans.) and James Strachey (ed.). New York: W.W. Norton & Co.

Gibson, J., J. Ivancevich and J. Donnelly (1991). *Organizations: Behaviour-Structure-Processes*, 7th edition. Homewood, IL: Richard D. Irwin, Inc.

Gilliland, B., R. James and J. Bowman (1989). *Theories and Strategies in Counselling and Psychotherapy.* Englewood Cliffs, NJ: Prentice Hall.

Glasser, William (1969). *Schools Without Failure.* New York: Harper & Row.

——— (1975). *The Identity Society*, revised edition. New York: Harper & Row.

——— (1975). *Reality Therapy: A New Approach to Psychiatry*. New York: Harper & Row.

——— (1976). *Positive Addiction*. New York: Harper & Row.

Glasser, William (1986). *Control Therapy-Reality Therapy Workbook*. Los Angeles: The Institute for Reality Therapy.

——— (1989). *Control Theory: A New Explanation of How We Control Our Lives*. New York: Harper & Row.

——— (1992) *The Quality School: Managing Students Without Coercion*, 2nd expanded edition. New York: HarperCollins.

——— (1993). *The Quality School Teacher*. New York: Harper Perennial.

Herzberg, F., B. Mausner and B. Synderdman (1959). *The Motivation to Work*. New York: John Wiley & Sons.

Hjelle, L. and D. Ziegler (1981). *Personality Theories: Basic Assumptions, Research and Applications*. New York: McGraw-Hill Book Co.

Hokanson, J.E. and M. Burgess (1962). "The Effects of Three Types of Aggression on Vascular Processes." *Journal of Abnormal and Social Psychology* 64: 446–449.

Joy, L.A., M.M. Kimbal and M.C. Zabrack (1986). "Television and Aggressive Behaviour." Pp. 303–360 in T.M. Williams (ed.), *The Impact of Television: A Natural Experiment Involving Three Towns*. New York: Academic Press.

Levinger, G. (1986). "Editor's Page." *Journal of Social Issues* 42: 3.

Liebert, Robert and Michael Spiegler (1990). *Personality: Strategies and Issues*, 6th edition. Pacific Grove, CA: Brooks/Cole Publishing.

Maslow, Abraham (1972). *The Farther Reaches of Human Nature*. New York: Penguin Books.

——— (1987). *Motivation and Personality*, 3rd edition. New York: Harper & Row.

McClelland, David (1962). "Business Drive and National Achievement." *Harvard Business Review* (July-August): 99–112.

McGregor, Douglas (1967). *The Human Side of Enterprise*. New York: McGraw-Hill.

Monte, Christopher (1987). *Beneath the Mask: An Introduction to Theories of Personality*, 3rd edition. Fort Worth: Holt, Rinehart and Winston.

Murray, R. (1943). *Thematic Apperception Test Pictures and Manual*. Cambridge, MA: Harvard University Press.

Ryckman, Richard M. (1989). *Theories of Personality*, 4th edition. Pacific Grove, CA: Brooks/Cole Publishing.

Schultz, Diane (1977). *Growth Psychology: Models of the Healthy Personality*. New York: D. Van Nostrand Co.

Smith, Barry D. and Harold J. Vetter (1991). *Theories of Personality*, 2nd edition. Englewood Cliffs, NJ: Prentice Hall.

Chapter 10

Chesney, M.A. and R.H. Rosenman (eds.) (1985). *Anger and Hostility in Cardio-Vascular and Behavioral Disorders*. Washington: Hemisphere.

Colletti, Lorraine et al. (1984). *System for Creating Organizational and Personal Effectiveness: Leader's Manual*. Plymouth, MI: Human Synergistics.

Coon, Dennis (1991). *Essentials of Psychology: Exploration and Application*, 5th edition. St. Paul: West Publishing.

Davis, M., E. Eschelman and M. McKay (1988). *The Relaxation and Stress Reduction Workbook*, 3rd edition. Oakland, CA: New Harbinger Publications.

Delongis, A. et al. (1982). "Relationship of Daily Hassles, Uplifts, and Major Life Events to Health Status." *Health Psychology* 1 (January): 119–136.

Ellis, Albert (1962). *Reason and Emotion in Psychotherapy*. New York: Lyle Stuart.

——— (1973). *Humanistic Psychotherapy: The Rational-Emotive Approach*. New York: The Julian Press.

Friedman, M. et al. (1984). "Alteration of Type A Behaviour and Reduction in Cardiac Recurrence in Postmyocardial Infarction Patients." *American Heart Journal* 10(2): 237–248.

Friedman, Meyer and Ray Rosenman (1974). *Type A Behaviour and Your Heart*. New York: Random House Inc.

Freedman, A.S. and S. Booth-Kewley (1987). "The Disease-Prone Personality." *American Psychologist* 43(1): 2–14.

Greenberg, Jerrold (1990). *Comprehensive Stress Management*, 3rd edition. Dubuque, IA: Wm. C. Brown Publishers.

Holmes, T.H. and R.H. Rahe (1967). "Social Readjustment Rating Scale." *Journal of Psychosomatic Research* 11: 216.

Lafferty, Clayton et al. (1984). *Stress Processing Report*. Plymouth, MI: Human Synergistics.

Lazarus, R.S. (1981). "Little Hassles Can Be Dangerous to Health." *Psychology Today* 15 (July): 58–62.

Lazarus, R.S. and S. Folkman (1984). *Stress, Appraisal and Coping*. New York: Springer.

Napoli, Vince, James M. Kilbride and Donald Tebbs (1992). *Adjustment and Growth in a Changing World*, 4th edition. St. Paul: West Publishing.

Pelletier, Kenneth (1992). *Mind as Healer, Mind as Slayer*. New York: Bantam Doubleday Dell Publishing Group Inc.

Selye, Hans (1974). *Stress Without Distress*. Philadelphia: J.B. Lippincott Co.

——— (1976). *The Stress of Life*. New York: McGraw-Hill Book Co.

Weiten, Wayne (1988). "Pressure as a Form of Stress in Its Relationship to Psychological Symptomatology." *Journal of Social and Clinical Psychology* 61): 127–139.

Weiten, W. and J. Dixon (1984). "Measurement of Pressure as a Form of Stress." Paper presented at the meeting of the American Psychological Association, Toronto, Ontario.

Weiten, Wayne and Margaret Lloyd (1994). *Psychology Applied to Modern Life*, 4th edition. Pacific Grove CA: Brooks/Cole Publishing Co.

————— (1991). *Psychology Applied to Modern Life*, 3rd edition. Pacific Grove CA: Brooks/Cole Publishing Co.

Wright, L. (1988). "The Type A Behaviour Pattern and Coronary Artery Disease: Quest for the Active Ingredients and the Elusive Mechanism." *American Psychologist* 43(1): 2–14.

Chapter 11

Baron, Renee and Elizabeth Wagele (1994). *The Enneagram Made Easy*. New York: HarperSanFrancisco.

Beesing, Maria, Robert Nogosek and Patrick O'Leary (1984). *The Enneagram: A Journey of Self-Discovery*. Denville, NJ: Dimension Books.

Frankl, Viktor (1963). *Man's Search for Meaning*. New York: Washington Square Press.

————— (1973). *The Doctor and the Soul: From Psychotherapy to Logotherapy*. New York: Vintage Books.

————— (1978). *The Unheard Cry for Meaning*. New York: Simon & Schuster.

Houston, Jean (1987). *The Search for the Beloved: Journeys in Sacred Psychology*. New York: St. Martin's Press.

Keyes, Margaret Frings (1992). *Emotions and the Enneagram: Working Through Your Shadow Lifescript*, revised edition. Muir Beach, CA: Molysdatur Publications.

Loomis, Mary E. (1991). *Dancing the Wheel of Psychological Types*. Wilmette, IL: Chiron Publications.

Pearson, Carol (1991). *Awakening the Heroes Within: Twelve Archetypes to Help Us Find Ourselves and Transform Our World*. New York: Harper SanFrancisco.

————— (1993). *For Journey Guides: An Awakening the Heroes Within Handbook for Helping Professionals*. College Park, MD: A Meristem Project.

Pearson, Carol and Katherine Pope (1981). *The Female Hero in American and British Literature*. New York: R.R. Bowker Co.

Pearson, Carol, Donna L. Shavlik and Judith G. Touchton (eds.) (1989). *Educating The Majority: Women Challenge Tradition in Higher Education*. New York: MacMillan Publishing Co.

Pearson, Carol and Sharon V. Seivert (1988). *Heroes at Work*. College Park, MD: A Meristem Project.

Riso, Don Richard (1987). *Personality Types: Using the Enneagram for Self-Discovery*. Boston: Houghton Mifflin.

———— (1990). *Understanding the Enneagram: The Practical Guide to Personality Types*. Boston: Houghton Mifflin.

———— (1992). *Discovering Your Personality Type: The Enneagram Questionnaire*. Boston: Houghton Mifflin.

———— (1993). *Enneagram Transformations: Releases and Affirmations for Healing Your Personality Type*. Boston: Houghton Mifflin.

Riso, Don Richard and Russ Hudson (1994). *The Riso-Hudson Enneagram Type Indicator (Version 2.0)*. New York: Enneagram Personality Types Inc.

———— (1996). *The Riso-Hudson Enneagram Type Indicator* (Version 2.0). New York: Enneagram Personality Types Inc.

Rohr, Richard and Andreas Ebert (1992). *Experiencing the Enneagram*. New York: Crossroads.

Schultz, Duane (1977). *Growth Psychology: Models of the Healthy Personality*. New York: D. Van Nostrand Company.

INDEX

Photo Credits

Page 2, PH Merrill Publishing/Scott Cunningham; page 4, Corbis-Bettmann; page 9, Corbis Bettmann; page 10, The Slide Farm/Al Harvey; page 14, PH Merrill Publishing/ Tom Wilcox; page15, Corbis-Bettmann; page 16, Corbis-Bettmann; page 17, The Slide Farm/Al Harvey; page 30, PhotoEdit/Michael Newman; page 35, PH Merrill Publishing; page 36, Prentice Hall Archives; page 43, Prentice Hall Archives; page 48, UPI/Bettmann; page 52, The Slide Farm/Al Harvey; page 68, The Slide Farm/Al Harvey; page 73, Corbis-Bettmann; page 86, The Slide Farm/Al Harvey; page 93, Nikki Abraham; page 97, Toronto Sun; page 100, Dr. Ray Pagtakhan; page 120, Michael Gibson-Stills Guy; page 122, UPI/Bettmann; page 128, Toronto Sun/Richard Cole; page 129, National Film Board of Canada; page 141, Nikki Abraham; page 150, The Slide Farm/Al Harvey; page 162, Toronto Sun/Mike Cassese; page 165, UPI/Bettmann; page 183, Dick Hemingway; page 194, Tony Stone Images/Christopher Bissell; page 206, Tony Stone Images/Bruce Ayres; page 207, Canapress/Chuck Stoody; page 218, Prentice Hall Archives; page 228, Dick Hemingway; page 236, The Slide Farm/Al Harvey; page 243, NASA; page 252, The Slide Farm/Al Harvey; page 264, Tony Stone Images/Chip Henderson; page 283, Dick Hemingway; page 292, Dick Hemingway; page 306, The Slide Farm/Al Harvey; page 329, Corbis-Bettmann; page 338, Dick Hemingway; page 340, Corbis-Bettmann; page 342, Corbis-Bettmann; page 345, Dr. Albert Bandura; page 348, William Glasser; page 350, The Slide Farm/Al Harvey; page 362, Canapress/Diana Nethercott; page 372, Canapress; page 378, Toronto Sun/Paul Henry; page 385, UPI/Bettmann; page 387, Lorrine Colletti and Robert Phillips; page 397, Canapress; page 408, Toronto Sun/G. Reekie; page 433, The Slide Farm/Al Harvey